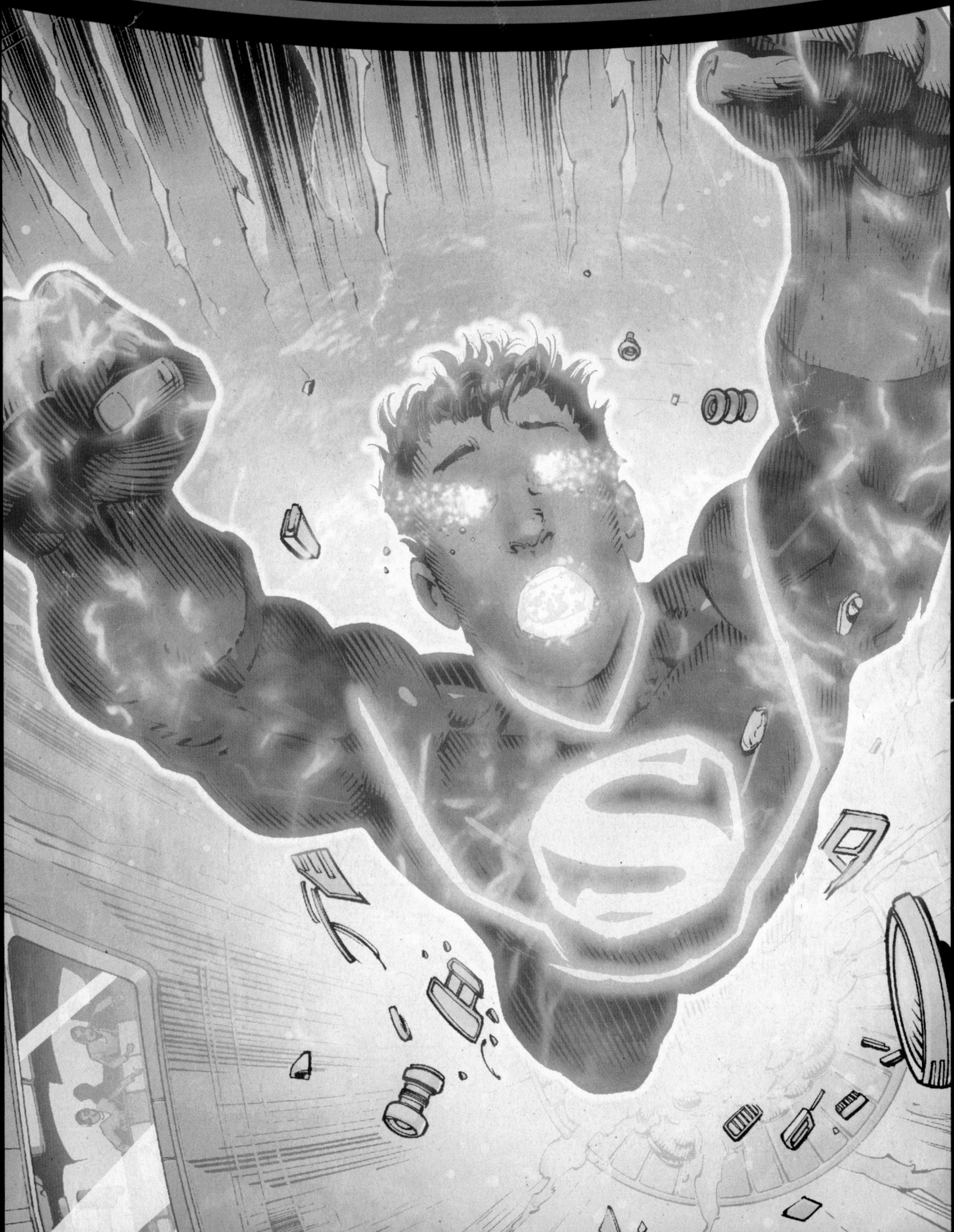

NEW SUPER-MAN

VOL.1 MADE IN CHINA

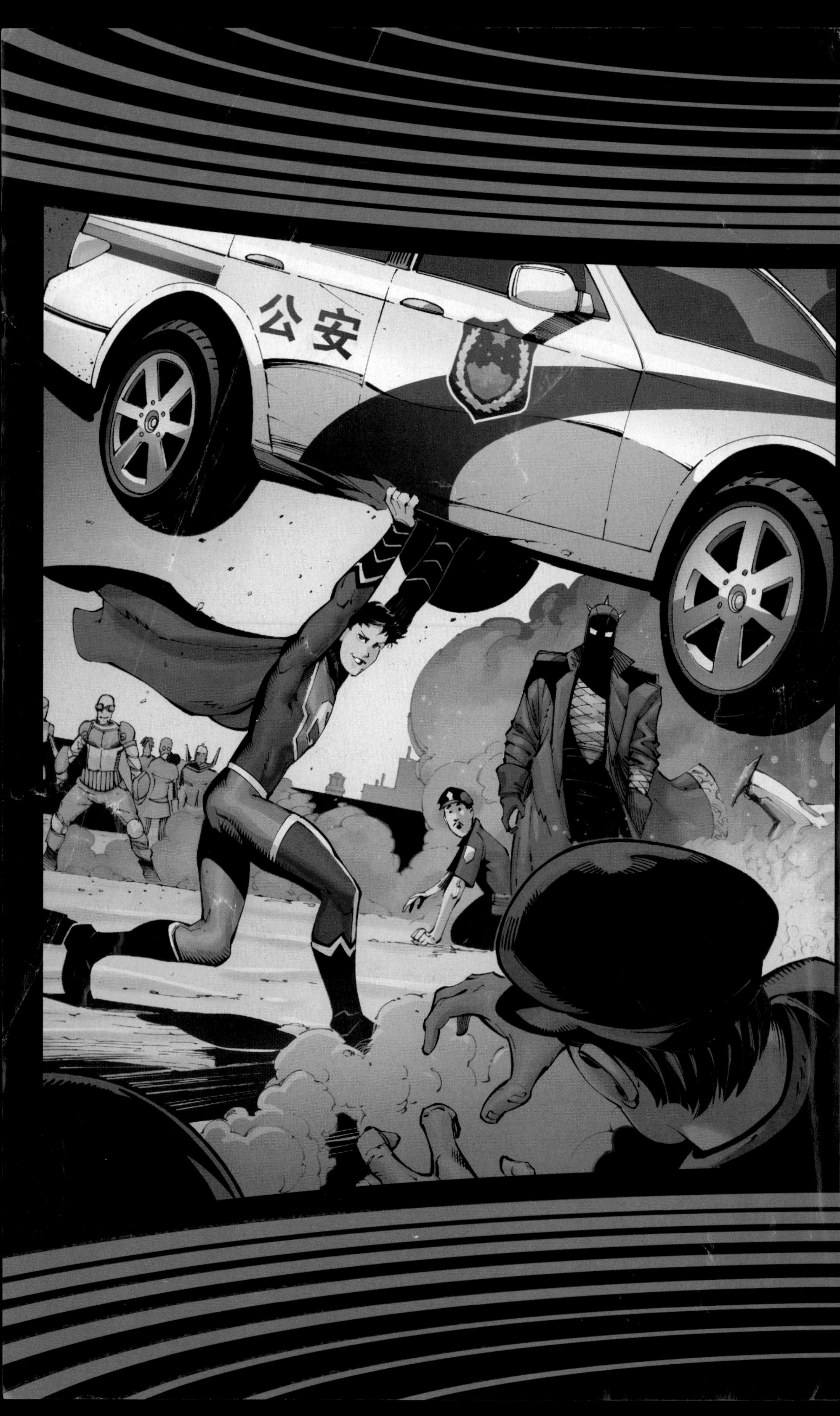
公安

NEW SUPER-MAN
VOL.1 MADE IN CHINA

GENE LUEN YANG
writer

VIKTOR BOGDANOVIC
penciller

RICHARD FRIEND
inker

HI-FI
colorist

DAVE SHARPE
letterer

VIKTOR BOGDANOVIC and KELSEY SHANNON
collection cover artists

SUPERMAN created by **JERRY SIEGEL** and **JOE SHUSTER**
By special arrangement with the Jerry Siegel family

PAUL KAMINSKI Editor - Original Series

JEB WOODARD Group Editor - Collected Editions ✳ **ERIKA ROTHBERG** Editor - Collected Edition
STEVE COOK Design Director - Books ✳ **MONIQUE GRUSPE** Publication Design

BOB HARRAS Senior VP - Editor-in-Chief, DC Comics

DIANE NELSON President ✳ **DAN DiDIO** Publisher ✳ **JIM LEE** Publisher ✳ **GEOFF JOHNS** President & Chief Creative Officer
AMIT DESAI Executive VP - Business & Marketing Strategy, Direct to Consumer & Global Franchise Management ✳ **SAM ADES** Senior VP - Direct to Consumer
BOBBIE CHASE VP - Talent Development ✳ **MARK CHIARELLO** Senior VP - Art, Design & Collected Editions
JOHN CUNNINGHAM Senior VP - Sales & Trade Marketing ✳ **ANNE DePIES** Senior VP - Business Strategy, Finance & Administration
DON FALLETTI VP - Manufacturing Operations ✳ **LAWRENCE GANEM** VP - Editorial Administration & Talent Relations
ALISON GILL Senior VP - Manufacturing & Operations ✳ **HANK KANALZ** Senior VP - Editorial Strategy & Administration
JAY KOGAN VP - Legal Affairs ✳ **THOMAS LOFTUS** VP - Business Affairs
JACK MAHAN VP - Business Affairs ✳ **NICK J. NAPOLITANO** VP - Manufacturing Administration
EDDIE SCANNELL VP - Consumer Marketing ✳ **COURTNEY SIMMONS** Senior VP - Publicity & Communications
JIM (SKI) SOKOLOWSKI VP - Comic Book Specialty Sales & Trade Marketing ✳ **NANCY SPEARS** VP - Mass, Book, Digital Sales & Trade Marketing

NEW SUPER-MAN VOL. 1: MADE IN CHINA

Published by DC Comics. Compilation and all new material Copyright © 2017 DC Comics. All Rights Reserved.
Originally published in single magazine form in NEW SUPER-MAN 1-6. Copyright © 2016, 2017 DC Comics.
SUPERMAN, DC UNIVERSE REBIRTH and all related characters and elements © & ™ DC Comics.
The stories, characters and incidents featured in this publication are entirely fictional.
DC Comics does not read or accept unsolicited submissions of ideas, stories or artwork.

DC Comics, 2900 West Alameda Ave., Burbank, CA 91505.
Printed by Solisco Printers, Scott, QC, Canada. 5/19/17. First Printing.
ISBN: 978-1-4012-7093-3

Library of Congress Cataloging-in-Publication Data is available.

PEFC Certified

This product is from
sustainably managed
forests, recycled and
controlled sources

PEFC/26-31-02   www.pefc.org

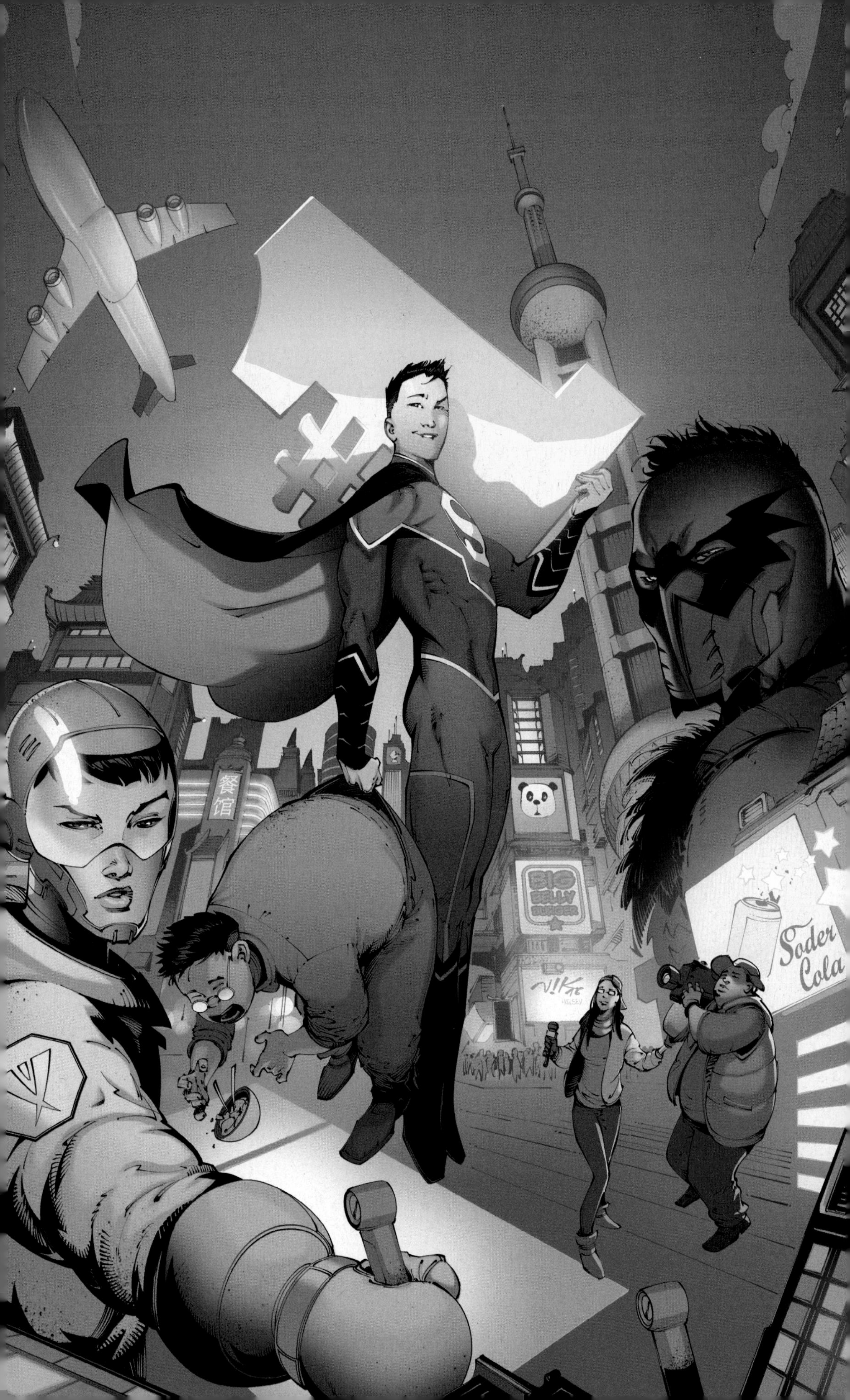
餐馆
BIG BELLY BURGER
Soder Cola

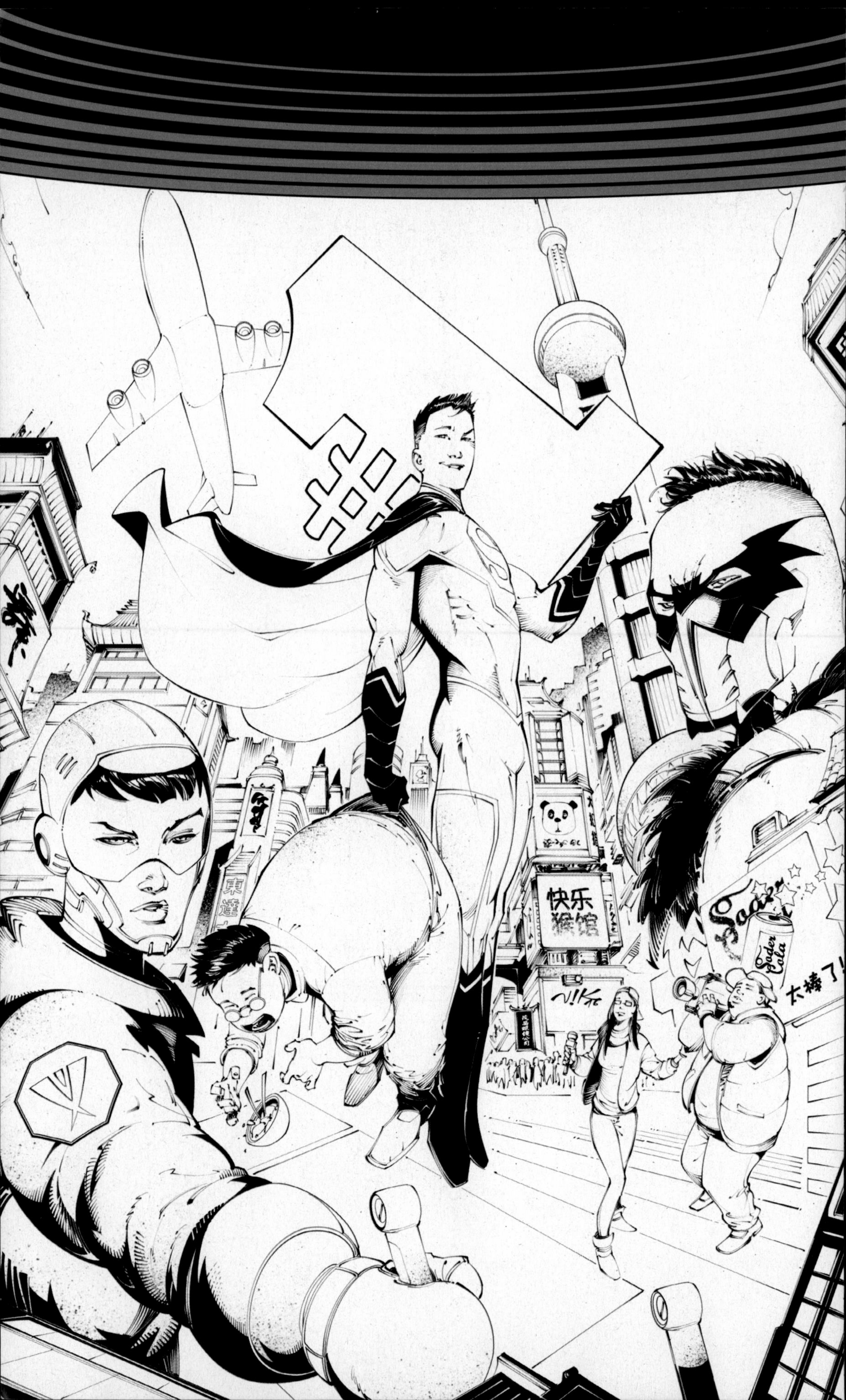
快乐
猴馆
Soder Cola
太棒了!

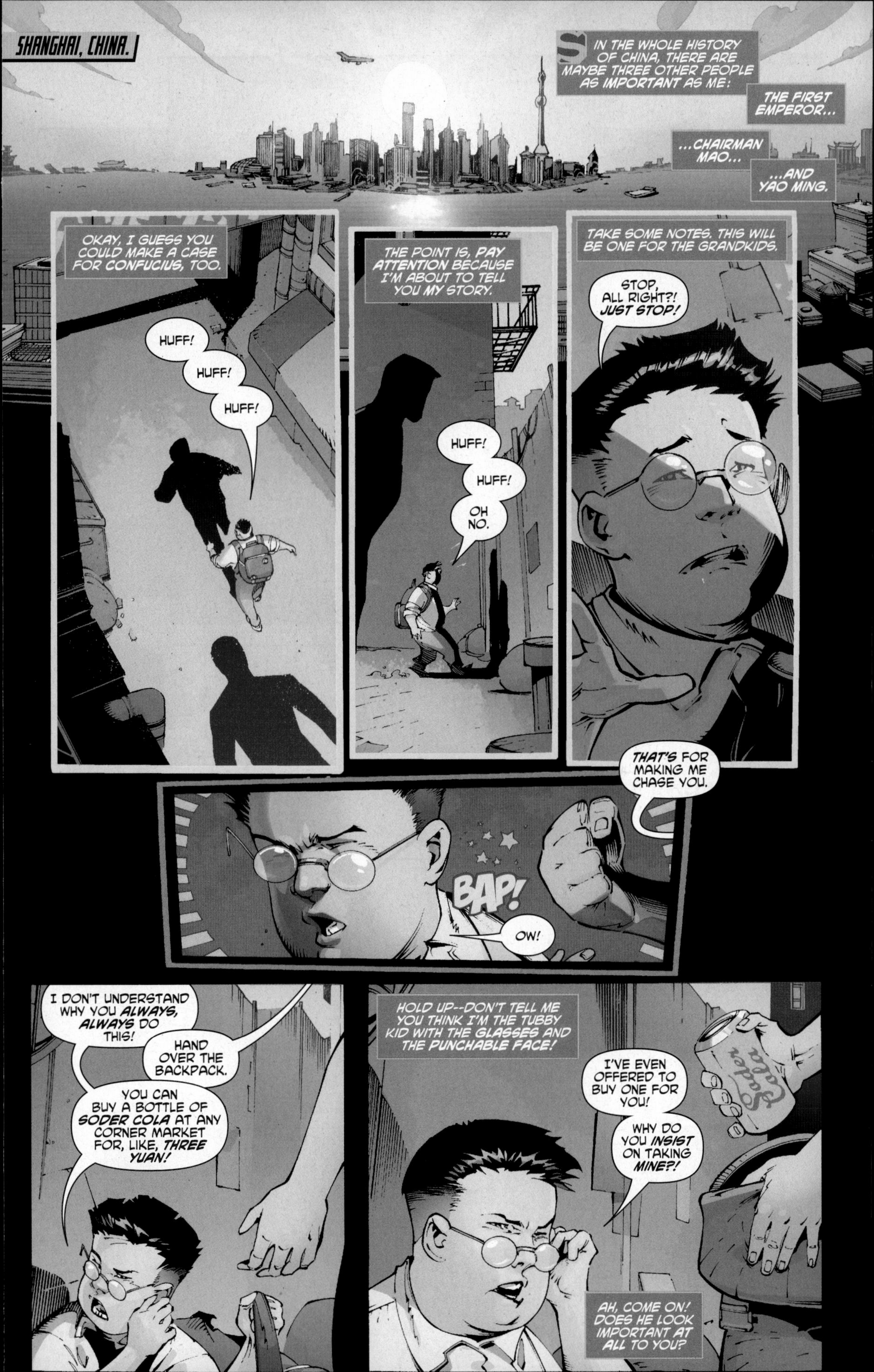
SHANGHAI, CHINA.
IN THE WHOLE HISTORY OF CHINA, THERE ARE MAYBE THREE OTHER PEOPLE AS IMPORTANT AS ME:
THE FIRST EMPEROR...
...CHAIRMAN MAO...
...AND YAO MING.
OKAY, I GUESS YOU COULD MAKE A CASE FOR CONFUCIUS, TOO.
HUFF!
HUFF!
HUFF!
THE POINT IS, PAY ATTENTION BECAUSE I'M ABOUT TO TELL YOU MY STORY.
HUFF!
HUFF!
OH NO.
TAKE SOME NOTES. THIS WILL BE ONE FOR THE GRANDKIDS.
STOP, ALL RIGHT?! JUST STOP!
THAT'S FOR MAKING ME CHASE YOU.
BAP!
OW!
I DON'T UNDERSTAND WHY YOU ALWAYS, ALWAYS DO THIS!
HAND OVER THE BACKPACK.
YOU CAN BUY A BOTTLE OF SODER COLA AT ANY CORNER MARKET FOR, LIKE, THREE YUAN!
HOLD UP--DON'T TELL ME YOU THINK I'M THE TUBBY KID WITH THE GLASSES AND THE PUNCHABLE FACE!
I'VE EVEN OFFERED TO BUY ONE FOR YOU!
Soder Cola
WHY DO YOU INSIST ON TAKING MINE?!
AH, COME ON! DOES HE LOOK IMPORTANT AT ALL TO YOU?

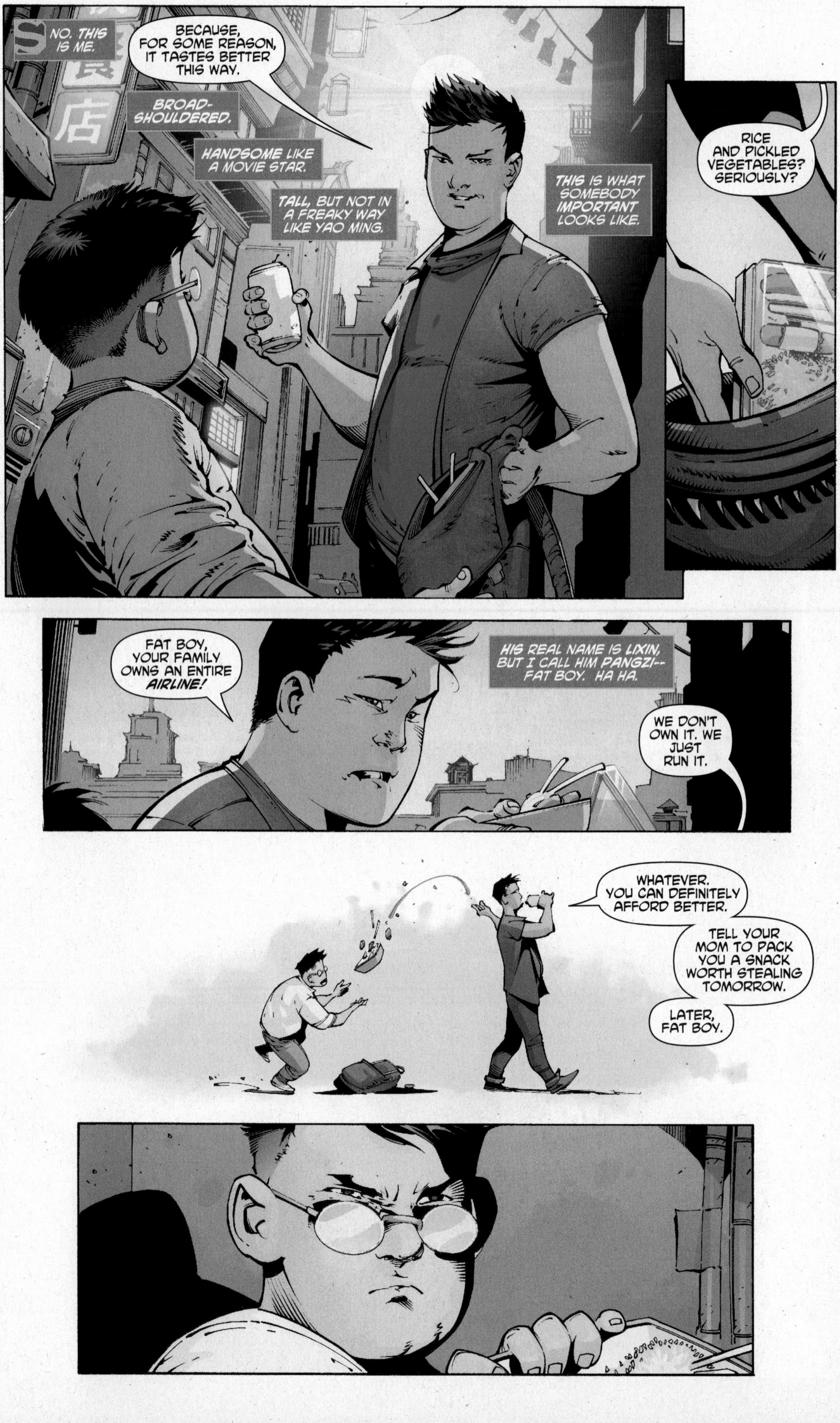

NO. THIS IS ME.
BECAUSE, FOR SOME REASON, IT TASTES BETTER THIS WAY.
BROAD-SHOULDERED.
HANDSOME LIKE A MOVIE STAR.
TALL, BUT NOT IN A FREAKY WAY LIKE YAO MING.
THIS IS WHAT SOMEBODY IMPORTANT LOOKS LIKE.
RICE AND PICKLED VEGETABLES? SERIOUSLY?
FAT BOY, YOUR FAMILY OWNS AN ENTIRE AIRLINE!
HIS REAL NAME IS LIXIN, BUT I CALL HIM PANGZI-- FAT BOY. HA HA.
WE DON'T OWN IT. WE JUST RUN IT.
WHATEVER. YOU CAN DEFINITELY AFFORD BETTER.
TELL YOUR MOM TO PACK YOU A SNACK WORTH STEALING TOMORROW.
LATER, FAT BOY.

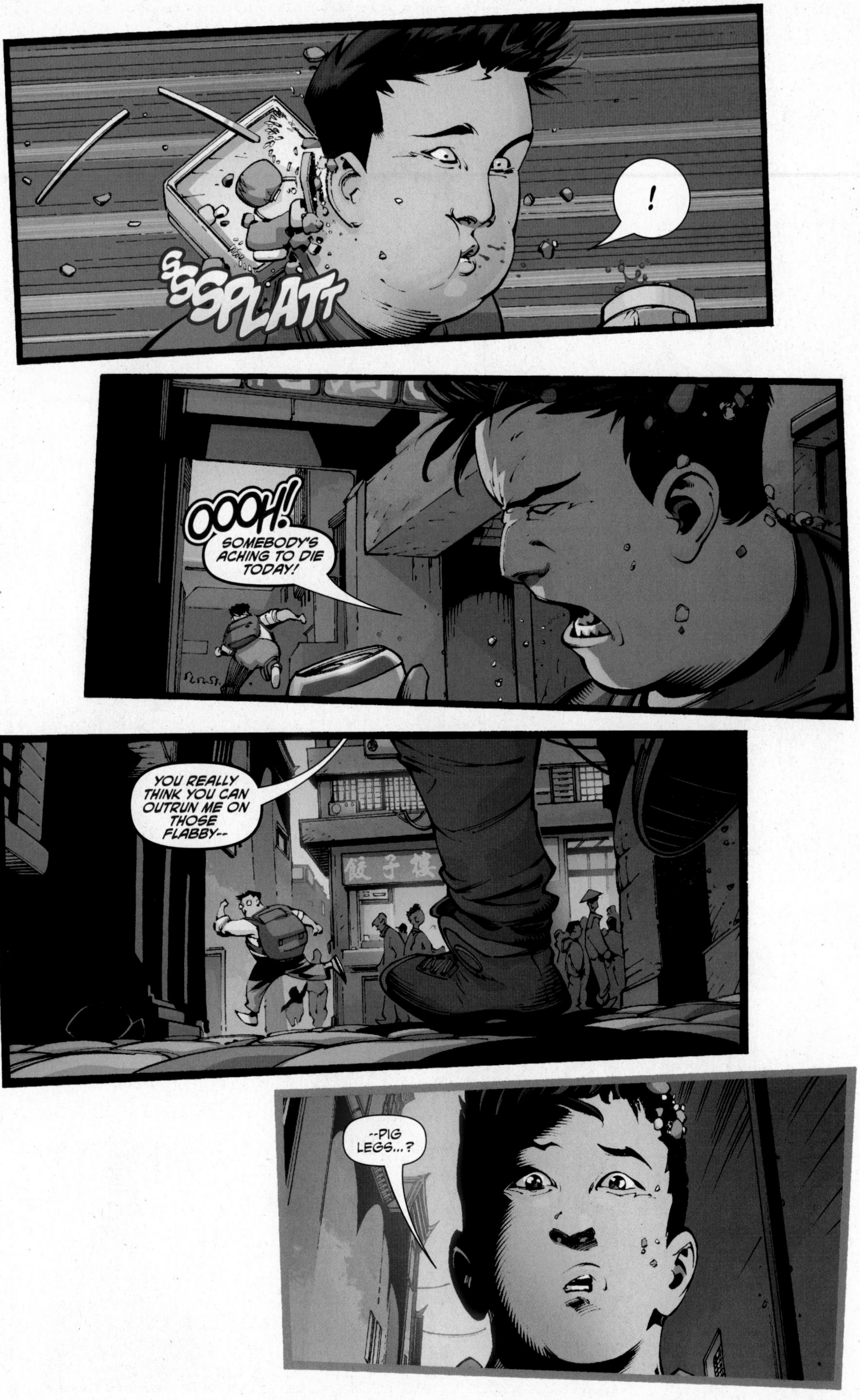
!
SSSPLATT
OOOH!
SOMEBODY'S ACHING TO DIE TODAY!
YOU REALLY THINK YOU CAN OUTRUN ME ON THOSE FLABBY--
--PIG LEGS...?

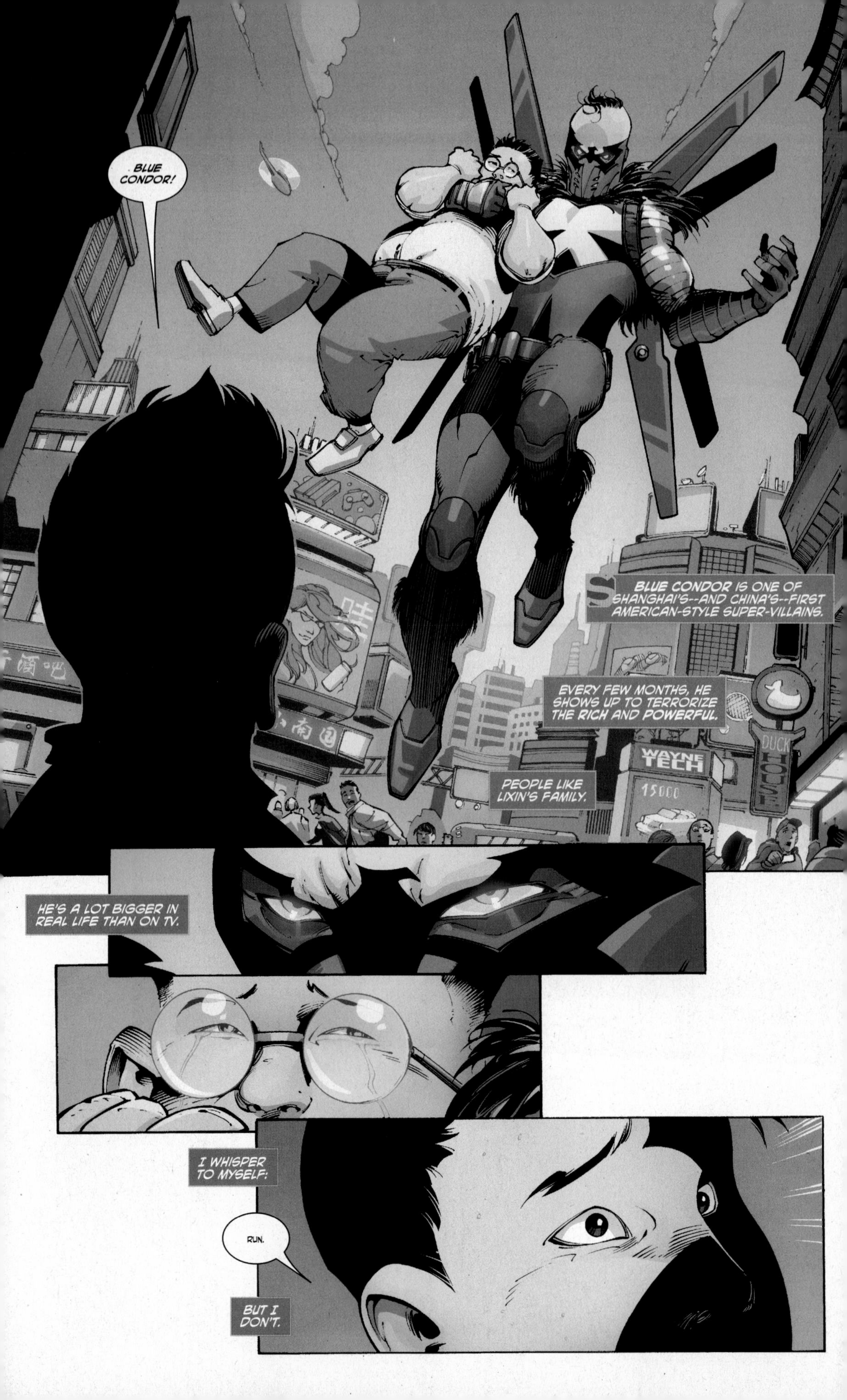
BLUE CONDOR!
BLUE CONDOR IS ONE OF SHANGHAI'S--AND CHINA'S--FIRST AMERICAN-STYLE SUPER-VILLAINS.
EVERY FEW MONTHS, HE SHOWS UP TO TERRORIZE THE RICH AND POWERFUL.
PEOPLE LIKE LIXIN'S FAMILY.
WAYNE TECH
DUCK HOUSE
HE'S A LOT BIGGER IN REAL LIFE THAN ON TV.
I WHISPER TO MYSELF:
RUN.
BUT I DON'T.

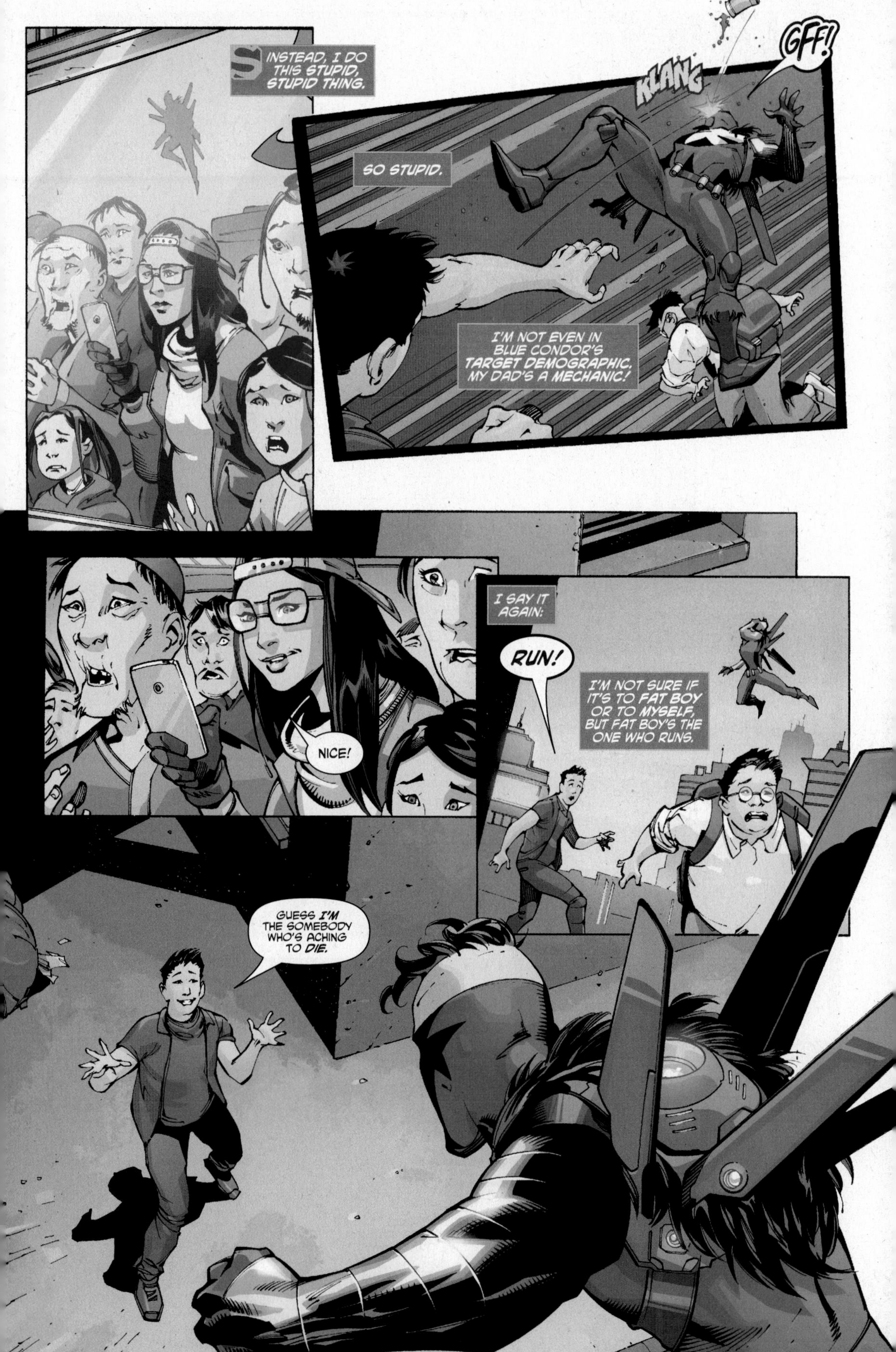
INSTEAD, I DO THIS STUPID, STUPID THING.
KLANG
GFF!
SO STUPID.
I'M NOT EVEN IN BLUE CONDOR'S TARGET DEMOGRAPHIC. MY DAD'S A MECHANIC!
NICE!
I SAY IT AGAIN:
RUN!
I'M NOT SURE IF IT'S TO FAT BOY OR TO MYSELF, BUT FAT BOY'S THE ONE WHO RUNS.
GUESS I'M THE SOMEBODY WHO'S ACHING TO DIE.

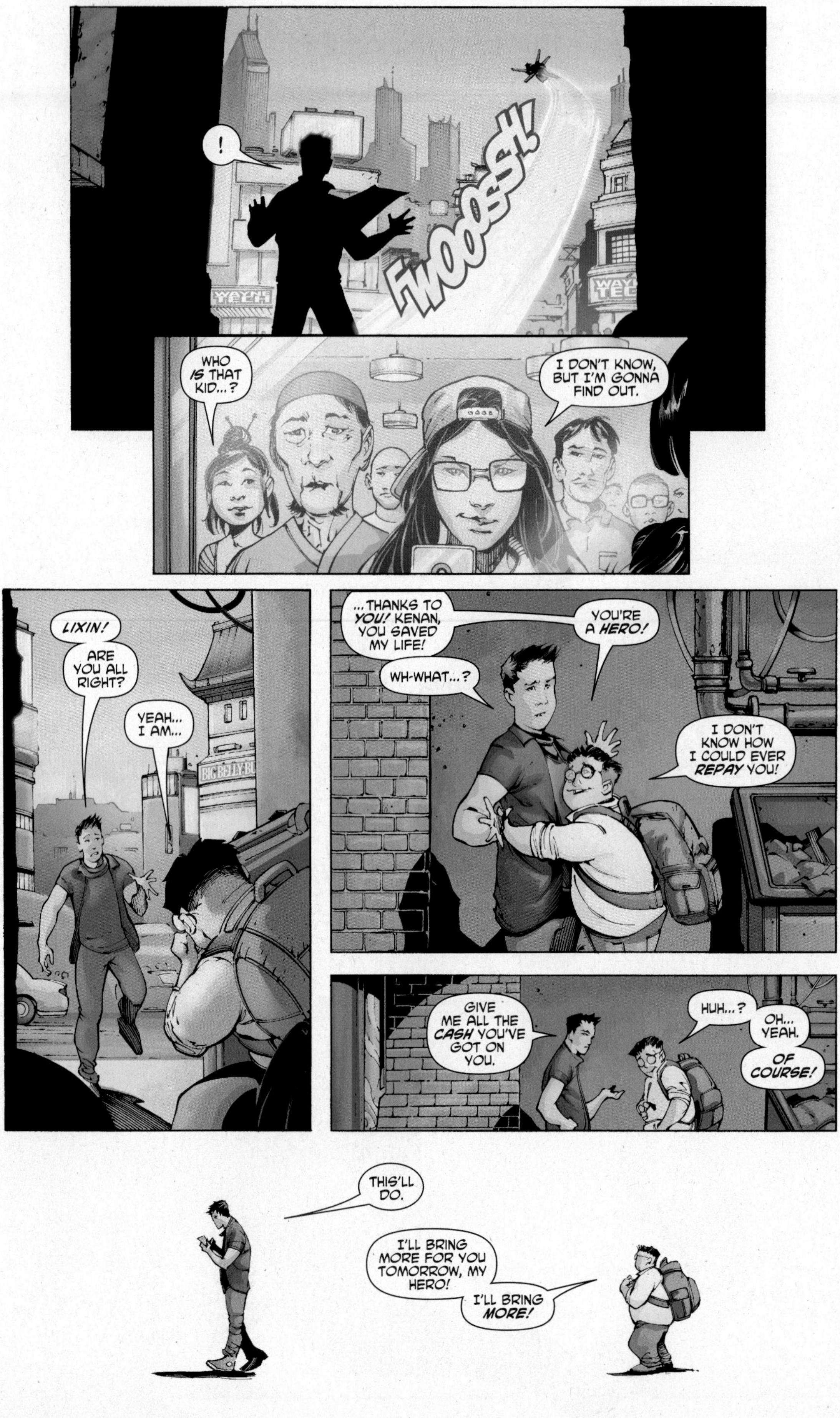
!
FWOOSSH!
WAYNE TECH
WHO IS THAT KID...?
I DON'T KNOW, BUT I'M GONNA FIND OUT.
LIXIN!
ARE YOU ALL RIGHT?
YEAH... I AM...
BIG BELLY BU
...THANKS TO YOU! KENAN, YOU SAVED MY LIFE!
YOU'RE A HERO!
WH-WHAT...?
I DON'T KNOW HOW I COULD EVER REPAY YOU!
GIVE ME ALL THE CASH YOU'VE GOT ON YOU.
HUH...?
OH... YEAH.
OF COURSE!
THIS'LL DO.
I'LL BRING MORE FOR YOU TOMORROW, MY HERO!
I'LL BRING MORE!

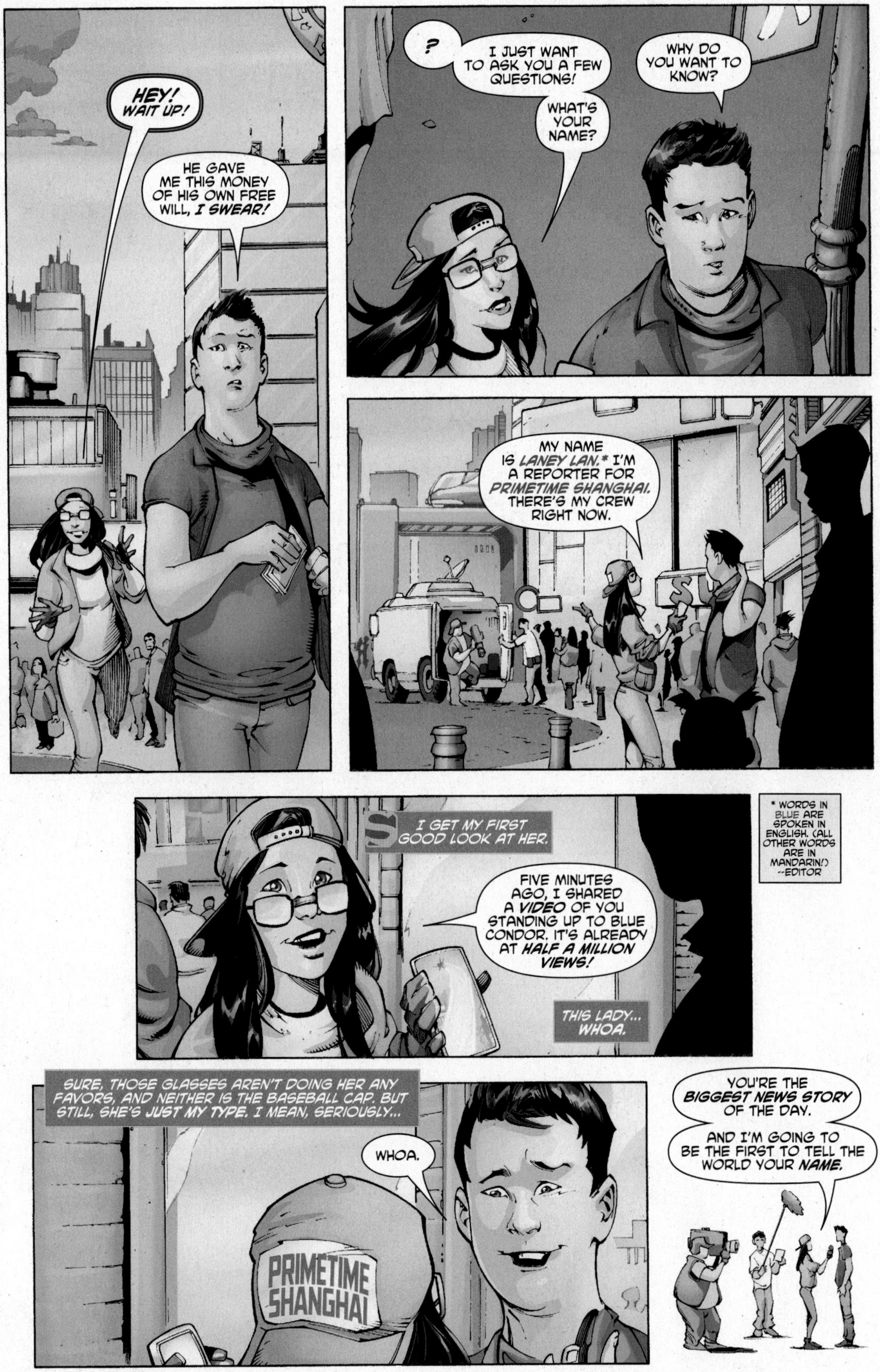
HEY! WAIT UP!
HE GAVE ME THIS MONEY OF HIS OWN FREE WILL, I SWEAR!
?
I JUST WANT TO ASK YOU A FEW QUESTIONS!
WHAT'S YOUR NAME?
WHY DO YOU WANT TO KNOW?
MY NAME IS LANEY LAN.* I'M A REPORTER FOR PRIMETIME SHANGHAI. THERE'S MY CREW RIGHT NOW.
I GET MY FIRST GOOD LOOK AT HER.
FIVE MINUTES AGO, I SHARED A VIDEO OF YOU STANDING UP TO BLUE CONDOR. IT'S ALREADY AT HALF A MILLION VIEWS!
THIS LADY... WHOA.
* WORDS IN BLUE ARE SPOKEN IN ENGLISH. (ALL OTHER WORDS ARE IN MANDARIN!) --EDITOR
SURE, THOSE GLASSES AREN'T DOING HER ANY FAVORS, AND NEITHER IS THE BASEBALL CAP. BUT STILL, SHE'S JUST MY TYPE. I MEAN, SERIOUSLY...
WHOA.
PRIMETIME SHANGHAI
YOU'RE THE BIGGEST NEWS STORY OF THE DAY.
AND I'M GOING TO BE THE FIRST TO TELL THE WORLD YOUR NAME.

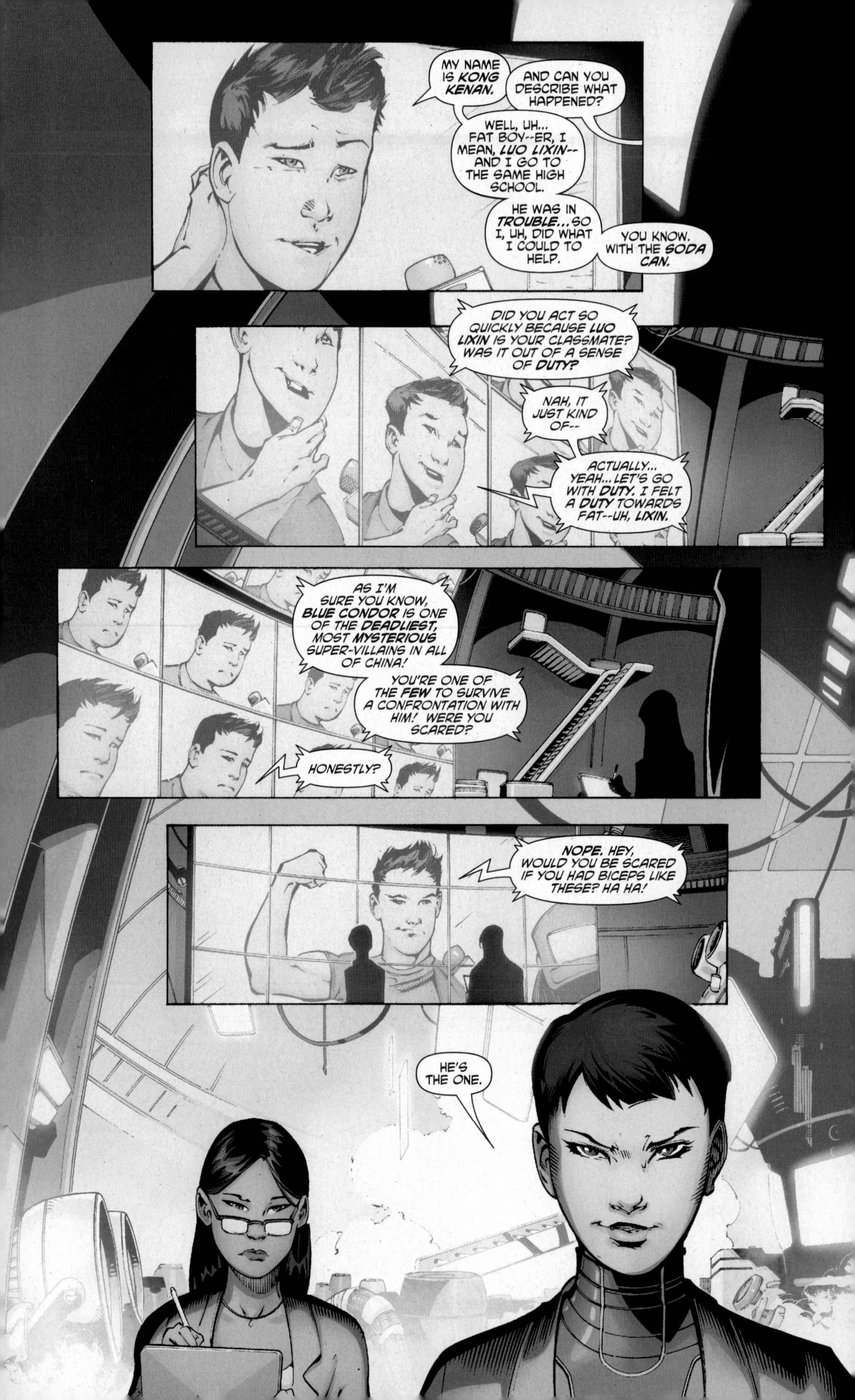
MY NAME IS KONG KENAN.
AND CAN YOU DESCRIBE WHAT HAPPENED?
WELL, UH... FAT BOY--ER, I MEAN, LUO LIXIN--AND I GO TO THE SAME HIGH SCHOOL.
HE WAS IN TROUBLE... SO I, UH, DID WHAT I COULD TO HELP.
YOU KNOW. WITH THE SODA CAN.
DID YOU ACT SO QUICKLY BECAUSE LUO LIXIN IS YOUR CLASSMATE? WAS IT OUT OF A SENSE OF DUTY?
NAH, IT JUST KIND OF--
ACTUALLY... YEAH... LET'S GO WITH DUTY. I FELT A DUTY TOWARDS FAT--UH, LIXIN.
AS I'M SURE YOU KNOW, BLUE CONDOR IS ONE OF THE DEADLIEST, MOST MYSTERIOUS SUPER-VILLAINS IN ALL OF CHINA!
YOU'RE ONE OF THE FEW TO SURVIVE A CONFRONTATION WITH HIM! WERE YOU SCARED?
HONESTLY?
NOPE. HEY, WOULD YOU BE SCARED IF YOU HAD BICEPS LIKE THESE? HA HA!
HE'S THE ONE.

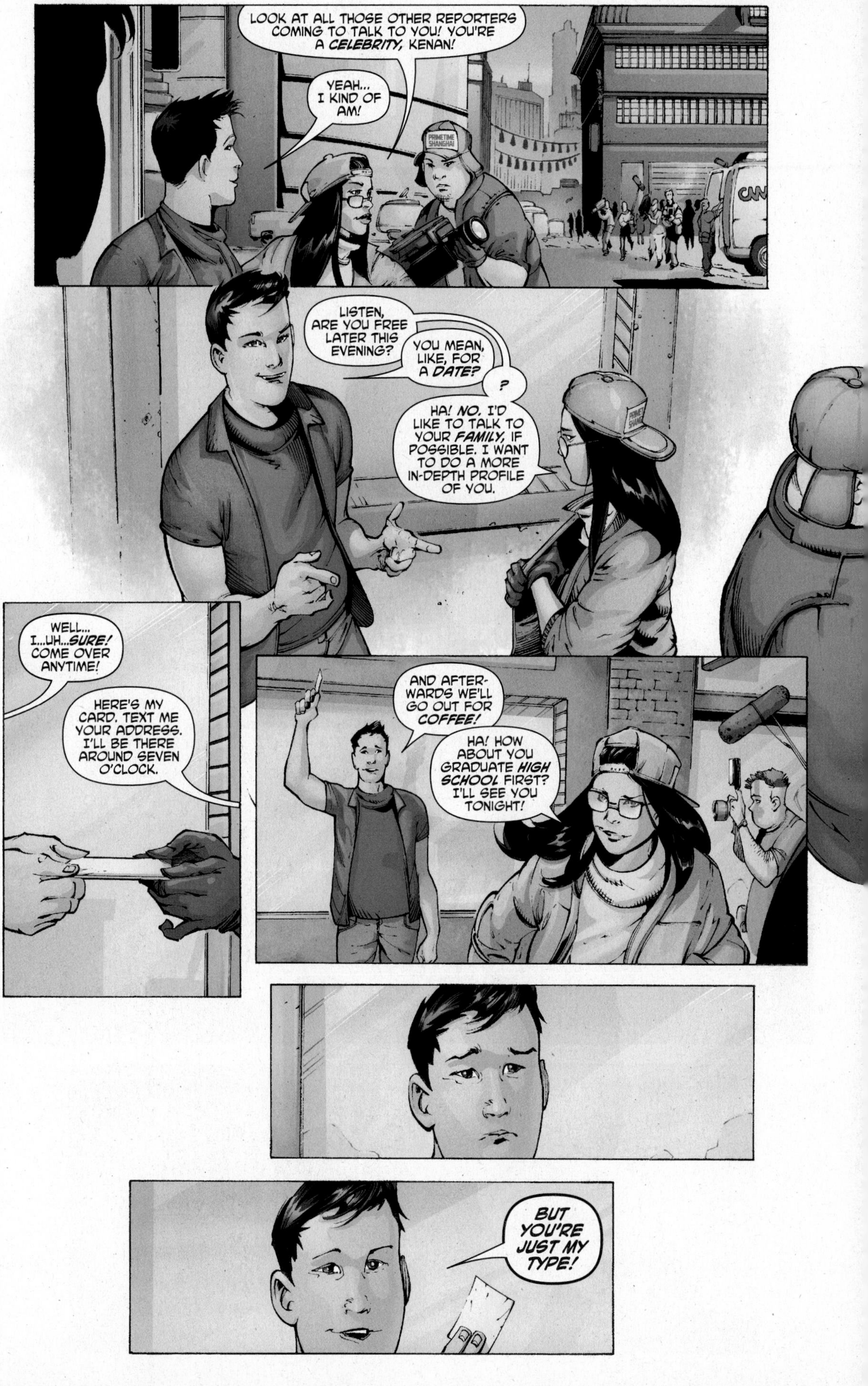
LOOK AT ALL THOSE OTHER REPORTERS COMING TO TALK TO YOU! YOU'RE A *CELEBRITY,* KENAN!
YEAH... I KIND OF AM!
PRIMETIME SHANGHAI
CNN
LISTEN, ARE YOU FREE LATER THIS EVENING?
YOU MEAN, LIKE, FOR A *DATE?*
?
HA! *NO.* I'D LIKE TO TALK TO YOUR *FAMILY,* IF POSSIBLE. I WANT TO DO A MORE IN-DEPTH PROFILE OF YOU.
WELL... I...UH...*SURE!* COME OVER ANYTIME!
HERE'S MY CARD. TEXT ME YOUR ADDRESS. I'LL BE THERE AROUND SEVEN O'CLOCK.
AND AFTER-WARDS WE'LL GO OUT FOR *COFFEE!*
HA! HOW ABOUT YOU GRADUATE *HIGH SCHOOL* FIRST? I'LL SEE YOU TONIGHT!
BUT YOU'RE JUST MY TYPE!

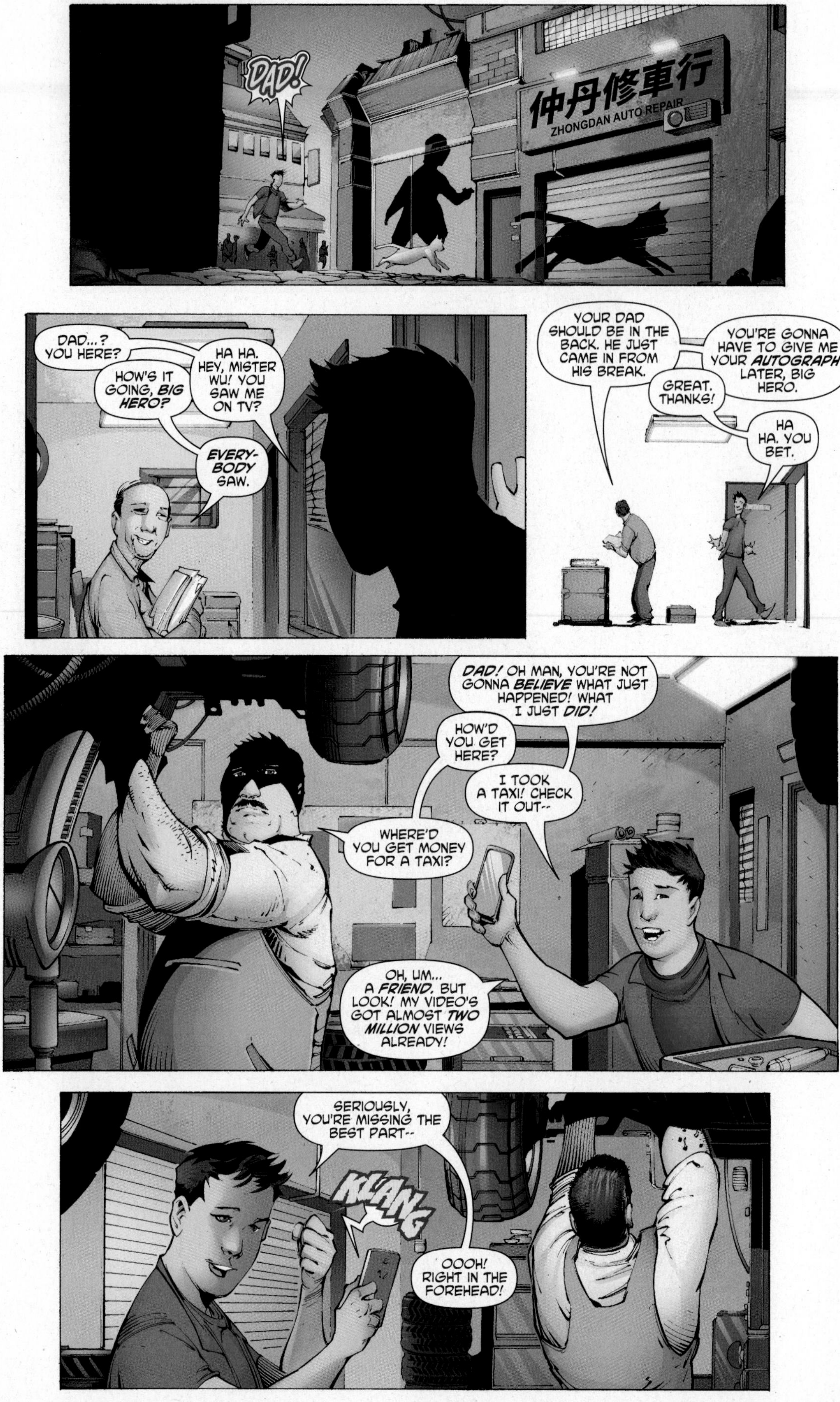
DAD!
仲丹修車行
ZHONGDAN AUTO REPAIR
DAD...? YOU HERE?
HOW'S IT GOING, BIG HERO?
HA HA. HEY, MISTER WU! YOU SAW ME ON TV?
EVERY-BODY SAW.
YOUR DAD SHOULD BE IN THE BACK. HE JUST CAME IN FROM HIS BREAK.
GREAT. THANKS!
YOU'RE GONNA HAVE TO GIVE ME YOUR AUTOGRAPH LATER, BIG HERO.
HA HA. YOU BET.
DAD! OH MAN, YOU'RE NOT GONNA BELIEVE WHAT JUST HAPPENED! WHAT I JUST DID!
HOW'D YOU GET HERE?
I TOOK A TAXI! CHECK IT OUT--
WHERE'D YOU GET MONEY FOR A TAXI?
OH, UM... A FRIEND. BUT LOOK! MY VIDEO'S GOT ALMOST TWO MILLION VIEWS ALREADY!
SERIOUSLY, YOU'RE MISSING THE BEST PART--
KLANG
OOOH! RIGHT IN THE FOREHEAD!

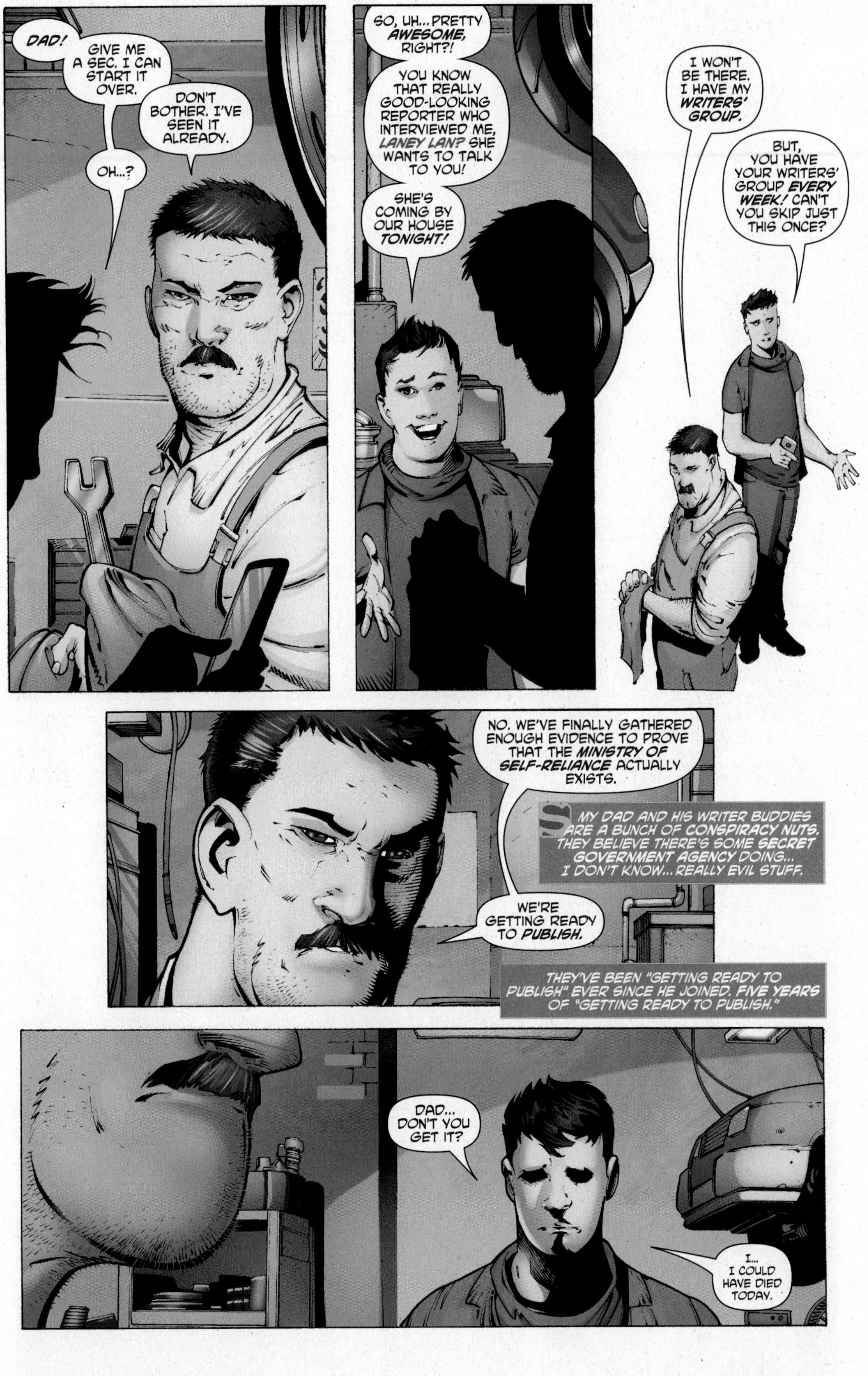
DAD!
GIVE ME A SEC. I CAN START IT OVER.
DON'T BOTHER. I'VE SEEN IT ALREADY.
OH...?
SO, UH... PRETTY AWESOME, RIGHT?!
YOU KNOW THAT REALLY GOOD-LOOKING REPORTER WHO INTERVIEWED ME, LANEY LAN? SHE WANTS TO TALK TO YOU!
SHE'S COMING BY OUR HOUSE TONIGHT!
I WON'T BE THERE. I HAVE MY WRITERS' GROUP.
BUT, YOU HAVE YOUR WRITERS' GROUP EVERY WEEK! CAN'T YOU SKIP JUST THIS ONCE?
NO. WE'VE FINALLY GATHERED ENOUGH EVIDENCE TO PROVE THAT THE MINISTRY OF SELF-RELIANCE ACTUALLY EXISTS.
MY DAD AND HIS WRITER BUDDIES ARE A BUNCH OF CONSPIRACY NUTS. THEY BELIEVE THERE'S SOME SECRET GOVERNMENT AGENCY DOING... I DON'T KNOW... REALLY EVIL STUFF.
WE'RE GETTING READY TO PUBLISH.
THEY'VE BEEN "GETTING READY TO PUBLISH" EVER SINCE HE JOINED. FIVE YEARS OF "GETTING READY TO PUBLISH."
DAD... DON'T YOU GET IT?
I... I COULD HAVE DIED TODAY.

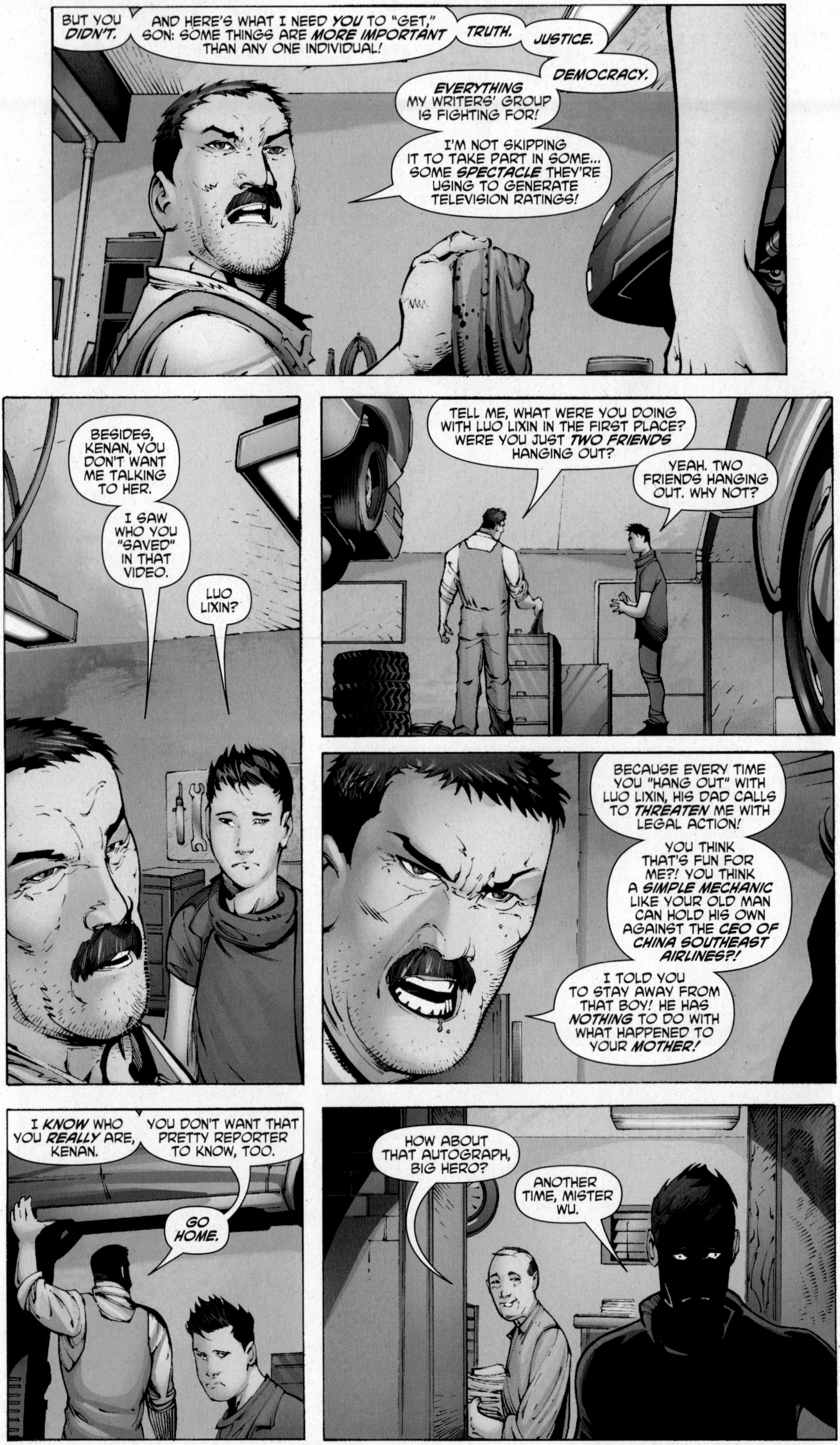

BUT YOU *DIDN'T.*
AND HERE'S WHAT I NEED *YOU* TO "GET," SON: SOME THINGS ARE *MORE IMPORTANT* THAN ANY ONE INDIVIDUAL!
TRUTH.
JUSTICE.
DEMOCRACY.
EVERYTHING MY WRITERS' GROUP IS FIGHTING FOR!
I'M NOT SKIPPING IT TO TAKE PART IN SOME... SOME *SPECTACLE* THEY'RE USING TO GENERATE TELEVISION RATINGS!
BESIDES, KENAN, YOU DON'T WANT ME TALKING TO HER.
I SAW WHO YOU "SAVED" IN THAT VIDEO.
LUO LIXIN?
TELL ME, WHAT WERE YOU DOING WITH LUO LIXIN IN THE FIRST PLACE? WERE YOU JUST *TWO FRIENDS* HANGING OUT?
YEAH. TWO FRIENDS HANGING OUT. WHY NOT?
BECAUSE EVERY TIME YOU "HANG OUT" WITH LUO LIXIN, HIS DAD CALLS TO *THREATEN* ME WITH LEGAL ACTION!
YOU THINK THAT'S FUN FOR ME?! YOU THINK A *SIMPLE MECHANIC* LIKE YOUR OLD MAN CAN HOLD HIS OWN AGAINST THE *CEO OF CHINA SOUTHEAST AIRLINES?!*
I TOLD YOU TO STAY AWAY FROM THAT BOY! HE HAS *NOTHING* TO DO WITH WHAT HAPPENED TO YOUR *MOTHER!*
I *KNOW* WHO YOU *REALLY* ARE, KENAN.
YOU DON'T WANT THAT PRETTY REPORTER TO KNOW, TOO.
GO HOME.
HOW ABOUT THAT AUTOGRAPH, BIG HERO?
ANOTHER TIME, MISTER WU.

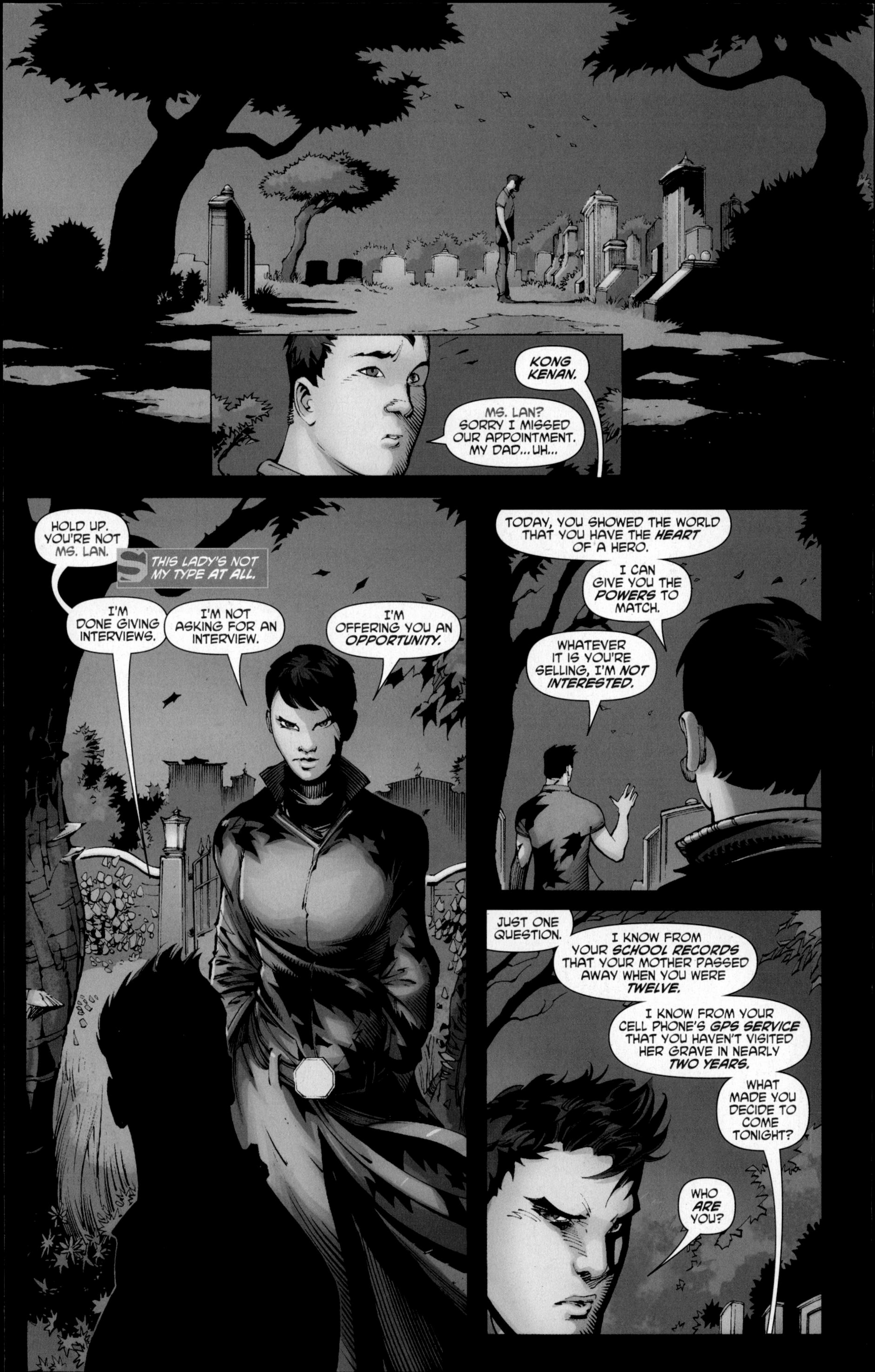
KONG KENAN.
MS. LAN? SORRY I MISSED OUR APPOINTMENT. MY DAD... UH...
HOLD UP. YOU'RE NOT MS. LAN.
THIS LADY'S NOT MY TYPE AT ALL.
I'M DONE GIVING INTERVIEWS.
I'M NOT ASKING FOR AN INTERVIEW.
I'M OFFERING YOU AN OPPORTUNITY.
TODAY, YOU SHOWED THE WORLD THAT YOU HAVE THE HEART OF A HERO.
I CAN GIVE YOU THE POWERS TO MATCH.
WHATEVER IT IS YOU'RE SELLING, I'M NOT INTERESTED.
JUST ONE QUESTION.
I KNOW FROM YOUR SCHOOL RECORDS THAT YOUR MOTHER PASSED AWAY WHEN YOU WERE TWELVE.
I KNOW FROM YOUR CELL PHONE'S GPS SERVICE THAT YOU HAVEN'T VISITED HER GRAVE IN NEARLY TWO YEARS.
WHAT MADE YOU DECIDE TO COME TONIGHT?
WHO ARE YOU?

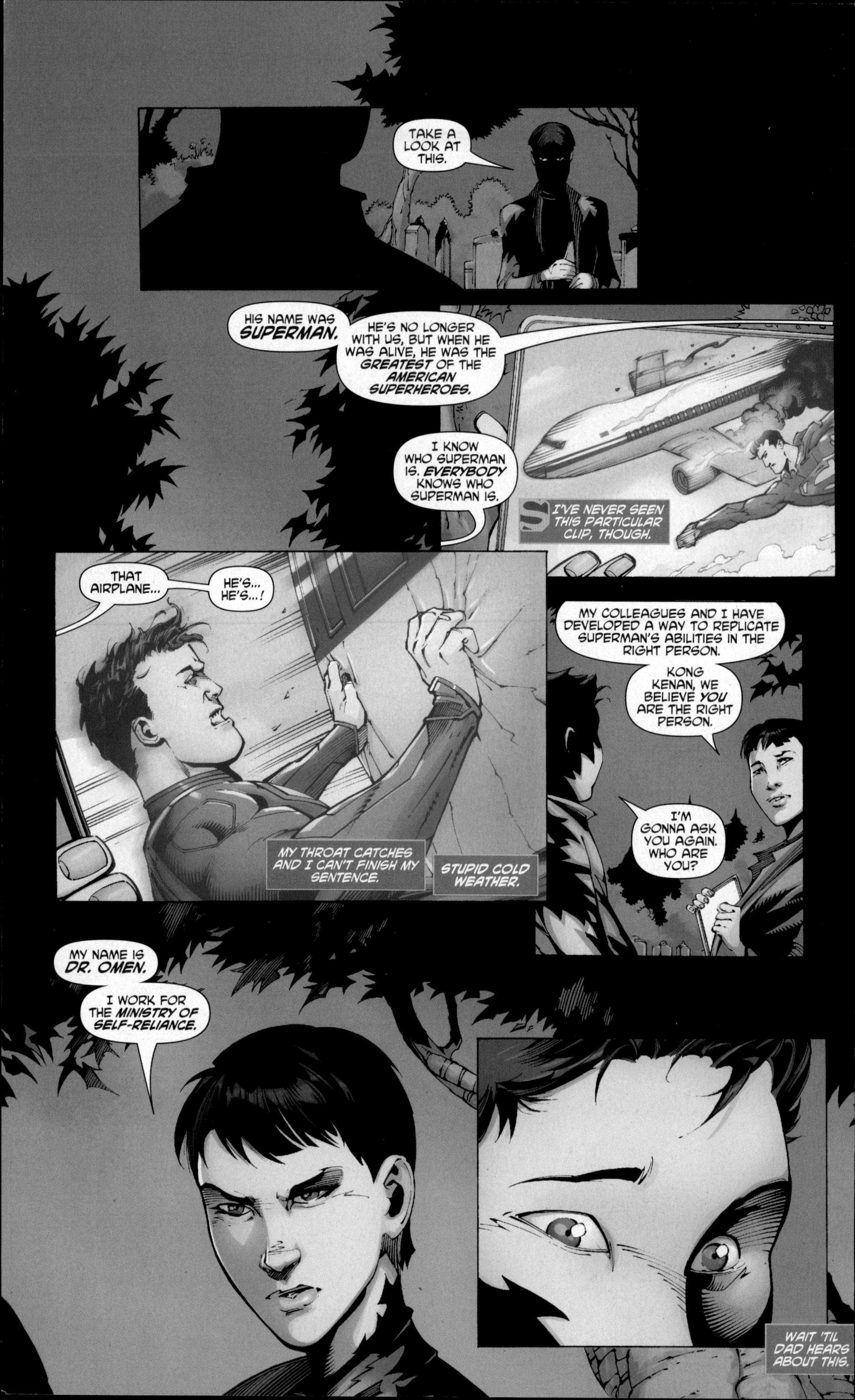
TAKE A LOOK AT THIS.
HIS NAME WAS SUPERMAN.
HE'S NO LONGER WITH US, BUT WHEN HE WAS ALIVE, HE WAS THE GREATEST OF THE AMERICAN SUPERHEROES.
I KNOW WHO SUPERMAN IS. EVERYBODY KNOWS WHO SUPERMAN IS.
I'VE NEVER SEEN THIS PARTICULAR CLIP, THOUGH.
THAT AIRPLANE...
HE'S... HE'S...!
MY THROAT CATCHES AND I CAN'T FINISH MY SENTENCE.
STUPID COLD WEATHER.
MY COLLEAGUES AND I HAVE DEVELOPED A WAY TO REPLICATE SUPERMAN'S ABILITIES IN THE RIGHT PERSON.
KONG KENAN, WE BELIEVE YOU ARE THE RIGHT PERSON.
I'M GONNA ASK YOU AGAIN. WHO ARE YOU?
MY NAME IS DR. OMEN.
I WORK FOR THE MINISTRY OF SELF-RELIANCE.
WAIT 'TIL DAD HEARS ABOUT THIS.

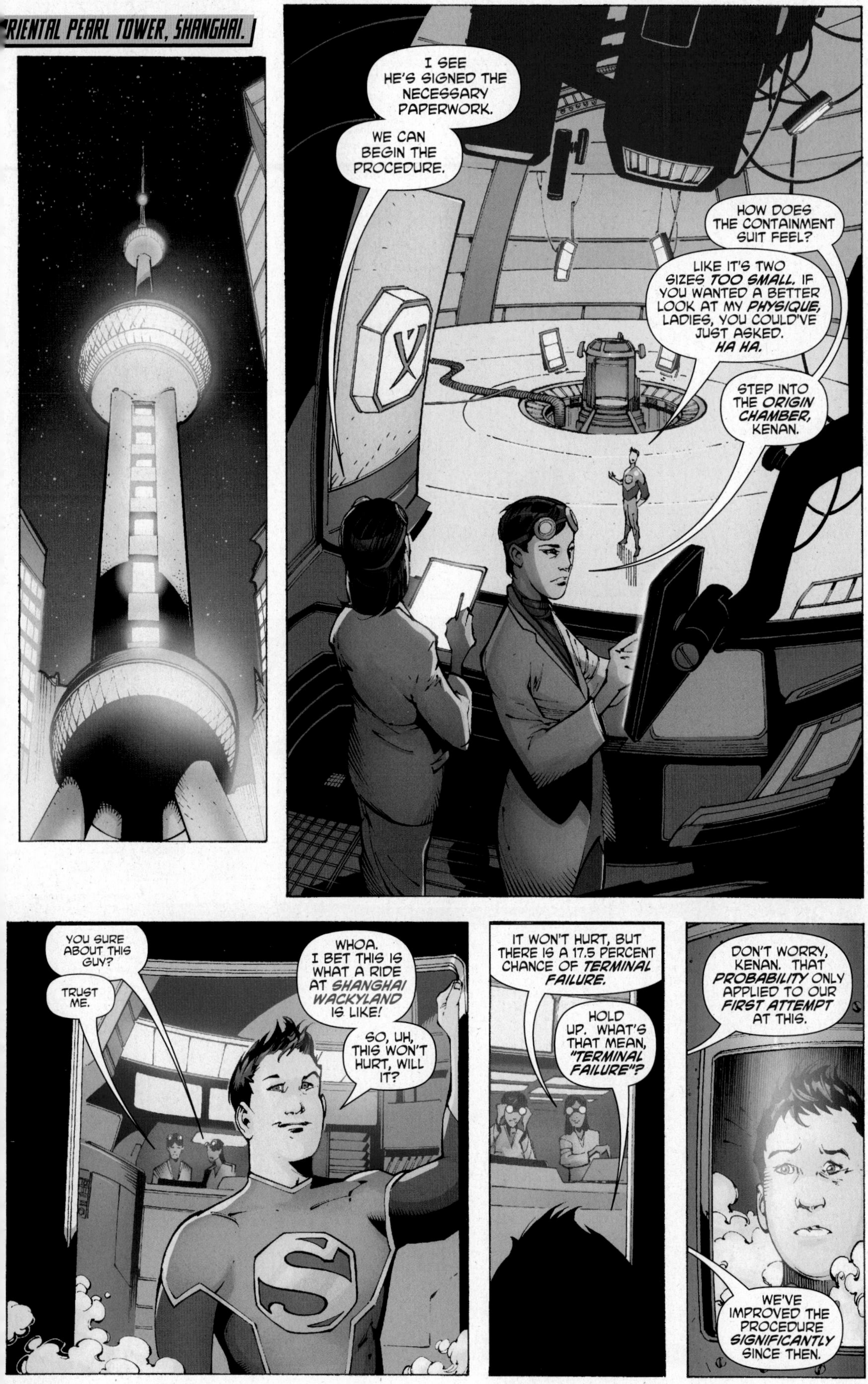

RIENTAL PEARL TOWER, SHANGHAI.
I SEE HE'S SIGNED THE NECESSARY PAPERWORK.
WE CAN BEGIN THE PROCEDURE.
HOW DOES THE CONTAINMENT SUIT FEEL?
LIKE IT'S TWO SIZES TOO SMALL. IF YOU WANTED A BETTER LOOK AT MY PHYSIQUE, LADIES, YOU COULD'VE JUST ASKED. HA HA.
STEP INTO THE ORIGIN CHAMBER, KENAN.
YOU SURE ABOUT THIS GUY?
TRUST ME.
WHOA. I BET THIS IS WHAT A RIDE AT SHANGHAI WACKYLAND IS LIKE!
SO, UH, THIS WON'T HURT, WILL IT?
IT WON'T HURT, BUT THERE IS A 17.5 PERCENT CHANCE OF TERMINAL FAILURE.
HOLD UP. WHAT'S THAT MEAN, "TERMINAL FAILURE"?
DON'T WORRY, KENAN. THAT PROBABILITY ONLY APPLIED TO OUR FIRST ATTEMPT AT THIS.
WE'VE IMPROVED THE PROCEDURE SIGNIFICANTLY SINCE THEN.

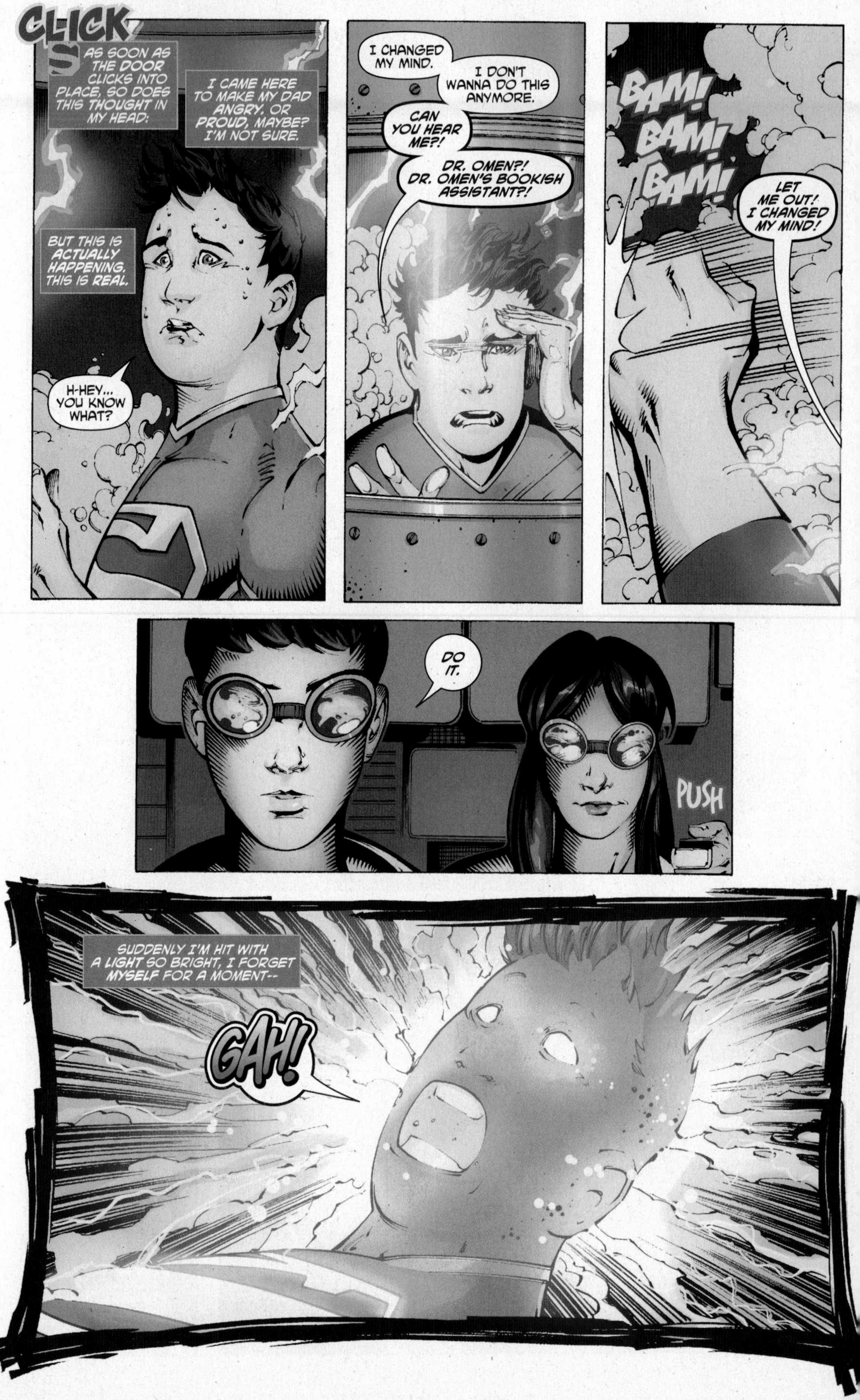
CLICK
AS SOON AS THE DOOR CLICKS INTO PLACE, SO DOES THIS THOUGHT IN MY HEAD:
I CAME HERE TO MAKE MY DAD ANGRY. OR PROUD, MAYBE? I'M NOT SURE.
BUT THIS IS ACTUALLY HAPPENING. THIS IS REAL.
H-HEY... YOU KNOW WHAT?
I CHANGED MY MIND.
I DON'T WANNA DO THIS ANYMORE.
CAN YOU HEAR ME?!
DR. OMEN?! DR. OMEN'S BOOKISH ASSISTANT?!
BAM! BAM! BAM!
LET ME OUT! I CHANGED MY MIND!
DO IT.
PUSH
SUDDENLY I'M HIT WITH A LIGHT SO BRIGHT, I FORGET MYSELF FOR A MOMENT--
GAH!

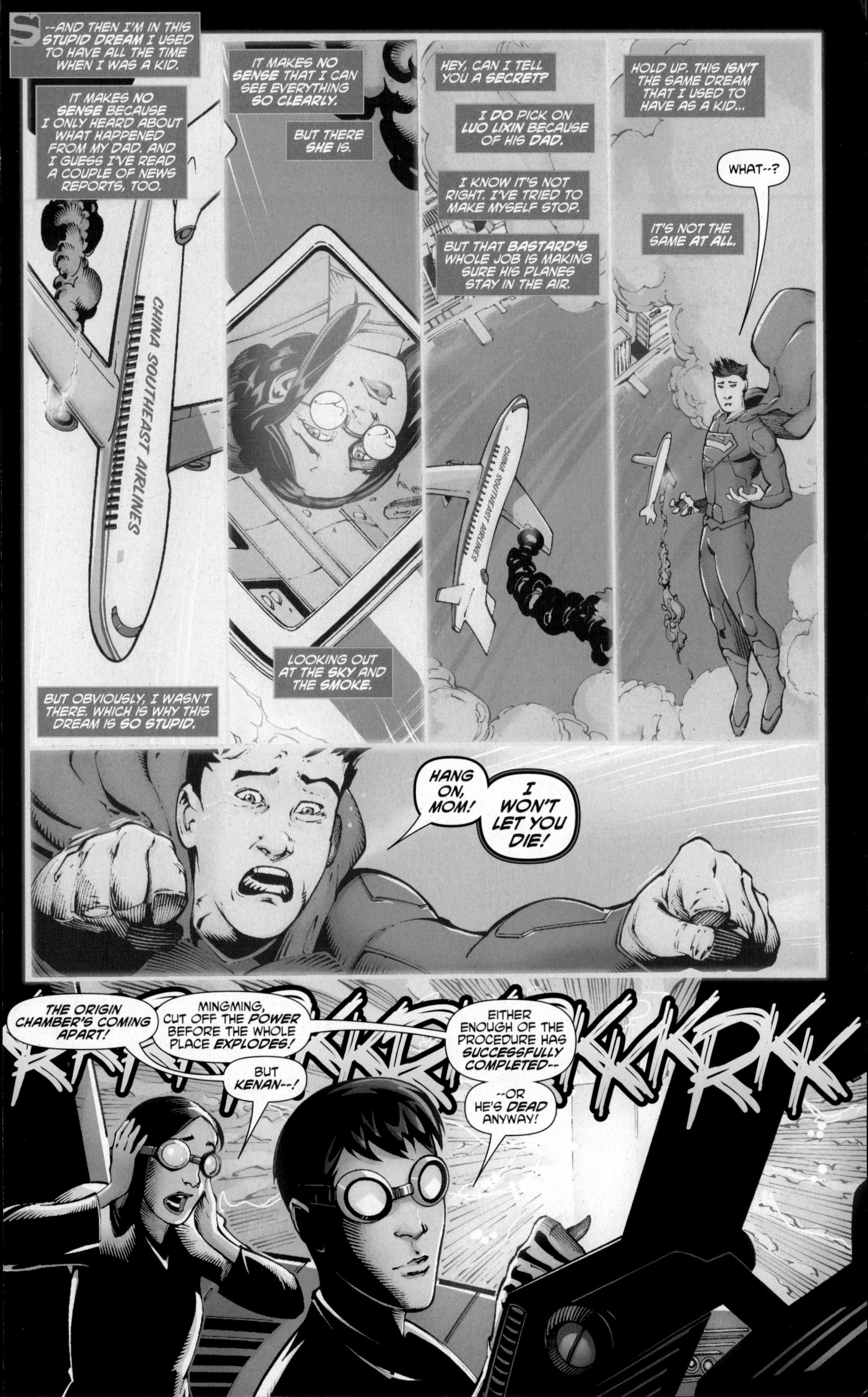
--AND THEN I'M IN THIS STUPID DREAM I USED TO HAVE ALL THE TIME WHEN I WAS A KID.
IT MAKES NO SENSE BECAUSE I ONLY HEARD ABOUT WHAT HAPPENED FROM MY DAD. AND I GUESS I'VE READ A COUPLE OF NEWS REPORTS, TOO.
CHINA SOUTHEAST AIRLINES
BUT OBVIOUSLY, I WASN'T THERE. WHICH IS WHY THIS DREAM IS SO STUPID.
IT MAKES NO SENSE THAT I CAN SEE EVERYTHING SO CLEARLY.
BUT THERE SHE IS.
LOOKING OUT AT THE SKY AND THE SMOKE.
HEY, CAN I TELL YOU A SECRET?
I DO PICK ON LUO LIXIN BECAUSE OF HIS DAD.
I KNOW IT'S NOT RIGHT. I'VE TRIED TO MAKE MYSELF STOP.
BUT THAT BASTARD'S WHOLE JOB IS MAKING SURE HIS PLANES STAY IN THE AIR.
CHINA SOUTHEAST AIRLINES
HOLD UP. THIS ISN'T THE SAME DREAM THAT I USED TO HAVE AS A KID...
WHAT--?
IT'S NOT THE SAME AT ALL.
HANG ON, MOM!
I WON'T LET YOU DIE!
THE ORIGIN CHAMBER'S COMING APART!
MINGMING, CUT OFF THE POWER BEFORE THE WHOLE PLACE EXPLODES!
BUT KENAN--!
EITHER ENOUGH OF THE PROCEDURE HAS SUCCESSFULLY COMPLETED--
--OR HE'S DEAD ANYWAY!
KRKKKKKKKKRKK

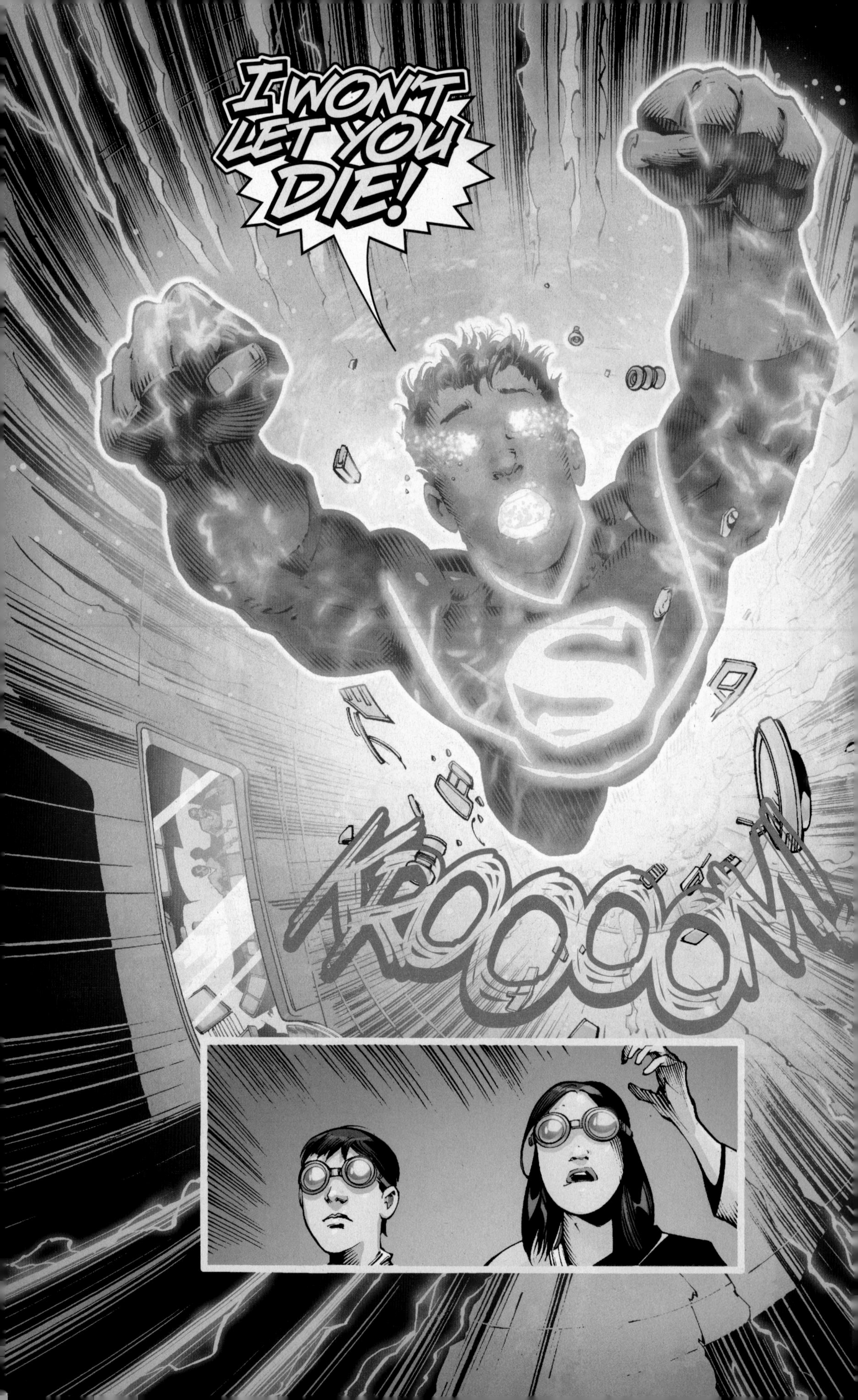
I WON'T LET YOU DIE!
KROOOOM

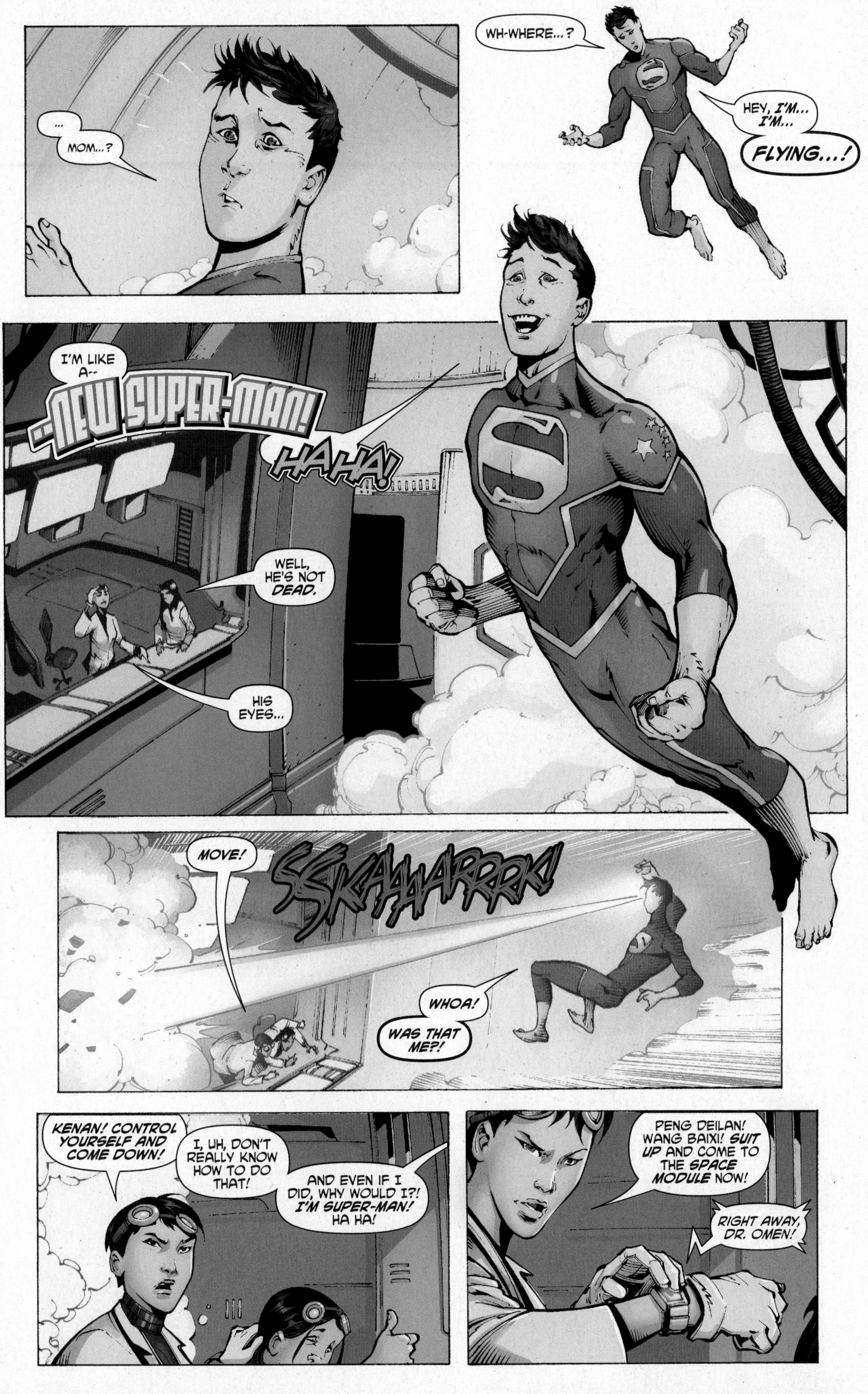
...
MOM...?
WH-WHERE...?
HEY, I'M... I'M...
FLYING...!
I'M LIKE A--
--NEW SUPER-MAN!
HAHA!
WELL, HE'S NOT DEAD.
HIS EYES...
MOVE!
SSKAAAARRRK!
WHOA!
WAS THAT ME?!
KENAN! CONTROL YOURSELF AND COME DOWN!
I, UH, DON'T REALLY KNOW HOW TO DO THAT!
AND EVEN IF I DID, WHY WOULD I?! I'M SUPER-MAN! HA HA!
PENG DEILAN! WANG BAIXI! SUIT UP AND COME TO THE SPACE MODULE NOW!
RIGHT AWAY, DR. OMEN!

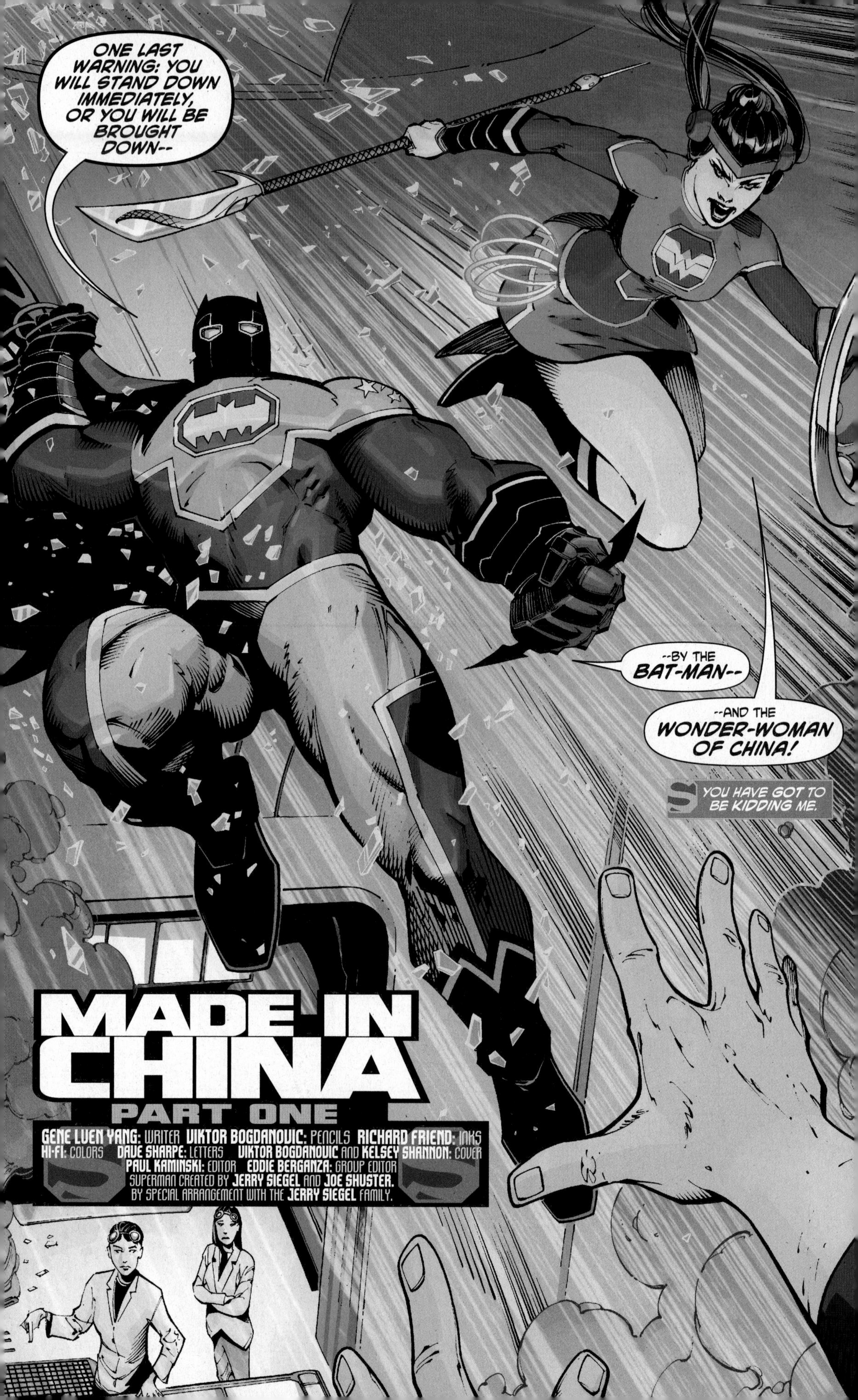
ONE LAST WARNING: YOU WILL STAND DOWN IMMEDIATELY, OR YOU WILL BE BROUGHT DOWN--
--BY THE BAT-MAN--
--AND THE WONDER-WOMAN OF CHINA!
YOU HAVE GOT TO BE KIDDING ME.
MADE IN CHINA
PART ONE
GENE LUEN YANG: WRITER VIKTOR BOGDANOVIC: PENCILS RICHARD FRIEND: INKS
HI-FI: COLORS DAVE SHARPE: LETTERS VIKTOR BOGDANOVIC AND KELSEY SHANNON: COVER
PAUL KAMINSKI: EDITOR EDDIE BERGANZA: GROUP EDITOR
SUPERMAN CREATED BY JERRY SIEGEL AND JOE SHUSTER.
BY SPECIAL ARRANGEMENT WITH THE JERRY SIEGEL FAMILY.

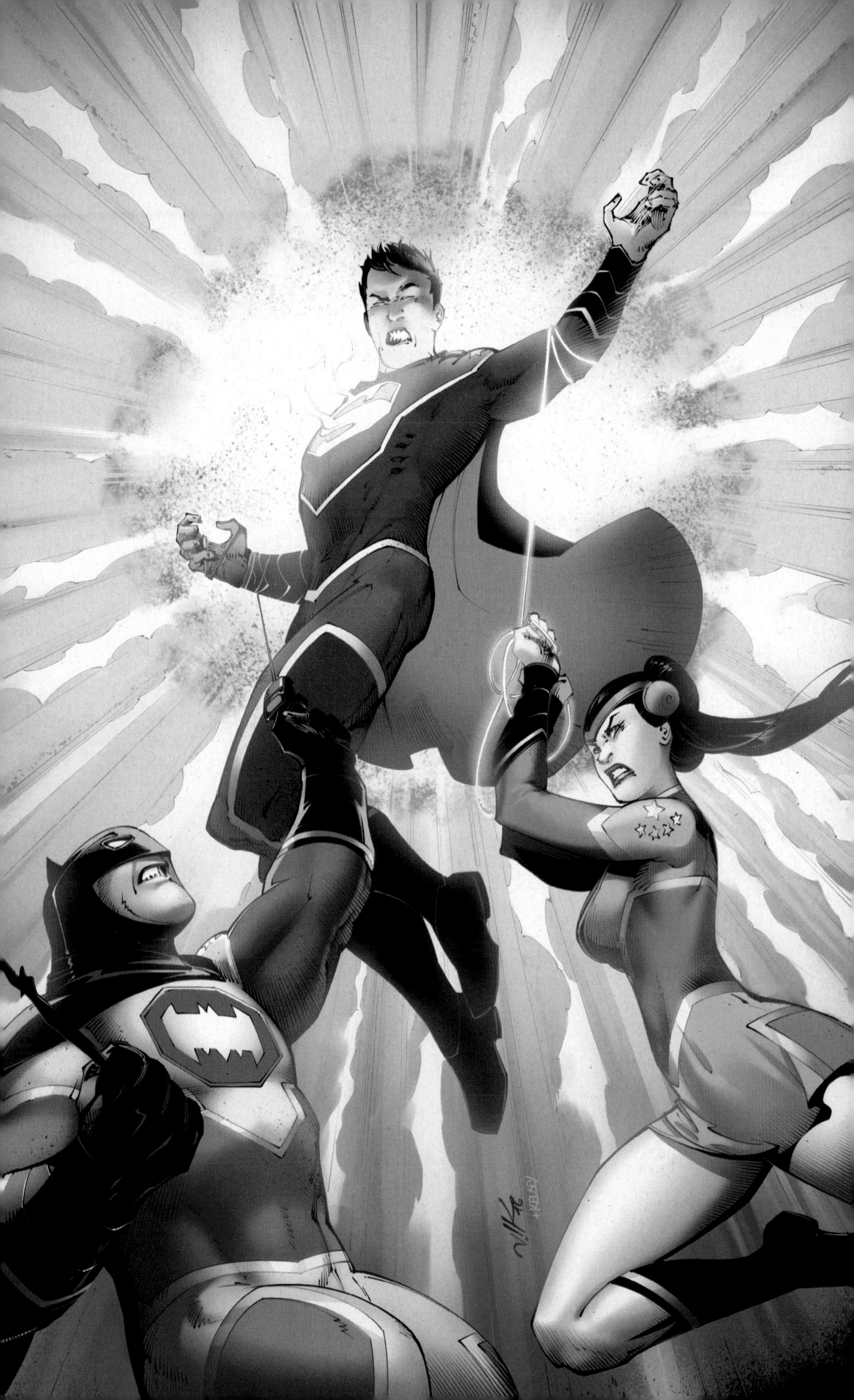

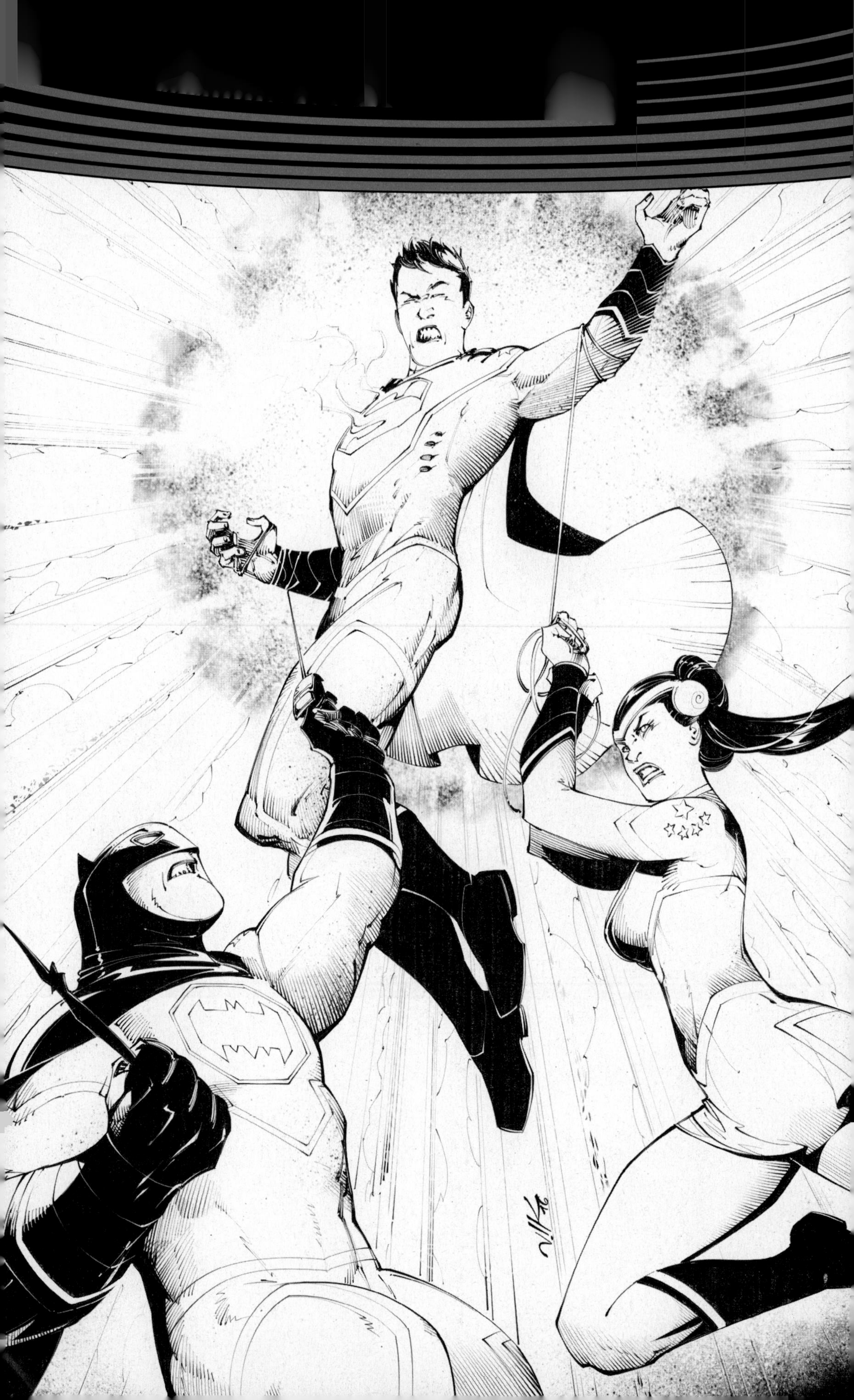

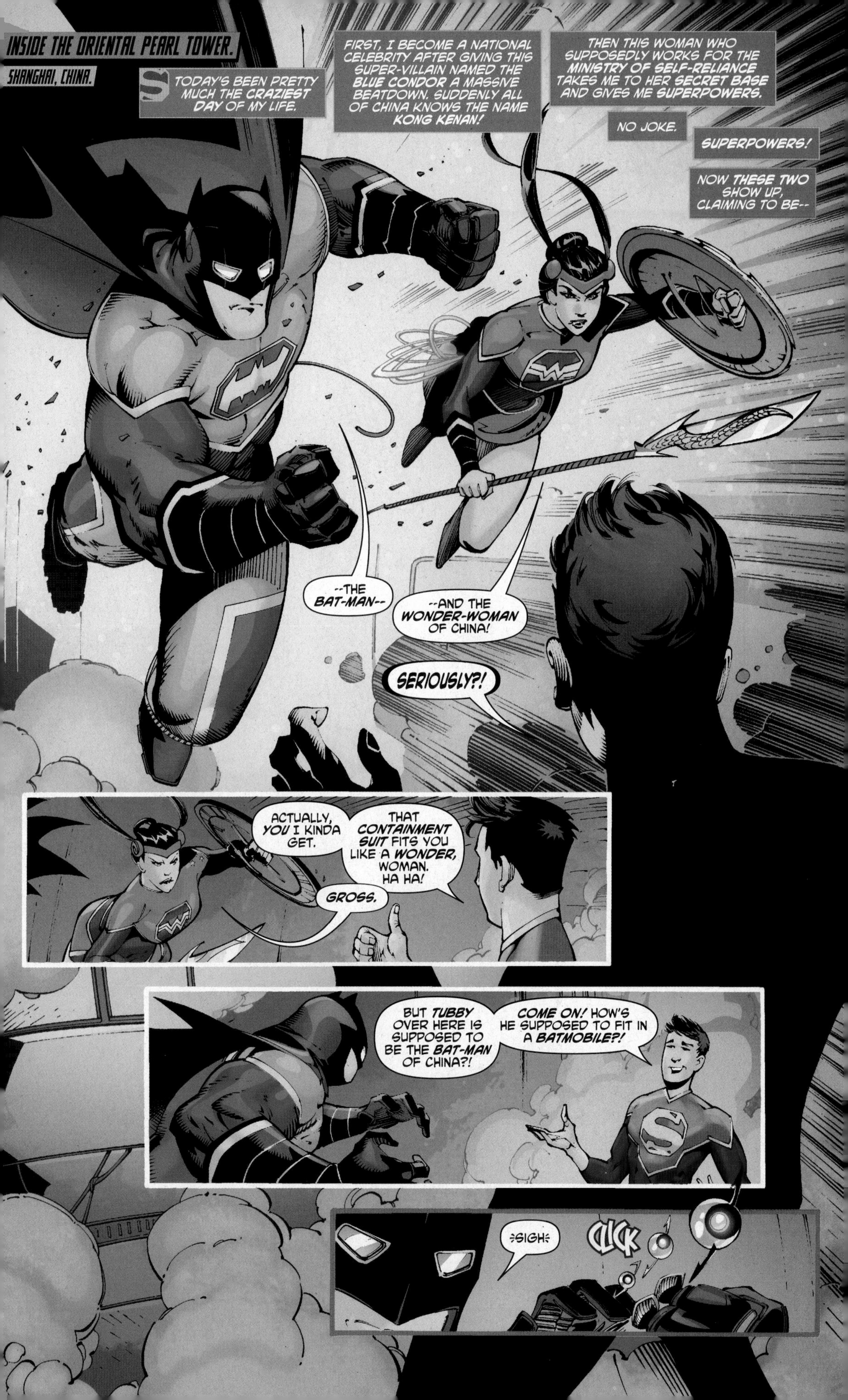
INSIDE THE ORIENTAL PEARL TOWER.
SHANGHAI, CHINA.
TODAY'S BEEN PRETTY MUCH THE CRAZIEST DAY OF MY LIFE.
FIRST, I BECOME A NATIONAL CELEBRITY AFTER GIVING THIS SUPER-VILLAIN NAMED THE BLUE CONDOR A MASSIVE BEATDOWN. SUDDENLY ALL OF CHINA KNOWS THE NAME KONG KENAN!
THEN THIS WOMAN WHO SUPPOSEDLY WORKS FOR THE MINISTRY OF SELF-RELIANCE TAKES ME TO HER SECRET BASE AND GIVES ME SUPERPOWERS.
NO JOKE.
SUPERPOWERS!
NOW THESE TWO SHOW UP, CLAIMING TO BE--
--THE BAT-MAN--
--AND THE WONDER-WOMAN OF CHINA!
SERIOUSLY?!
ACTUALLY, YOU I KINDA GET.
THAT CONTAINMENT SUIT FITS YOU LIKE A WONDER, WOMAN. HA HA!
GROSS.
BUT TUBBY OVER HERE IS SUPPOSED TO BE THE BAT-MAN OF CHINA?!
COME ON! HOW'S HE SUPPOSED TO FIT IN A BATMOBILE?!
SIGH
CLICK

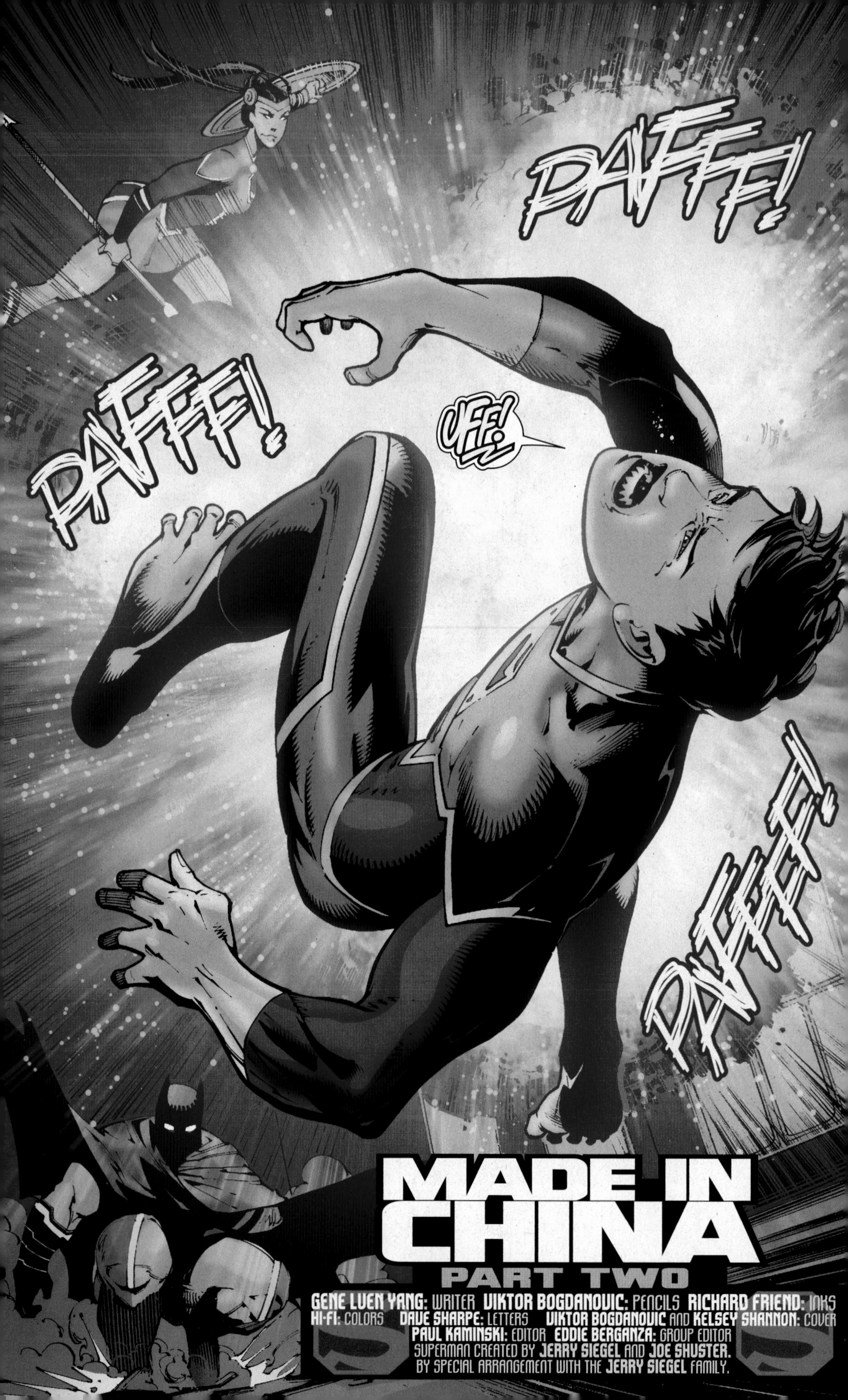
DAFFF!
DAFFF!
UFF!
DAFFF!
MADE IN CHINA
PART TWO
GENE LUEN YANG: WRITER VIKTOR BOGDANOVIC: PENCILS RICHARD FRIEND: INKS
HI-FI: COLORS DAVE SHARPE: LETTERS VIKTOR BOGDANOVIC AND KELSEY SHANNON: COVER
PAUL KAMINSKI: EDITOR EDDIE BERGANZA: GROUP EDITOR
SUPERMAN CREATED BY JERRY SIEGEL AND JOE SHUSTER.
BY SPECIAL ARRANGEMENT WITH THE JERRY SIEGEL FAMILY.

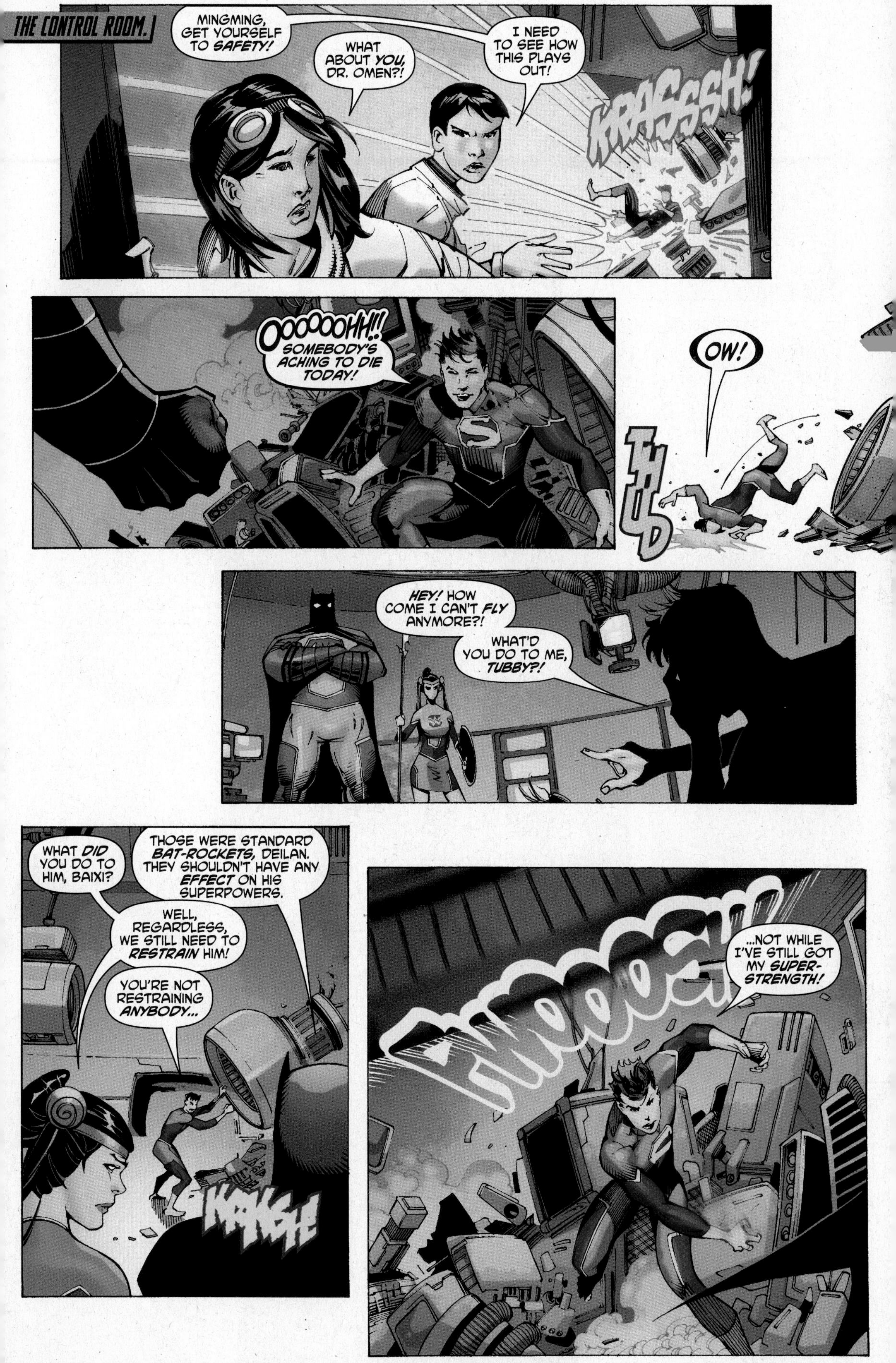
THE CONTROL ROOM.
MINGMING, GET YOURSELF TO SAFETY!
WHAT ABOUT YOU, DR. OMEN?!
I NEED TO SEE HOW THIS PLAYS OUT!
KRASSSH!
OOOOOOHH!! SOMEBODY'S ACHING TO DIE TODAY!
OW!
THUD
HEY! HOW COME I CAN'T FLY ANYMORE?!
WHAT'D YOU DO TO ME, TUBBY?!
WHAT DID YOU DO TO HIM, BAIXI?
THOSE WERE STANDARD BAT-ROCKETS, DEILAN. THEY SHOULDN'T HAVE ANY EFFECT ON HIS SUPERPOWERS.
WELL, REGARDLESS, WE STILL NEED TO RESTRAIN HIM!
YOU'RE NOT RESTRAINING ANYBODY...
KRASH!
FWOOOSH!
...NOT WHILE I'VE STILL GOT MY SUPER-STRENGTH!

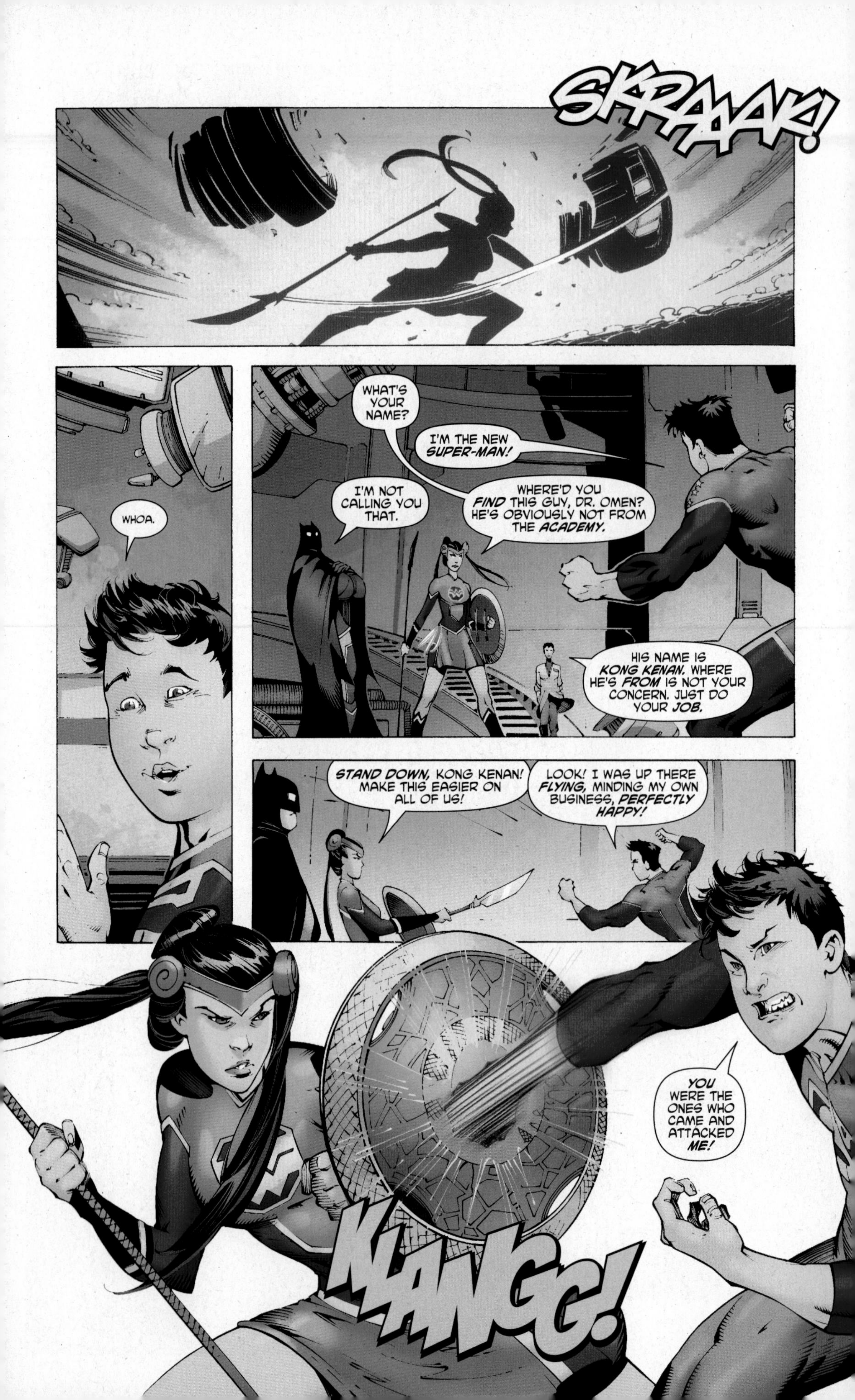
SKRAAAK!
WHOA.
WHAT'S YOUR NAME?
I'M THE NEW SUPER-MAN!
I'M NOT CALLING YOU THAT.
WHERE'D YOU FIND THIS GUY, DR. OMEN? HE'S OBVIOUSLY NOT FROM THE ACADEMY.
HIS NAME IS KONG KENAN. WHERE HE'S FROM IS NOT YOUR CONCERN. JUST DO YOUR JOB.
STAND DOWN, KONG KENAN! MAKE THIS EASIER ON ALL OF US!
LOOK! I WAS UP THERE FLYING, MINDING MY OWN BUSINESS, PERFECTLY HAPPY!
YOU WERE THE ONES WHO CAME AND ATTACKED ME!
KLANGG!

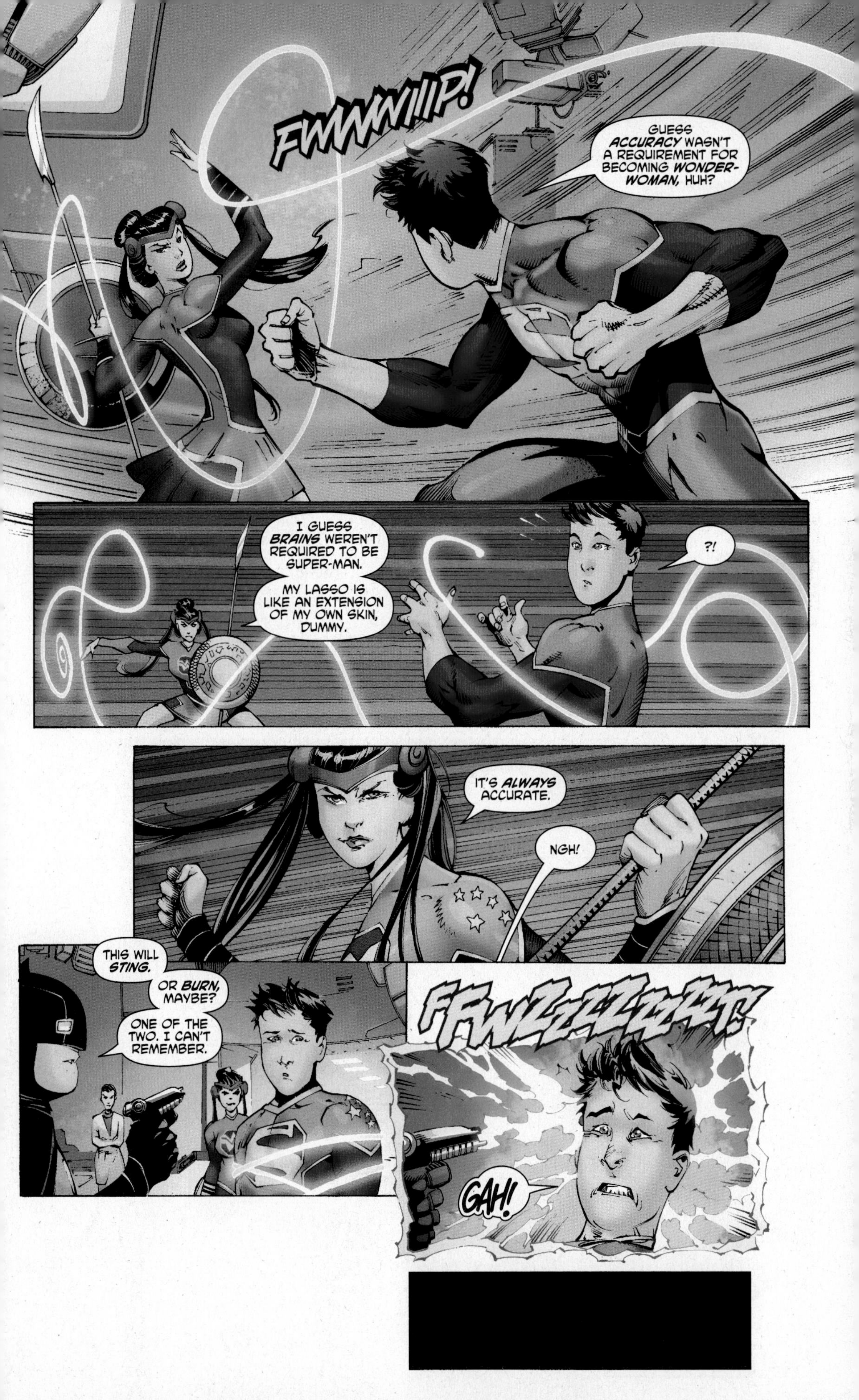
FWWWIIIP!
GUESS ACCURACY WASN'T A REQUIREMENT FOR BECOMING WONDER-WOMAN, HUH?
I GUESS BRAINS WEREN'T REQUIRED TO BE SUPER-MAN.
MY LASSO IS LIKE AN EXTENSION OF MY OWN SKIN, DUMMY.
?!
IT'S ALWAYS ACCURATE.
NGH!
THIS WILL STING.
OR BURN, MAYBE?
ONE OF THE TWO. I CAN'T REMEMBER.
FFWZZZZZZZT!
GAH!
[redacted]

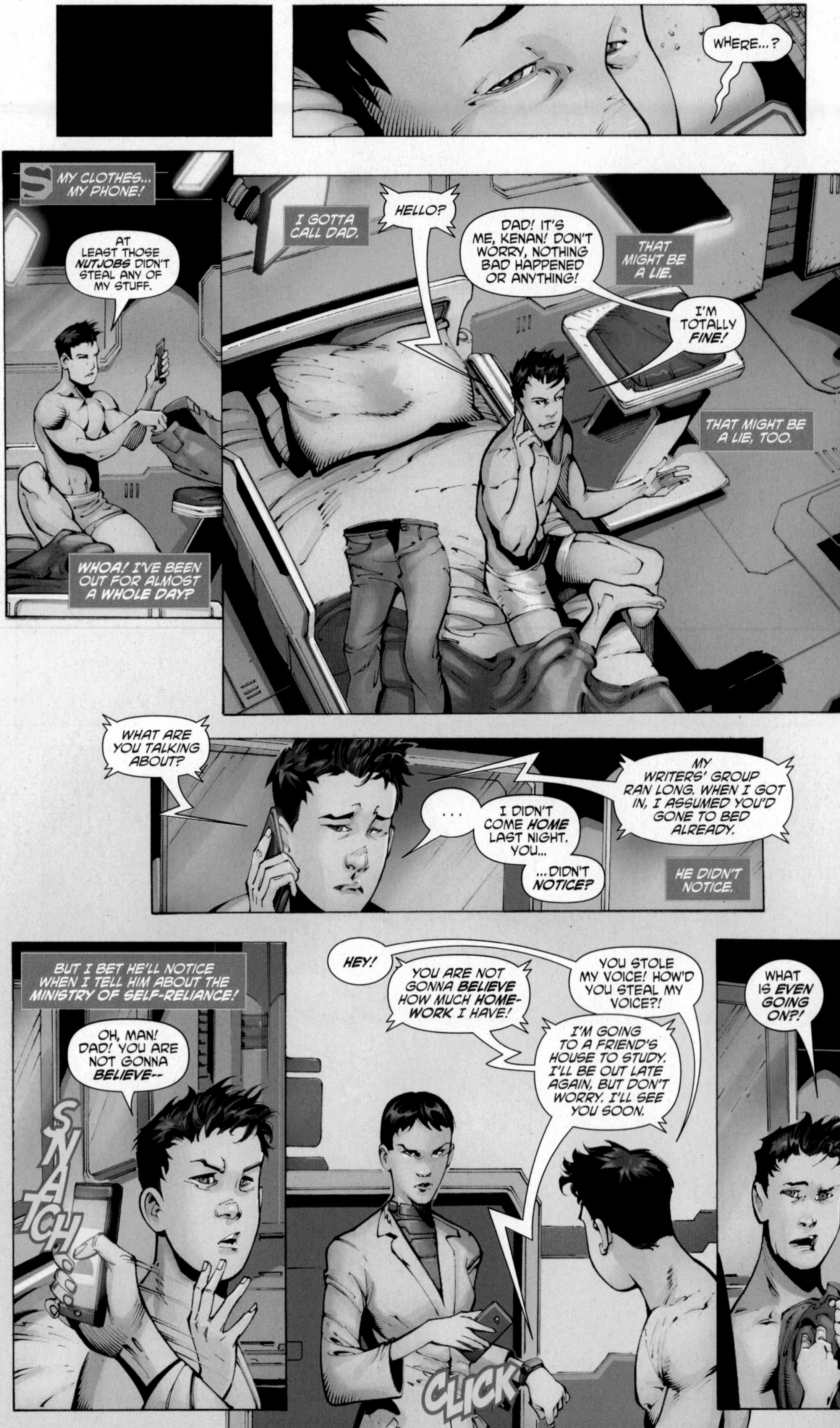
WHERE...?
MY CLOTHES... MY PHONE!
AT LEAST THOSE NUTJOBS DIDN'T STEAL ANY OF MY STUFF.
WHOA! I'VE BEEN OUT FOR ALMOST A WHOLE DAY?
I GOTTA CALL DAD.
HELLO?
DAD! IT'S ME, KENAN! DON'T WORRY, NOTHING BAD HAPPENED OR ANYTHING!
THAT MIGHT BE A LIE.
I'M TOTALLY FINE!
THAT MIGHT BE A LIE, TOO.
WHAT ARE YOU TALKING ABOUT?
...
I DIDN'T COME HOME LAST NIGHT. YOU...
...DIDN'T NOTICE?
MY WRITERS' GROUP RAN LONG. WHEN I GOT IN, I ASSUMED YOU'D GONE TO BED ALREADY.
HE DIDN'T NOTICE.
BUT I BET HE'LL NOTICE WHEN I TELL HIM ABOUT THE MINISTRY OF SELF-RELIANCE!
OH, MAN! DAD! YOU ARE NOT GONNA BELIEVE--
SNATCH
HEY!
YOU ARE NOT GONNA BELIEVE HOW MUCH HOME-WORK I HAVE!
YOU STOLE MY VOICE! HOW'D YOU STEAL MY VOICE?!
I'M GOING TO A FRIEND'S HOUSE TO STUDY. I'LL BE OUT LATE AGAIN, BUT DON'T WORRY. I'LL SEE YOU SOON.
CLICK
WHAT IS EVEN GOING ON?!

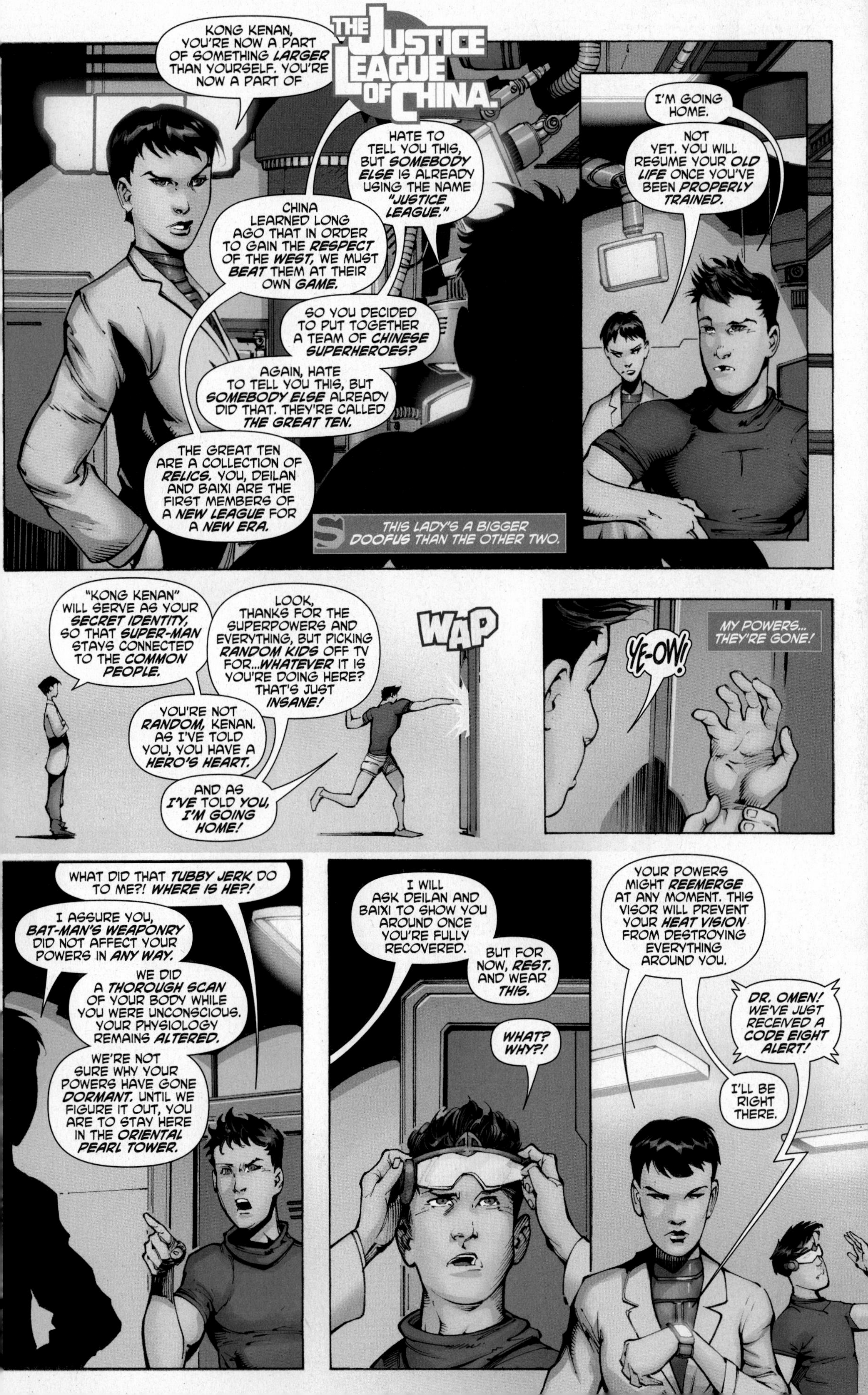
KONG KENAN, YOU'RE NOW A PART OF SOMETHING LARGER THAN YOURSELF. YOU'RE NOW A PART OF
THE JUSTICE LEAGUE OF CHINA.
HATE TO TELL YOU THIS, BUT SOMEBODY ELSE IS ALREADY USING THE NAME "JUSTICE LEAGUE."
CHINA LEARNED LONG AGO THAT IN ORDER TO GAIN THE RESPECT OF THE WEST, WE MUST BEAT THEM AT THEIR OWN GAME.
SO YOU DECIDED TO PUT TOGETHER A TEAM OF CHINESE SUPERHEROES?
AGAIN, HATE TO TELL YOU THIS, BUT SOMEBODY ELSE ALREADY DID THAT. THEY'RE CALLED THE GREAT TEN.
THE GREAT TEN ARE A COLLECTION OF RELICS. YOU, DEILAN AND BAIXI ARE THE FIRST MEMBERS OF A NEW LEAGUE FOR A NEW ERA.
THIS LADY'S A BIGGER DOOFUS THAN THE OTHER TWO.
I'M GOING HOME.
NOT YET. YOU WILL RESUME YOUR OLD LIFE ONCE YOU'VE BEEN PROPERLY TRAINED.
"KONG KENAN" WILL SERVE AS YOUR SECRET IDENTITY, SO THAT SUPER-MAN STAYS CONNECTED TO THE COMMON PEOPLE.
LOOK, THANKS FOR THE SUPERPOWERS AND EVERYTHING, BUT PICKING RANDOM KIDS OFF TV FOR...WHATEVER IT IS YOU'RE DOING HERE? THAT'S JUST INSANE!
YOU'RE NOT RANDOM, KENAN. AS I'VE TOLD YOU, YOU HAVE A HERO'S HEART.
AND AS I'VE TOLD YOU, I'M GOING HOME!
WAP
YE-OW!
MY POWERS... THEY'RE GONE!
WHAT DID THAT TUBBY JERK DO TO ME?! WHERE IS HE?!
I ASSURE YOU, BAT-MAN'S WEAPONRY DID NOT AFFECT YOUR POWERS IN ANY WAY.
WE DID A THOROUGH SCAN OF YOUR BODY WHILE YOU WERE UNCONSCIOUS. YOUR PHYSIOLOGY REMAINS ALTERED.
WE'RE NOT SURE WHY YOUR POWERS HAVE GONE DORMANT. UNTIL WE FIGURE IT OUT, YOU ARE TO STAY HERE IN THE ORIENTAL PEARL TOWER.
I WILL ASK DEILAN AND BAIXI TO SHOW YOU AROUND ONCE YOU'RE FULLY RECOVERED.
BUT FOR NOW, REST. AND WEAR THIS.
WHAT? WHY?!
YOUR POWERS MIGHT REEMERGE AT ANY MOMENT. THIS VISOR WILL PREVENT YOUR HEAT VISION FROM DESTROYING EVERYTHING AROUND YOU.
DR. OMEN! WE'VE JUST RECEIVED A CODE EIGHT ALERT!
I'LL BE RIGHT THERE.

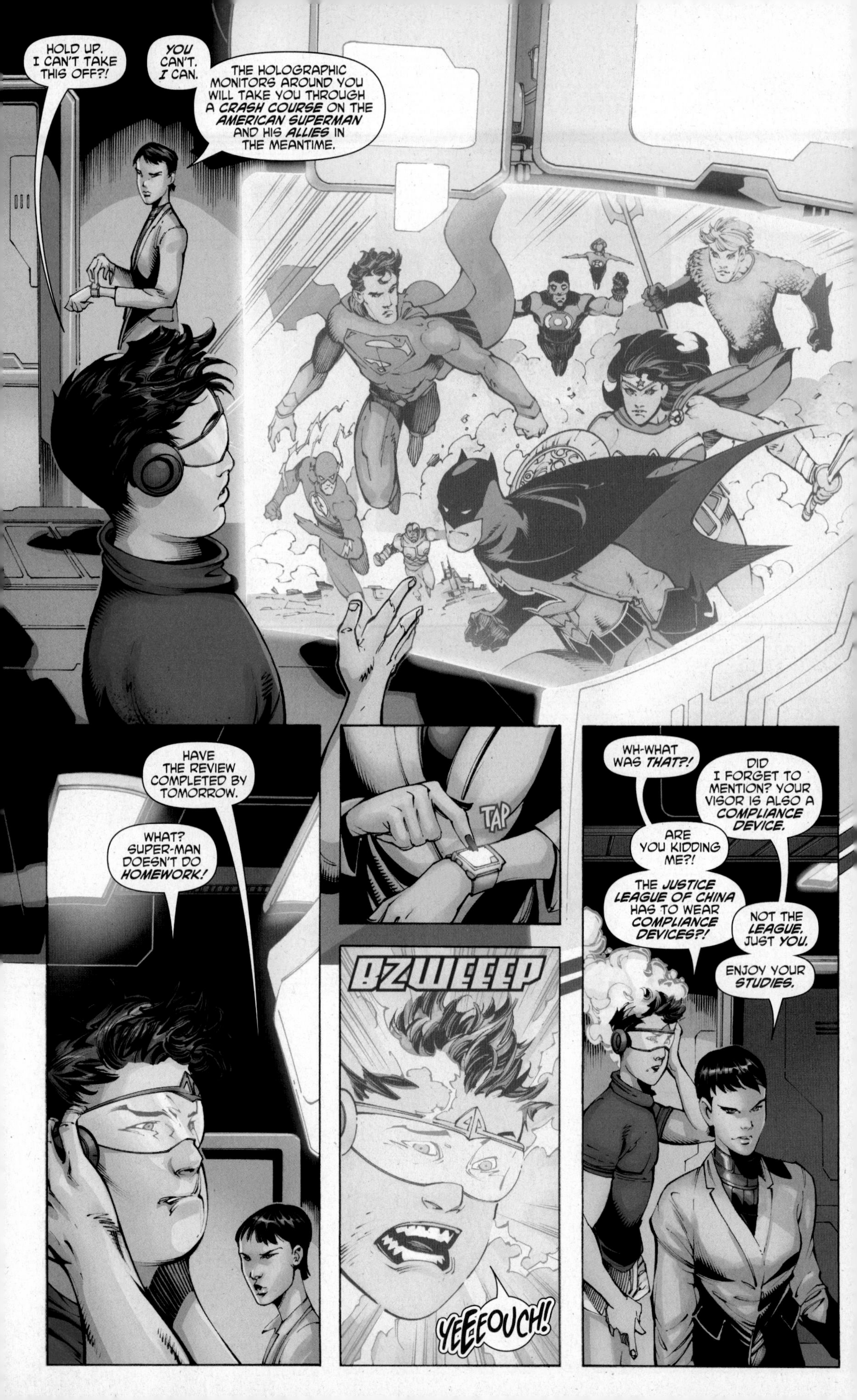
HOLD UP. I CAN'T TAKE THIS OFF?!
YOU CAN'T. I CAN.
THE HOLOGRAPHIC MONITORS AROUND YOU WILL TAKE YOU THROUGH A CRASH COURSE ON THE AMERICAN SUPERMAN AND HIS ALLIES IN THE MEANTIME.
HAVE THE REVIEW COMPLETED BY TOMORROW.
WHAT? SUPER-MAN DOESN'T DO HOMEWORK!
TAP
BZWEEEP
YEEEOUCH!
WH-WHAT WAS THAT?!
DID I FORGET TO MENTION? YOUR VISOR IS ALSO A COMPLIANCE DEVICE.
ARE YOU KIDDING ME?!
THE JUSTICE LEAGUE OF CHINA HAS TO WEAR COMPLIANCE DEVICES?!
NOT THE LEAGUE. JUST YOU.
ENJOY YOUR STUDIES.

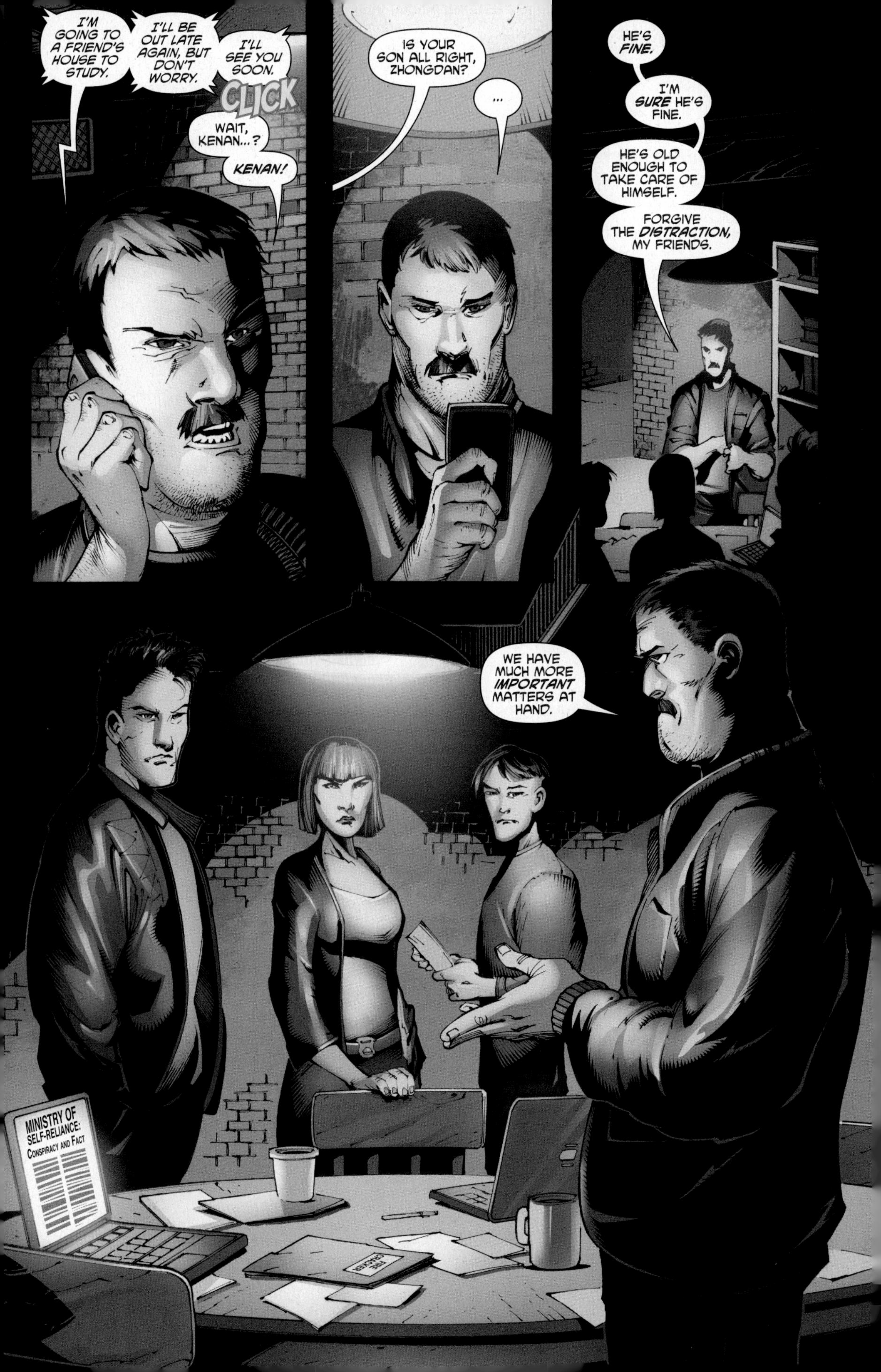
I'M GOING TO A FRIEND'S HOUSE TO STUDY.
I'LL BE OUT LATE AGAIN, BUT DON'T WORRY.
I'LL SEE YOU SOON.
CLICK
WAIT, KENAN...?
KENAN!
IS YOUR SON ALL RIGHT, ZHONGDAN?
...
HE'S FINE.
I'M SURE HE'S FINE.
HE'S OLD ENOUGH TO TAKE CARE OF HIMSELF.
FORGIVE THE DISTRACTION, MY FRIENDS.
WE HAVE MUCH MORE IMPORTANT MATTERS AT HAND.
MINISTRY OF SELF-RELIANCE: CONSPIRACY AND FACT

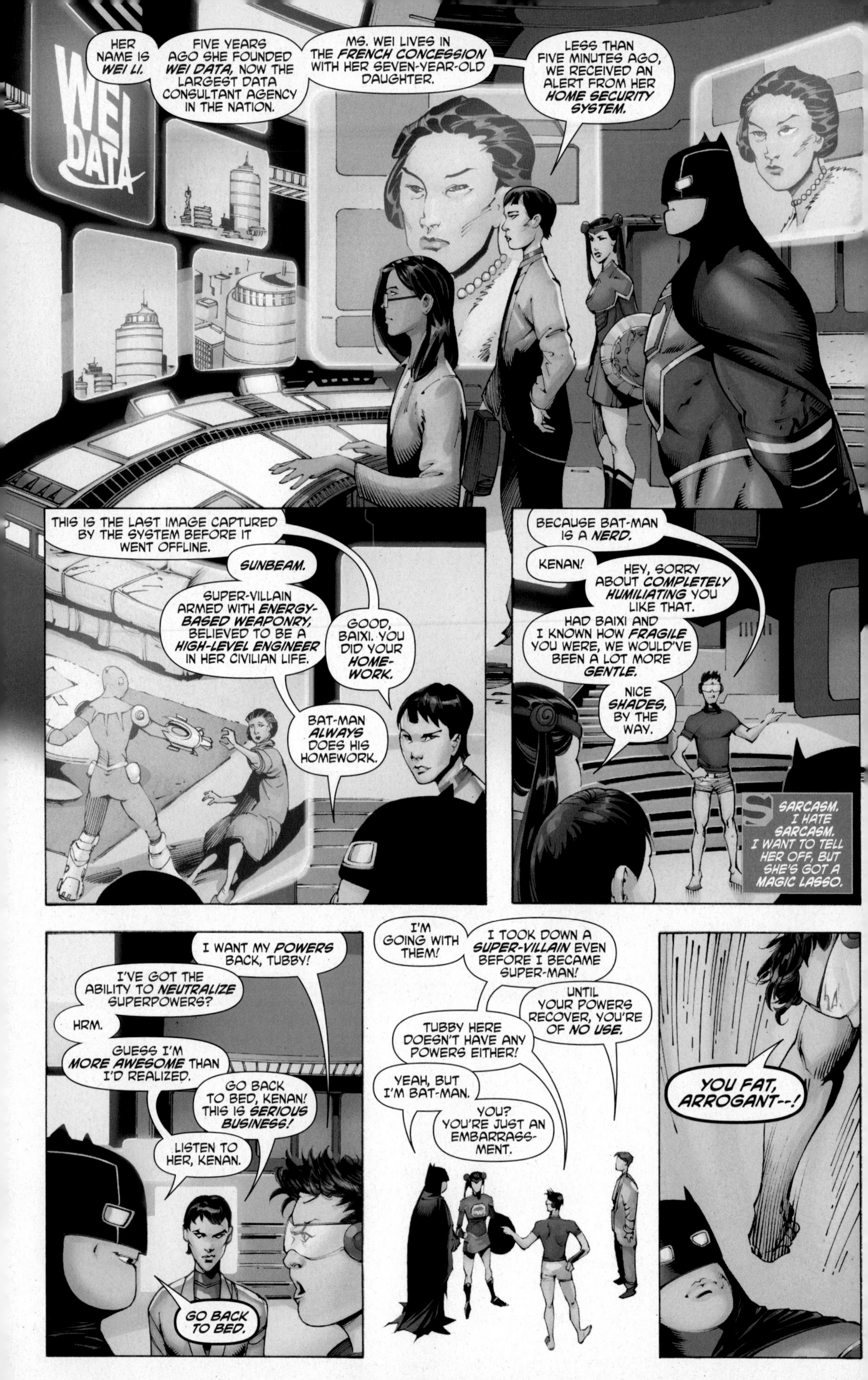
HER NAME IS WEI LI.
FIVE YEARS AGO SHE FOUNDED WEI DATA, NOW THE LARGEST DATA CONSULTANT AGENCY IN THE NATION.
MS. WEI LIVES IN THE FRENCH CONCESSION WITH HER SEVEN-YEAR-OLD DAUGHTER.
LESS THAN FIVE MINUTES AGO, WE RECEIVED AN ALERT FROM HER HOME SECURITY SYSTEM.
WEI DATA
THIS IS THE LAST IMAGE CAPTURED BY THE SYSTEM BEFORE IT WENT OFFLINE.
SUNBEAM.
SUPER-VILLAIN ARMED WITH ENERGY-BASED WEAPONRY, BELIEVED TO BE A HIGH-LEVEL ENGINEER IN HER CIVILIAN LIFE.
GOOD, BAIXI. YOU DID YOUR HOME-WORK.
BAT-MAN ALWAYS DOES HIS HOMEWORK.
BECAUSE BAT-MAN IS A NERD.
KENAN!
HEY, SORRY ABOUT COMPLETELY HUMILIATING YOU LIKE THAT.
HAD BAIXI AND I KNOWN HOW FRAGILE YOU WERE, WE WOULD'VE BEEN A LOT MORE GENTLE.
NICE SHADES, BY THE WAY.
SARCASM. I HATE SARCASM. I WANT TO TELL HER OFF, BUT SHE'S GOT A MAGIC LASSO.
I WANT MY POWERS BACK, TUBBY!
I'VE GOT THE ABILITY TO NEUTRALIZE SUPERPOWERS?
HRM.
GUESS I'M MORE AWESOME THAN I'D REALIZED.
GO BACK TO BED, KENAN! THIS IS SERIOUS BUSINESS!
LISTEN TO HER, KENAN.
GO BACK TO BED.
I'M GOING WITH THEM!
I TOOK DOWN A SUPER-VILLAIN EVEN BEFORE I BECAME SUPER-MAN!
UNTIL YOUR POWERS RECOVER, YOU'RE OF NO USE.
TUBBY HERE DOESN'T HAVE ANY POWERS EITHER!
YEAH, BUT I'M BAT-MAN.
YOU? YOU'RE JUST AN EMBARRASS-MENT.
YOU FAT, ARROGANT--!

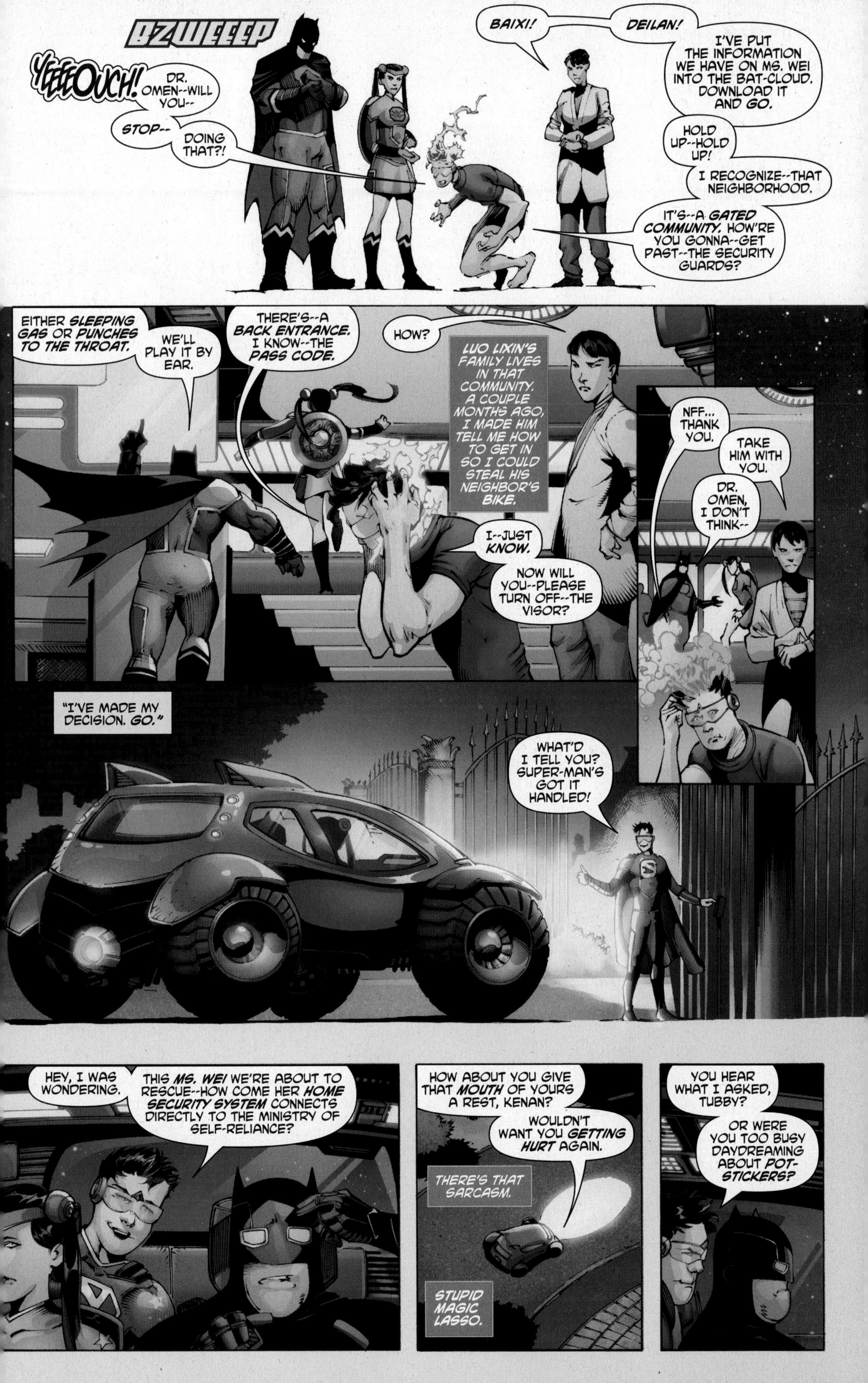
BZWEEEP
YEEEOUCH!
DR. OMEN--WILL YOU--
STOP--
DOING THAT?!
BAIXI!
DEILAN!
I'VE PUT THE INFORMATION WE HAVE ON MS. WEI INTO THE BAT-CLOUD. DOWNLOAD IT AND GO.
HOLD UP--HOLD UP!
I RECOGNIZE--THAT NEIGHBORHOOD.
IT'S--A GATED COMMUNITY. HOW'RE YOU GONNA--GET PAST--THE SECURITY GUARDS?
EITHER SLEEPING GAS OR PUNCHES TO THE THROAT.
WE'LL PLAY IT BY EAR.
THERE'S--A BACK ENTRANCE. I KNOW--THE PASS CODE.
HOW?
LUO LIXIN'S FAMILY LIVES IN THAT COMMUNITY. A COUPLE MONTHS AGO, I MADE HIM TELL ME HOW TO GET IN SO I COULD STEAL HIS NEIGHBOR'S BIKE.
I--JUST KNOW.
NOW WILL YOU--PLEASE TURN OFF--THE VISOR?
NFF... THANK YOU.
TAKE HIM WITH YOU.
DR. OMEN, I DON'T THINK--
"I'VE MADE MY DECISION. GO."
WHAT'D I TELL YOU? SUPER-MAN'S GOT IT HANDLED!
HEY, I WAS WONDERING.
THIS MS. WEI WE'RE ABOUT TO RESCUE--HOW COME HER HOME SECURITY SYSTEM CONNECTS DIRECTLY TO THE MINISTRY OF SELF-RELIANCE?
HOW ABOUT YOU GIVE THAT MOUTH OF YOURS A REST, KENAN?
WOULDN'T WANT YOU GETTING HURT AGAIN.
THERE'S THAT SARCASM.
STUPID MAGIC LASSO.
YOU HEAR WHAT I ASKED, TUBBY?
OR WERE YOU TOO BUSY DAYDREAMING ABOUT POT-STICKERS?

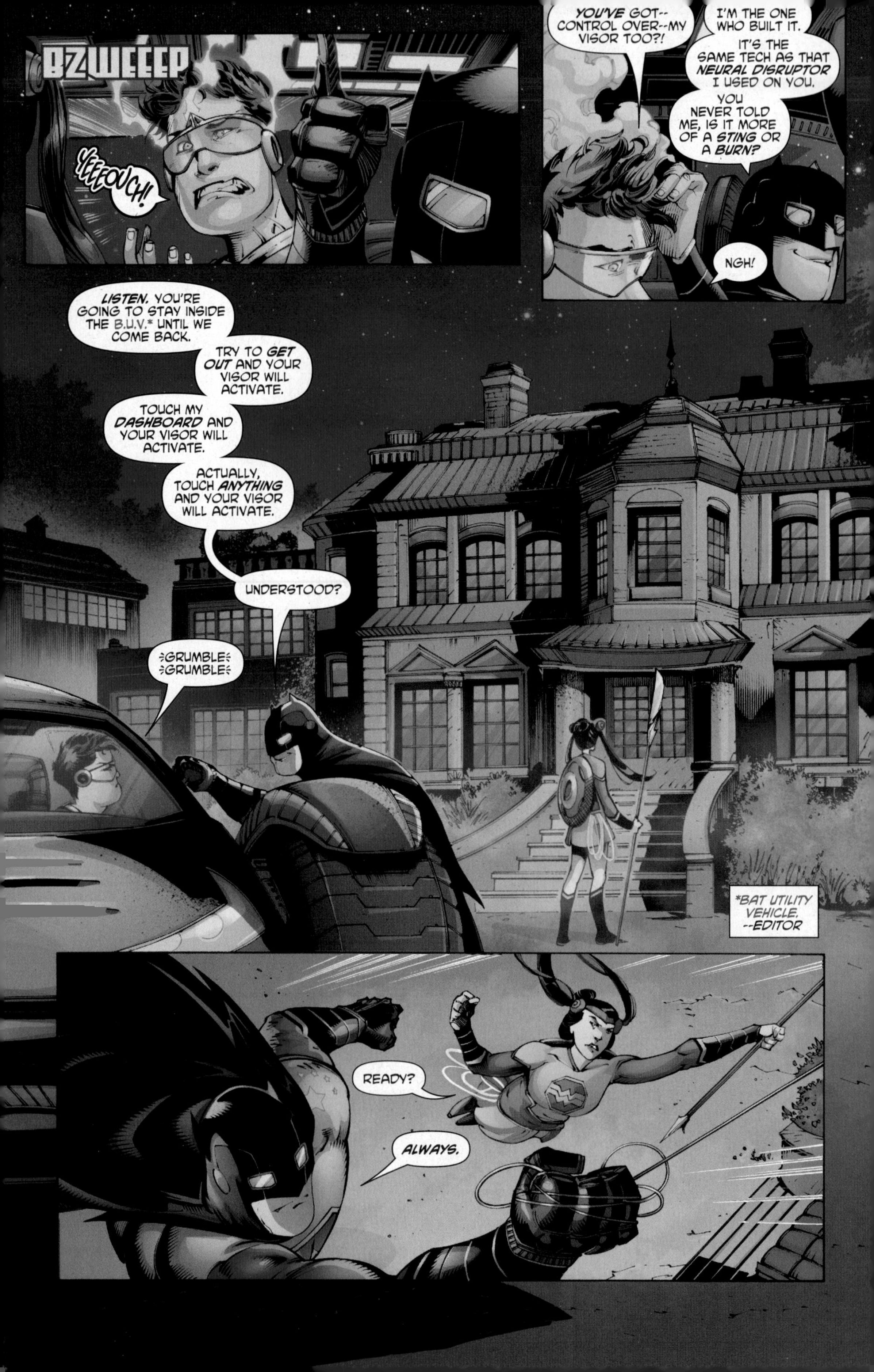
BZWEEEP
YEEEOUCH!
YOU'VE GOT-- CONTROL OVER--MY VISOR TOO?!
I'M THE ONE WHO BUILT IT.
IT'S THE SAME TECH AS THAT NEURAL DISRUPTOR I USED ON YOU.
YOU NEVER TOLD ME, IS IT MORE OF A STING OR A BURN?
NGH!
LISTEN. YOU'RE GOING TO STAY INSIDE THE B.U.V.* UNTIL WE COME BACK.
TRY TO GET OUT AND YOUR VISOR WILL ACTIVATE.
TOUCH MY DASHBOARD AND YOUR VISOR WILL ACTIVATE.
ACTUALLY, TOUCH ANYTHING AND YOUR VISOR WILL ACTIVATE.
UNDERSTOOD?
GRUMBLE GRUMBLE
*BAT UTILITY VEHICLE. --EDITOR
READY?
ALWAYS.

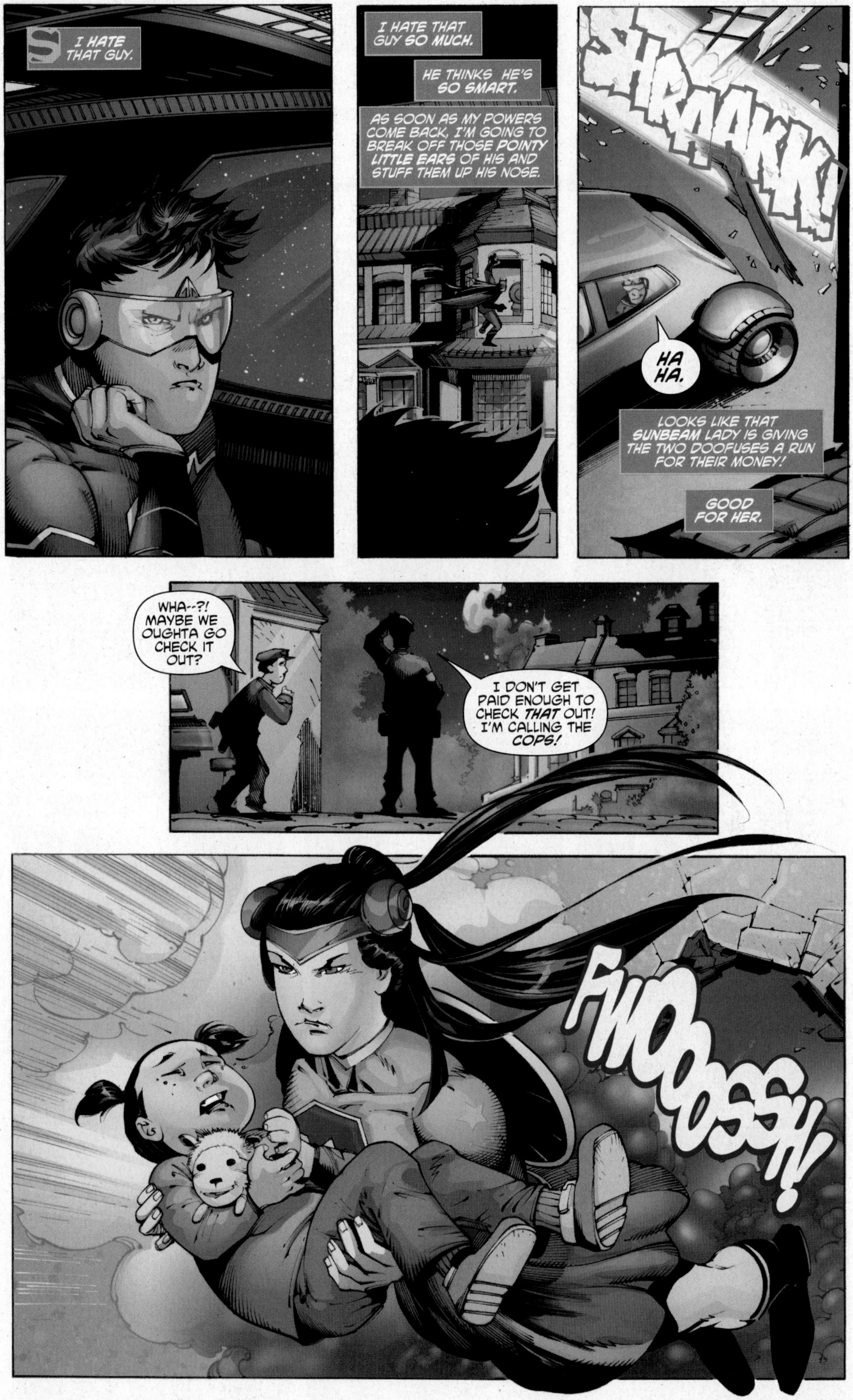
I HATE THAT GUY.
I HATE THAT GUY SO MUCH.
HE THINKS HE'S SO SMART.
AS SOON AS MY POWERS COME BACK, I'M GOING TO BREAK OFF THOSE POINTY LITTLE EARS OF HIS AND STUFF THEM UP HIS NOSE.
SHRAAKK!
HA HA.
LOOKS LIKE THAT SUNBEAM LADY IS GIVING THE TWO DOOFUSES A RUN FOR THEIR MONEY!
GOOD FOR HER.
WHA--?! MAYBE WE OUGHTA GO CHECK IT OUT?
I DON'T GET PAID ENOUGH TO CHECK THAT OUT! I'M CALLING THE COPS!
FWOOOSSH!

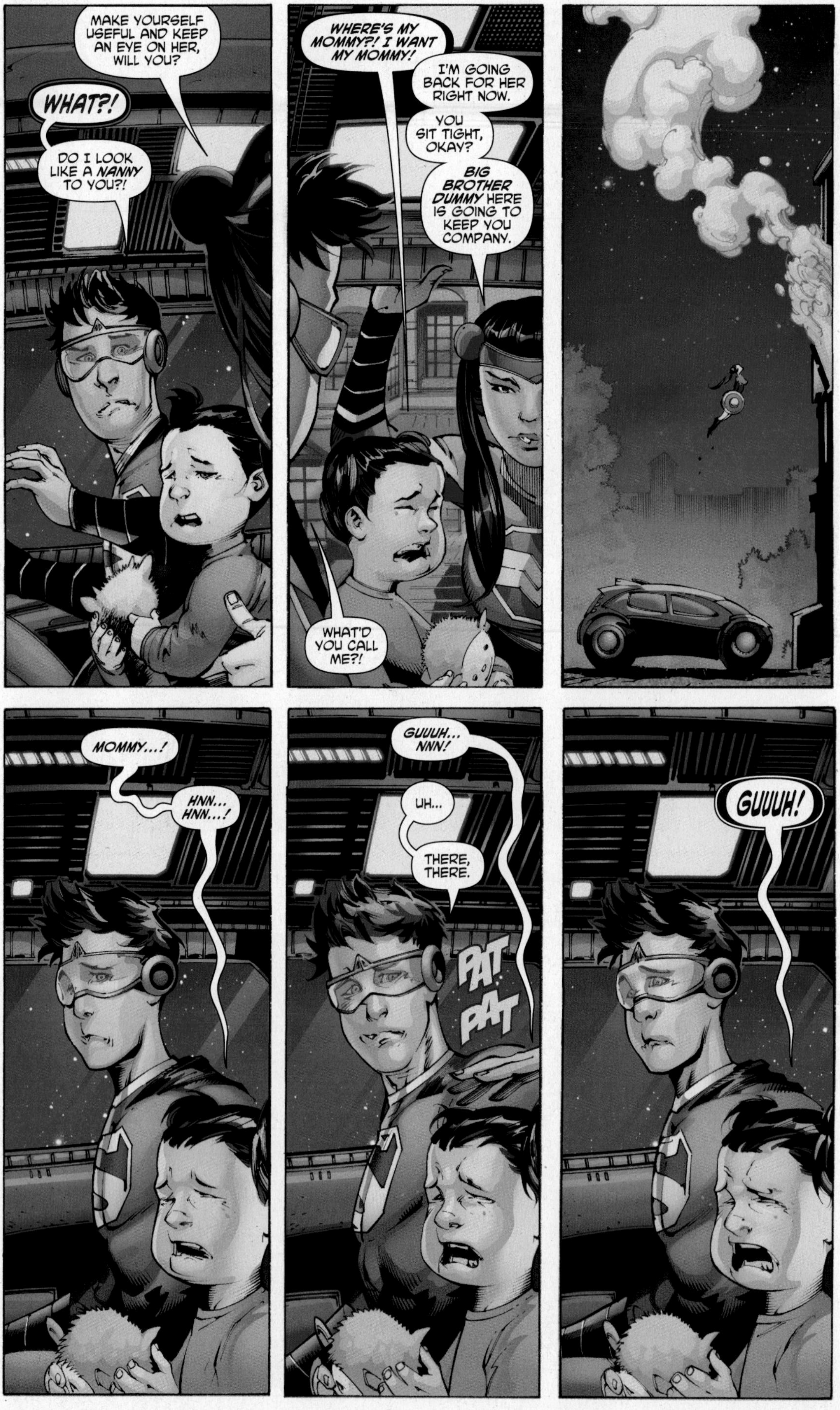
MAKE YOURSELF USEFUL AND KEEP AN EYE ON HER, WILL YOU?
WHAT?!
DO I LOOK LIKE A NANNY TO YOU?!
WHERE'S MY MOMMY?! I WANT MY MOMMY!
I'M GOING BACK FOR HER RIGHT NOW.
YOU SIT TIGHT, OKAY?
BIG BROTHER DUMMY HERE IS GOING TO KEEP YOU COMPANY.
WHAT'D YOU CALL ME?!
MOMMY...!
HNN... HNN...!
GUUUH... NNN!
UH...
THERE, THERE.
PAT PAT
GUUUH!

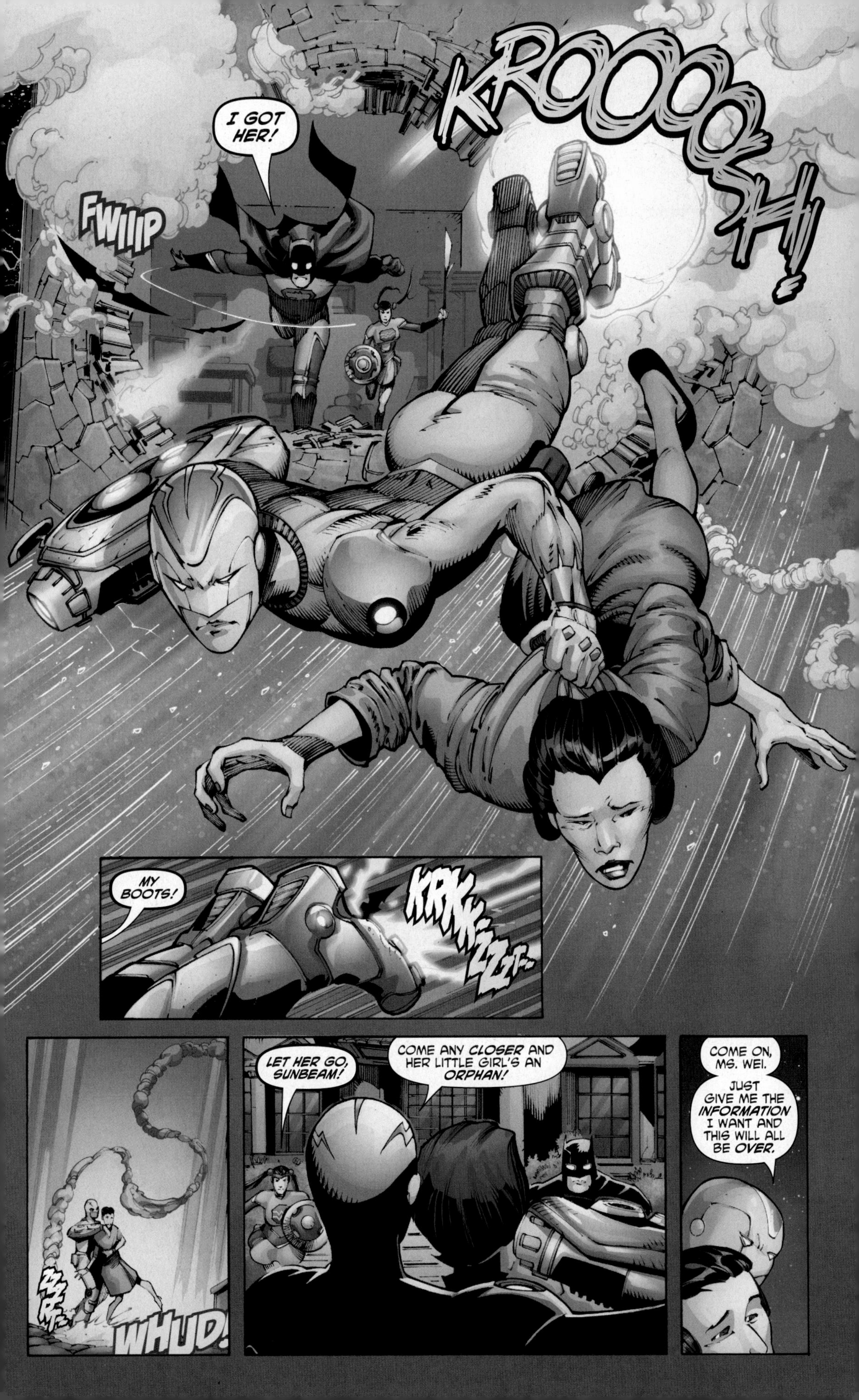

KROOOOSH!
I GOT HER!
FWIIIP
MY BOOTS!
KRKK-ZZZT-
ZZZRT-
WHUD!
LET HER GO, SUNBEAM!
COME ANY CLOSER AND HER LITTLE GIRL'S AN ORPHAN!
COME ON, MS. WEI.
JUST GIVE ME THE INFORMATION I WANT AND THIS WILL ALL BE OVER.

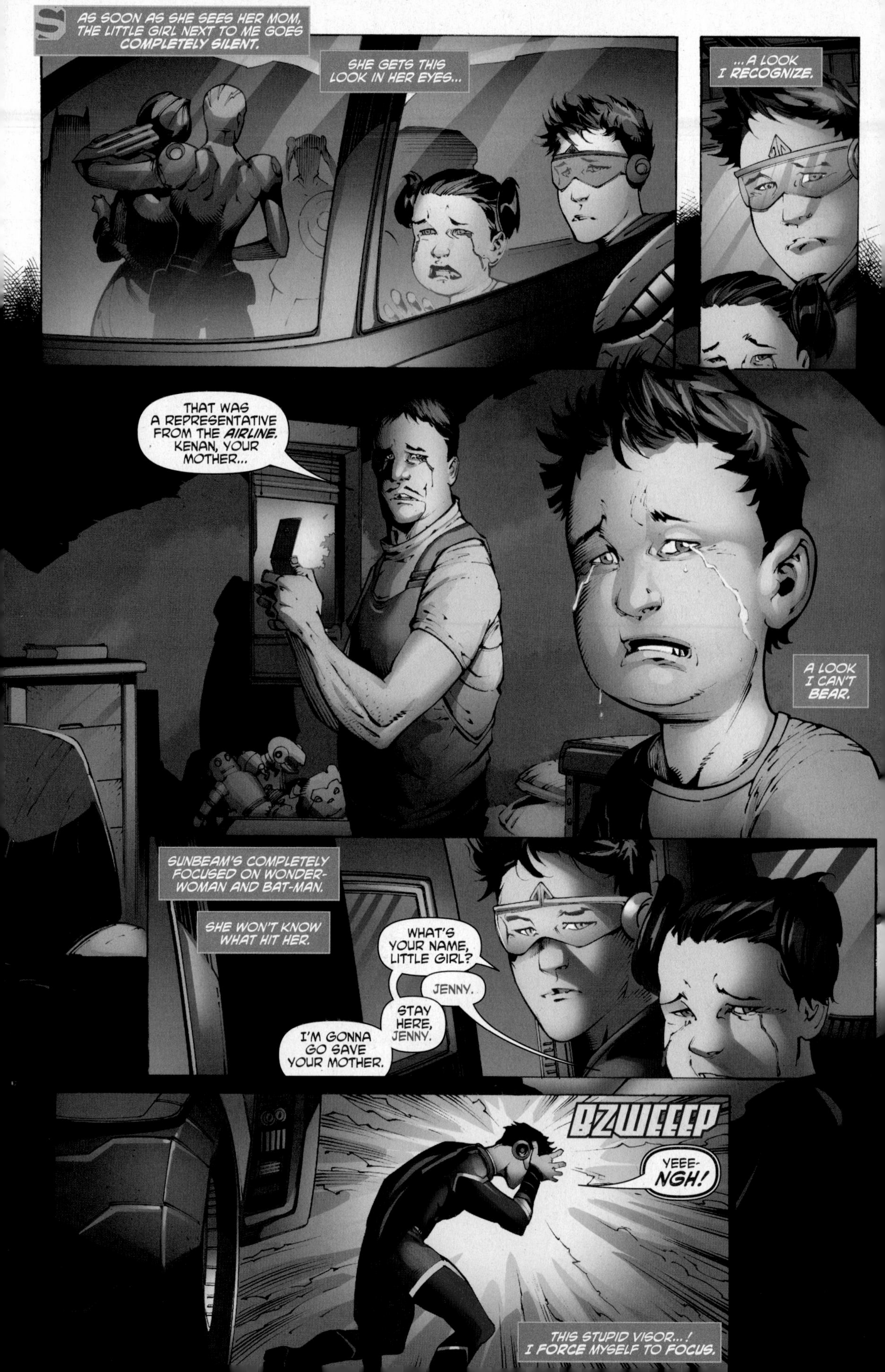

AS SOON AS SHE SEES HER MOM, THE LITTLE GIRL NEXT TO ME GOES COMPLETELY SILENT.
SHE GETS THIS LOOK IN HER EYES...
...A LOOK I RECOGNIZE.
THAT WAS A REPRESENTATIVE FROM THE AIRLINE. KENAN, YOUR MOTHER...
A LOOK I CAN'T BEAR.
SUNBEAM'S COMPLETELY FOCUSED ON WONDER-WOMAN AND BAT-MAN.
SHE WON'T KNOW WHAT HIT HER.
WHAT'S YOUR NAME, LITTLE GIRL?
JENNY.
STAY HERE, JENNY.
I'M GONNA GO SAVE YOUR MOTHER.
BZWEEEP
YEEE-NGH!
THIS STUPID VISOR...! I FORCE MYSELF TO FOCUS.

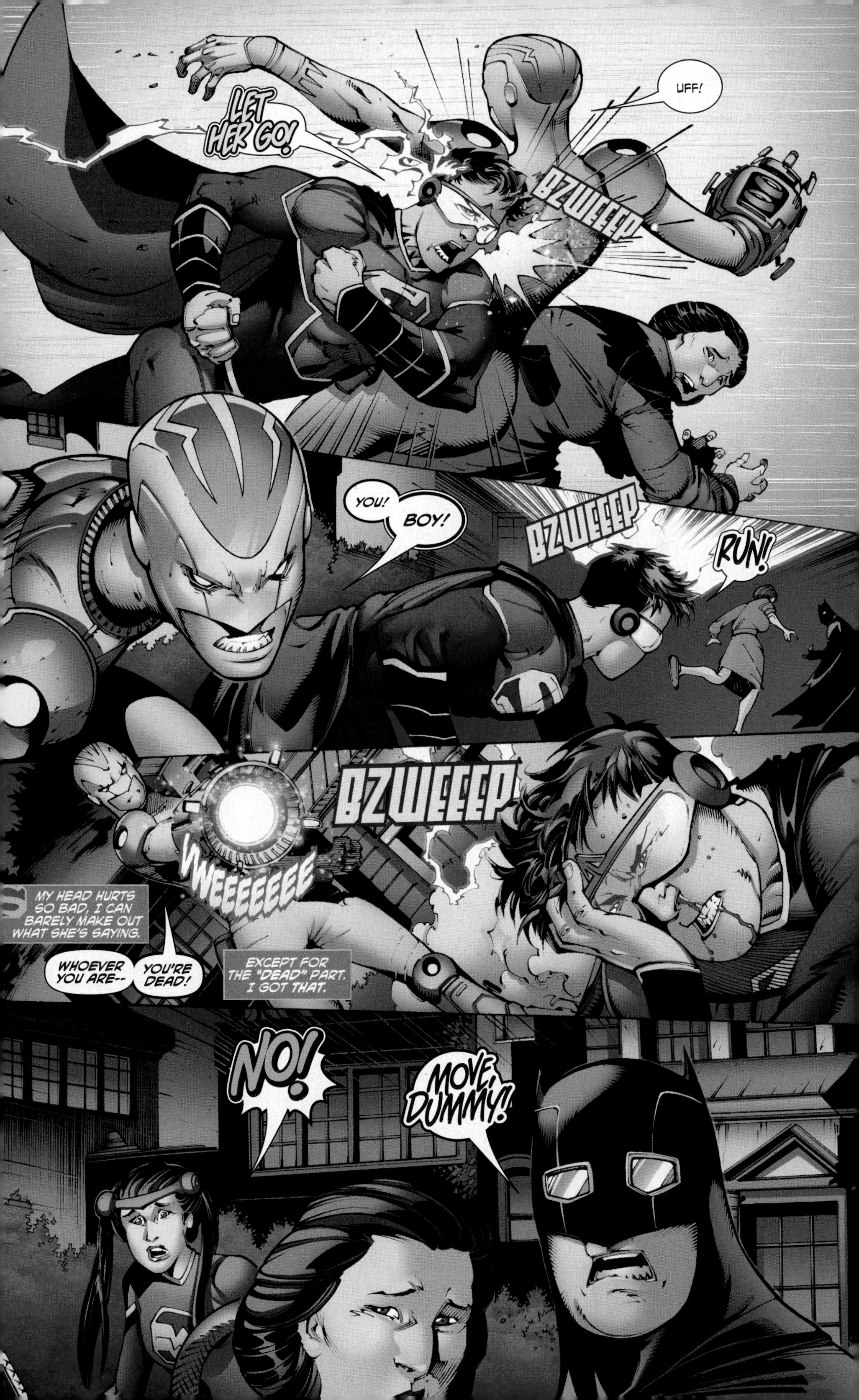
LET HER GO!
UFF!
BZWEEEP
YOU!
BOY!
BZWEEEP
RUN!
BZWEEEP
VWEEEEEEE
MY HEAD HURTS SO BAD, I CAN BARELY MAKE OUT WHAT SHE'S SAYING.
WHOEVER YOU ARE--
YOU'RE DEAD!
EXCEPT FOR THE "DEAD" PART. I GOT THAT.
NO!
MOVE, DUMMY!

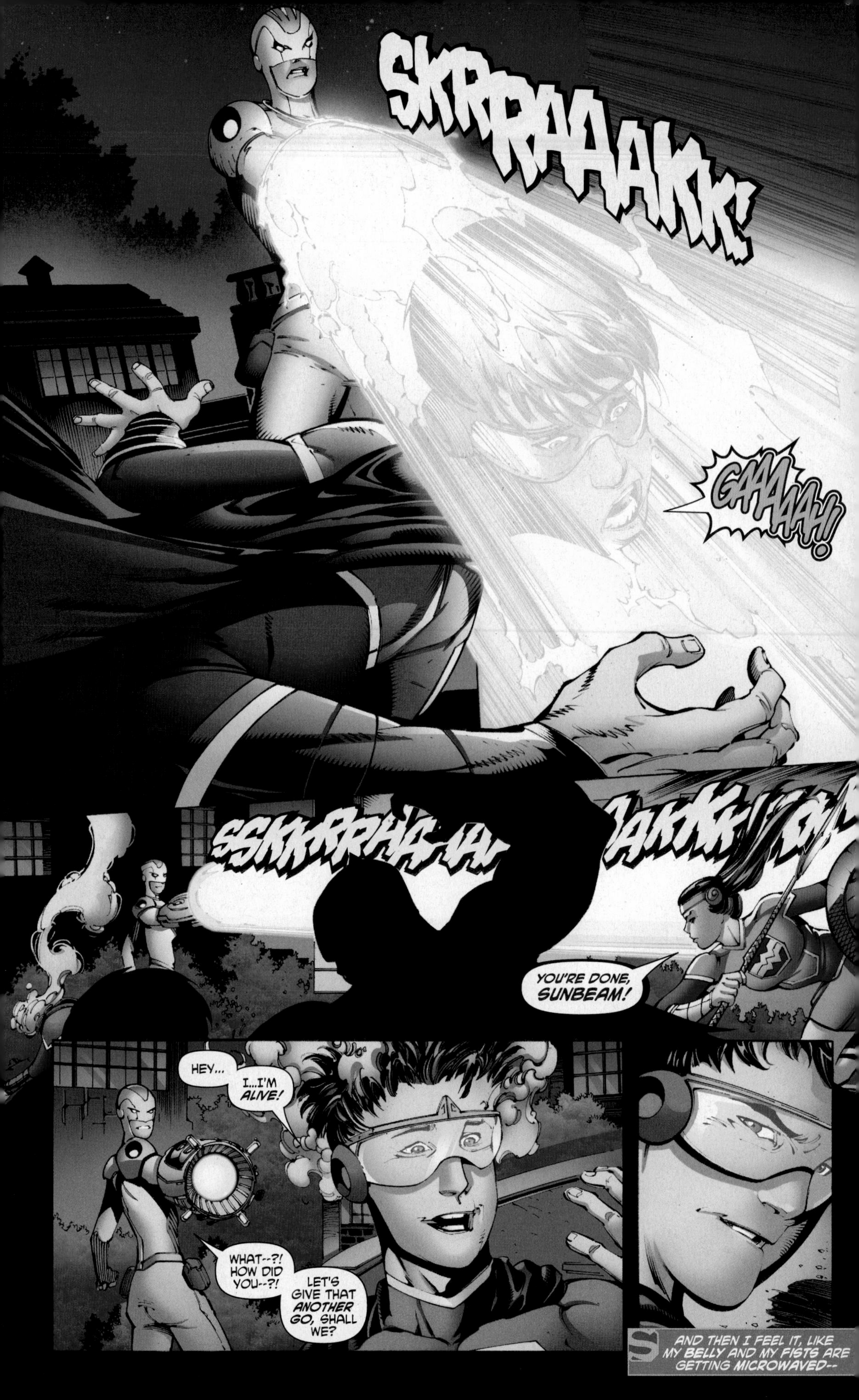
SKRRAAAKK!
GAAAAAH!
SSKKRRHAAAAKKK
YOU'RE DONE, SUNBEAM!
HEY...
I...I'M ALIVE!
WHAT--?! HOW DID YOU--?!
LET'S GIVE THAT ANOTHER GO, SHALL WE?
AND THEN I FEEL IT, LIKE MY BELLY AND MY FISTS ARE GETTING MICROWAVED--

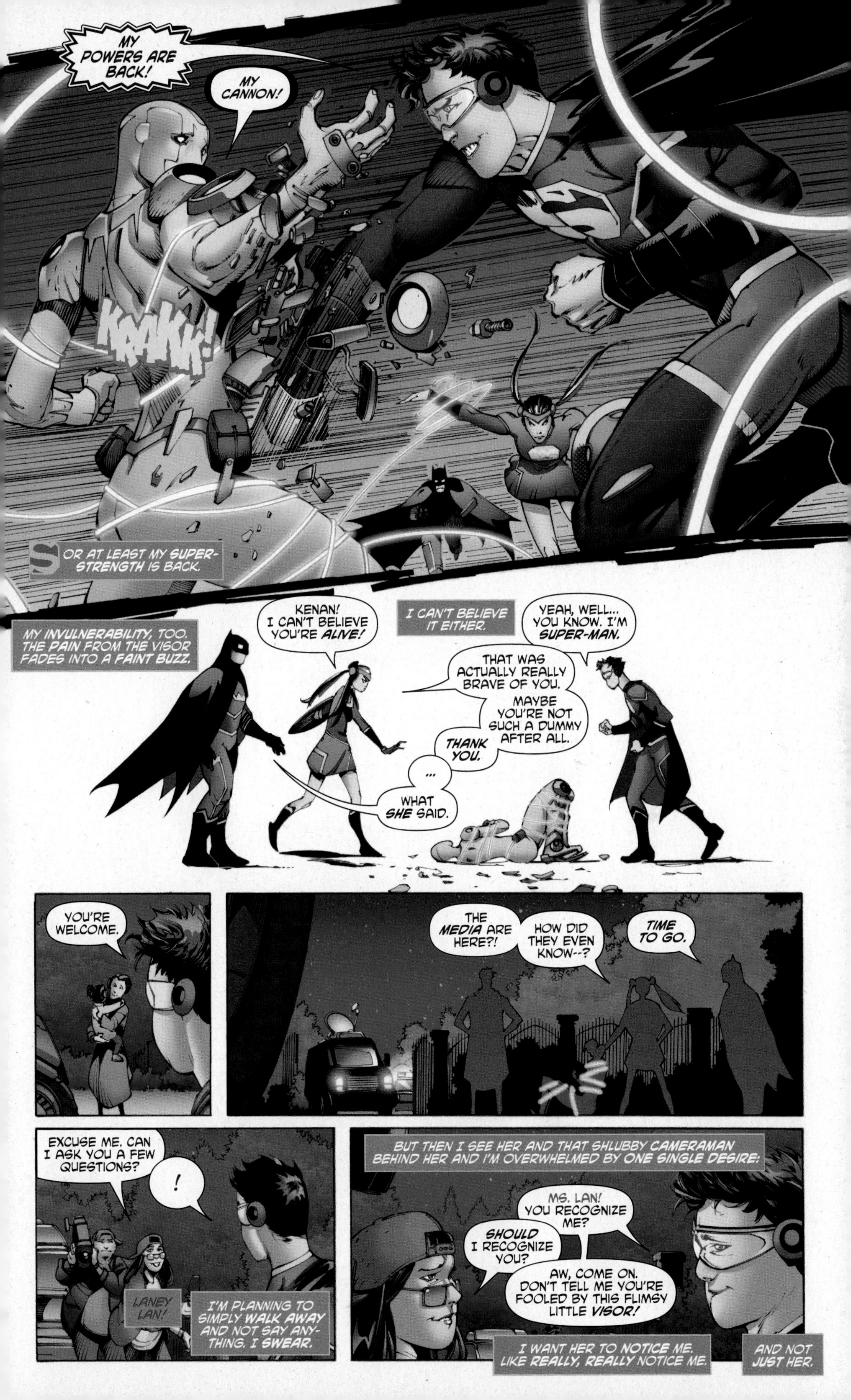
MY POWERS ARE BACK!
MY CANNON!
KRAKK!
OR AT LEAST MY SUPER-STRENGTH IS BACK.
MY INVULNERABILITY, TOO. THE PAIN FROM THE VISOR FADES INTO A FAINT BUZZ.
KENAN! I CAN'T BELIEVE YOU'RE ALIVE!
I CAN'T BELIEVE IT EITHER.
YEAH, WELL... YOU KNOW. I'M SUPER-MAN.
THAT WAS ACTUALLY REALLY BRAVE OF YOU.
MAYBE YOU'RE NOT SUCH A DUMMY AFTER ALL.
THANK YOU.
...
WHAT SHE SAID.
YOU'RE WELCOME.
THE MEDIA ARE HERE?!
HOW DID THEY EVEN KNOW--?
TIME TO GO.
EXCUSE ME. CAN I ASK YOU A FEW QUESTIONS?
!
LANEY LAN!
I'M PLANNING TO SIMPLY WALK AWAY AND NOT SAY ANY-THING. I SWEAR.
BUT THEN I SEE HER AND THAT SHLUBBY CAMERAMAN BEHIND HER AND I'M OVERWHELMED BY ONE SINGLE DESIRE:
MS. LAN! YOU RECOGNIZE ME?
SHOULD I RECOGNIZE YOU?
AW, COME ON. DON'T TELL ME YOU'RE FOOLED BY THIS FLIMSY LITTLE VISOR!
I WANT HER TO NOTICE ME. LIKE REALLY, REALLY NOTICE ME.
AND NOT JUST HER.

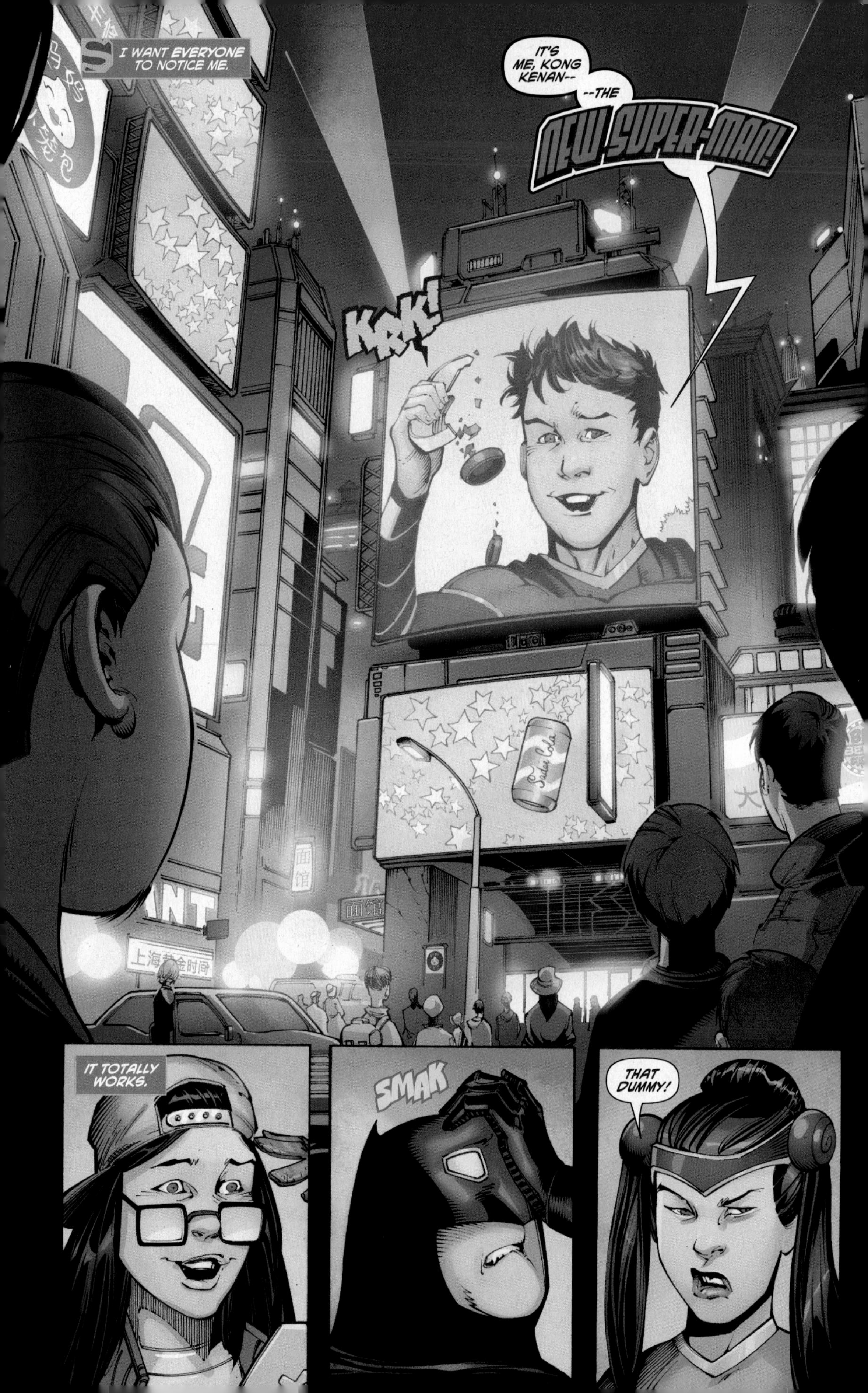

I WANT EVERYONE TO NOTICE ME.
IT'S ME, KONG KENAN--
--THE NEW SUPER-MAN!
KRK!
IT TOTALLY WORKS.
SMAK
THAT DUMMY!

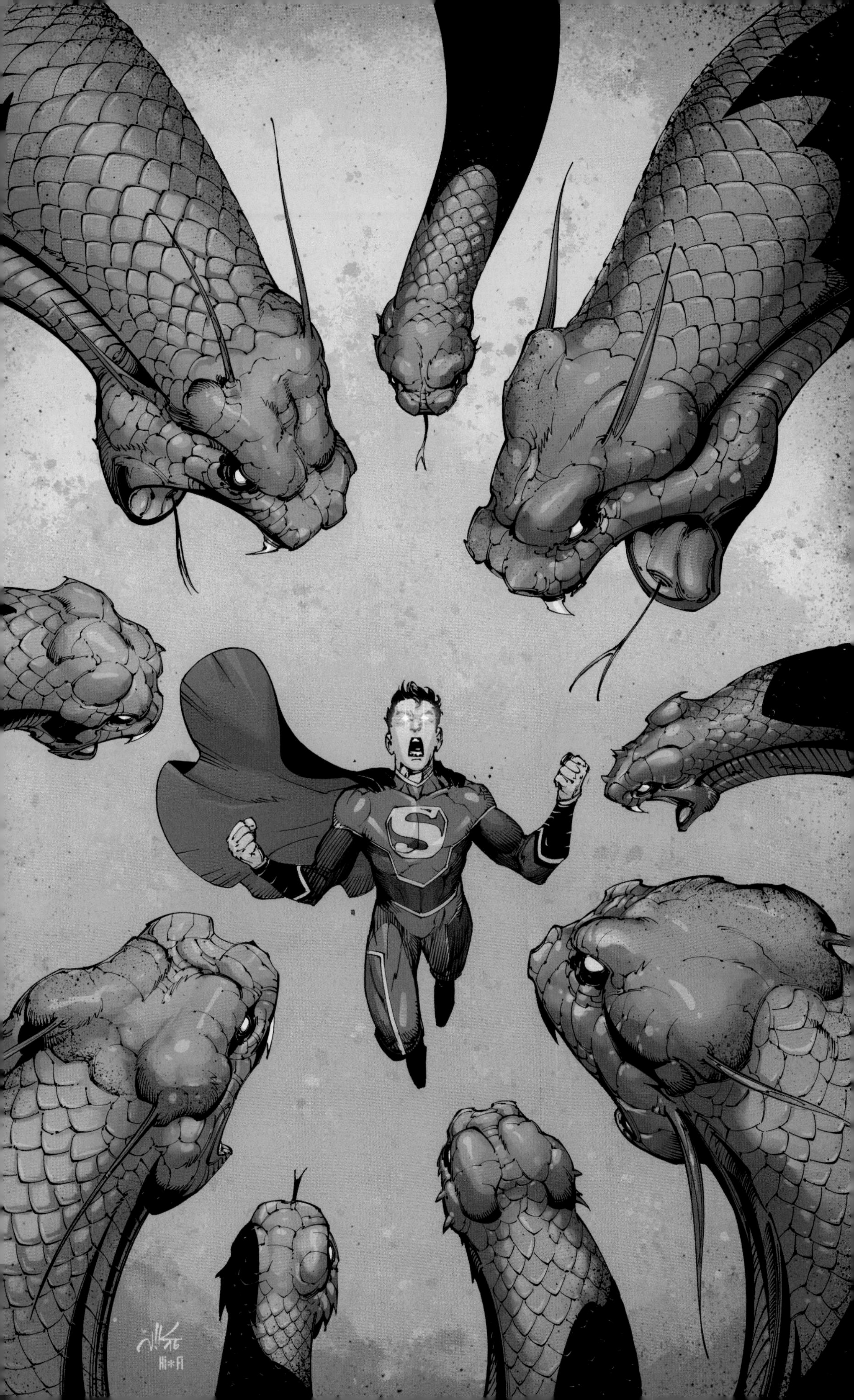
Hi*Fi

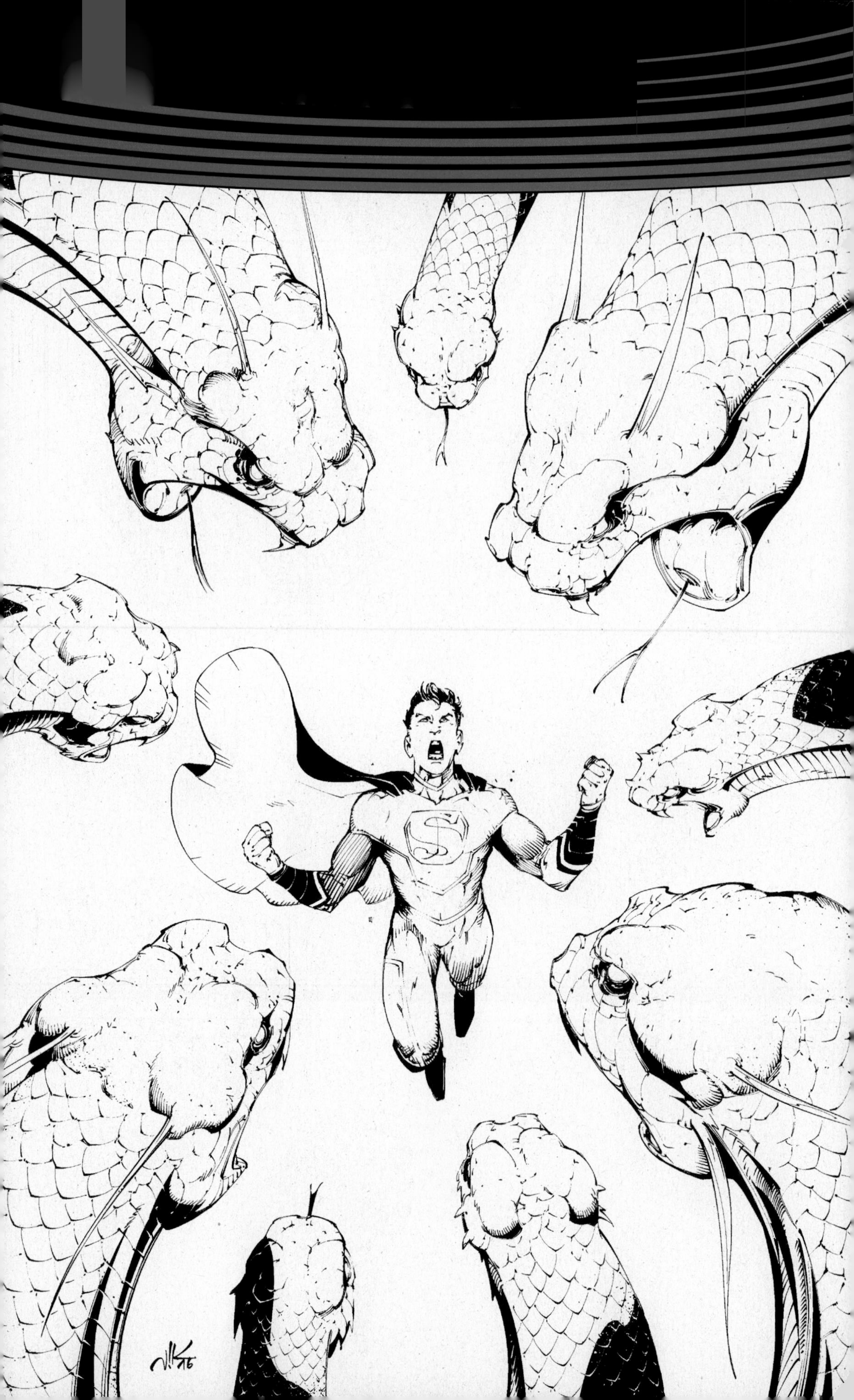

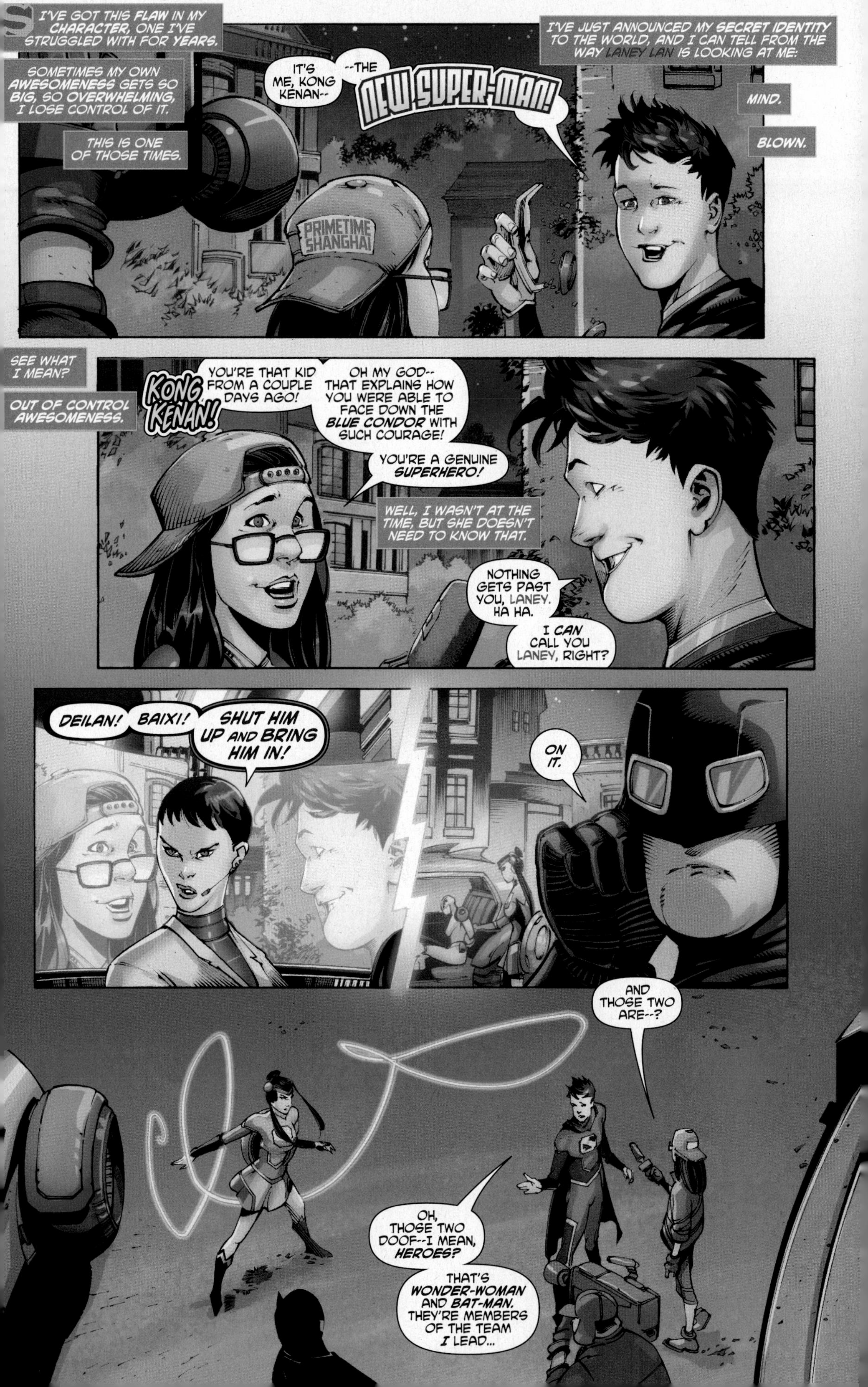

I'VE GOT THIS FLAW IN MY CHARACTER, ONE I'VE STRUGGLED WITH FOR YEARS.
SOMETIMES MY OWN AWESOMENESS GETS SO BIG, SO OVERWHELMING, I LOSE CONTROL OF IT.
THIS IS ONE OF THOSE TIMES.
IT'S ME, KONG KENAN--
--THE NEW SUPER-MAN!
PRIMETIME SHANGHAI
I'VE JUST ANNOUNCED MY SECRET IDENTITY TO THE WORLD, AND I CAN TELL FROM THE WAY LANEY LAN IS LOOKING AT ME:
MIND.
BLOWN.
SEE WHAT I MEAN?
OUT OF CONTROL AWESOMENESS.
KONG KENAN!
YOU'RE THAT KID FROM A COUPLE DAYS AGO!
OH MY GOD-- THAT EXPLAINS HOW YOU WERE ABLE TO FACE DOWN THE BLUE CONDOR WITH SUCH COURAGE!
YOU'RE A GENUINE SUPERHERO!
WELL, I WASN'T AT THE TIME, BUT SHE DOESN'T NEED TO KNOW THAT.
NOTHING GETS PAST YOU, LANEY. HA HA.
I CAN CALL YOU LANEY, RIGHT?
DEILAN!
BAIXI!
SHUT HIM UP AND BRING HIM IN!
ON IT.
AND THOSE TWO ARE--?
OH, THOSE TWO DOOF--I MEAN, HEROES?
THAT'S WONDER-WOMAN AND BAT-MAN. THEY'RE MEMBERS OF THE TEAM I LEAD...

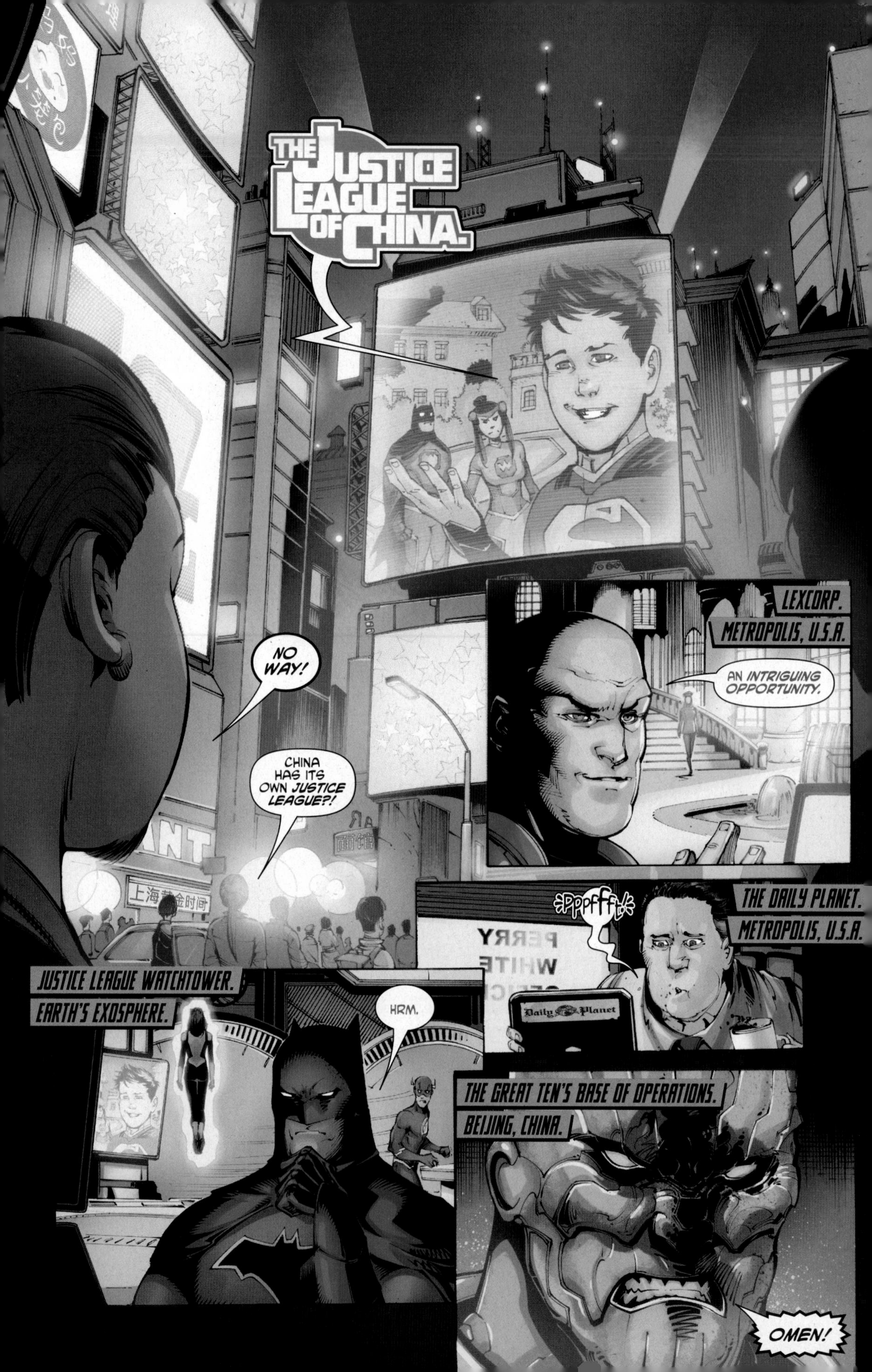
THE JUSTICE LEAGUE OF CHINA.
NO WAY!
CHINA HAS ITS OWN JUSTICE LEAGUE?!
上海黄金时间
LEXCORP.
METROPOLIS, U.S.A.
AN INTRIGUING OPPORTUNITY.
THE DAILY PLANET.
METROPOLIS, U.S.A.
PPPFFFT!
PERRY WHITE
Daily Planet
JUSTICE LEAGUE WATCHTOWER.
EARTH'S EXOSPHERE.
HRM.
THE GREAT TEN'S BASE OF OPERATIONS.
BEIJING, CHINA.
OMEN!

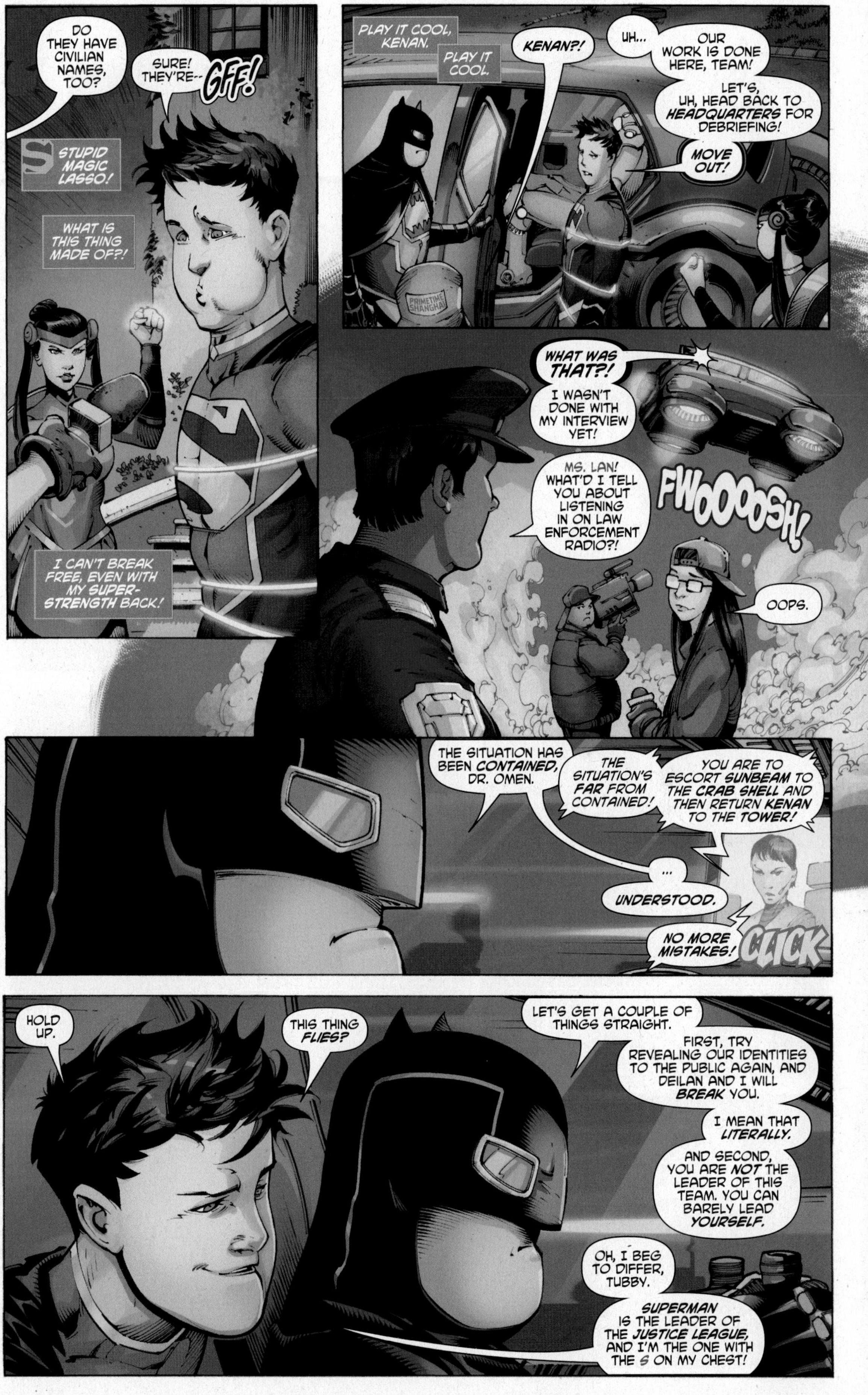

DO THEY HAVE CIVILIAN NAMES, TOO?
SURE! THEY'RE--
GFF!
STUPID MAGIC LASSO!
WHAT IS THIS THING MADE OF?!
I CAN'T BREAK FREE, EVEN WITH MY SUPER-STRENGTH BACK!
PLAY IT COOL, KENAN.
PLAY IT COOL.
KENAN?!
UH...
OUR WORK IS DONE HERE, TEAM!
LET'S, UH, HEAD BACK TO HEADQUARTERS FOR DEBRIEFING!
MOVE OUT!
PRIMETIME SHANGHAI
WHAT WAS THAT?!
I WASN'T DONE WITH MY INTERVIEW YET!
MS. LAN! WHAT'D I TELL YOU ABOUT LISTENING IN ON LAW ENFORCEMENT RADIO?!
FWOOOOSH!
OOPS.
THE SITUATION HAS BEEN CONTAINED, DR. OMEN.
THE SITUATION'S FAR FROM CONTAINED!
YOU ARE TO ESCORT SUNBEAM TO THE CRAB SHELL AND THEN RETURN KENAN TO THE TOWER!
...
UNDERSTOOD.
NO MORE MISTAKES!
CLICK
HOLD UP.
THIS THING FLIES?
LET'S GET A COUPLE OF THINGS STRAIGHT.
FIRST, TRY REVEALING OUR IDENTITIES TO THE PUBLIC AGAIN, AND DEILAN AND I WILL BREAK YOU.
I MEAN THAT LITERALLY.
AND SECOND, YOU ARE NOT THE LEADER OF THIS TEAM. YOU CAN BARELY LEAD YOURSELF.
OH, I BEG TO DIFFER, TUBBY.
SUPERMAN IS THE LEADER OF THE JUSTICE LEAGUE, AND I'M THE ONE WITH THE S ON MY CHEST!

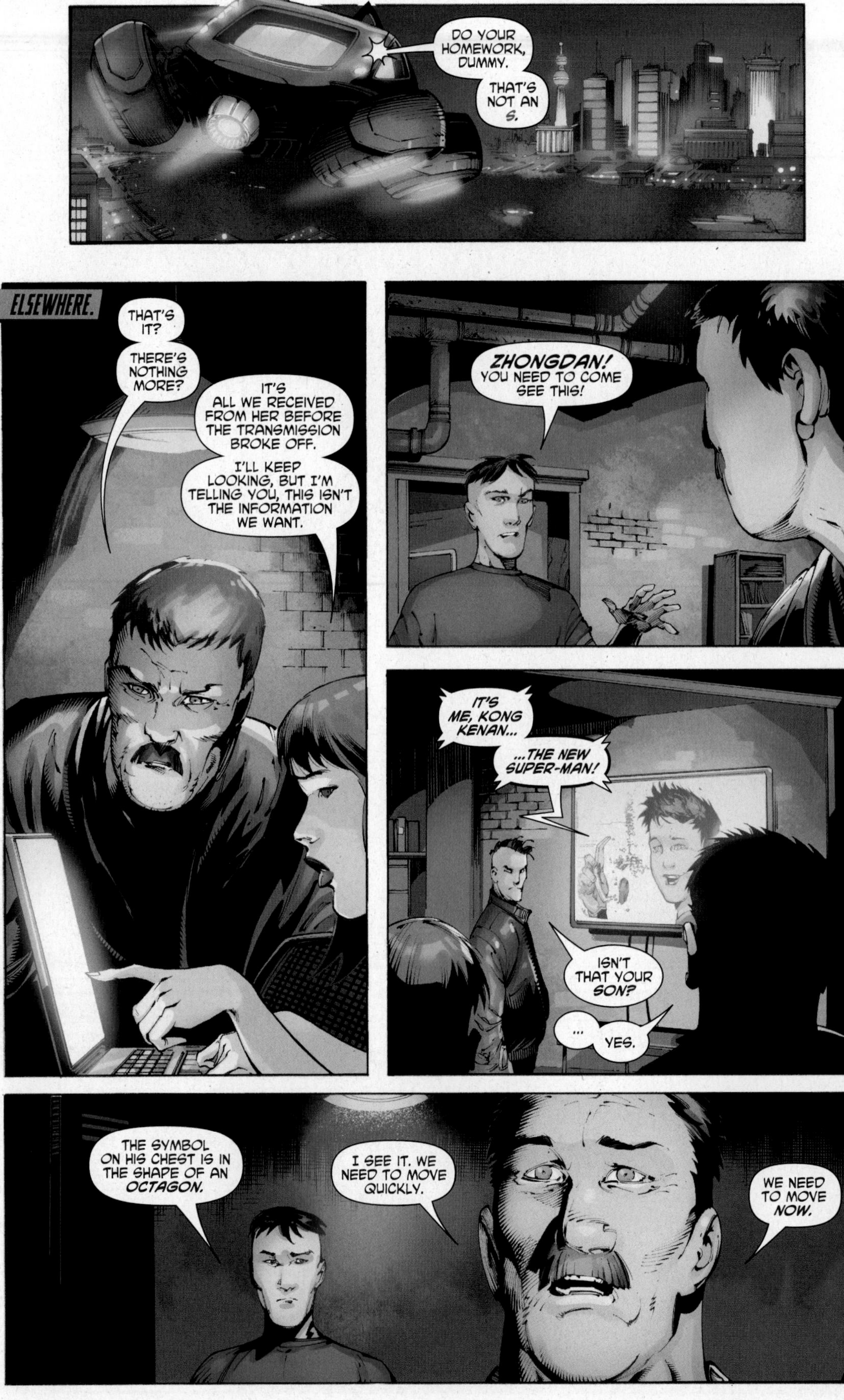
DO YOUR HOMEWORK, DUMMY.
THAT'S NOT AN S.
ELSEWHERE.
THAT'S IT?
THERE'S NOTHING MORE?
IT'S ALL WE RECEIVED FROM HER BEFORE THE TRANSMISSION BROKE OFF.
I'LL KEEP LOOKING, BUT I'M TELLING YOU, THIS ISN'T THE INFORMATION WE WANT.
ZHONGDAN! YOU NEED TO COME SEE THIS!
IT'S ME, KONG KENAN...
...THE NEW SUPER-MAN!
ISN'T THAT YOUR SON?
...
YES.
THE SYMBOL ON HIS CHEST IS IN THE SHAPE OF AN OCTAGON.
I SEE IT. WE NEED TO MOVE QUICKLY.
WE NEED TO MOVE NOW.

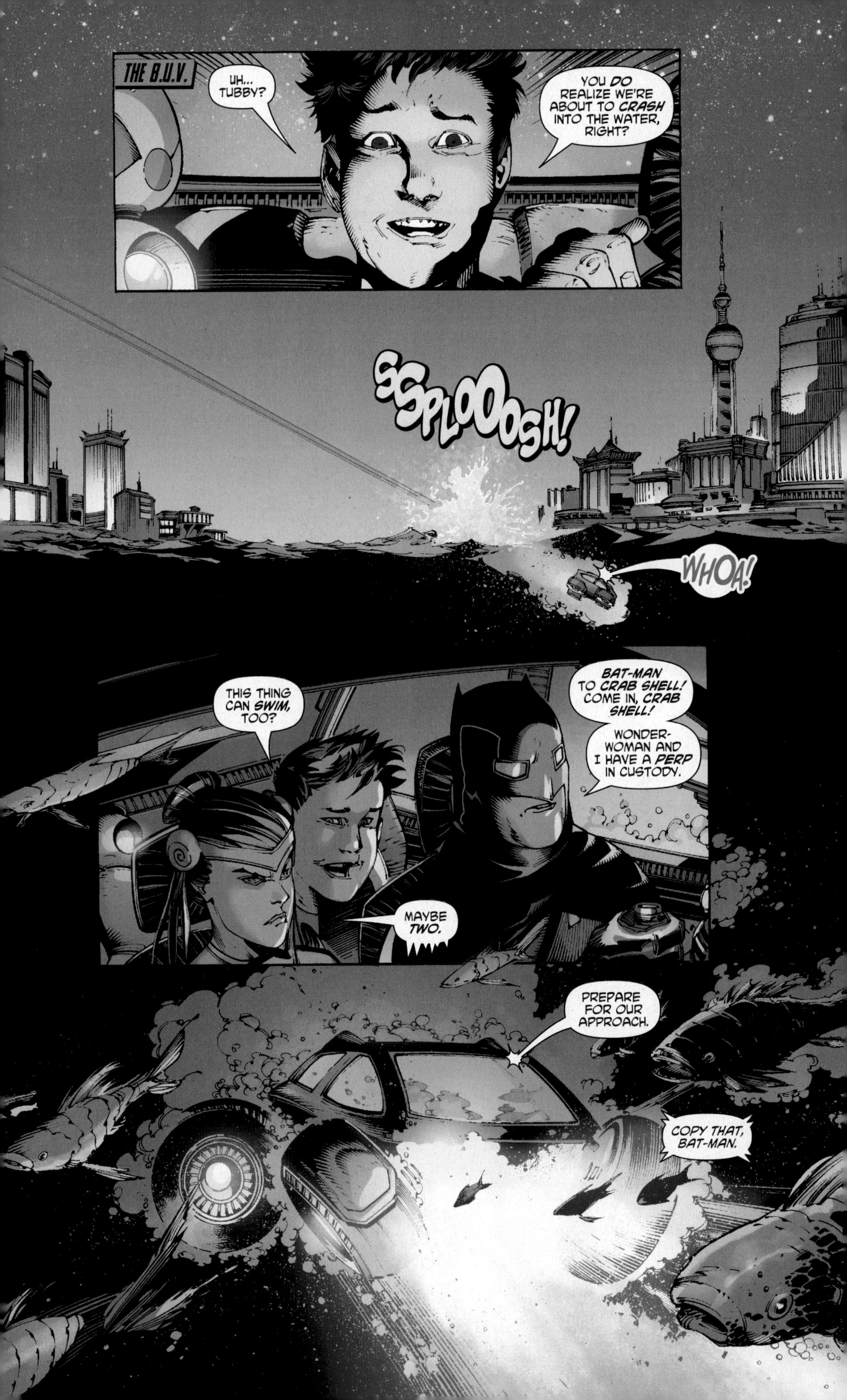
THE B.U.V.
UH... TUBBY?
YOU DO REALIZE WE'RE ABOUT TO CRASH INTO THE WATER, RIGHT?
SSPLOOOOSH!
WHOA!
THIS THING CAN SWIM, TOO?
BAT-MAN TO CRAB SHELL! COME IN, CRAB SHELL!
WONDER-WOMAN AND I HAVE A PERP IN CUSTODY.
MAYBE TWO.
PREPARE FOR OUR APPROACH.
COPY THAT, BAT-MAN.

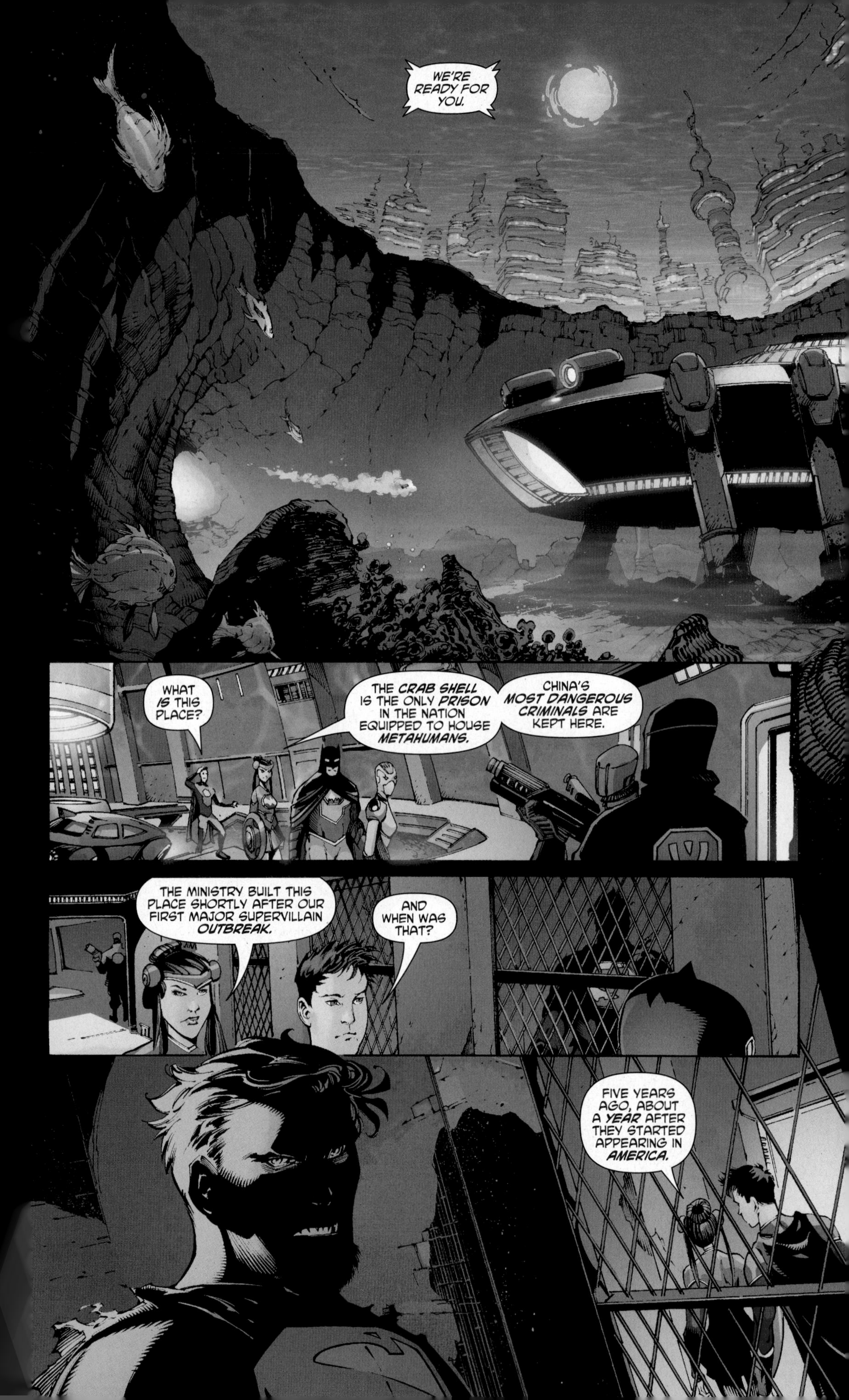
WE'RE READY FOR YOU.
WHAT IS THIS PLACE?
THE CRAB SHELL IS THE ONLY PRISON IN THE NATION EQUIPPED TO HOUSE METAHUMANS.
CHINA'S MOST DANGEROUS CRIMINALS ARE KEPT HERE.
THE MINISTRY BUILT THIS PLACE SHORTLY AFTER OUR FIRST MAJOR SUPERVILLAIN OUTBREAK.
AND WHEN WAS THAT?
FIVE YEARS AGO, ABOUT A YEAR AFTER THEY STARTED APPEARING IN AMERICA.

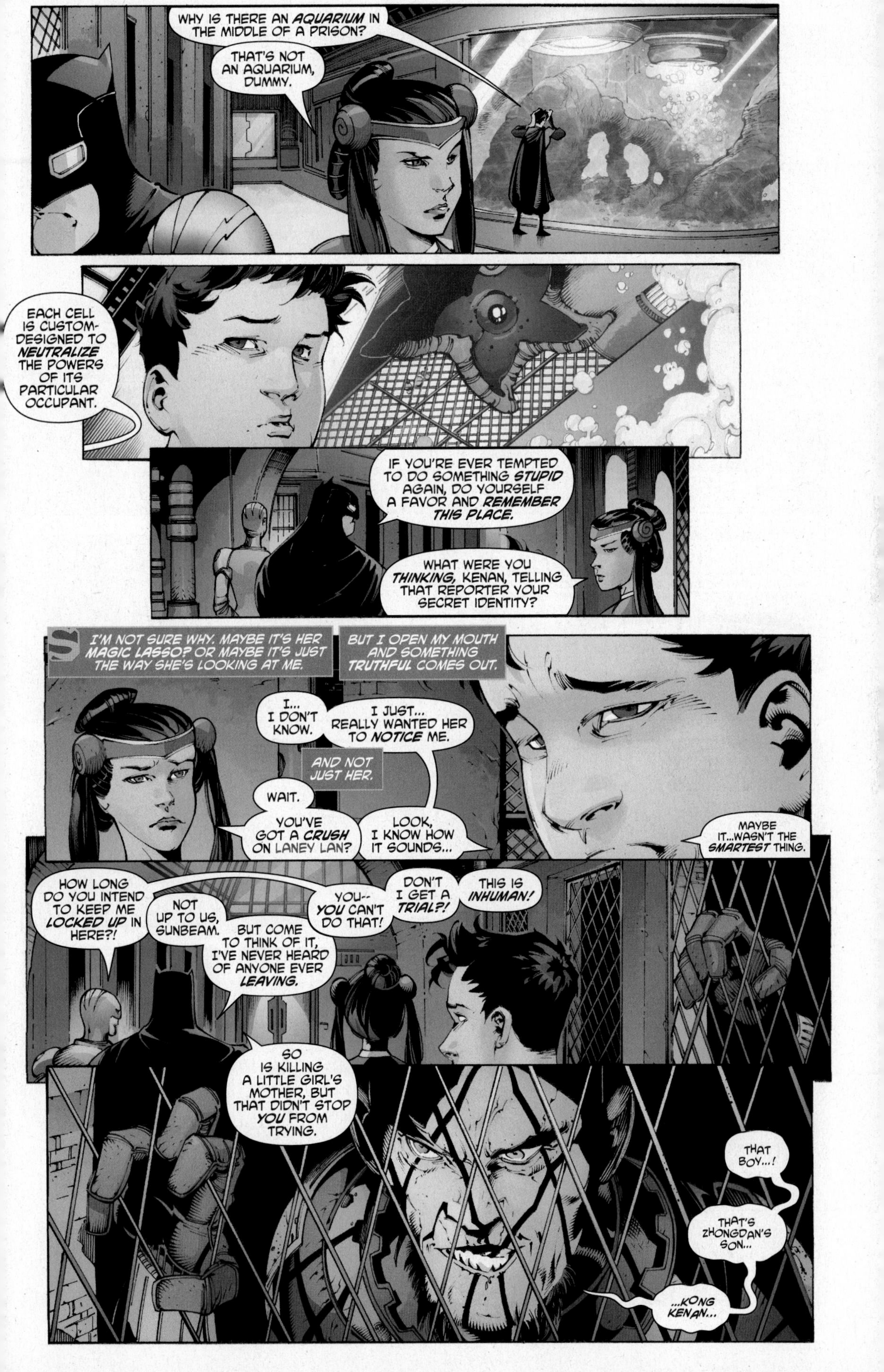
WHY IS THERE AN AQUARIUM IN THE MIDDLE OF A PRISON?
THAT'S NOT AN AQUARIUM, DUMMY.
EACH CELL IS CUSTOM-DESIGNED TO NEUTRALIZE THE POWERS OF ITS PARTICULAR OCCUPANT.
IF YOU'RE EVER TEMPTED TO DO SOMETHING STUPID AGAIN, DO YOURSELF A FAVOR AND REMEMBER THIS PLACE.
WHAT WERE YOU THINKING, KENAN, TELLING THAT REPORTER YOUR SECRET IDENTITY?
I'M NOT SURE WHY. MAYBE IT'S HER MAGIC LASSO? OR MAYBE IT'S JUST THE WAY SHE'S LOOKING AT ME.
BUT I OPEN MY MOUTH AND SOMETHING TRUTHFUL COMES OUT.
I... I DON'T KNOW.
I JUST... REALLY WANTED HER TO NOTICE ME.
AND NOT JUST HER.
WAIT.
YOU'VE GOT A CRUSH ON LANEY LAN?
LOOK, I KNOW HOW IT SOUNDS...
MAYBE IT...WASN'T THE SMARTEST THING.
HOW LONG DO YOU INTEND TO KEEP ME LOCKED UP IN HERE?!
NOT UP TO US, SUNBEAM.
BUT COME TO THINK OF IT, I'VE NEVER HEARD OF ANYONE EVER LEAVING.
YOU-- YOU CAN'T DO THAT!
DON'T I GET A TRIAL?!
THIS IS INHUMAN!
SO IS KILLING A LITTLE GIRL'S MOTHER, BUT THAT DIDN'T STOP YOU FROM TRYING.
THAT BOY...!
THAT'S ZHONGDAN'S SON...
...KONG KENAN...

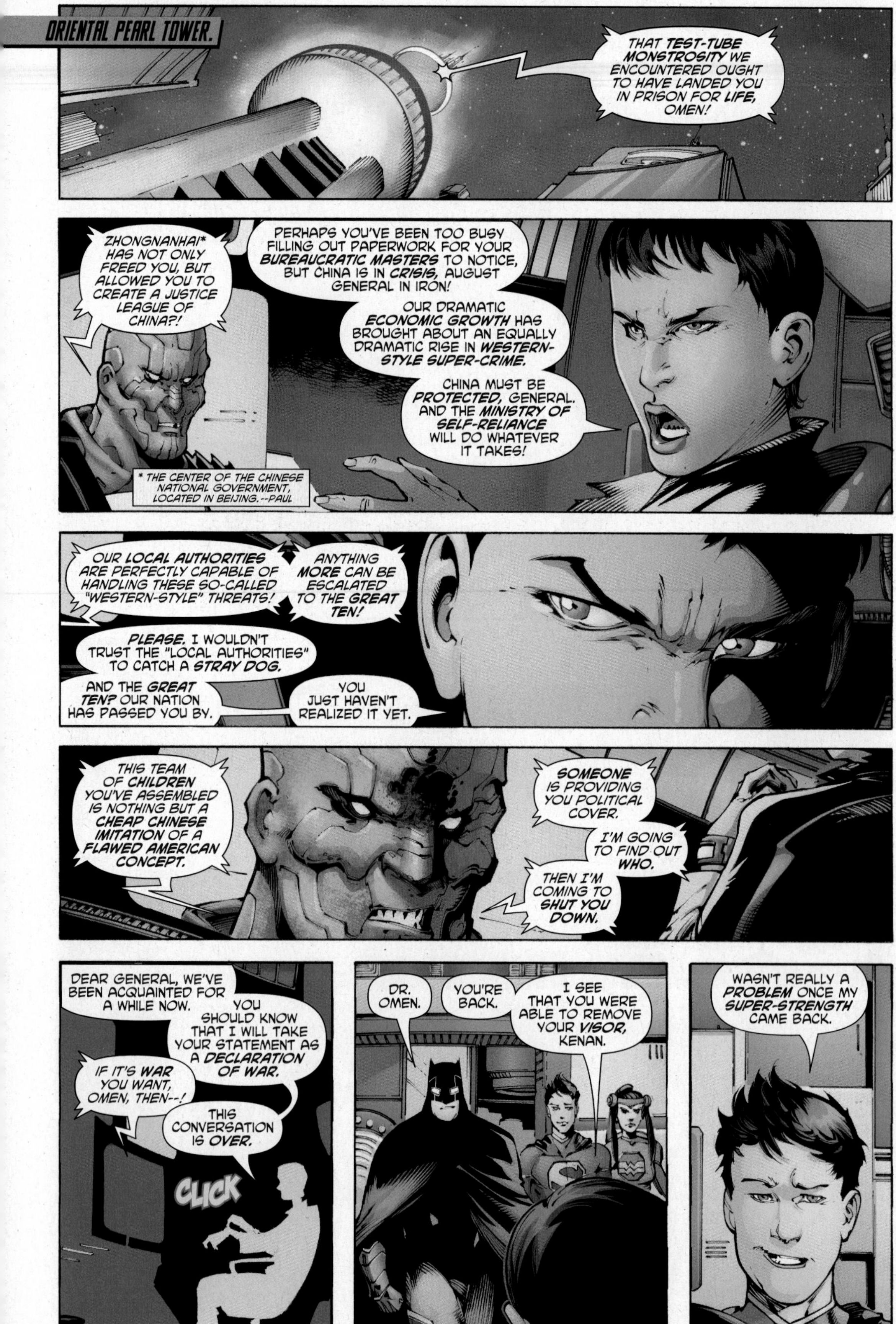
ORIENTAL PEARL TOWER.
THAT TEST-TUBE MONSTROSITY WE ENCOUNTERED OUGHT TO HAVE LANDED YOU IN PRISON FOR LIFE, OMEN!
ZHONGNANHAI* HAS NOT ONLY FREED YOU, BUT ALLOWED YOU TO CREATE A JUSTICE LEAGUE OF CHINA?!
PERHAPS YOU'VE BEEN TOO BUSY FILLING OUT PAPERWORK FOR YOUR BUREAUCRATIC MASTERS TO NOTICE, BUT CHINA IS IN CRISIS, AUGUST GENERAL IN IRON!
OUR DRAMATIC ECONOMIC GROWTH HAS BROUGHT ABOUT AN EQUALLY DRAMATIC RISE IN WESTERN-STYLE SUPER-CRIME.
CHINA MUST BE PROTECTED, GENERAL. AND THE MINISTRY OF SELF-RELIANCE WILL DO WHATEVER IT TAKES!
* THE CENTER OF THE CHINESE NATIONAL GOVERNMENT, LOCATED IN BEIJING.--PAUL
OUR LOCAL AUTHORITIES ARE PERFECTLY CAPABLE OF HANDLING THESE SO-CALLED "WESTERN-STYLE" THREATS!
ANYTHING MORE CAN BE ESCALATED TO THE GREAT TEN!
PLEASE. I WOULDN'T TRUST THE "LOCAL AUTHORITIES" TO CATCH A STRAY DOG.
AND THE GREAT TEN? OUR NATION HAS PASSED YOU BY.
YOU JUST HAVEN'T REALIZED IT YET.
THIS TEAM OF CHILDREN YOU'VE ASSEMBLED IS NOTHING BUT A CHEAP CHINESE IMITATION OF A FLAWED AMERICAN CONCEPT.
SOMEONE IS PROVIDING YOU POLITICAL COVER.
I'M GOING TO FIND OUT WHO.
THEN I'M COMING TO SHUT YOU DOWN.
DEAR GENERAL, WE'VE BEEN ACQUAINTED FOR A WHILE NOW.
YOU SHOULD KNOW THAT I WILL TAKE YOUR STATEMENT AS A DECLARATION OF WAR.
IF IT'S WAR YOU WANT, OMEN, THEN--!
THIS CONVERSATION IS OVER.
CLICK
DR. OMEN.
YOU'RE BACK.
I SEE THAT YOU WERE ABLE TO REMOVE YOUR VISOR, KENAN.
WASN'T REALLY A PROBLEM ONCE MY SUPER-STRENGTH CAME BACK.

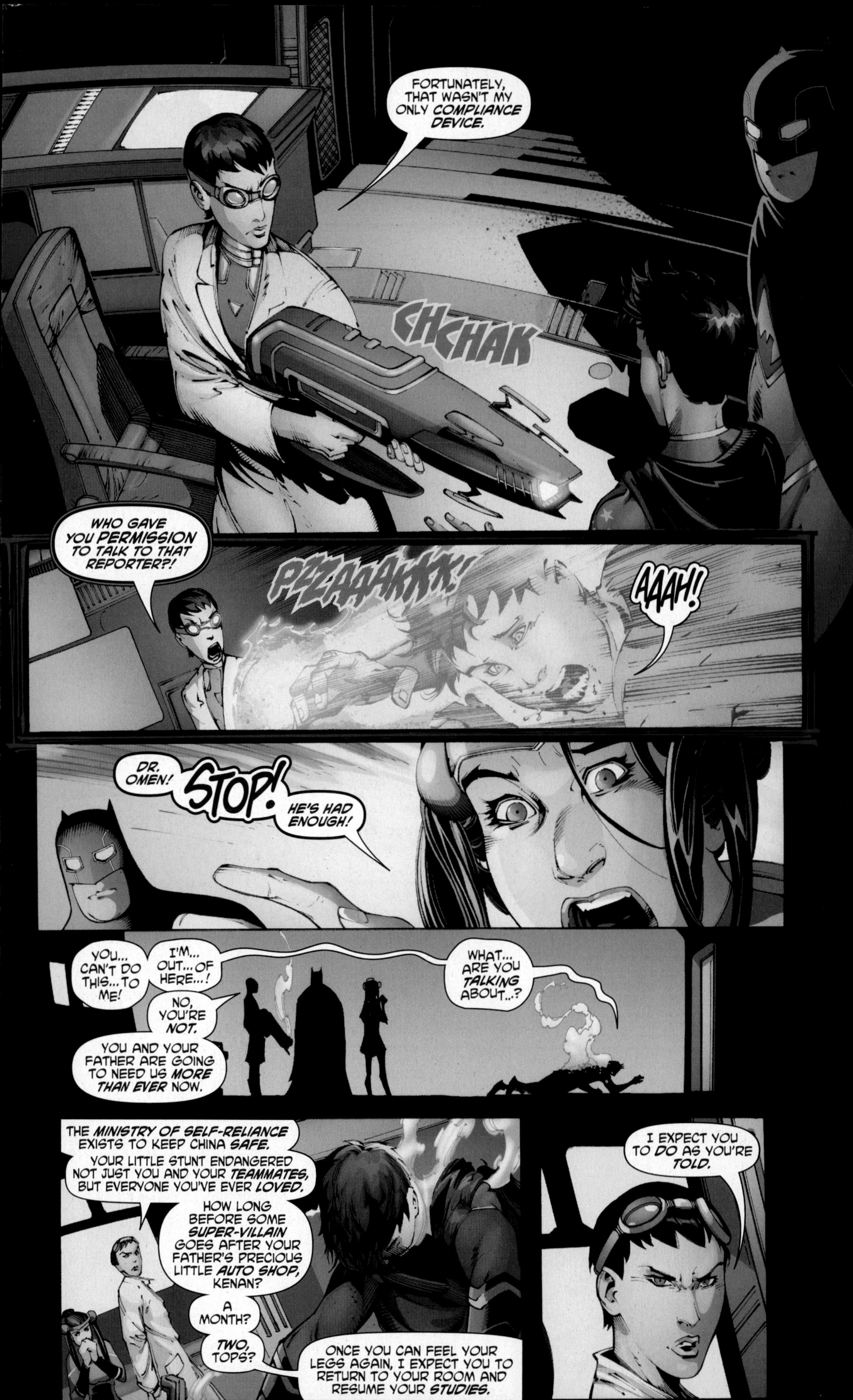
FORTUNATELY, THAT WASN'T MY ONLY COMPLIANCE DEVICE.
CHCHAK
WHO GAVE YOU PERMISSION TO TALK TO THAT REPORTER?!
PZZAAAKKK!
AAAH!
DR. OMEN!
STOP!
HE'S HAD ENOUGH!
YOU... CAN'T DO THIS... TO ME!
I'M... OUT... OF HERE...!
NO, YOU'RE NOT.
YOU AND YOUR FATHER ARE GOING TO NEED US MORE THAN EVER NOW.
WHAT... ARE YOU TALKING ABOUT...?
THE MINISTRY OF SELF-RELIANCE EXISTS TO KEEP CHINA SAFE.
YOUR LITTLE STUNT ENDANGERED NOT JUST YOU AND YOUR TEAMMATES, BUT EVERYONE YOU'VE EVER LOVED.
HOW LONG BEFORE SOME SUPER-VILLAIN GOES AFTER YOUR FATHER'S PRECIOUS LITTLE AUTO SHOP, KENAN?
A MONTH?
TWO, TOPS?
ONCE YOU CAN FEEL YOUR LEGS AGAIN, I EXPECT YOU TO RETURN TO YOUR ROOM AND RESUME YOUR STUDIES.
I EXPECT YOU TO DO AS YOU'RE TOLD.

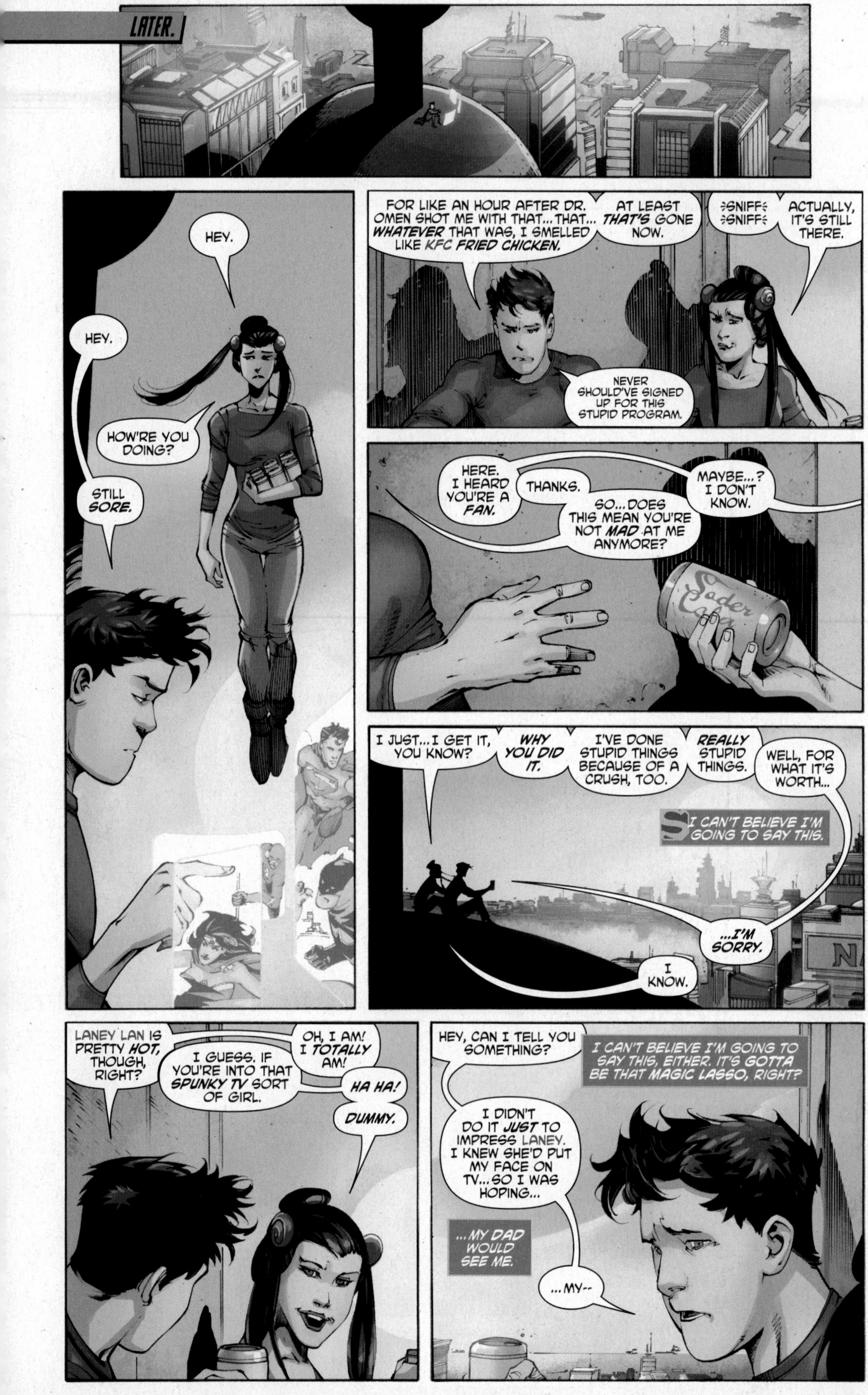
LATER.
HEY.
HEY.
HOW'RE YOU DOING?
STILL SORE.
FOR LIKE AN HOUR AFTER DR. OMEN SHOT ME WITH THAT...THAT... WHATEVER THAT WAS, I SMELLED LIKE KFC FRIED CHICKEN.
AT LEAST THAT'S GONE NOW.
SNIFF *SNIFF*
ACTUALLY, IT'S STILL THERE.
NEVER SHOULD'VE SIGNED UP FOR THIS STUPID PROGRAM.
HERE. I HEARD YOU'RE A FAN.
THANKS.
SO...DOES THIS MEAN YOU'RE NOT MAD AT ME ANYMORE?
MAYBE...? I DON'T KNOW.
Soder Cola
I JUST...I GET IT, YOU KNOW?
WHY YOU DID IT.
I'VE DONE STUPID THINGS BECAUSE OF A CRUSH, TOO.
REALLY STUPID THINGS.
WELL, FOR WHAT IT'S WORTH...
I CAN'T BELIEVE I'M GOING TO SAY THIS.
...I'M SORRY.
I KNOW.
LANEY LAN IS PRETTY HOT, THOUGH, RIGHT?
I GUESS. IF YOU'RE INTO THAT SPUNKY TV SORT OF GIRL.
OH, I AM! I TOTALLY AM!
HA HA!
DUMMY.
HEY, CAN I TELL YOU SOMETHING?
I CAN'T BELIEVE I'M GOING TO SAY THIS, EITHER. IT'S GOTTA BE THAT MAGIC LASSO, RIGHT?
I DIDN'T DO IT JUST TO IMPRESS LANEY. I KNEW SHE'D PUT MY FACE ON TV...SO I WAS HOPING...
...MY DAD WOULD SEE ME.
...MY--

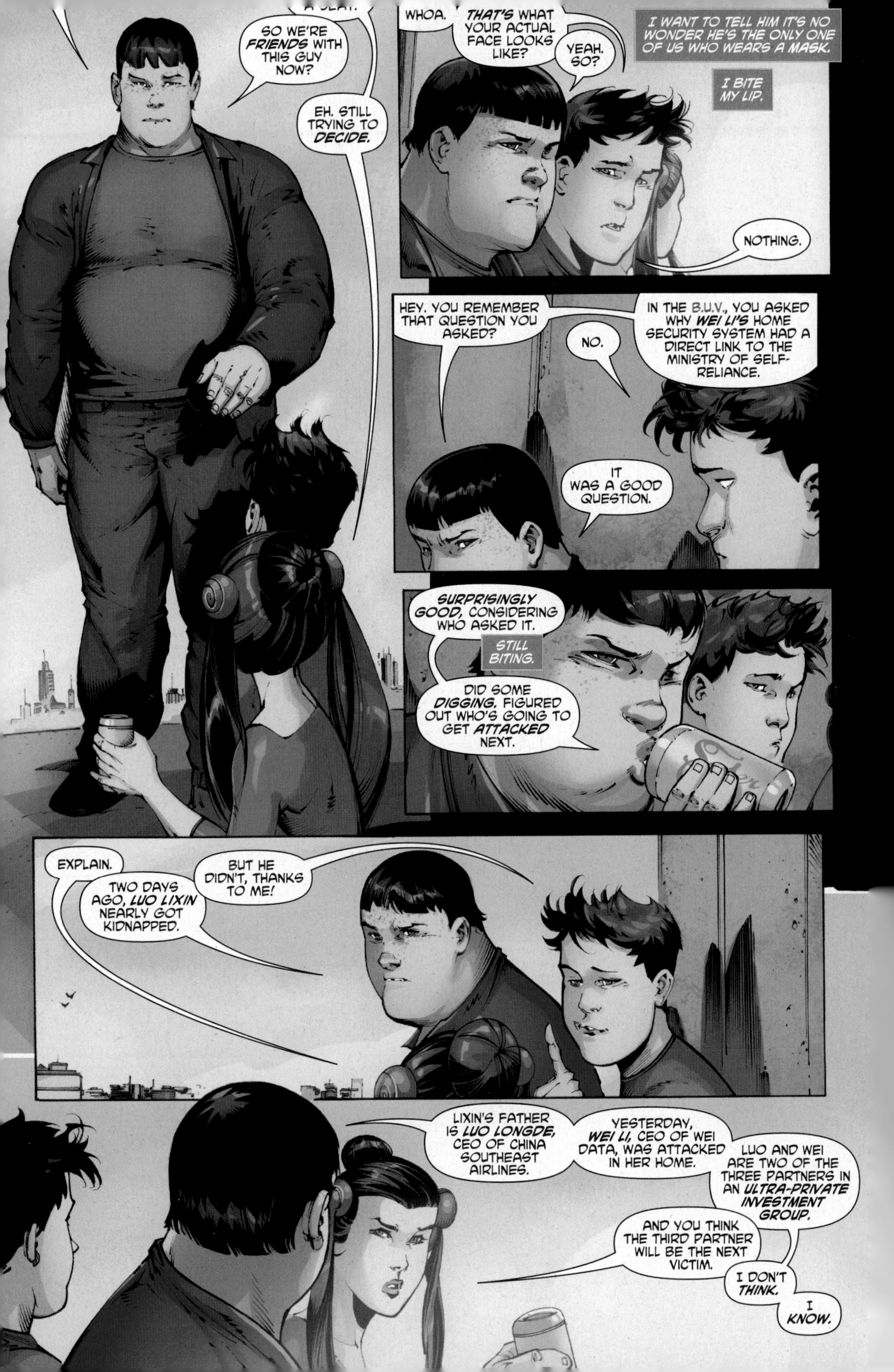
SO WE'RE FRIENDS WITH THIS GUY NOW?
EH. STILL TRYING TO DECIDE.
WHOA.
THAT'S WHAT YOUR ACTUAL FACE LOOKS LIKE?
YEAH. SO?
I WANT TO TELL HIM IT'S NO WONDER HE'S THE ONLY ONE OF US WHO WEARS A MASK.
I BITE MY LIP.
NOTHING.
HEY. YOU REMEMBER THAT QUESTION YOU ASKED?
NO.
IN THE B.U.V., YOU ASKED WHY WEI LI'S HOME SECURITY SYSTEM HAD A DIRECT LINK TO THE MINISTRY OF SELF-RELIANCE.
IT WAS A GOOD QUESTION.
SURPRISINGLY GOOD, CONSIDERING WHO ASKED IT.
STILL BITING.
DID SOME DIGGING. FIGURED OUT WHO'S GOING TO GET ATTACKED NEXT.
EXPLAIN.
TWO DAYS AGO, LUO LIXIN NEARLY GOT KIDNAPPED.
BUT HE DIDN'T, THANKS TO ME!
LIXIN'S FATHER IS LUO LONGDE, CEO OF CHINA SOUTHEAST AIRLINES.
YESTERDAY, WEI LI, CEO OF WEI DATA, WAS ATTACKED IN HER HOME.
LUO AND WEI ARE TWO OF THE THREE PARTNERS IN AN ULTRA-PRIVATE INVESTMENT GROUP.
AND YOU THINK THE THIRD PARTNER WILL BE THE NEXT VICTIM.
I DON'T THINK.
I KNOW.

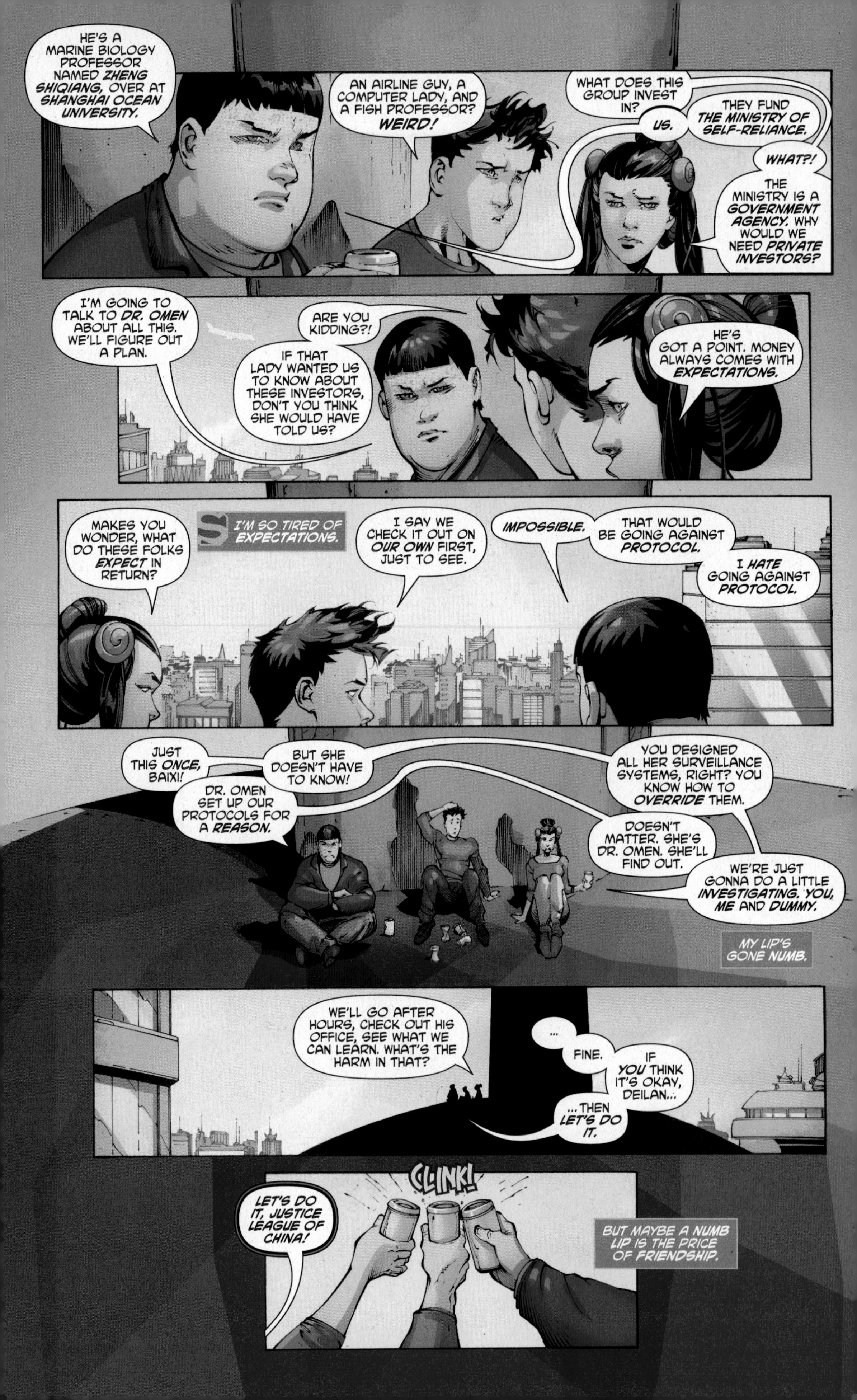
HE'S A MARINE BIOLOGY PROFESSOR NAMED ZHENG SHIQIANG, OVER AT SHANGHAI OCEAN UNIVERSITY.
AN AIRLINE GUY, A COMPUTER LADY, AND A FISH PROFESSOR? WEIRD!
WHAT DOES THIS GROUP INVEST IN?
US.
THEY FUND THE MINISTRY OF SELF-RELIANCE.
WHAT?!
THE MINISTRY IS A GOVERNMENT AGENCY. WHY WOULD WE NEED PRIVATE INVESTORS?
I'M GOING TO TALK TO DR. OMEN ABOUT ALL THIS. WE'LL FIGURE OUT A PLAN.
ARE YOU KIDDING?!
IF THAT LADY WANTED US TO KNOW ABOUT THESE INVESTORS, DON'T YOU THINK SHE WOULD HAVE TOLD US?
HE'S GOT A POINT. MONEY ALWAYS COMES WITH EXPECTATIONS.
MAKES YOU WONDER, WHAT DO THESE FOLKS EXPECT IN RETURN?
I'M SO TIRED OF EXPECTATIONS.
I SAY WE CHECK IT OUT ON OUR OWN FIRST, JUST TO SEE.
IMPOSSIBLE.
THAT WOULD BE GOING AGAINST PROTOCOL.
I HATE GOING AGAINST PROTOCOL.
JUST THIS ONCE, BAIXI!
BUT SHE DOESN'T HAVE TO KNOW!
DR. OMEN SET UP OUR PROTOCOLS FOR A REASON.
YOU DESIGNED ALL HER SURVEILLANCE SYSTEMS, RIGHT? YOU KNOW HOW TO OVERRIDE THEM.
DOESN'T MATTER. SHE'S DR. OMEN. SHE'LL FIND OUT.
WE'RE JUST GONNA DO A LITTLE INVESTIGATING. YOU, ME AND DUMMY.
MY LIP'S GONE NUMB.
WE'LL GO AFTER HOURS, CHECK OUT HIS OFFICE, SEE WHAT WE CAN LEARN. WHAT'S THE HARM IN THAT?
...
FINE.
IF YOU THINK IT'S OKAY, DEILAN...
...THEN LET'S DO IT.
CLINK!
LET'S DO IT, JUSTICE LEAGUE OF CHINA!
BUT MAYBE A NUMB LIP IS THE PRICE OF FRIENDSHIP.

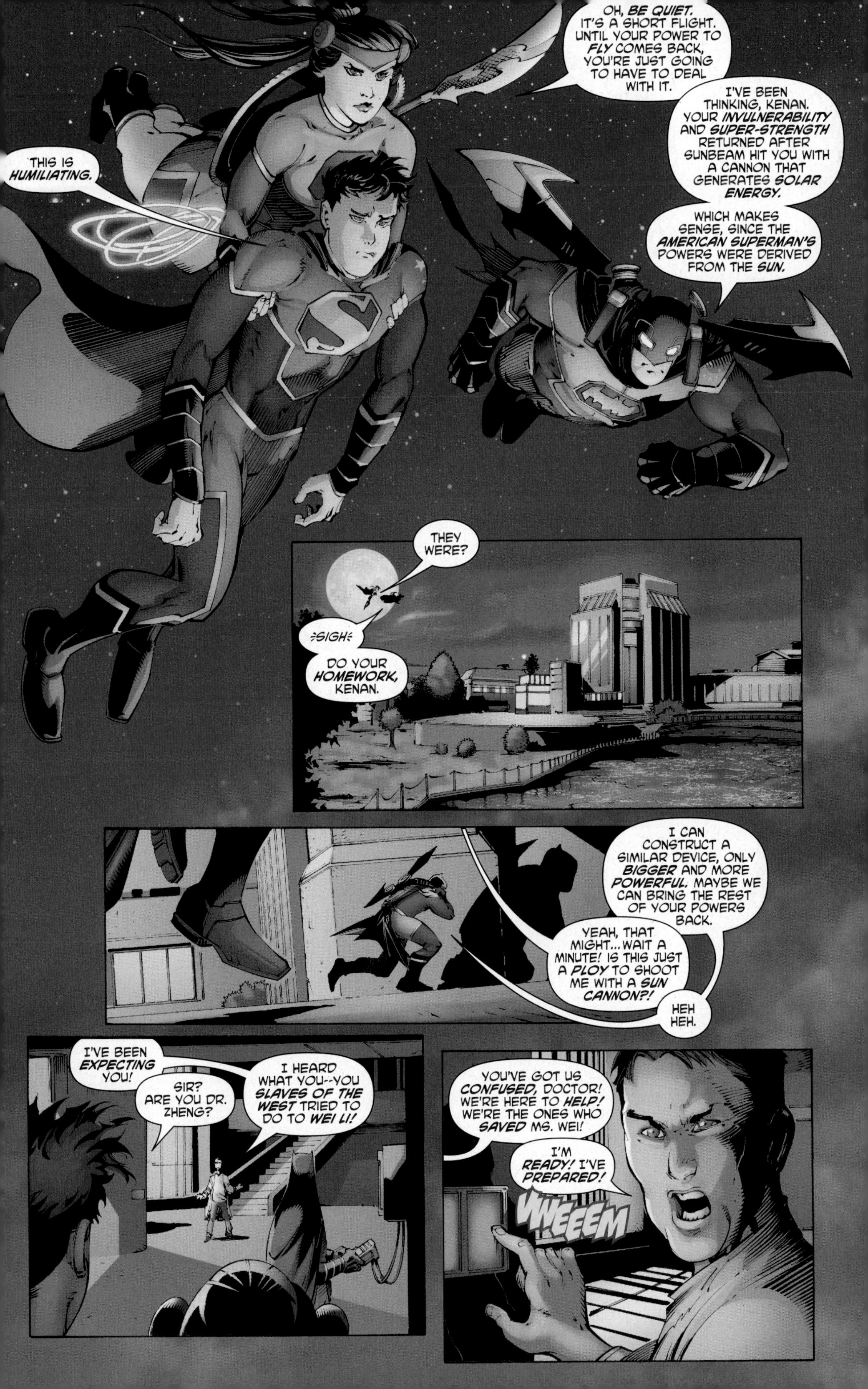
OH, BE QUIET. IT'S A SHORT FLIGHT. UNTIL YOUR POWER TO FLY COMES BACK, YOU'RE JUST GOING TO HAVE TO DEAL WITH IT.
THIS IS HUMILIATING.
I'VE BEEN THINKING, KENAN. YOUR INVULNERABILITY AND SUPER-STRENGTH RETURNED AFTER SUNBEAM HIT YOU WITH A CANNON THAT GENERATES SOLAR ENERGY.
WHICH MAKES SENSE, SINCE THE AMERICAN SUPERMAN'S POWERS WERE DERIVED FROM THE SUN.
THEY WERE?
SIGH
DO YOUR HOMEWORK, KENAN.
I CAN CONSTRUCT A SIMILAR DEVICE, ONLY BIGGER AND MORE POWERFUL. MAYBE WE CAN BRING THE REST OF YOUR POWERS BACK.
YEAH, THAT MIGHT... WAIT A MINUTE! IS THIS JUST A PLOY TO SHOOT ME WITH A SUN CANNON?!
HEH HEH.
I'VE BEEN EXPECTING YOU!
SIR? ARE YOU DR. ZHENG?
I HEARD WHAT YOU--YOU SLAVES OF THE WEST TRIED TO DO TO WEI LI!
YOU'VE GOT US CONFUSED, DOCTOR! WE'RE HERE TO HELP! WE'RE THE ONES WHO SAVED MS. WEI!
I'M READY! I'VE PREPARED!
VWEEEM

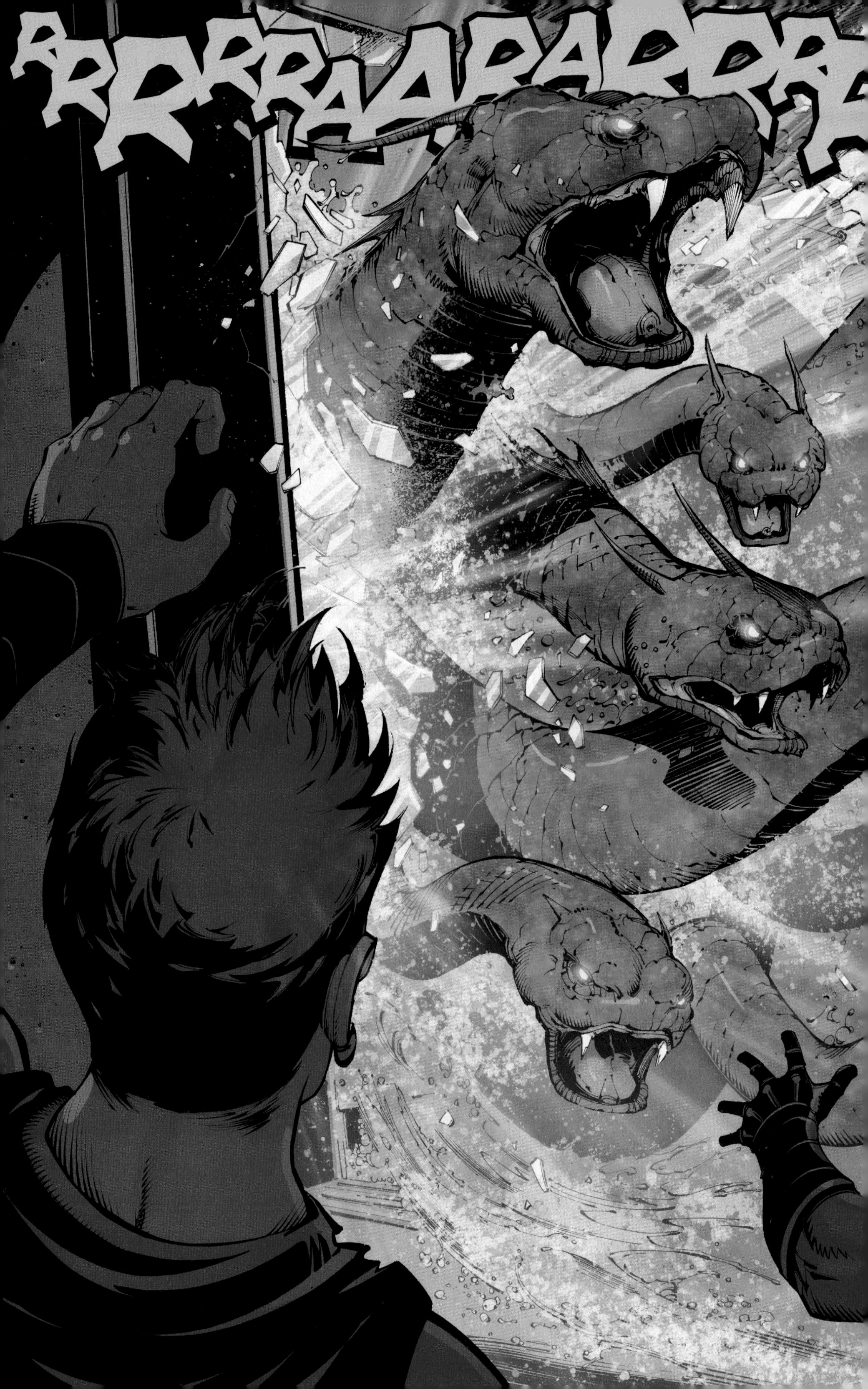
RRRRAARARRRR

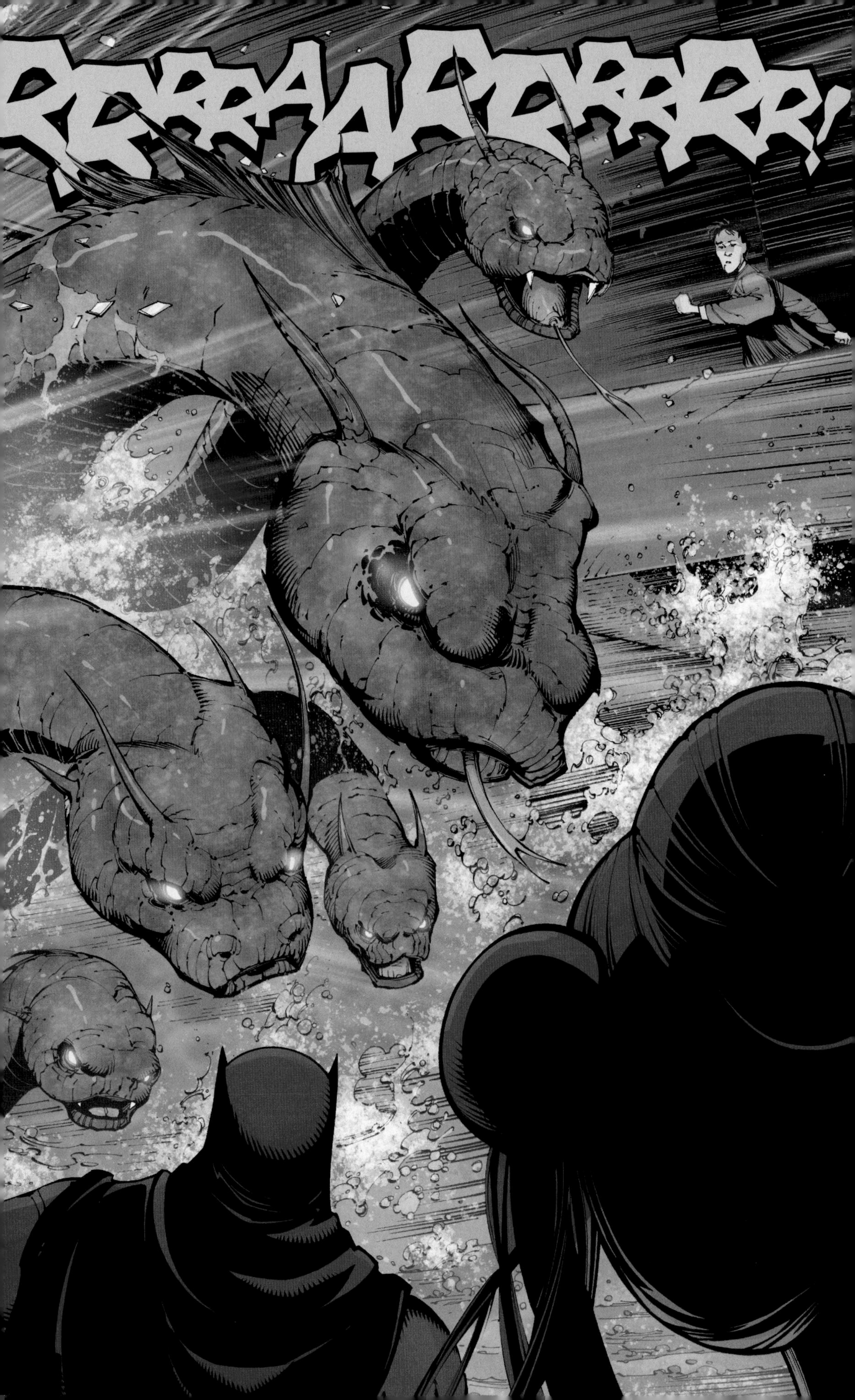
RRRAARRRRR!

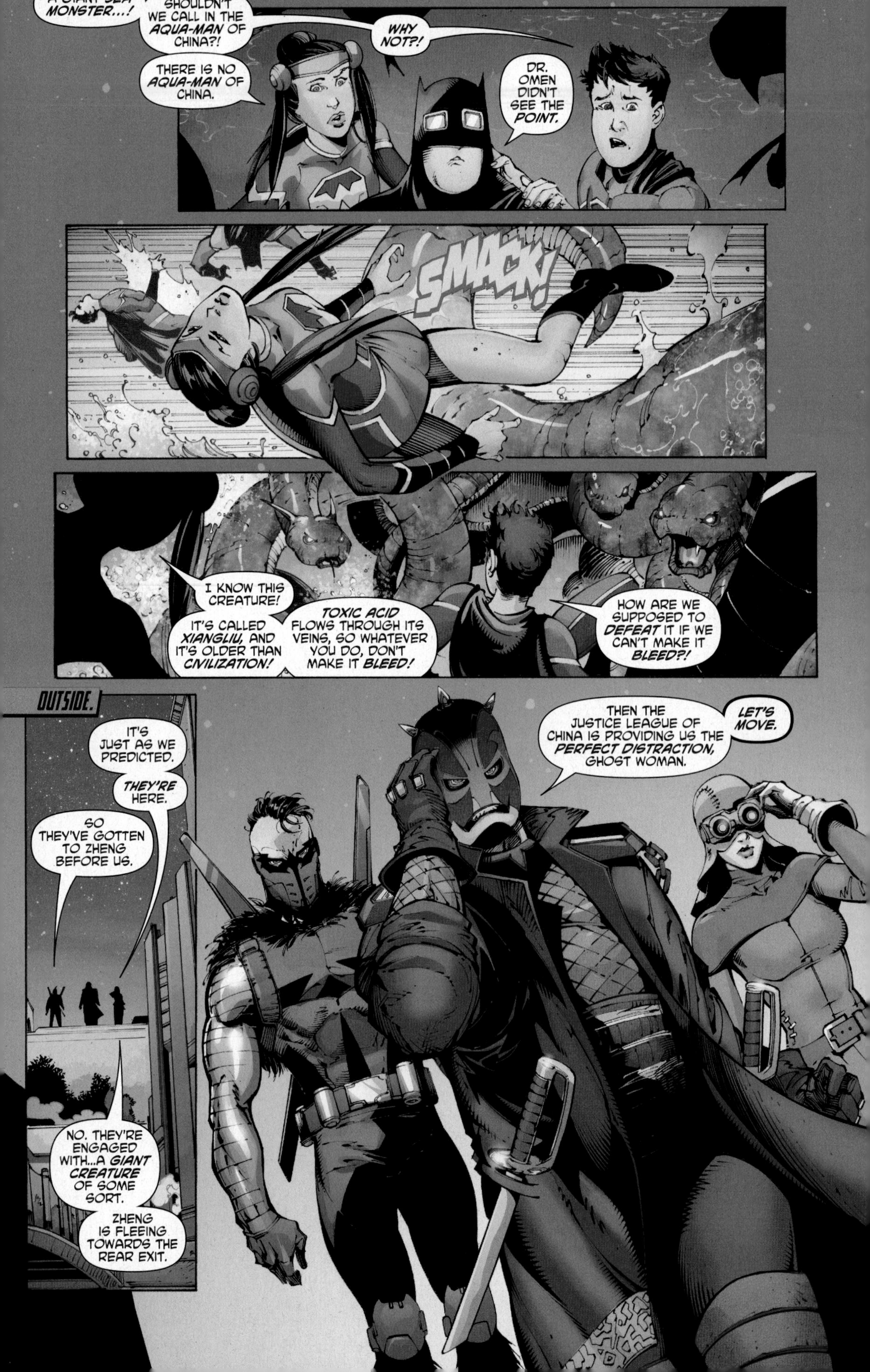
A GIANT SEA MONSTER...!
SHOULDN'T WE CALL IN THE AQUA-MAN OF CHINA?!
WHY NOT?!
THERE IS NO AQUA-MAN OF CHINA.
DR. OMEN DIDN'T SEE THE POINT.
SMACK!
I KNOW THIS CREATURE!
IT'S CALLED XIANGLIU, AND IT'S OLDER THAN CIVILIZATION!
TOXIC ACID FLOWS THROUGH ITS VEINS, SO WHATEVER YOU DO, DON'T MAKE IT BLEED!
HOW ARE WE SUPPOSED TO DEFEAT IT IF WE CAN'T MAKE IT BLEED?!
OUTSIDE.
IT'S JUST AS WE PREDICTED.
THEY'RE HERE.
SO THEY'VE GOTTEN TO ZHENG BEFORE US.
NO. THEY'RE ENGAGED WITH...A GIANT CREATURE OF SOME SORT.
ZHENG IS FLEEING TOWARDS THE REAR EXIT.
THEN THE JUSTICE LEAGUE OF CHINA IS PROVIDING US THE PERFECT DISTRACTION, GHOST WOMAN.
LET'S MOVE.

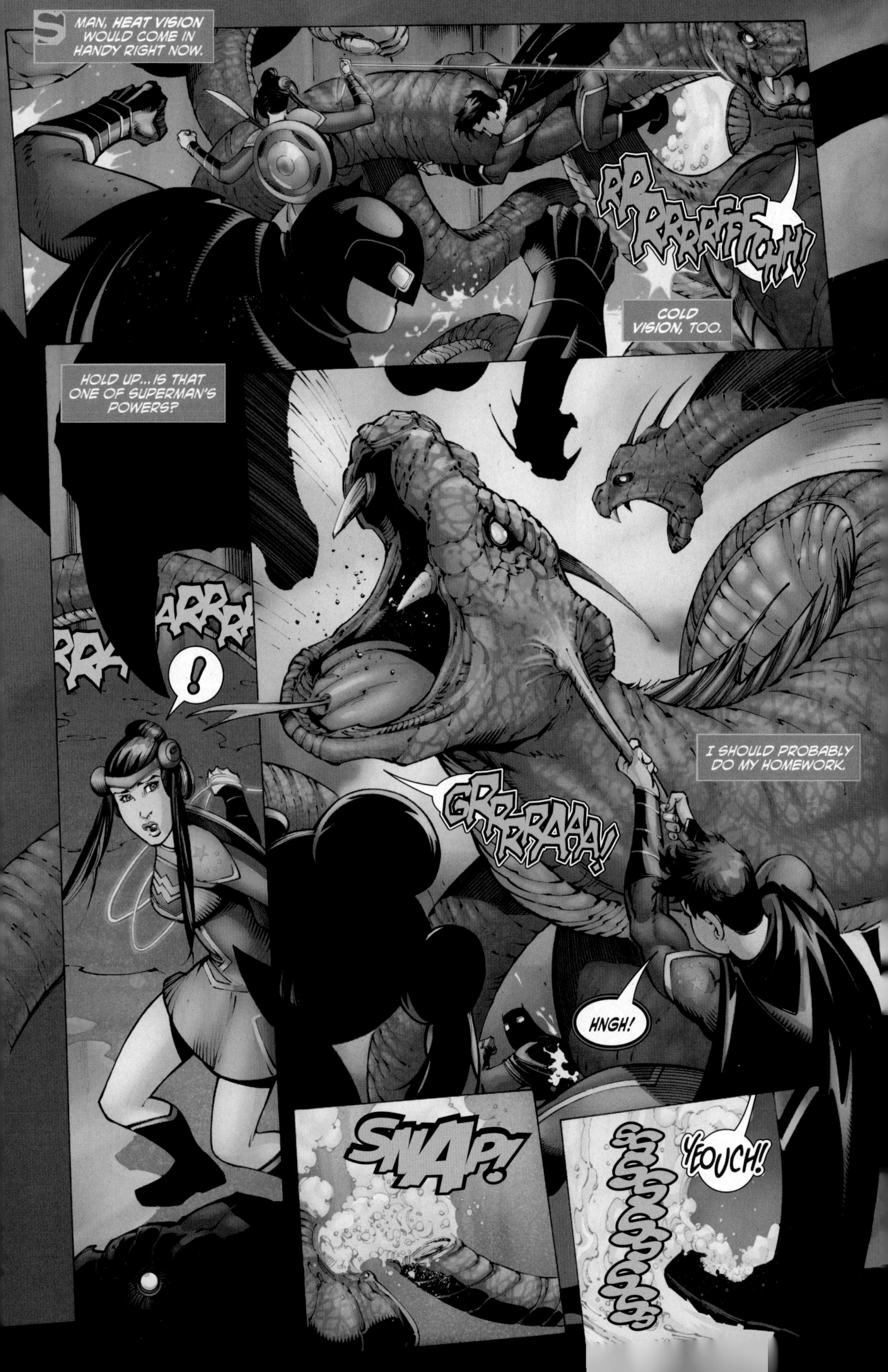
MAN, HEAT VISION WOULD COME IN HANDY RIGHT NOW.
RRRRRRAFFCHH!
COLD VISION, TOO.
HOLD UP...IS THAT ONE OF SUPERMAN'S POWERS?
ARRRK
!
I SHOULD PROBABLY DO MY HOMEWORK.
GRRRRAAA!
HNGH!
SNAP!
SSSSSSSSSS
YEOUCH!

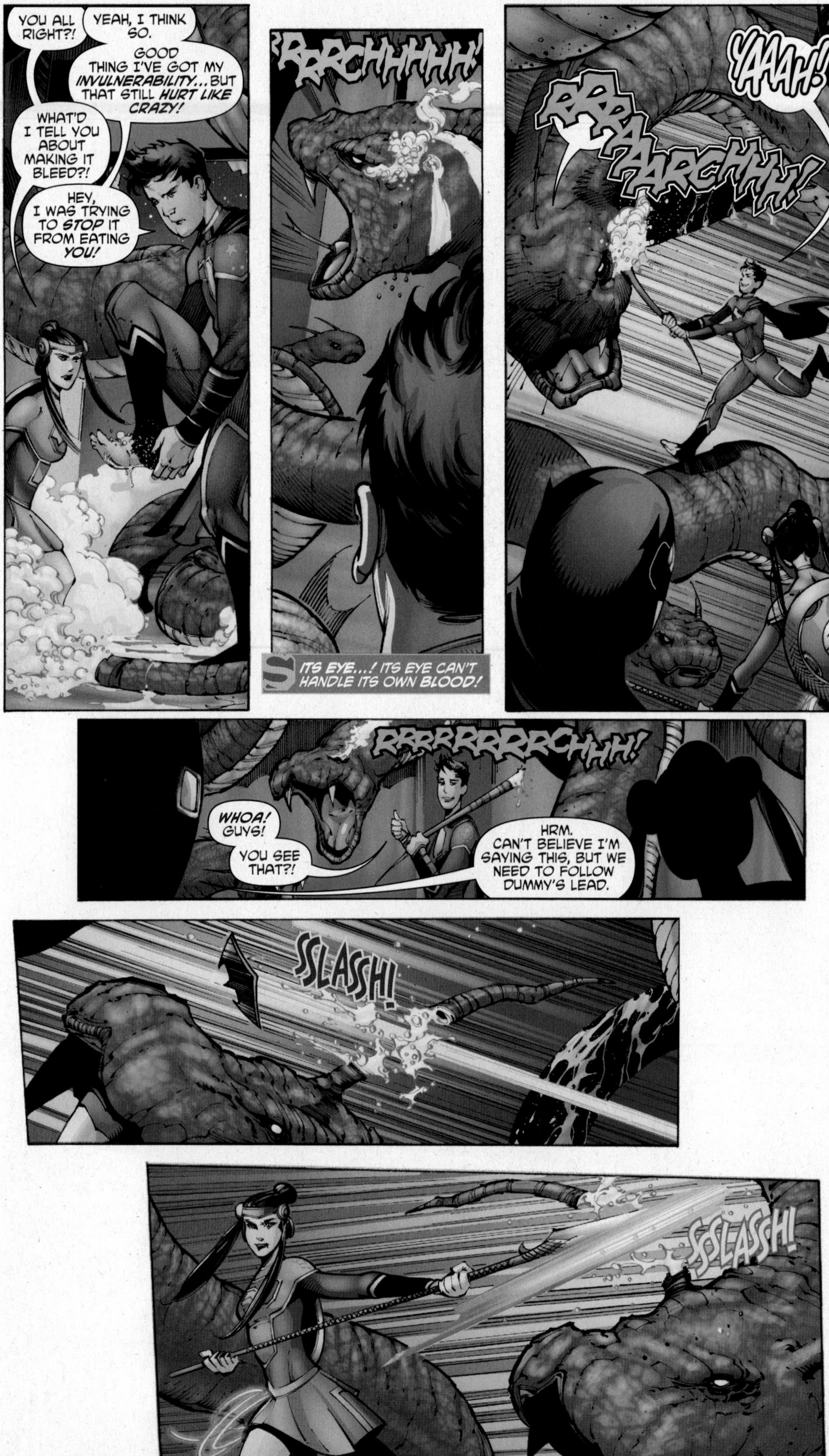
YOU ALL RIGHT?!
YEAH, I THINK SO.
GOOD THING I'VE GOT MY INVULNERABILITY... BUT THAT STILL HURT LIKE CRAZY!
WHAT'D I TELL YOU ABOUT MAKING IT BLEED?!
HEY, I WAS TRYING TO STOP IT FROM EATING YOU!
RRRCHHHHH!
ITS EYE...! ITS EYE CAN'T HANDLE ITS OWN BLOOD!
YAAAH!
RRRAAARCHHH!
RRRRRRRRCHHH!
WHOA! GUYS!
YOU SEE THAT?!
HRM. CAN'T BELIEVE I'M SAYING THIS, BUT WE NEED TO FOLLOW DUMMY'S LEAD.
SSLASSH!
SSLASSH!

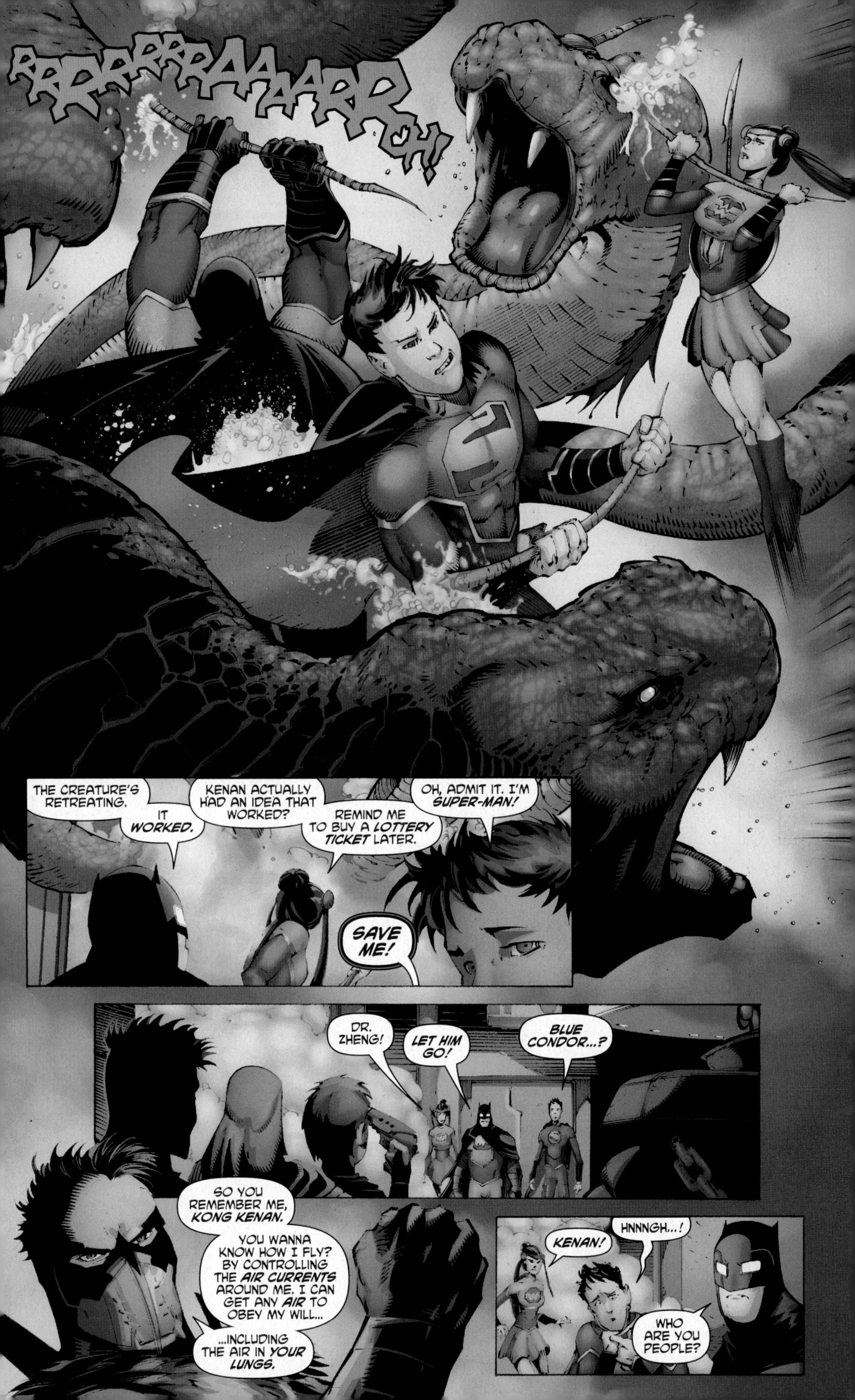

RRRRRRAAAARRRGH!
THE CREATURE'S RETREATING.
IT WORKED.
KENAN ACTUALLY HAD AN IDEA THAT WORKED?
REMIND ME TO BUY A LOTTERY TICKET LATER.
OH, ADMIT IT. I'M SUPER-MAN!
SAVE ME!
DR. ZHENG!
LET HIM GO!
BLUE CONDOR...?
SO YOU REMEMBER ME, KONG KENAN.
YOU WANNA KNOW HOW I FLY? BY CONTROLLING THE AIR CURRENTS AROUND ME. I CAN GET ANY AIR TO OBEY MY WILL...
...INCLUDING THE AIR IN YOUR LUNGS.
KENAN!
HNNNGH...!
WHO ARE YOU PEOPLE?

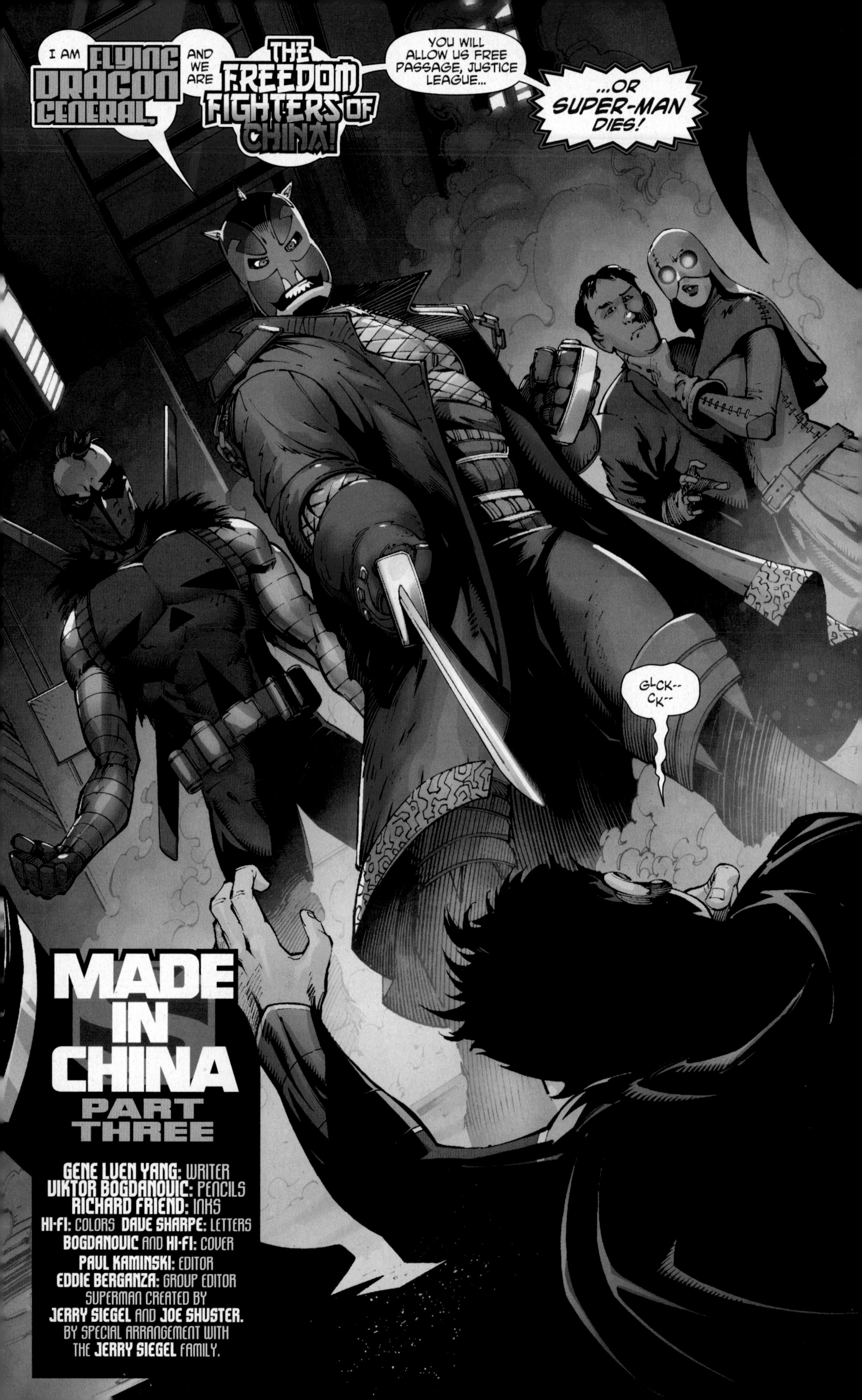
I AM FLYING DRAGON GENERAL,
AND WE ARE THE FREEDOM FIGHTERS OF CHINA!
YOU WILL ALLOW US FREE PASSAGE, JUSTICE LEAGUE...
...OR SUPER-MAN DIES!
GLCK--CK--
MADE IN CHINA
PART THREE
GENE LUEN YANG: WRITER
VIKTOR BOGDANOVIC: PENCILS
RICHARD FRIEND: INKS
HI-FI: COLORS DAVE SHARPE: LETTERS
BOGDANOVIC AND HI-FI: COVER
PAUL KAMINSKI: EDITOR
EDDIE BERGANZA: GROUP EDITOR
SUPERMAN CREATED BY
JERRY SIEGEL AND JOE SHUSTER.
BY SPECIAL ARRANGEMENT WITH
THE JERRY SIEGEL FAMILY.

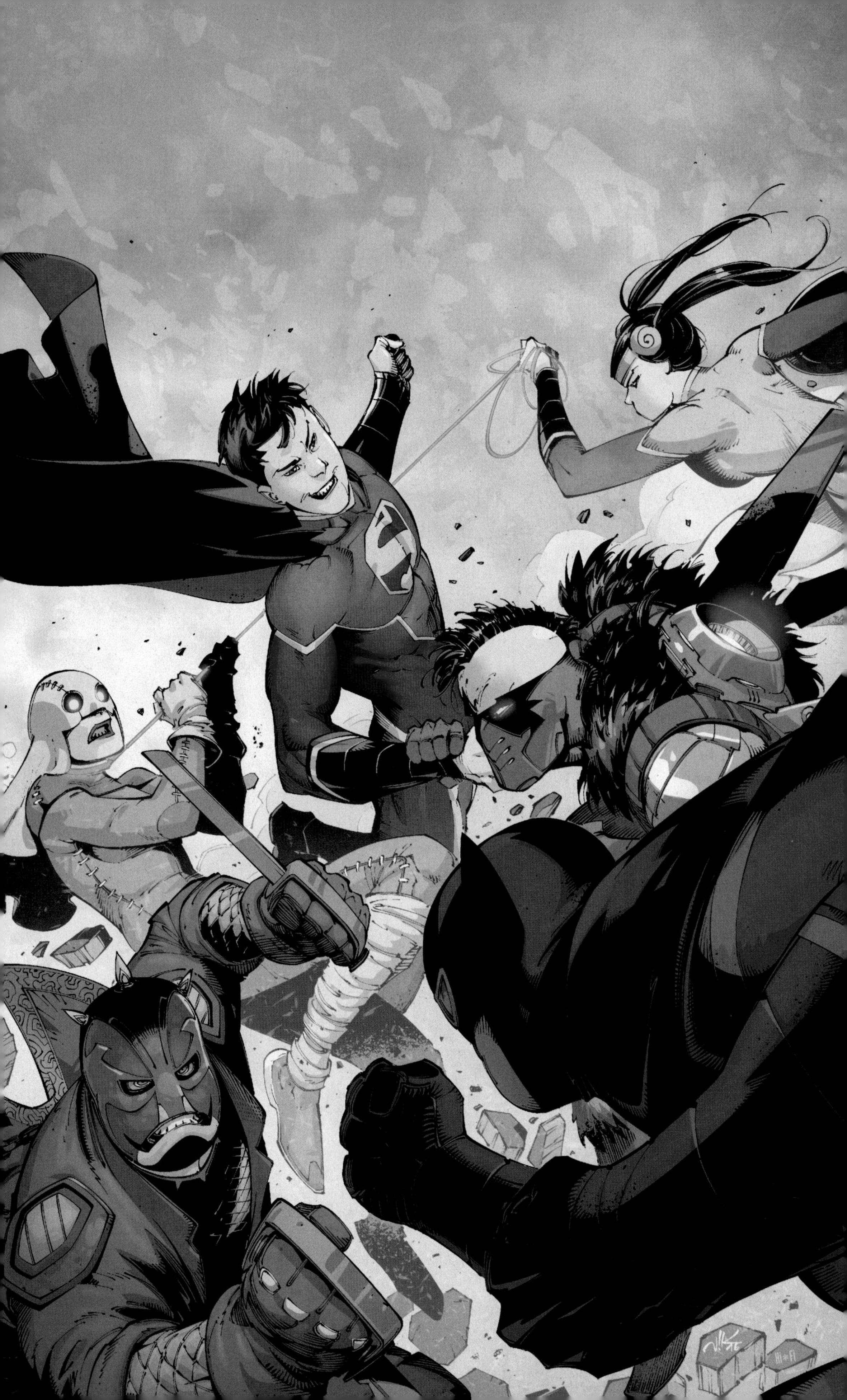

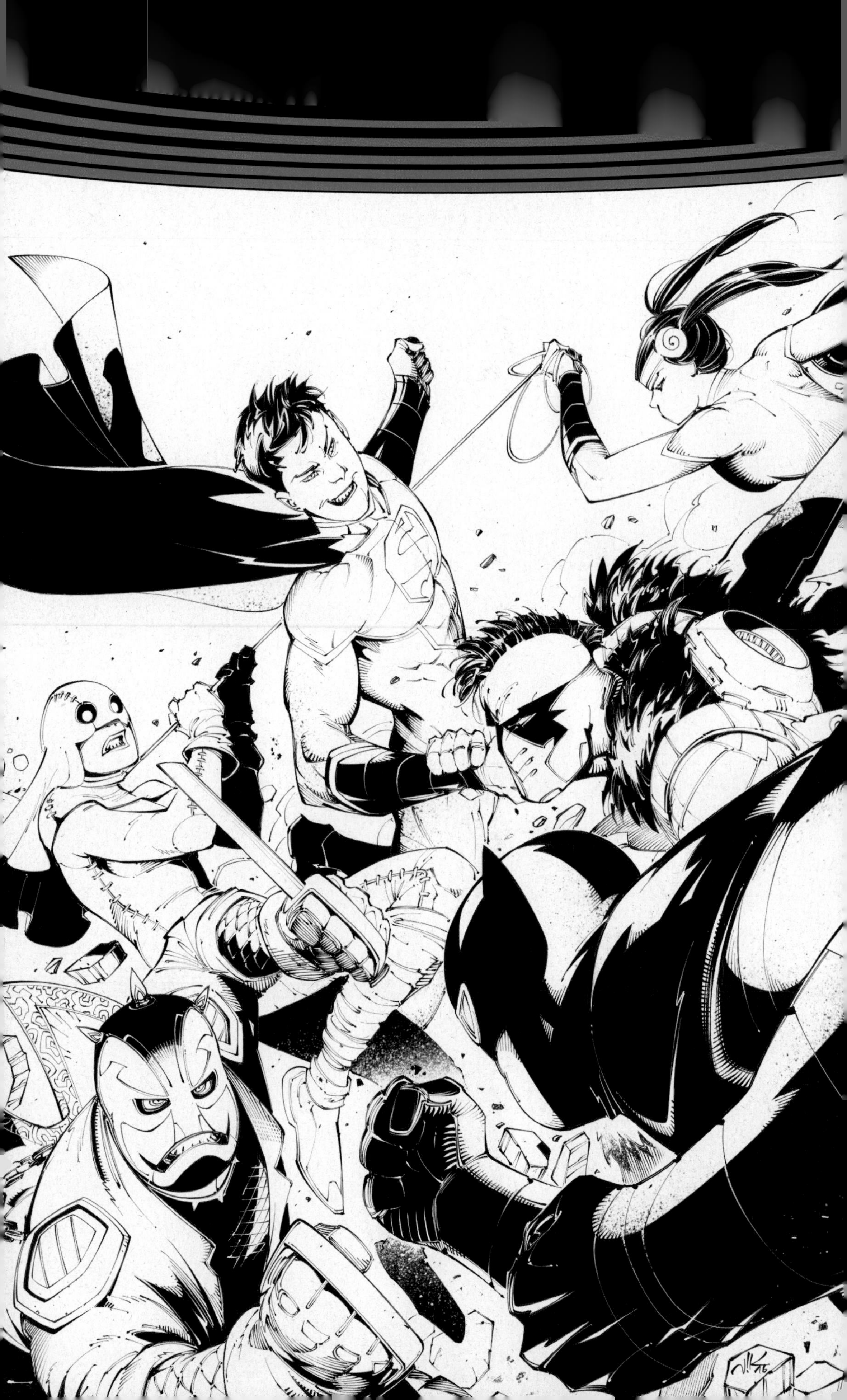

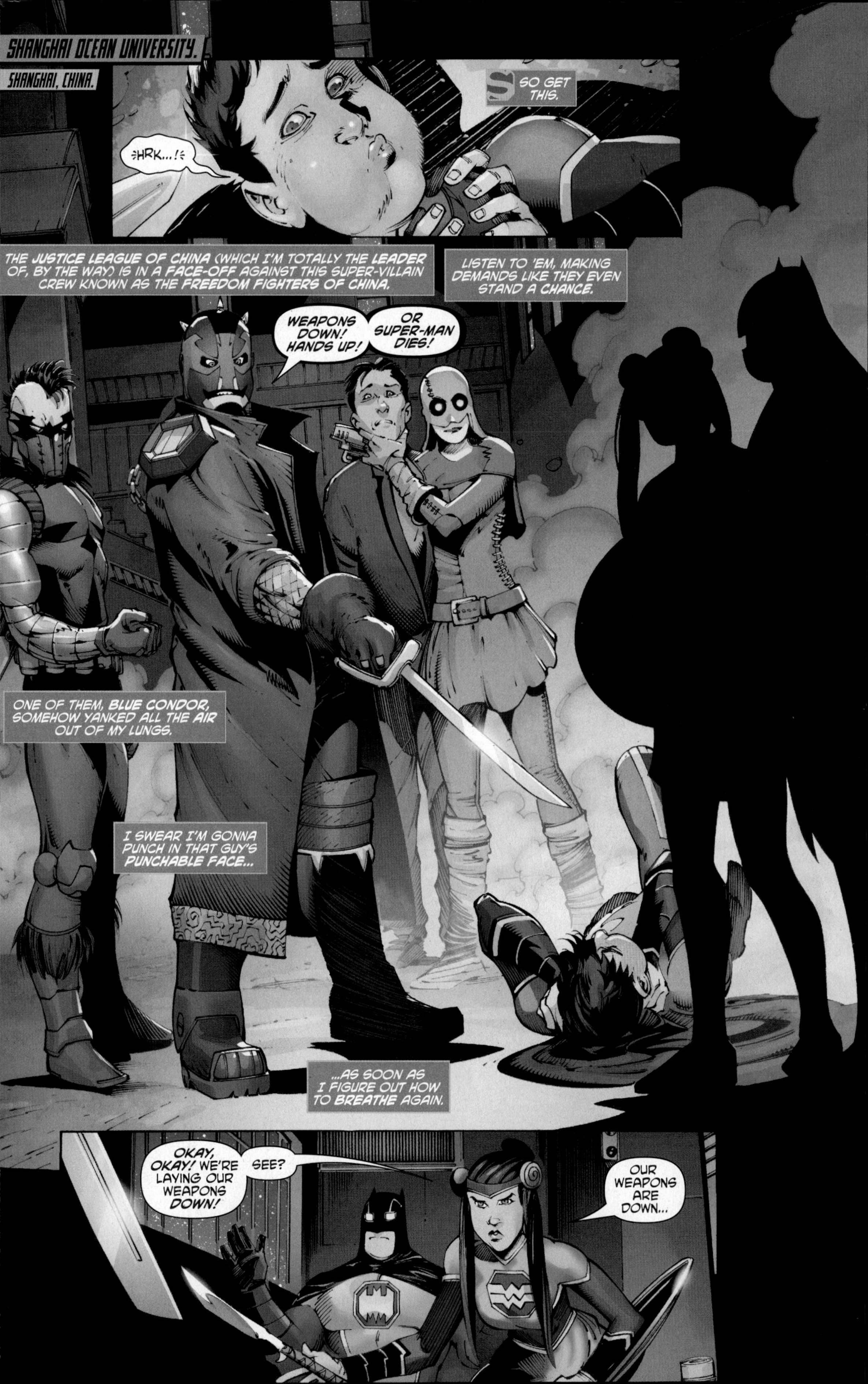
SHANGHAI OCEAN UNIVERSITY.
SHANGHAI, CHINA.
SO GET THIS.
HRK...!
THE JUSTICE LEAGUE OF CHINA (WHICH I'M TOTALLY THE LEADER OF, BY THE WAY) IS IN A FACE-OFF AGAINST THIS SUPER-VILLAIN CREW KNOWN AS THE FREEDOM FIGHTERS OF CHINA.
LISTEN TO 'EM, MAKING DEMANDS LIKE THEY EVEN STAND A CHANCE.
WEAPONS DOWN! HANDS UP!
OR SUPER-MAN DIES!
ONE OF THEM, BLUE CONDOR, SOMEHOW YANKED ALL THE AIR OUT OF MY LUNGS.
I SWEAR I'M GONNA PUNCH IN THAT GUY'S PUNCHABLE FACE...
...AS SOON AS I FIGURE OUT HOW TO BREATHE AGAIN.
OKAY, OKAY! WE'RE LAYING OUR WEAPONS DOWN!
SEE?
OUR WEAPONS ARE DOWN...

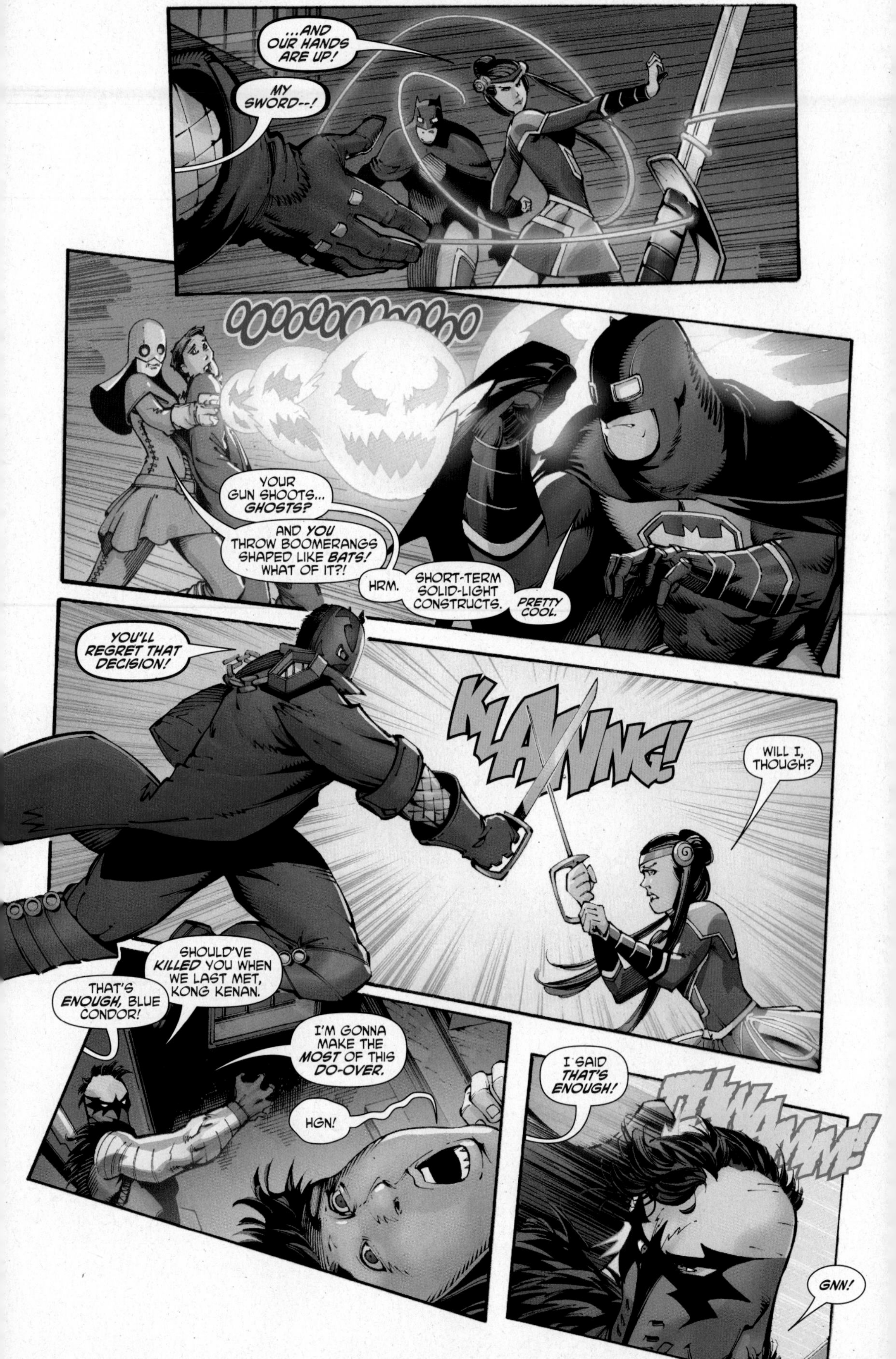
...AND OUR HANDS ARE UP!
MY SWORD--!
OOOOOOOOOOOOOOO
YOUR GUN SHOOTS... GHOSTS?
AND YOU THROW BOOMERANGS SHAPED LIKE BATS! WHAT OF IT?!
HRM.
SHORT-TERM SOLID-LIGHT CONSTRUCTS.
PRETTY COOL.
YOU'LL REGRET THAT DECISION!
KLANNG!
WILL I, THOUGH?
SHOULD'VE KILLED YOU WHEN WE LAST MET, KONG KENAN.
THAT'S ENOUGH, BLUE CONDOR!
I'M GONNA MAKE THE MOST OF THIS DO-OVER.
HGN!
I SAID THAT'S ENOUGH!
THWAMM!
GNN!

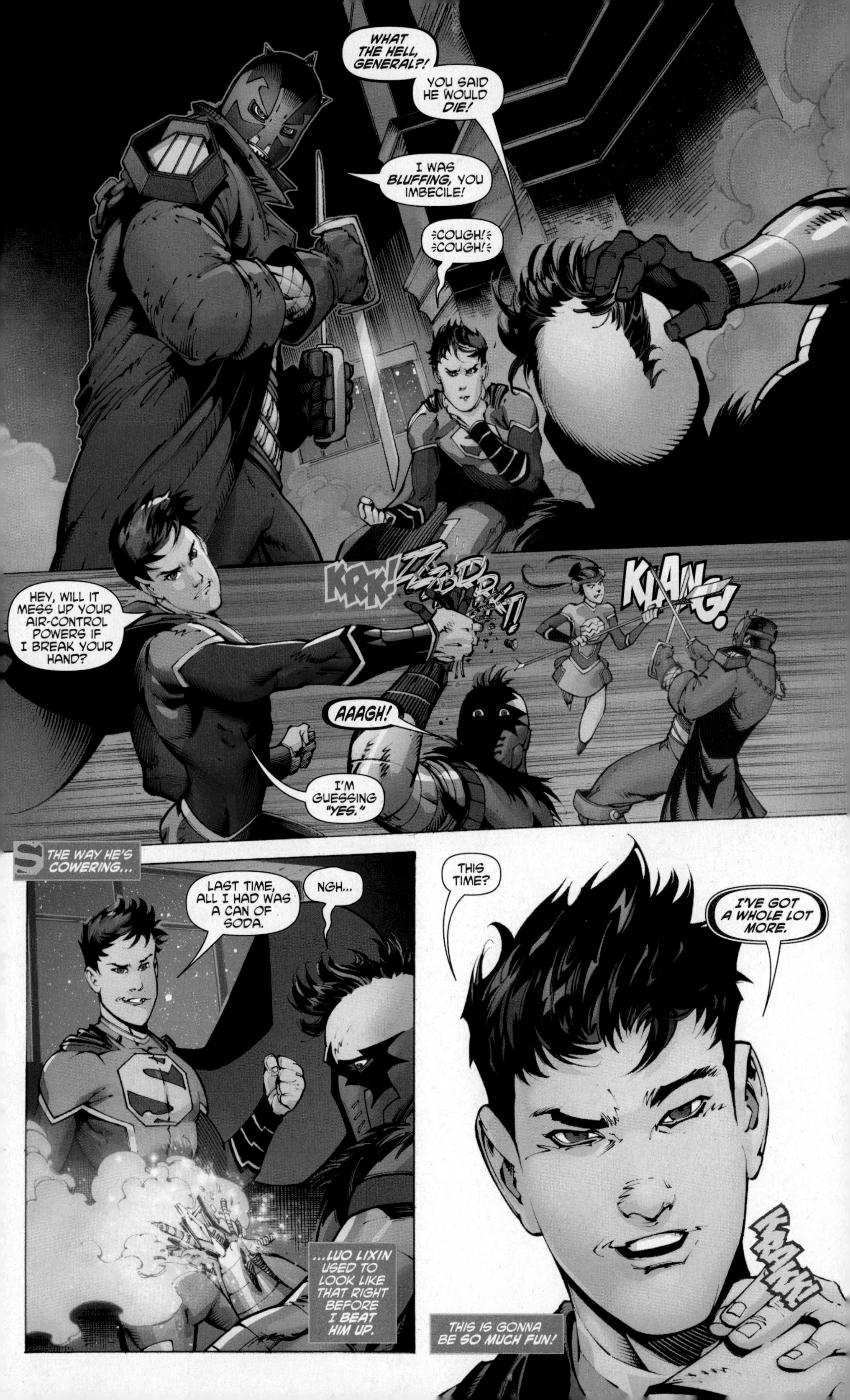
WHAT THE HELL, GENERAL?!
YOU SAID HE WOULD DIE!
I WAS BLUFFING, YOU IMBECILE!
COUGH! COUGH!
KRK! ZZDDRK!!
KLANG!
HEY, WILL IT MESS UP YOUR AIR-CONTROL POWERS IF I BREAK YOUR HAND?
AAAGH!
I'M GUESSING "YES."
THE WAY HE'S COWERING...
LAST TIME, ALL I HAD WAS A CAN OF SODA.
NGH...
...LUO LIXIN USED TO LOOK LIKE THAT RIGHT BEFORE I BEAT HIM UP.
THIS TIME?
I'VE GOT A WHOLE LOT MORE.
THIS IS GONNA BE SO MUCH FUN!

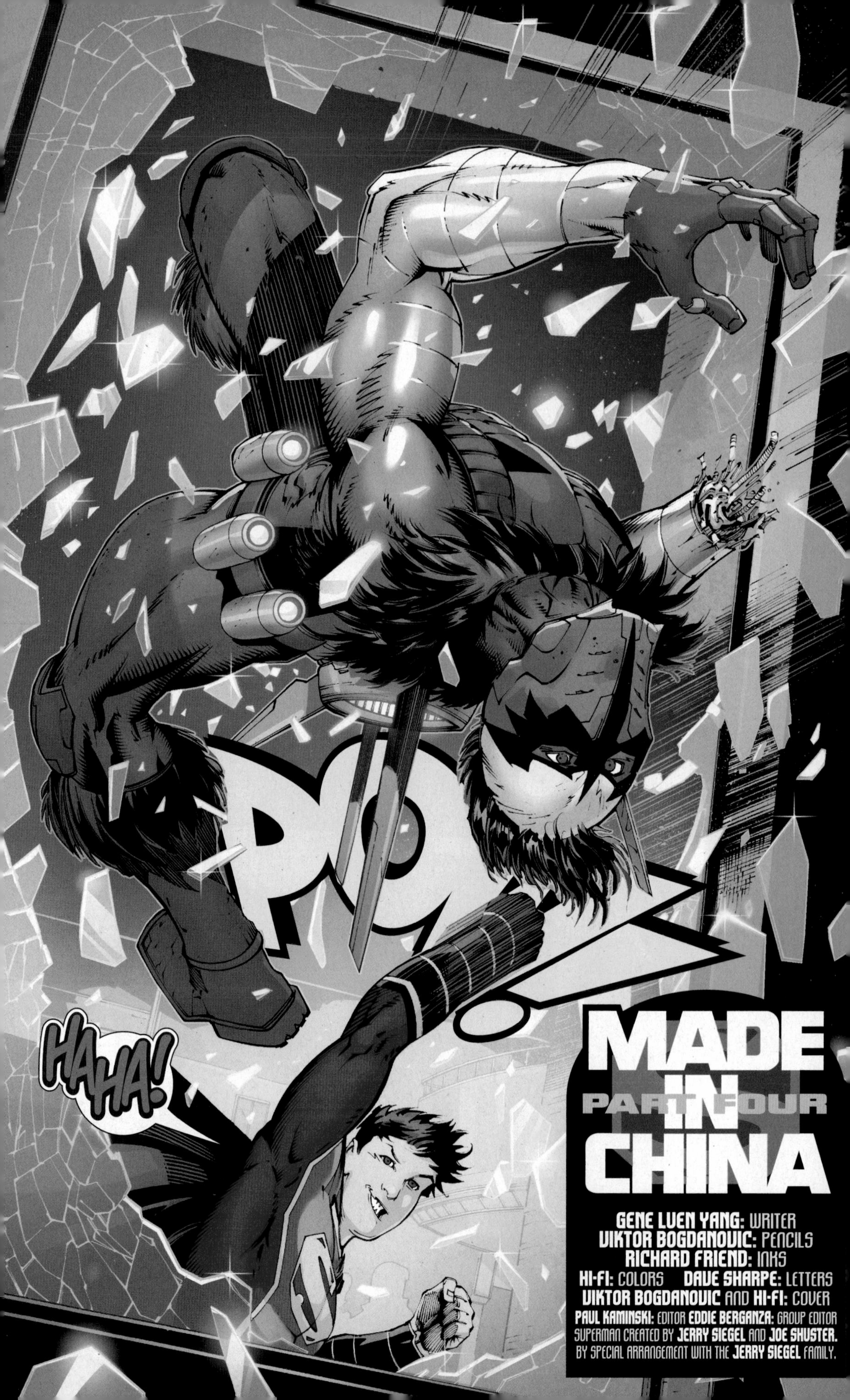

HAHA!
MADE IN CHINA
PART FOUR
GENE LUEN YANG: WRITER
VIKTOR BOGDANOVIC: PENCILS
RICHARD FRIEND: INKS
HI-FI: COLORS DAVE SHARPE: LETTERS
VIKTOR BOGDANOVIC AND HI-FI: COVER
PAUL KAMINSKI: EDITOR EDDIE BERGANZA: GROUP EDITOR
SUPERMAN CREATED BY JERRY SIEGEL AND JOE SHUSTER.
BY SPECIAL ARRANGEMENT WITH THE JERRY SIEGEL FAMILY.

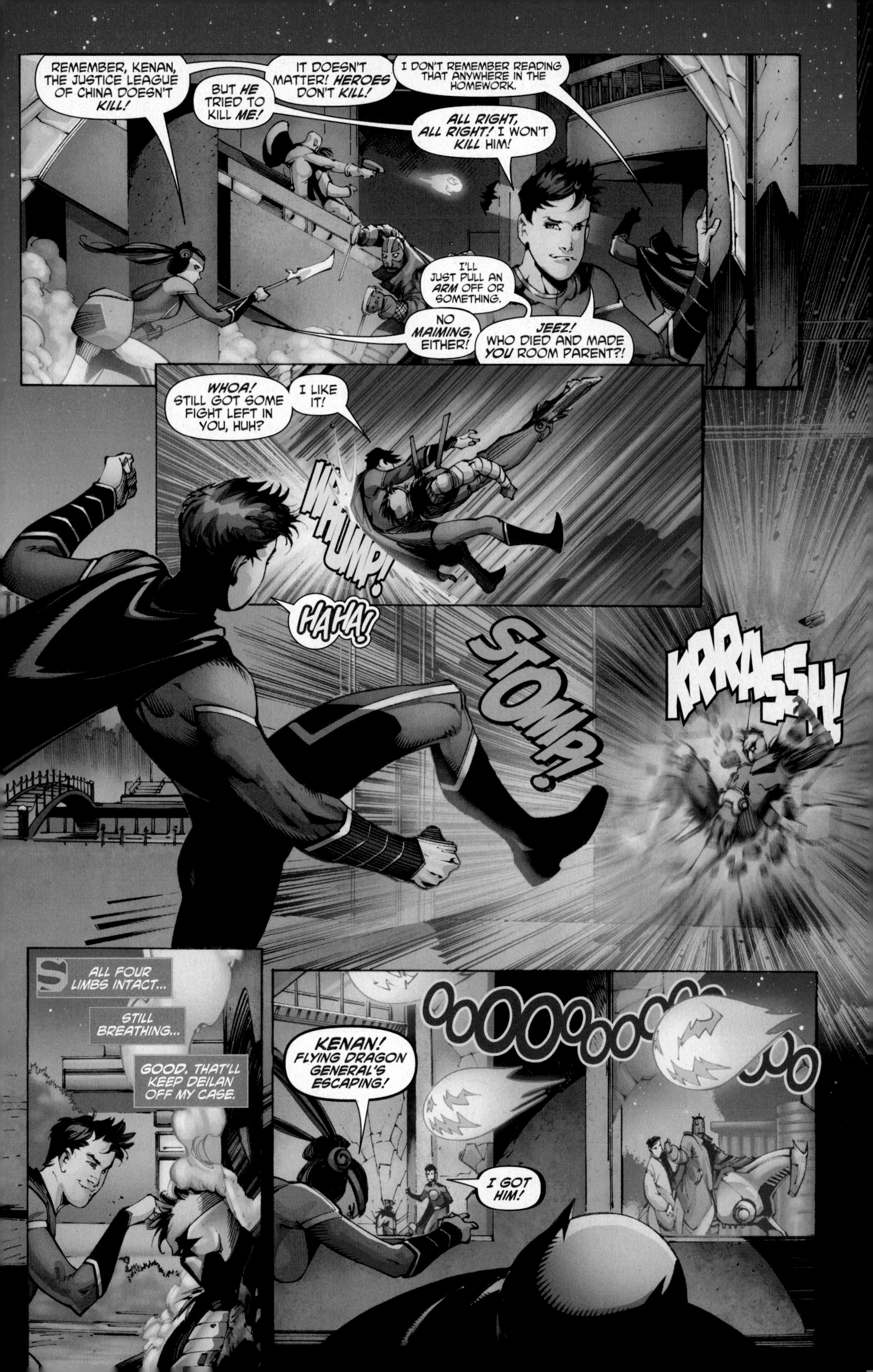
REMEMBER, KENAN, THE JUSTICE LEAGUE OF CHINA DOESN'T KILL!
BUT HE TRIED TO KILL ME!
IT DOESN'T MATTER! HEROES DON'T KILL!
I DON'T REMEMBER READING THAT ANYWHERE IN THE HOMEWORK.
ALL RIGHT, ALL RIGHT! I WON'T KILL HIM!
I'LL JUST PULL AN ARM OFF OR SOMETHING.
NO MAIMING, EITHER!
JEEZ! WHO DIED AND MADE YOU ROOM PARENT?!
WHOA! STILL GOT SOME FIGHT LEFT IN YOU, HUH?
I LIKE IT!
WHUMP!
HAHA!
STOMP!
KRRASSH!
ALL FOUR LIMBS INTACT...
STILL BREATHING...
GOOD. THAT'LL KEEP DEILAN OFF MY CASE.
OOOOOOOOOOOOO
KENAN! FLYING DRAGON GENERAL'S ESCAPING!
I GOT HIM!

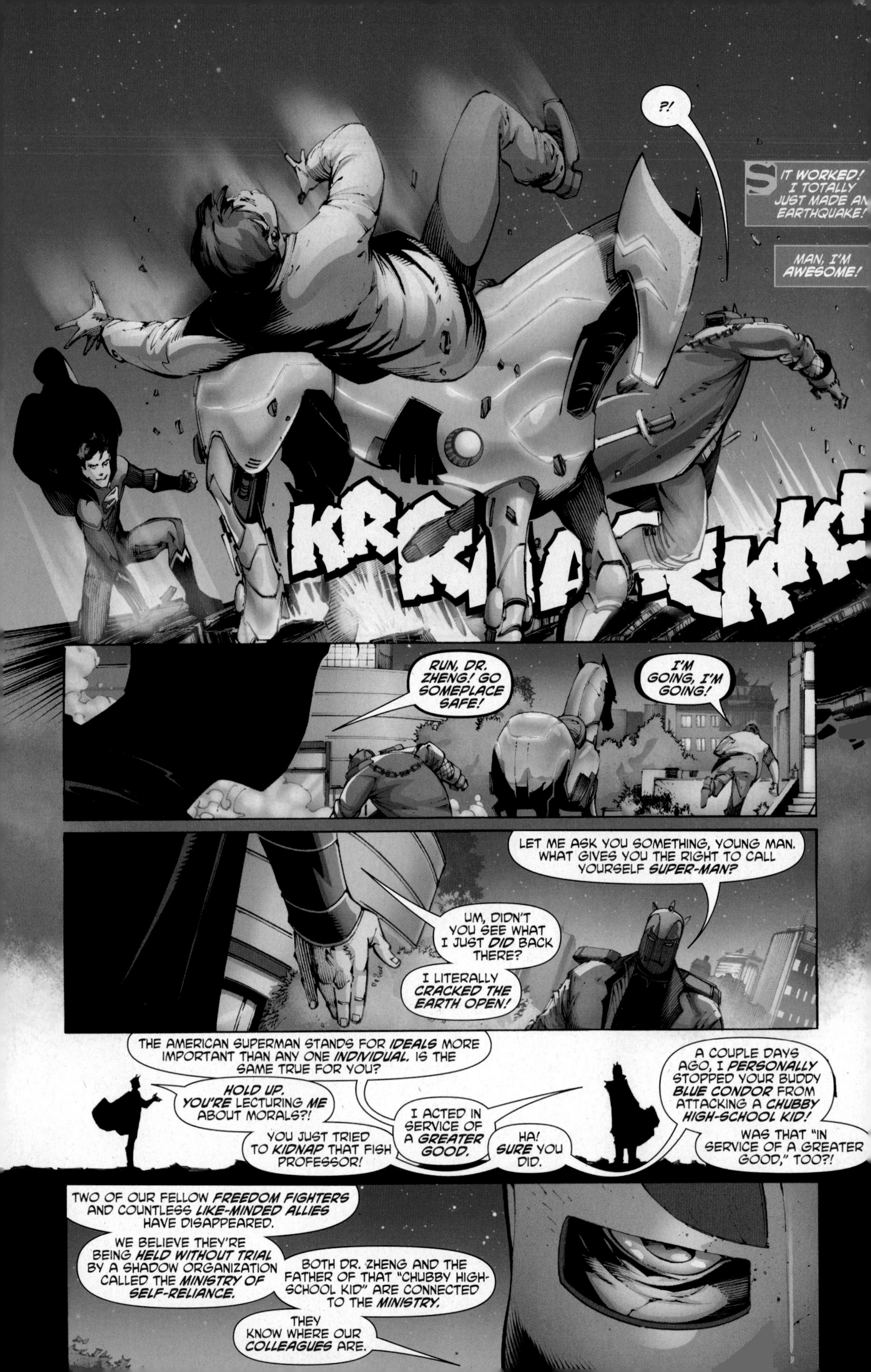
?!
IT WORKED! I TOTALLY JUST MADE AN EARTHQUAKE!
MAN, I'M AWESOME!
KRRAKK!
RUN, DR. ZHENG! GO SOMEPLACE SAFE!
I'M GOING, I'M GOING!
LET ME ASK YOU SOMETHING, YOUNG MAN. WHAT GIVES YOU THE RIGHT TO CALL YOURSELF SUPER-MAN?
UM, DIDN'T YOU SEE WHAT I JUST DID BACK THERE?
I LITERALLY CRACKED THE EARTH OPEN!
THE AMERICAN SUPERMAN STANDS FOR IDEALS MORE IMPORTANT THAN ANY ONE INDIVIDUAL. IS THE SAME TRUE FOR YOU?
HOLD UP. YOU'RE LECTURING ME ABOUT MORALS?!
YOU JUST TRIED TO KIDNAP THAT FISH PROFESSOR!
I ACTED IN SERVICE OF A GREATER GOOD.
HA! SURE YOU DID.
A COUPLE DAYS AGO, I PERSONALLY STOPPED YOUR BUDDY BLUE CONDOR FROM ATTACKING A CHUBBY HIGH-SCHOOL KID!
WAS THAT "IN SERVICE OF A GREATER GOOD," TOO?!
TWO OF OUR FELLOW FREEDOM FIGHTERS AND COUNTLESS LIKE-MINDED ALLIES HAVE DISAPPEARED.
WE BELIEVE THEY'RE BEING HELD WITHOUT TRIAL BY A SHADOW ORGANIZATION CALLED THE MINISTRY OF SELF-RELIANCE.
BOTH DR. ZHENG AND THE FATHER OF THAT "CHUBBY HIGH-SCHOOL KID" ARE CONNECTED TO THE MINISTRY.
THEY KNOW WHERE OUR COLLEAGUES ARE.

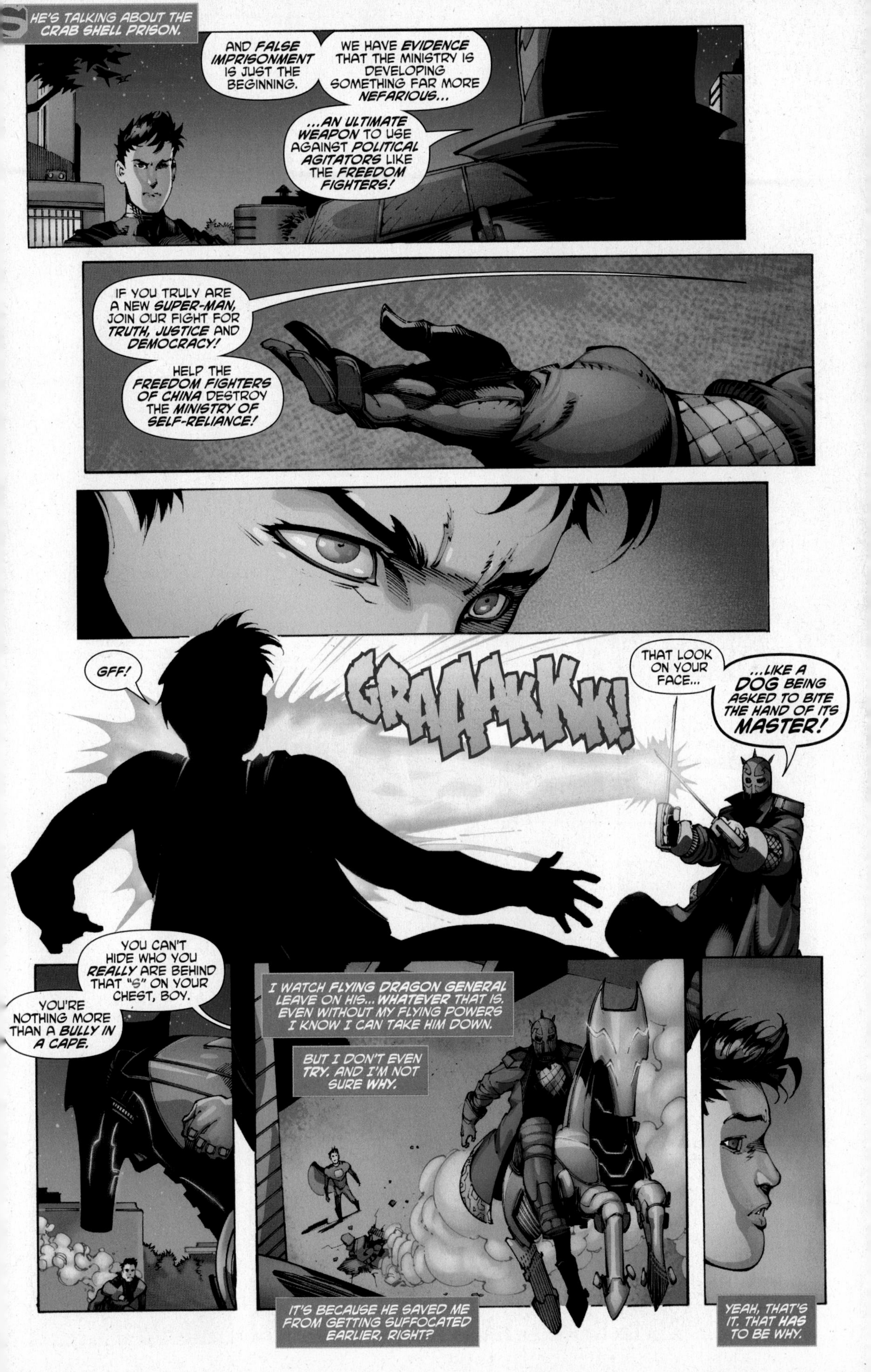
HE'S TALKING ABOUT THE CRAB SHELL PRISON.
AND FALSE IMPRISONMENT IS JUST THE BEGINNING.
WE HAVE EVIDENCE THAT THE MINISTRY IS DEVELOPING SOMETHING FAR MORE NEFARIOUS...
...AN ULTIMATE WEAPON TO USE AGAINST POLITICAL AGITATORS LIKE THE FREEDOM FIGHTERS!
IF YOU TRULY ARE A NEW SUPER-MAN, JOIN OUR FIGHT FOR TRUTH, JUSTICE AND DEMOCRACY!
HELP THE FREEDOM FIGHTERS OF CHINA DESTROY THE MINISTRY OF SELF-RELIANCE!
GFF!
GRAAAKKKK!
THAT LOOK ON YOUR FACE...
...LIKE A DOG BEING ASKED TO BITE THE HAND OF ITS MASTER!
YOU CAN'T HIDE WHO YOU REALLY ARE BEHIND THAT "S" ON YOUR CHEST, BOY.
YOU'RE NOTHING MORE THAN A BULLY IN A CAPE.
I WATCH FLYING DRAGON GENERAL LEAVE ON HIS... WHATEVER THAT IS. EVEN WITHOUT MY FLYING POWERS I KNOW I CAN TAKE HIM DOWN.
BUT I DON'T EVEN TRY. AND I'M NOT SURE WHY.
IT'S BECAUSE HE SAVED ME FROM GETTING SUFFOCATED EARLIER, RIGHT?
YEAH, THAT'S IT. THAT HAS TO BE WHY.

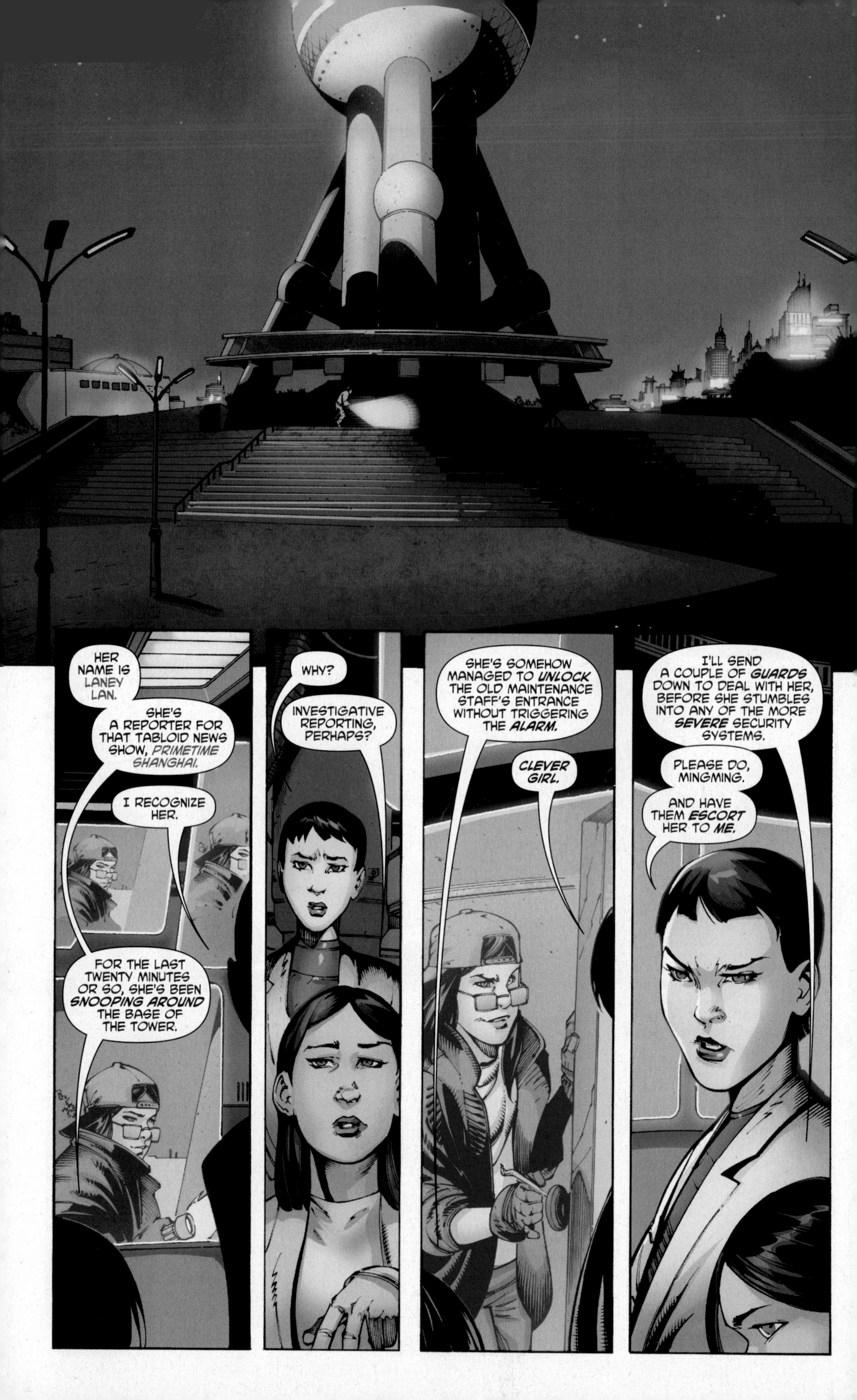
HER NAME IS LANEY LAN.
SHE'S A REPORTER FOR THAT TABLOID NEWS SHOW, PRIMETIME SHANGHAI.
I RECOGNIZE HER.
FOR THE LAST TWENTY MINUTES OR SO, SHE'S BEEN SNOOPING AROUND THE BASE OF THE TOWER.
WHY?
INVESTIGATIVE REPORTING, PERHAPS?
SHE'S SOMEHOW MANAGED TO UNLOCK THE OLD MAINTENANCE STAFF'S ENTRANCE WITHOUT TRIGGERING THE ALARM.
CLEVER GIRL.
I'LL SEND A COUPLE OF GUARDS DOWN TO DEAL WITH HER, BEFORE SHE STUMBLES INTO ANY OF THE MORE SEVERE SECURITY SYSTEMS.
PLEASE DO, MINGMING.
AND HAVE THEM ESCORT HER TO ME.

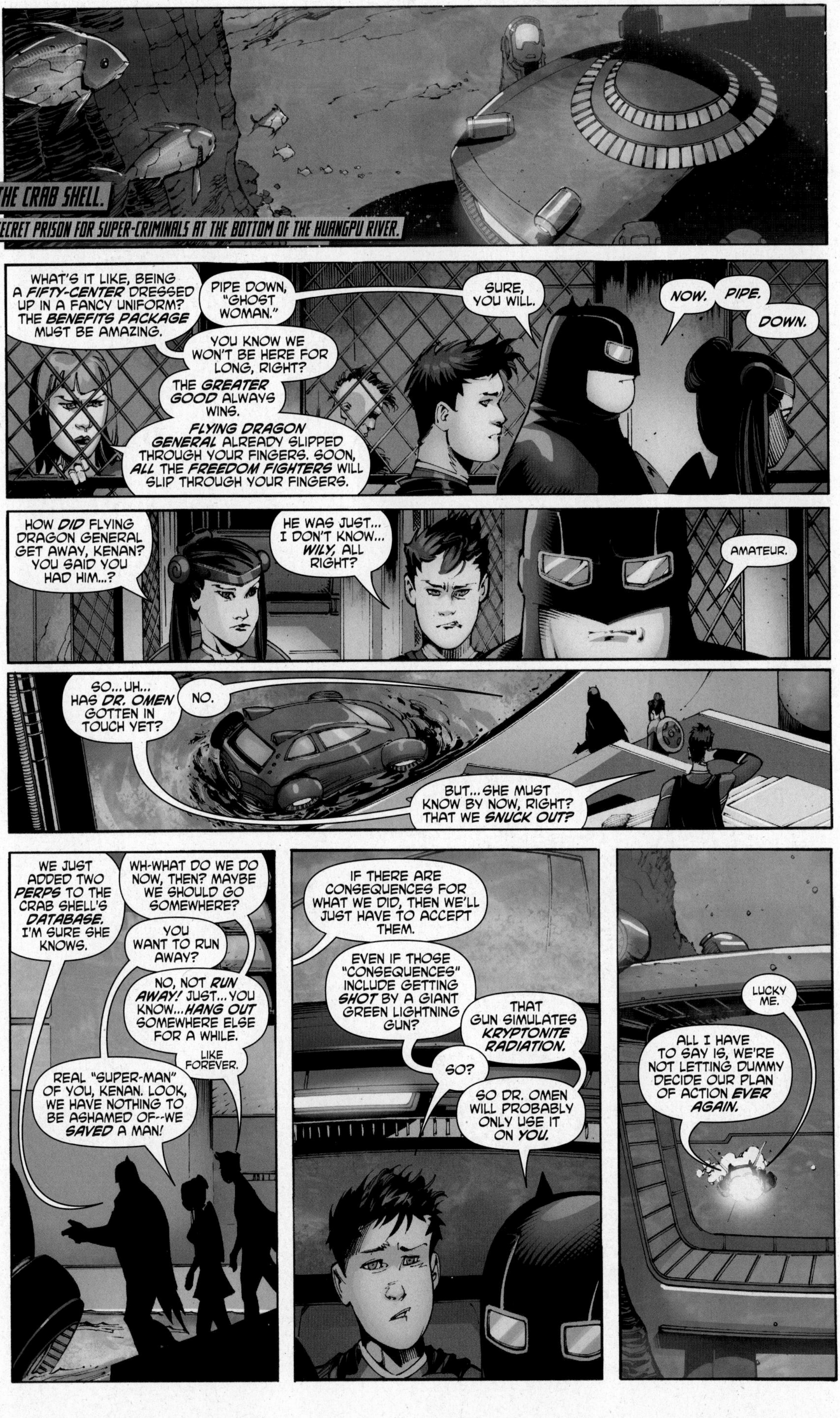
THE CRAB SHELL.
SECRET PRISON FOR SUPER-CRIMINALS AT THE BOTTOM OF THE HUANGPU RIVER.
WHAT'S IT LIKE, BEING A FIFTY-CENTER DRESSED UP IN A FANCY UNIFORM? THE BENEFITS PACKAGE MUST BE AMAZING.
PIPE DOWN, "GHOST WOMAN."
YOU KNOW WE WON'T BE HERE FOR LONG, RIGHT?
THE GREATER GOOD ALWAYS WINS.
FLYING DRAGON GENERAL ALREADY SLIPPED THROUGH YOUR FINGERS. SOON, ALL THE FREEDOM FIGHTERS WILL SLIP THROUGH YOUR FINGERS.
SURE, YOU WILL.
NOW. PIPE. DOWN.
HOW DID FLYING DRAGON GENERAL GET AWAY, KENAN? YOU SAID YOU HAD HIM...?
HE WAS JUST... I DON'T KNOW... WILY, ALL RIGHT?
AMATEUR.
SO...UH... HAS DR. OMEN GOTTEN IN TOUCH YET?
NO.
BUT...SHE MUST KNOW BY NOW, RIGHT? THAT WE SNUCK OUT?
WE JUST ADDED TWO PERPS TO THE CRAB SHELL'S DATABASE. I'M SURE SHE KNOWS.
WH-WHAT DO WE DO NOW, THEN? MAYBE WE SHOULD GO SOMEWHERE?
YOU WANT TO RUN AWAY?
NO, NOT RUN AWAY! JUST...YOU KNOW...HANG OUT SOMEWHERE ELSE FOR A WHILE.
LIKE FOREVER.
REAL "SUPER-MAN" OF YOU, KENAN. LOOK, WE HAVE NOTHING TO BE ASHAMED OF--WE SAVED A MAN!
IF THERE ARE CONSEQUENCES FOR WHAT WE DID, THEN WE'LL JUST HAVE TO ACCEPT THEM.
EVEN IF THOSE "CONSEQUENCES" INCLUDE GETTING SHOT BY A GIANT GREEN LIGHTNING GUN?
THAT GUN SIMULATES KRYPTONITE RADIATION.
SO?
SO DR. OMEN WILL PROBABLY ONLY USE IT ON YOU.
LUCKY ME.
ALL I HAVE TO SAY IS, WE'RE NOT LETTING DUMMY DECIDE OUR PLAN OF ACTION EVER AGAIN.

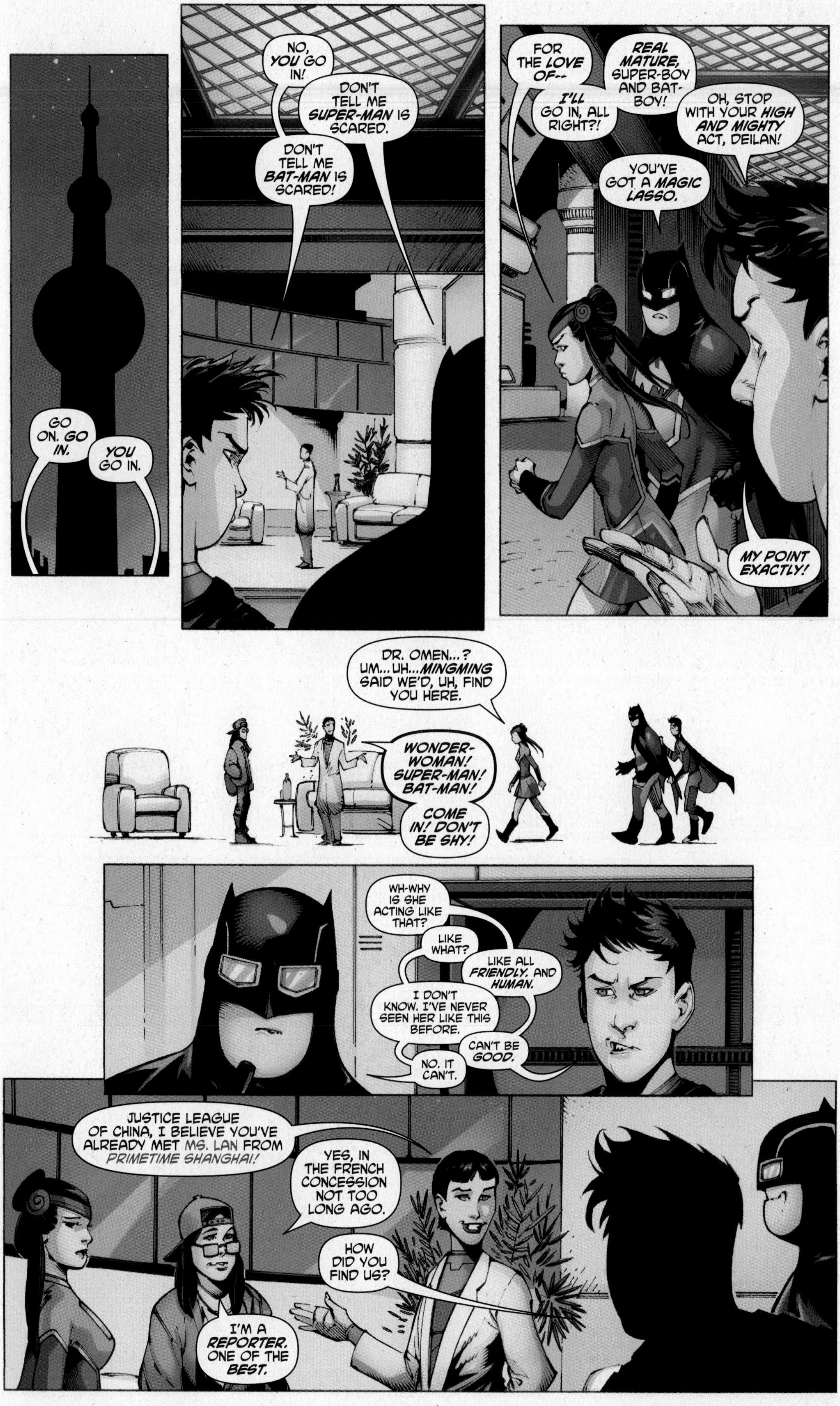

GO ON. GO IN.
YOU GO IN.
NO, YOU GO IN!
DON'T TELL ME SUPER-MAN IS SCARED.
DON'T TELL ME BAT-MAN IS SCARED!
FOR THE LOVE OF--
I'LL GO IN, ALL RIGHT?!
REAL MATURE, SUPER-BOY AND BAT-BOY!
OH, STOP WITH YOUR HIGH AND MIGHTY ACT, DEILAN!
YOU'VE GOT A MAGIC LASSO.
MY POINT EXACTLY!
DR. OMEN...? UM...UH...MINGMING SAID WE'D, UH, FIND YOU HERE.
WONDER-WOMAN! SUPER-MAN! BAT-MAN!
COME IN! DON'T BE SHY!
WH-WHY IS SHE ACTING LIKE THAT?
LIKE WHAT?
LIKE ALL FRIENDLY. AND HUMAN.
I DON'T KNOW. I'VE NEVER SEEN HER LIKE THIS BEFORE.
CAN'T BE GOOD.
NO. IT CAN'T.
JUSTICE LEAGUE OF CHINA, I BELIEVE YOU'VE ALREADY MET MS. LAN FROM PRIMETIME SHANGHAI!
YES, IN THE FRENCH CONCESSION NOT TOO LONG AGO.
HOW DID YOU FIND US?
I'M A REPORTER. ONE OF THE BEST.

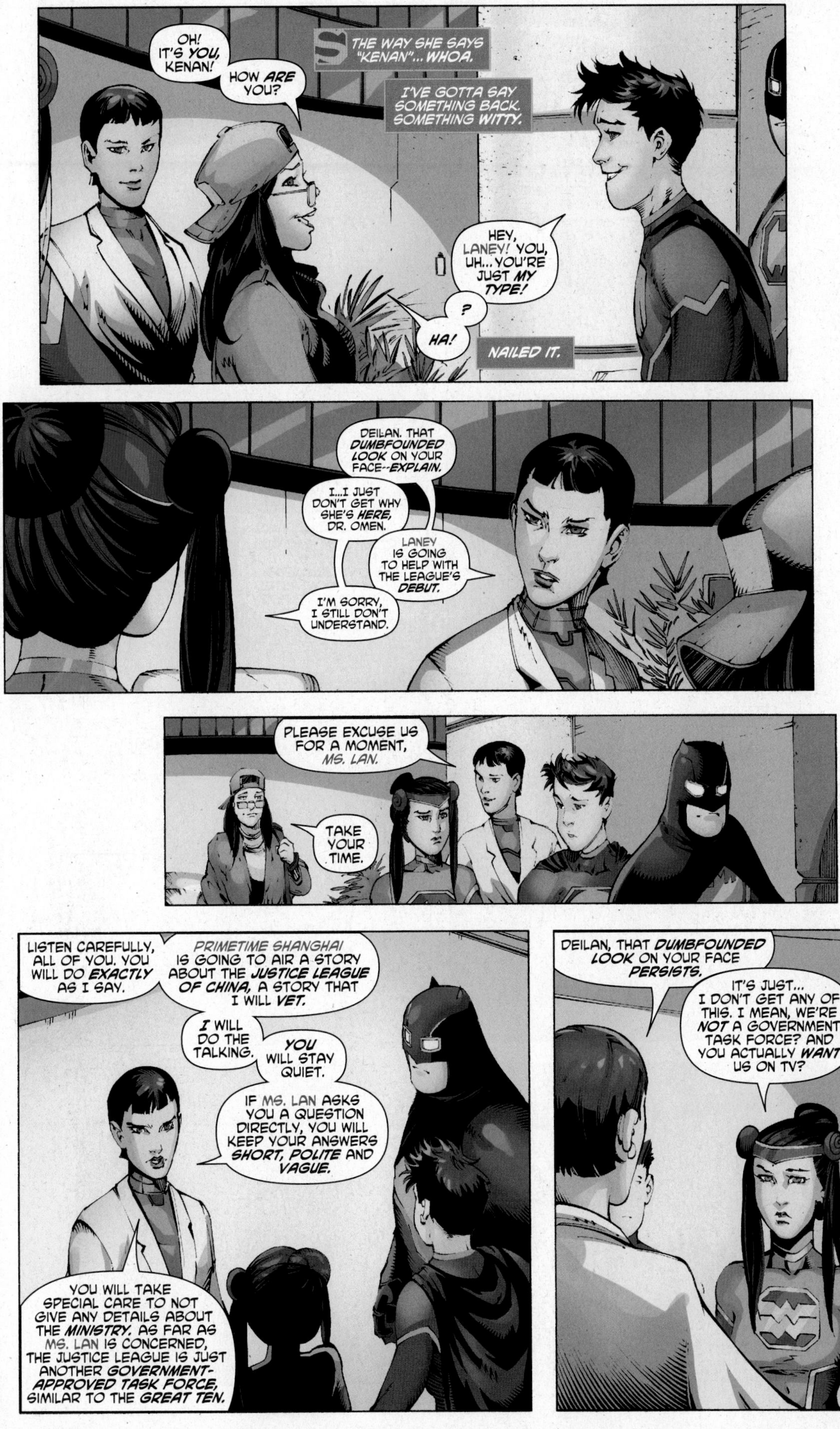
OH! IT'S YOU, KENAN!
HOW ARE YOU?
THE WAY SHE SAYS "KENAN"... WHOA.
I'VE GOTTA SAY SOMETHING BACK. SOMETHING WITTY.
HEY, LANEY! YOU, UH... YOU'RE JUST MY TYPE!
?
HA!
NAILED IT.
DEILAN. THAT DUMBFOUNDED LOOK ON YOUR FACE--EXPLAIN.
I...I JUST DON'T GET WHY SHE'S HERE, DR. OMEN.
LANEY IS GOING TO HELP WITH THE LEAGUE'S DEBUT.
I'M SORRY, I STILL DON'T UNDERSTAND.
PLEASE EXCUSE US FOR A MOMENT, MS. LAN.
TAKE YOUR TIME.
LISTEN CAREFULLY, ALL OF YOU. YOU WILL DO EXACTLY AS I SAY.
PRIMETIME SHANGHAI IS GOING TO AIR A STORY ABOUT THE JUSTICE LEAGUE OF CHINA, A STORY THAT I WILL VET.
I WILL DO THE TALKING.
YOU WILL STAY QUIET.
IF MS. LAN ASKS YOU A QUESTION DIRECTLY, YOU WILL KEEP YOUR ANSWERS SHORT, POLITE AND VAGUE.
YOU WILL TAKE SPECIAL CARE TO NOT GIVE ANY DETAILS ABOUT THE MINISTRY. AS FAR AS MS. LAN IS CONCERNED, THE JUSTICE LEAGUE IS JUST ANOTHER GOVERNMENT-APPROVED TASK FORCE, SIMILAR TO THE GREAT TEN.
DEILAN, THAT DUMBFOUNDED LOOK ON YOUR FACE PERSISTS.
IT'S JUST... I DON'T GET ANY OF THIS. I MEAN, WE'RE NOT A GOVERNMENT TASK FORCE? AND YOU ACTUALLY WANT US ON TV?

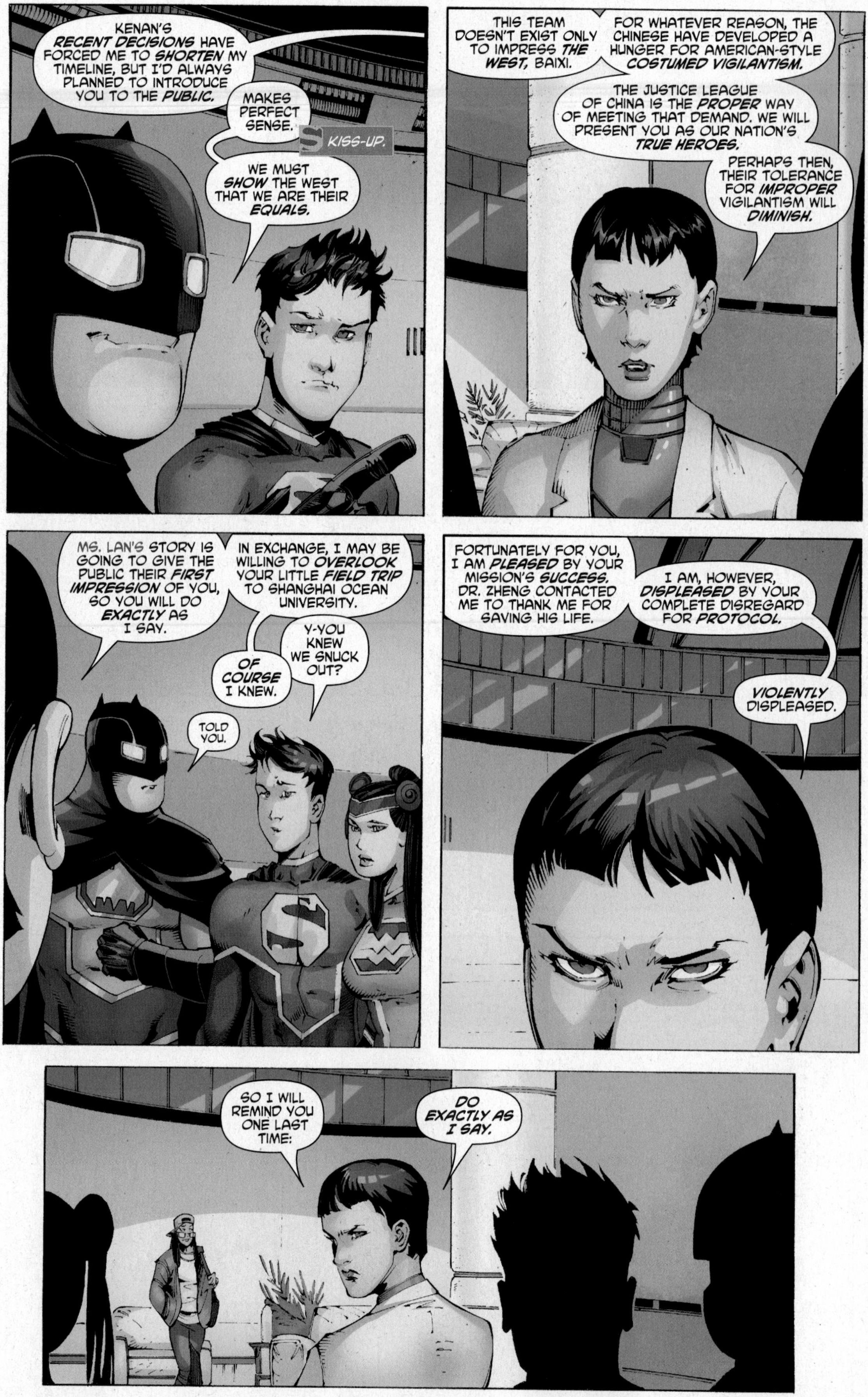
KENAN'S RECENT DECISIONS HAVE FORCED ME TO SHORTEN MY TIMELINE, BUT I'D ALWAYS PLANNED TO INTRODUCE YOU TO THE PUBLIC.
MAKES PERFECT SENSE.
KISS-UP.
WE MUST SHOW THE WEST THAT WE ARE THEIR EQUALS.
THIS TEAM DOESN'T EXIST ONLY TO IMPRESS THE WEST, BAIXI.
FOR WHATEVER REASON, THE CHINESE HAVE DEVELOPED A HUNGER FOR AMERICAN-STYLE COSTUMED VIGILANTISM.
THE JUSTICE LEAGUE OF CHINA IS THE PROPER WAY OF MEETING THAT DEMAND. WE WILL PRESENT YOU AS OUR NATION'S TRUE HEROES.
PERHAPS THEN, THEIR TOLERANCE FOR IMPROPER VIGILANTISM WILL DIMINISH.
MS. LAN'S STORY IS GOING TO GIVE THE PUBLIC THEIR FIRST IMPRESSION OF YOU, SO YOU WILL DO EXACTLY AS I SAY.
IN EXCHANGE, I MAY BE WILLING TO OVERLOOK YOUR LITTLE FIELD TRIP TO SHANGHAI OCEAN UNIVERSITY.
Y-YOU KNEW WE SNUCK OUT?
OF COURSE I KNEW.
TOLD YOU.
FORTUNATELY FOR YOU, I AM PLEASED BY YOUR MISSION'S SUCCESS. DR. ZHENG CONTACTED ME TO THANK ME FOR SAVING HIS LIFE.
I AM, HOWEVER, DISPLEASED BY YOUR COMPLETE DISREGARD FOR PROTOCOL.
VIOLENTLY DISPLEASED.
SO I WILL REMIND YOU ONE LAST TIME:
DO EXACTLY AS I SAY.

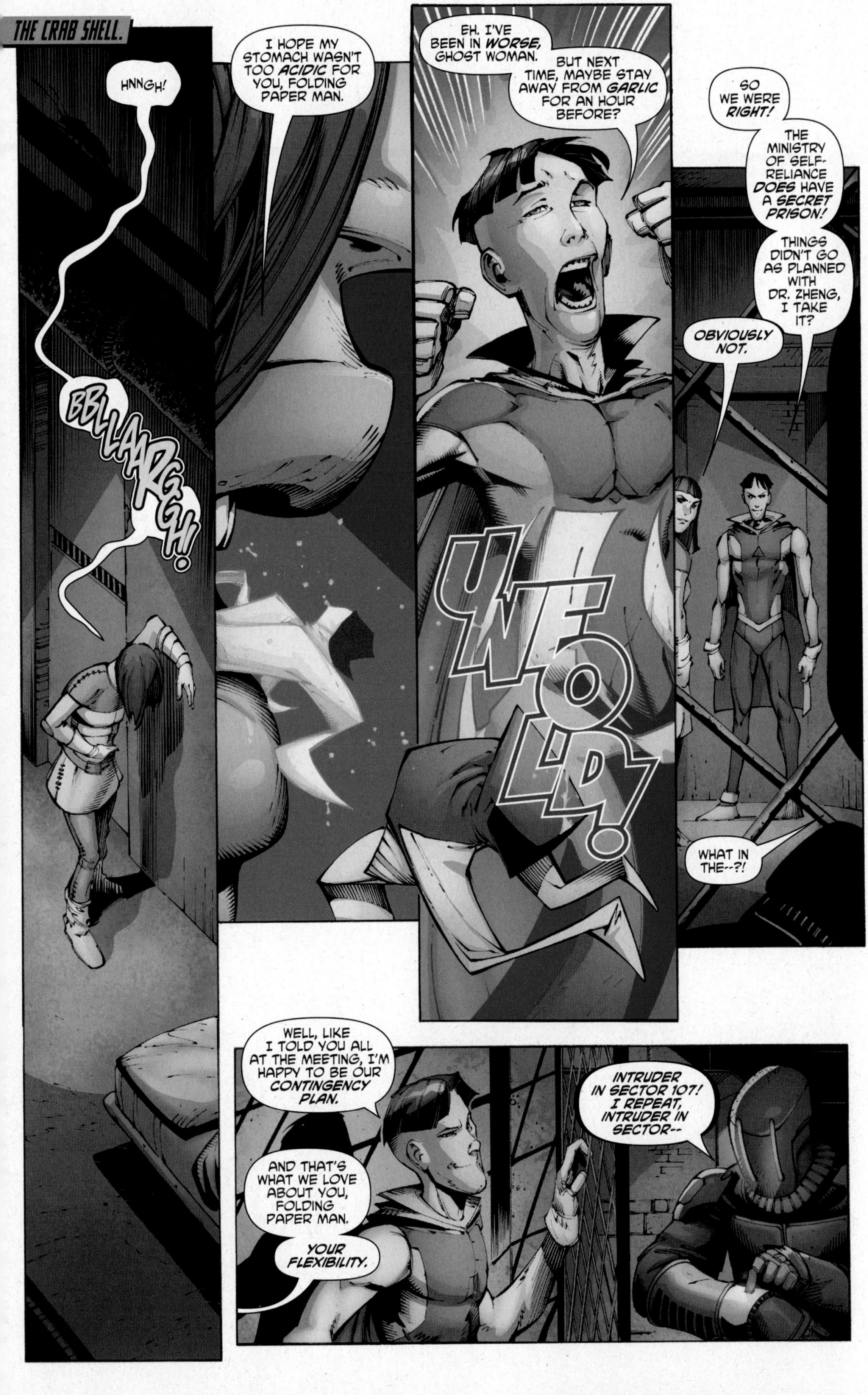
THE CRAB SHELL.
HNNGH!
BBLLAARGGH!
I HOPE MY STOMACH WASN'T TOO ACIDIC FOR YOU, FOLDING PAPER MAN.
EH. I'VE BEEN IN WORSE, GHOST WOMAN.
BUT NEXT TIME, MAYBE STAY AWAY FROM GARLIC FOR AN HOUR BEFORE?
UNFOLD!
SO WE WERE RIGHT!
THE MINISTRY OF SELF-RELIANCE DOES HAVE A SECRET PRISON!
THINGS DIDN'T GO AS PLANNED WITH DR. ZHENG, I TAKE IT?
OBVIOUSLY NOT.
WHAT IN THE--?!
WELL, LIKE I TOLD YOU ALL AT THE MEETING, I'M HAPPY TO BE OUR CONTINGENCY PLAN.
AND THAT'S WHAT WE LOVE ABOUT YOU, FOLDING PAPER MAN.
YOUR FLEXIBILITY.
INTRUDER IN SECTOR 107! I REPEAT, INTRUDER IN SECTOR--

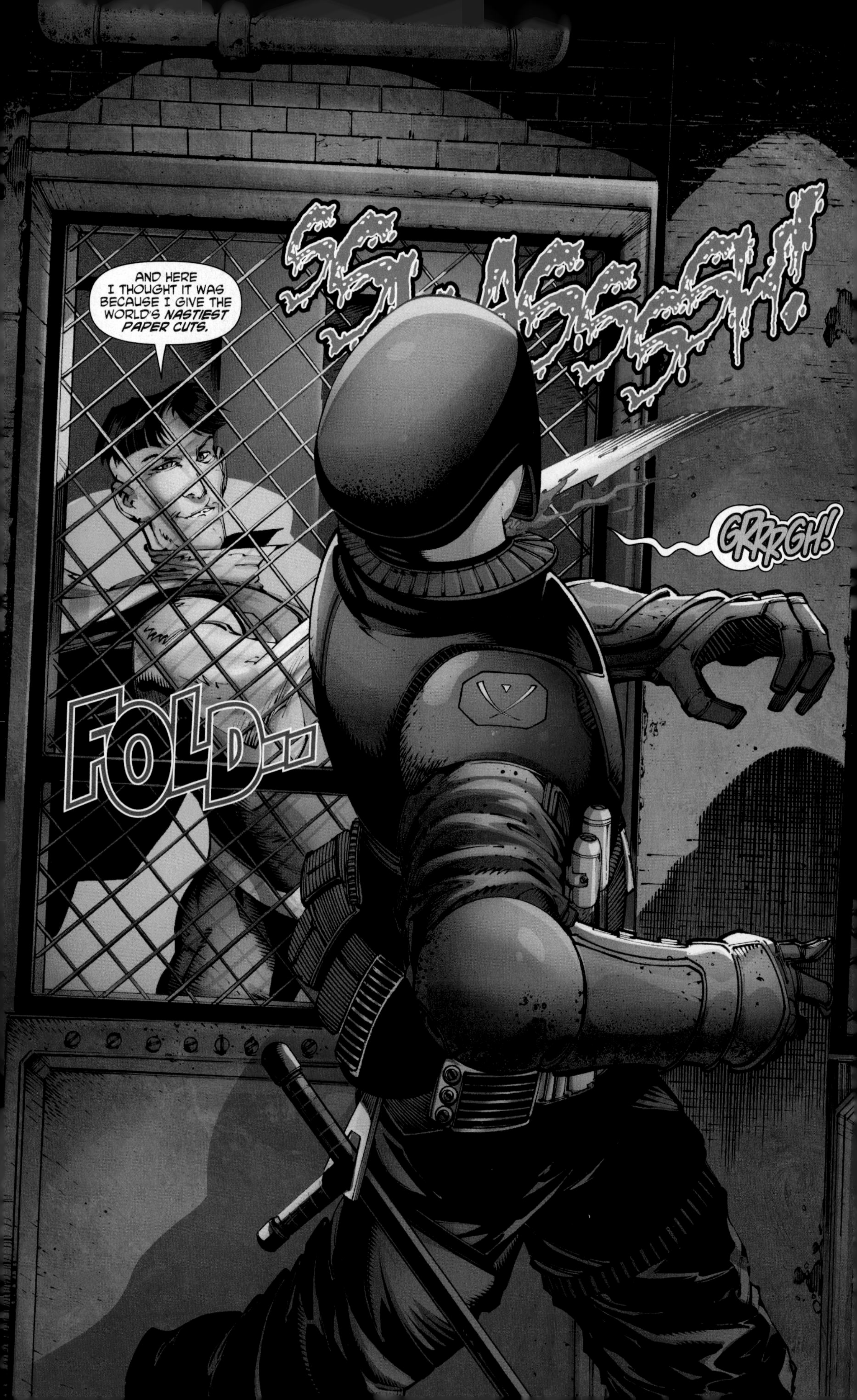
AND HERE I THOUGHT IT WAS BECAUSE I GIVE THE WORLD'S *NASTIEST PAPER CUTS.*
GRRRGH!
FOLD..

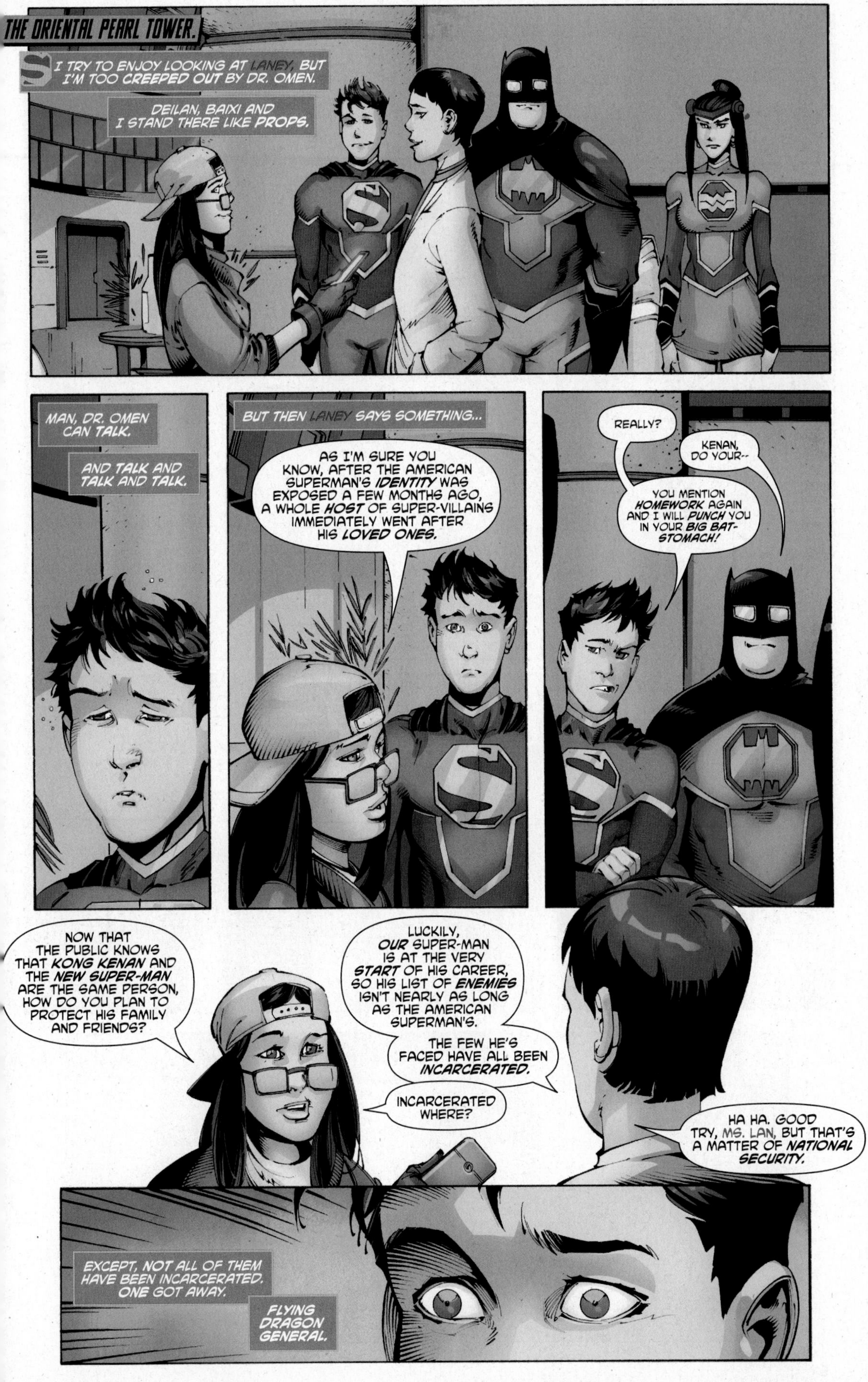
THE ORIENTAL PEARL TOWER.
I TRY TO ENJOY LOOKING AT LANEY, BUT I'M TOO CREEPED OUT BY DR. OMEN.
DEILAN, BAIXI AND I STAND THERE LIKE PROPS.
MAN, DR. OMEN CAN TALK.
AND TALK AND TALK AND TALK.
BUT THEN LANEY SAYS SOMETHING...
AS I'M SURE YOU KNOW, AFTER THE AMERICAN SUPERMAN'S IDENTITY WAS EXPOSED A FEW MONTHS AGO, A WHOLE HOST OF SUPER-VILLAINS IMMEDIATELY WENT AFTER HIS LOVED ONES.
REALLY?
KENAN, DO YOUR--
YOU MENTION HOMEWORK AGAIN AND I WILL PUNCH YOU IN YOUR BIG BAT-STOMACH!
NOW THAT THE PUBLIC KNOWS THAT KONG KENAN AND THE NEW SUPER-MAN ARE THE SAME PERSON, HOW DO YOU PLAN TO PROTECT HIS FAMILY AND FRIENDS?
LUCKILY, OUR SUPER-MAN IS AT THE VERY START OF HIS CAREER, SO HIS LIST OF ENEMIES ISN'T NEARLY AS LONG AS THE AMERICAN SUPERMAN'S.
THE FEW HE'S FACED HAVE ALL BEEN INCARCERATED.
INCARCERATED WHERE?
HA HA. GOOD TRY, MS. LAN, BUT THAT'S A MATTER OF NATIONAL SECURITY.
EXCEPT, NOT ALL OF THEM HAVE BEEN INCARCERATED. ONE GOT AWAY.
FLYING DRAGON GENERAL.

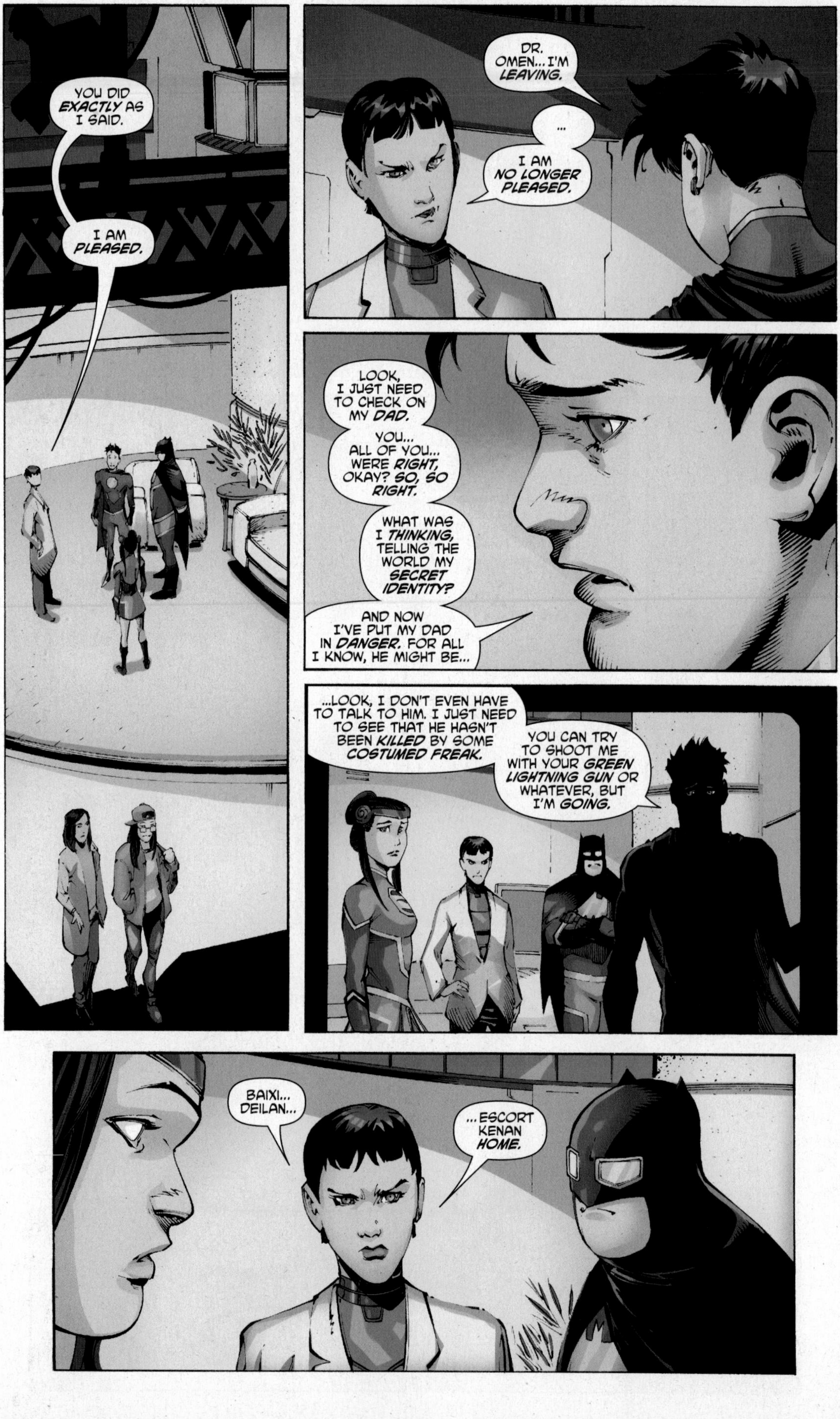
YOU DID EXACTLY AS I SAID.
I AM PLEASED.
DR. OMEN... I'M LEAVING.
...
I AM NO LONGER PLEASED.
LOOK, I JUST NEED TO CHECK ON MY DAD.
YOU... ALL OF YOU... WERE RIGHT, OKAY? SO, SO RIGHT.
WHAT WAS I THINKING, TELLING THE WORLD MY SECRET IDENTITY?
AND NOW I'VE PUT MY DAD IN DANGER. FOR ALL I KNOW, HE MIGHT BE...
...LOOK, I DON'T EVEN HAVE TO TALK TO HIM. I JUST NEED TO SEE THAT HE HASN'T BEEN KILLED BY SOME COSTUMED FREAK.
YOU CAN TRY TO SHOOT ME WITH YOUR GREEN LIGHTNING GUN OR WHATEVER, BUT I'M GOING.
BAIXI... DEILAN...
...ESCORT KENAN HOME.

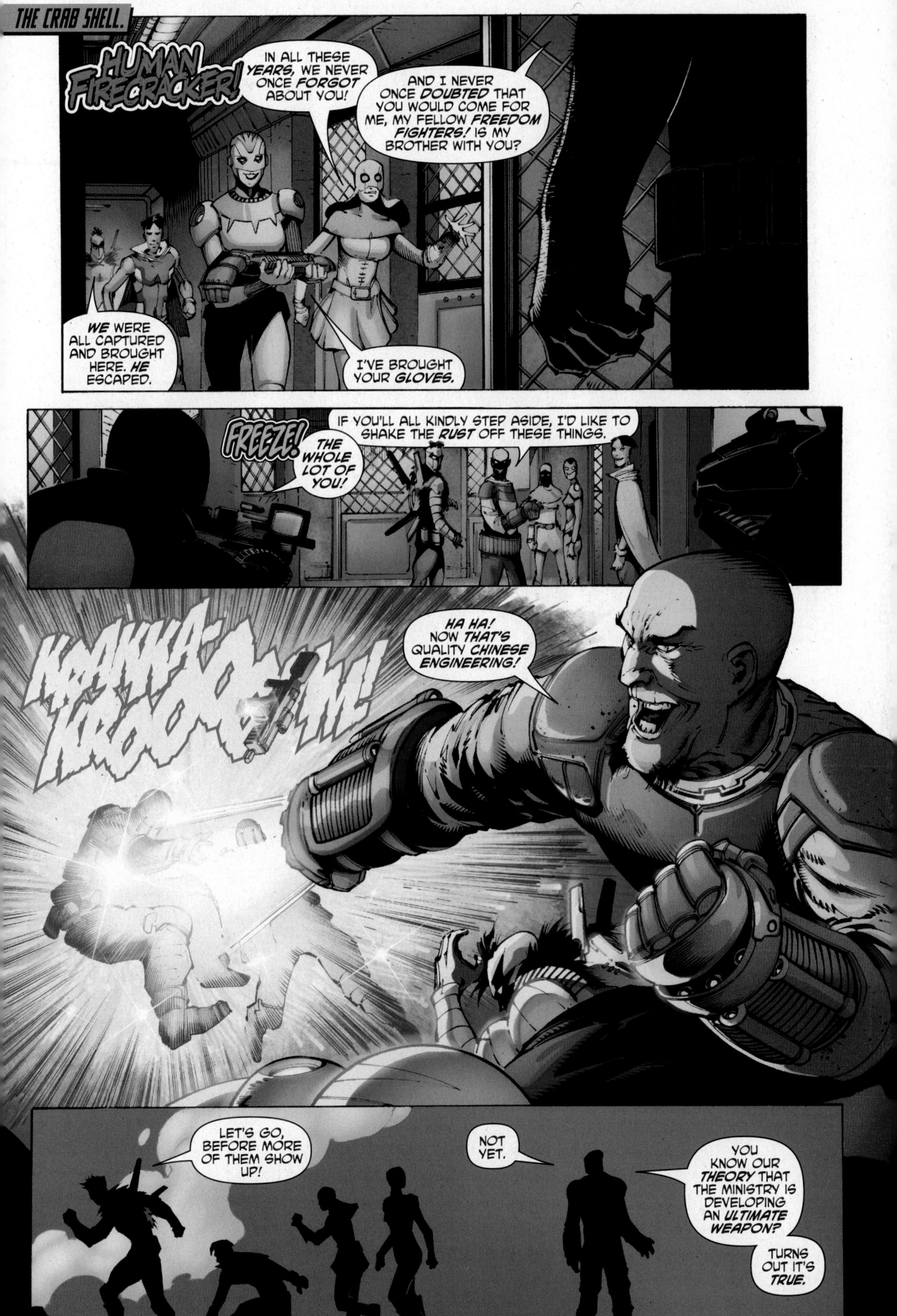
THE CRAB SHELL.
HUMAN FIRECRACKER!
IN ALL THESE YEARS, WE NEVER ONCE FORGOT ABOUT YOU!
AND I NEVER ONCE DOUBTED THAT YOU WOULD COME FOR ME, MY FELLOW FREEDOM FIGHTERS! IS MY BROTHER WITH YOU?
WE WERE ALL CAPTURED AND BROUGHT HERE. HE ESCAPED.
I'VE BROUGHT YOUR GLOVES.
IF YOU'LL ALL KINDLY STEP ASIDE, I'D LIKE TO SHAKE THE RUST OFF THESE THINGS.
FREEZE!
THE WHOLE LOT OF YOU!
HA HA! NOW THAT'S QUALITY CHINESE ENGINEERING!
LET'S GO, BEFORE MORE OF THEM SHOW UP!
NOT YET.
YOU KNOW OUR THEORY THAT THE MINISTRY IS DEVELOPING AN ULTIMATE WEAPON?
TURNS OUT IT'S TRUE.

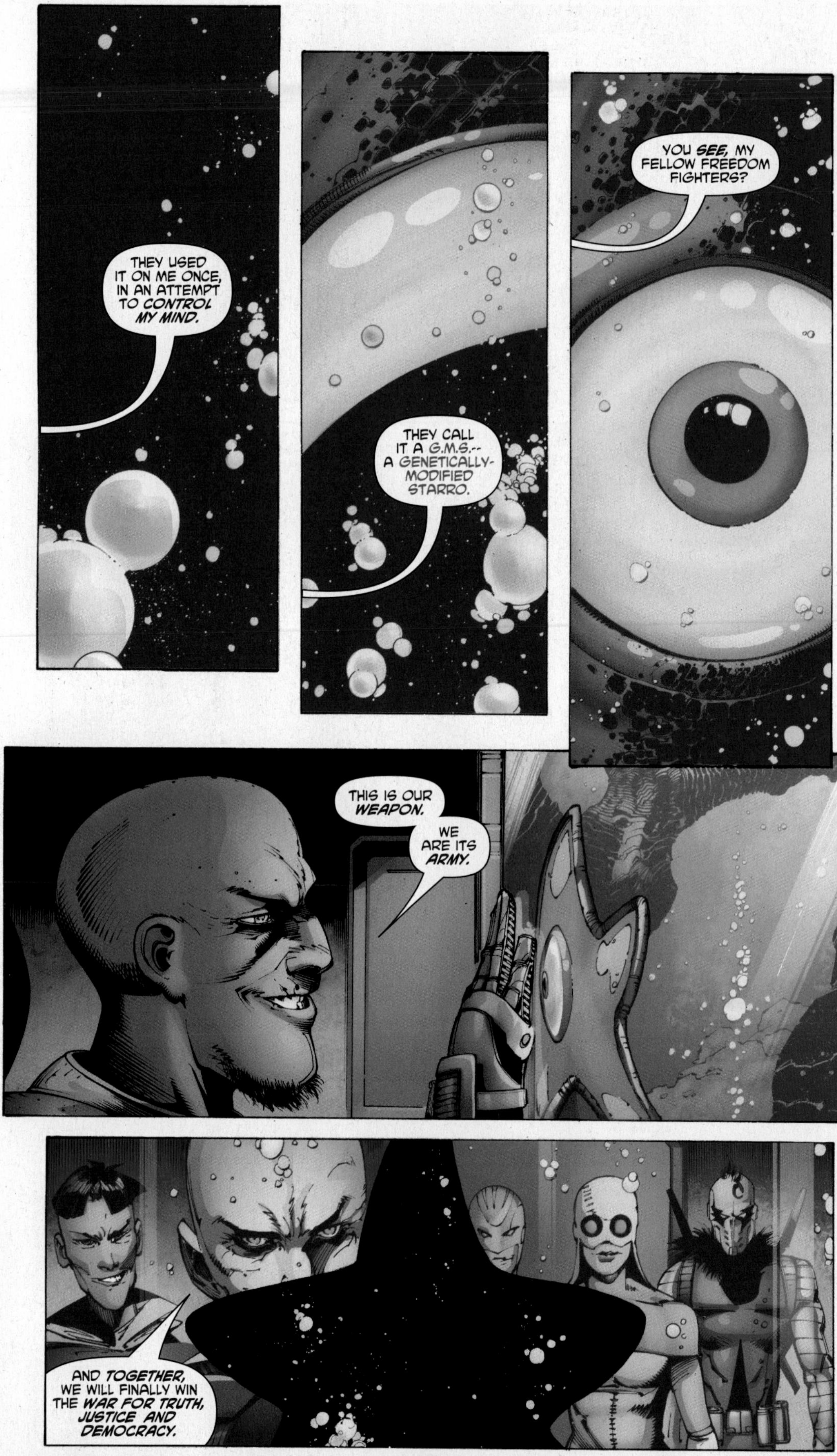
THEY USED IT ON ME ONCE, IN AN ATTEMPT TO CONTROL MY MIND.
THEY CALL IT A G.M.S.-- A GENETICALLY-MODIFIED STARRO.
YOU SEE, MY FELLOW FREEDOM FIGHTERS?
THIS IS OUR WEAPON.
WE ARE ITS ARMY.
AND TOGETHER, WE WILL FINALLY WIN THE WAR FOR TRUTH, JUSTICE AND DEMOCRACY.

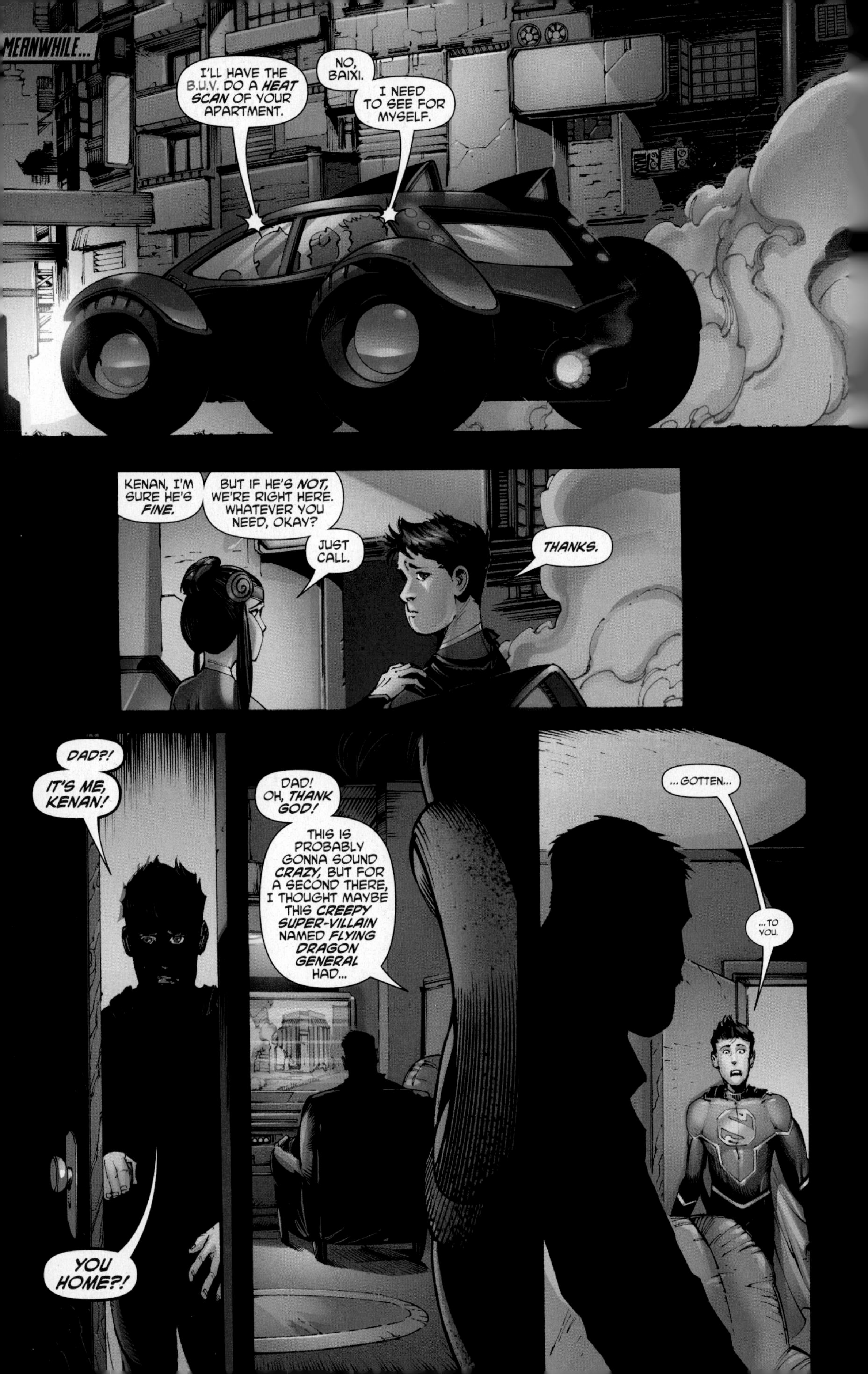

MEANWHILE...
I'LL HAVE THE B.U.V. DO A HEAT SCAN OF YOUR APARTMENT.
NO, BAIXI.
I NEED TO SEE FOR MYSELF.
KENAN, I'M SURE HE'S FINE.
BUT IF HE'S NOT, WE'RE RIGHT HERE. WHATEVER YOU NEED, OKAY?
JUST CALL.
THANKS.
DAD?!
IT'S ME, KENAN!
YOU HOME?!
DAD! OH, THANK GOD!
THIS IS PROBABLY GONNA SOUND CRAZY, BUT FOR A SECOND THERE, I THOUGHT MAYBE THIS CREEPY SUPER-VILLAIN NAMED FLYING DRAGON GENERAL HAD...
...GOTTEN...
...TO YOU.

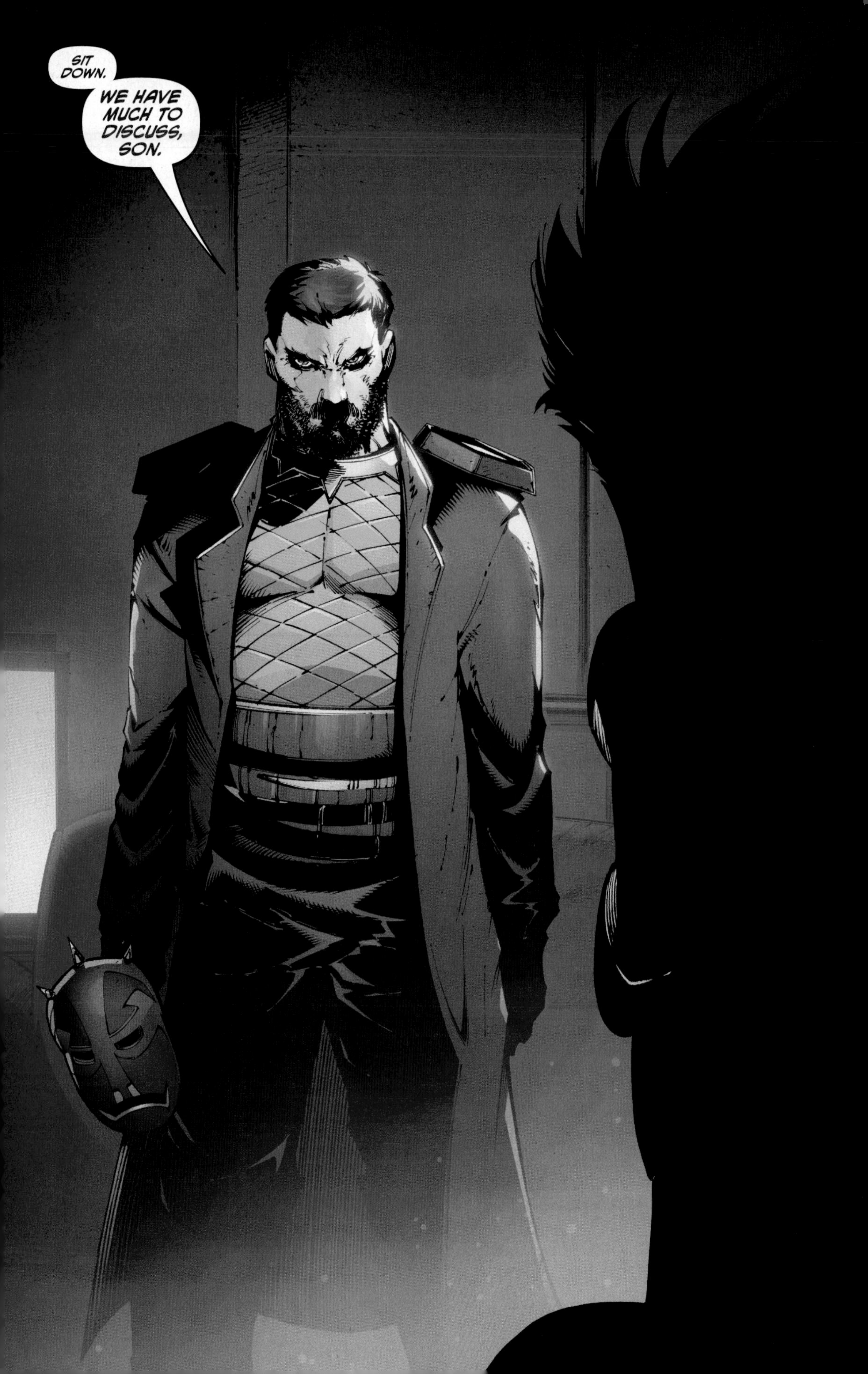
SIT DOWN.
WE HAVE MUCH TO DISCUSS, SON.

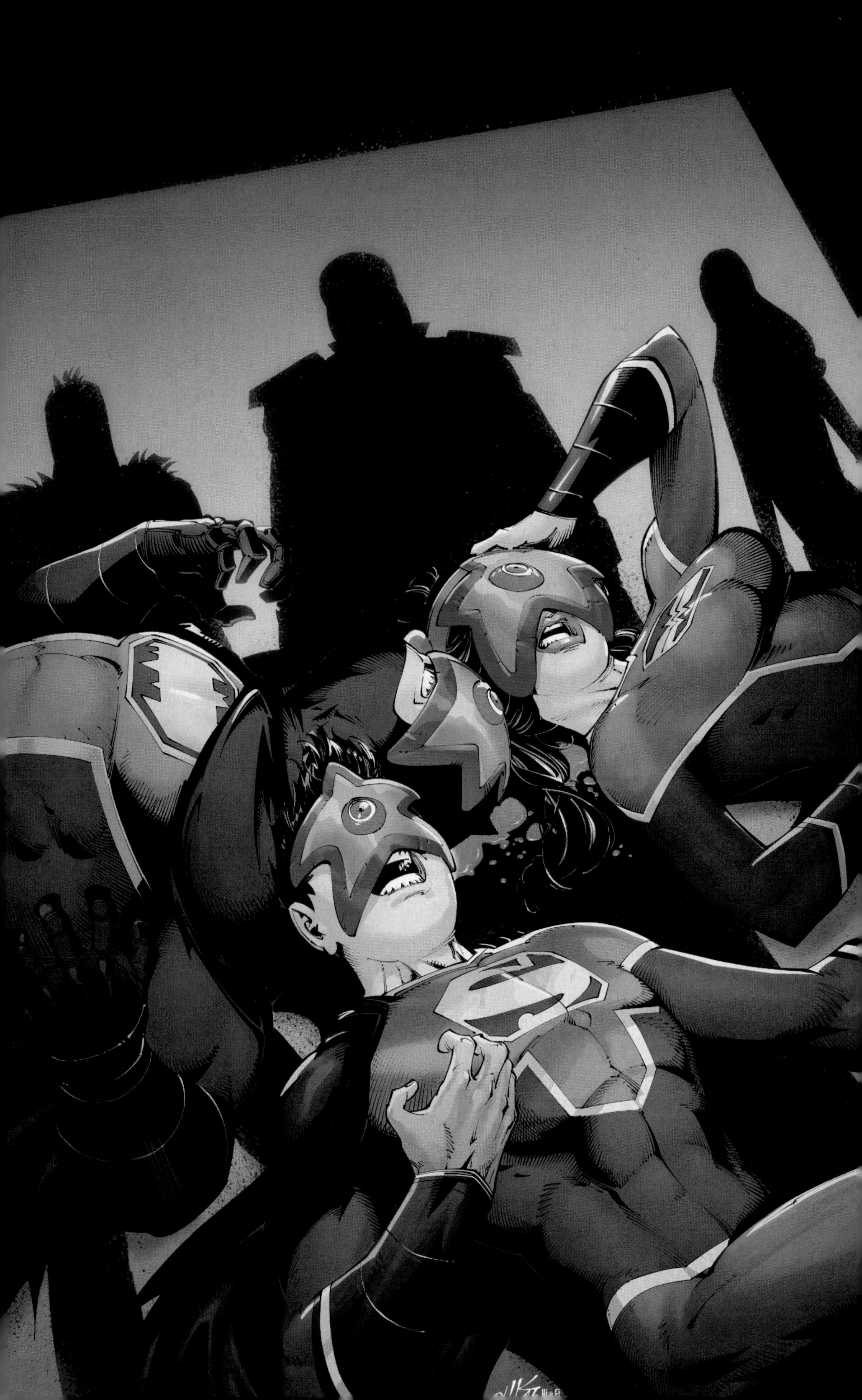

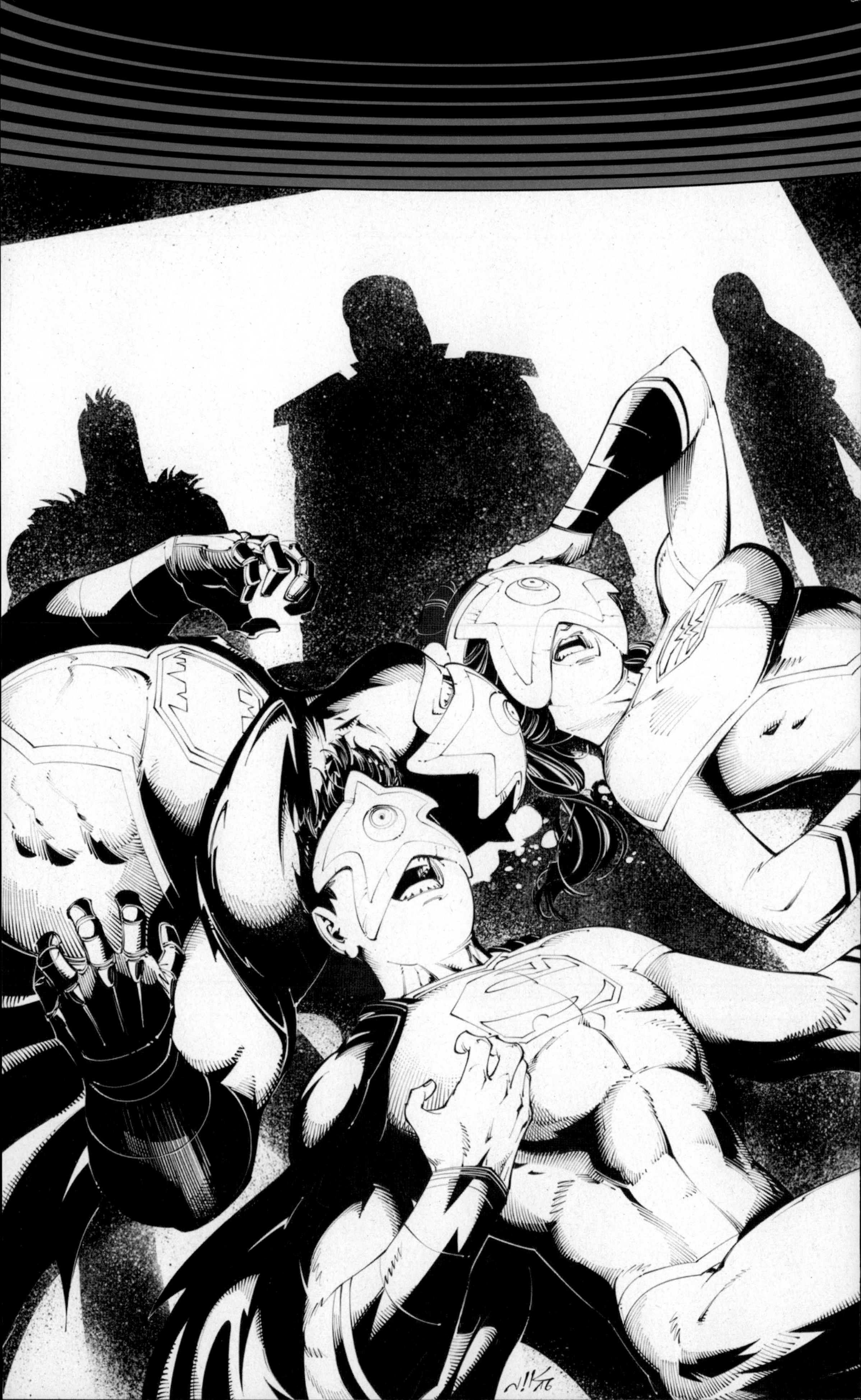

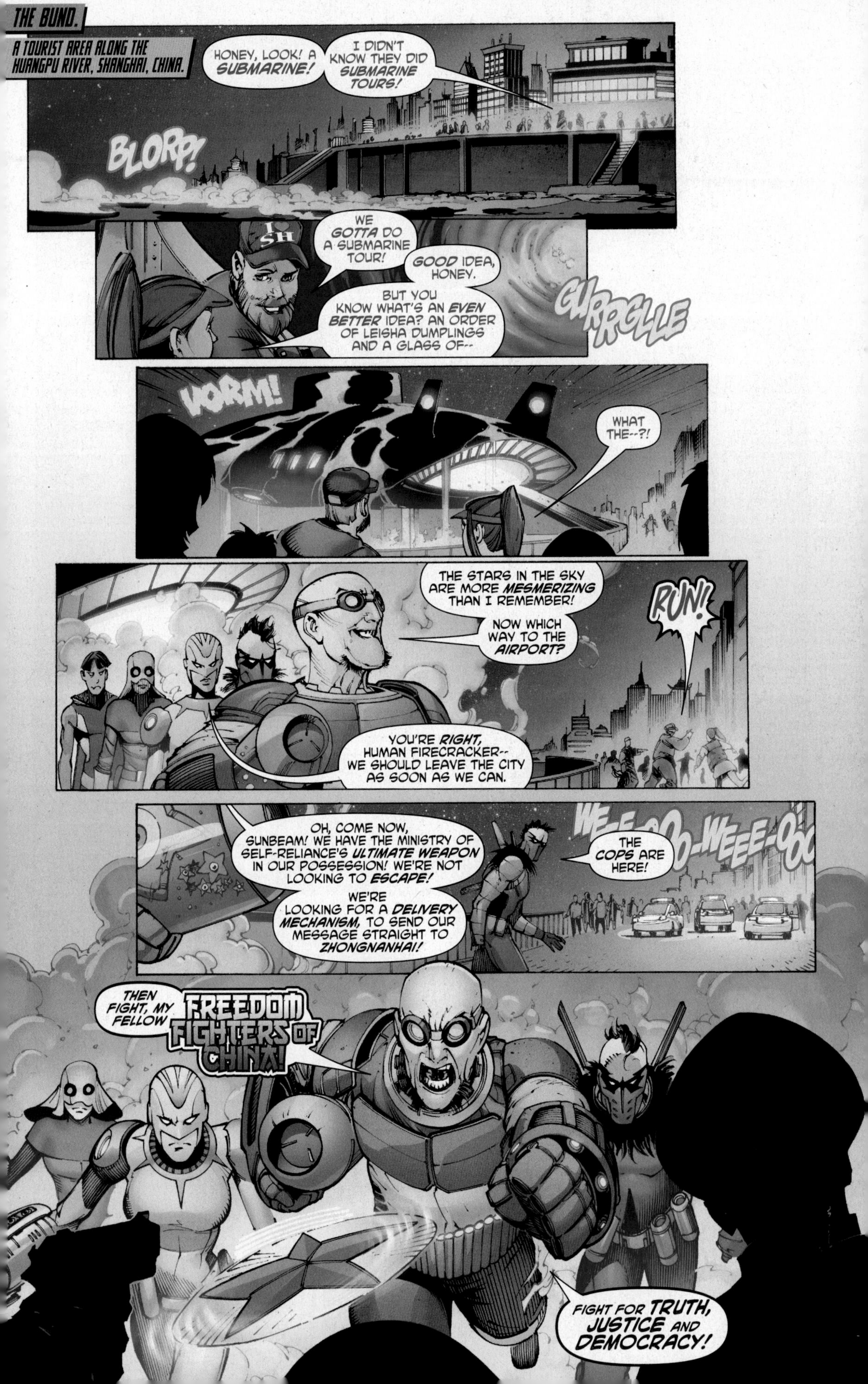
THE BUND.
A TOURIST AREA ALONG THE HUANGPU RIVER, SHANGHAI, CHINA.
HONEY, LOOK! A SUBMARINE!
I DIDN'T KNOW THEY DID SUBMARINE TOURS!
BLORP!
WE GOTTA DO A SUBMARINE TOUR!
GOOD IDEA, HONEY.
BUT YOU KNOW WHAT'S AN EVEN BETTER IDEA? AN ORDER OF LEISHA DUMPLINGS AND A GLASS OF--
GURRGLLE
VORM!
WHAT THE--?!
THE STARS IN THE SKY ARE MORE MESMERIZING THAN I REMEMBER!
NOW WHICH WAY TO THE AIRPORT?
RUN!
YOU'RE RIGHT, HUMAN FIRECRACKER-- WE SHOULD LEAVE THE CITY AS SOON AS WE CAN.
OH, COME NOW, SUNBEAM! WE HAVE THE MINISTRY OF SELF-RELIANCE'S ULTIMATE WEAPON IN OUR POSSESSION! WE'RE NOT LOOKING TO ESCAPE!
WE'RE LOOKING FOR A DELIVERY MECHANISM, TO SEND OUR MESSAGE STRAIGHT TO ZHONGNANHAI!
THE COPS ARE HERE!
THEN FIGHT, MY FELLOW FREEDOM FIGHTERS OF CHINA!
FIGHT FOR TRUTH, JUSTICE AND DEMOCRACY!

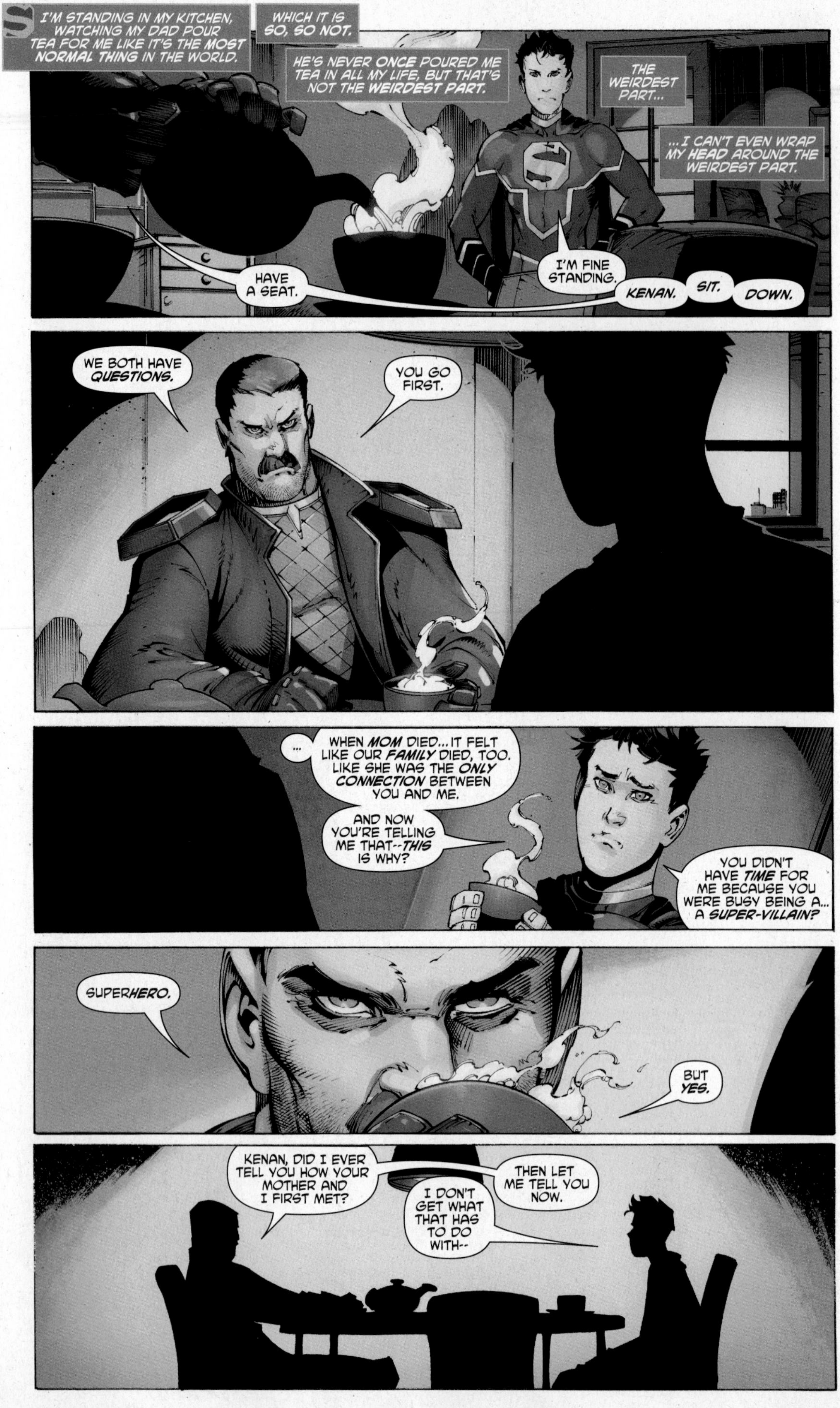
I'M STANDING IN MY KITCHEN, WATCHING MY DAD POUR TEA FOR ME LIKE IT'S THE MOST NORMAL THING IN THE WORLD.
WHICH IT IS SO, SO NOT.
HE'S NEVER ONCE POURED ME TEA IN ALL MY LIFE, BUT THAT'S NOT THE WEIRDEST PART.
THE WEIRDEST PART...
...I CAN'T EVEN WRAP MY HEAD AROUND THE WEIRDEST PART.
HAVE A SEAT.
I'M FINE STANDING.
KENAN.
SIT.
DOWN.
WE BOTH HAVE QUESTIONS.
YOU GO FIRST.
...
WHEN MOM DIED... IT FELT LIKE OUR FAMILY DIED, TOO. LIKE SHE WAS THE ONLY CONNECTION BETWEEN YOU AND ME.
AND NOW YOU'RE TELLING ME THAT--THIS IS WHY?
YOU DIDN'T HAVE TIME FOR ME BECAUSE YOU WERE BUSY BEING A... A SUPER-VILLAIN?
SUPERHERO.
BUT YES.
KENAN, DID I EVER TELL YOU HOW YOUR MOTHER AND I FIRST MET?
I DON'T GET WHAT THAT HAS TO DO WITH--
THEN LET ME TELL YOU NOW.

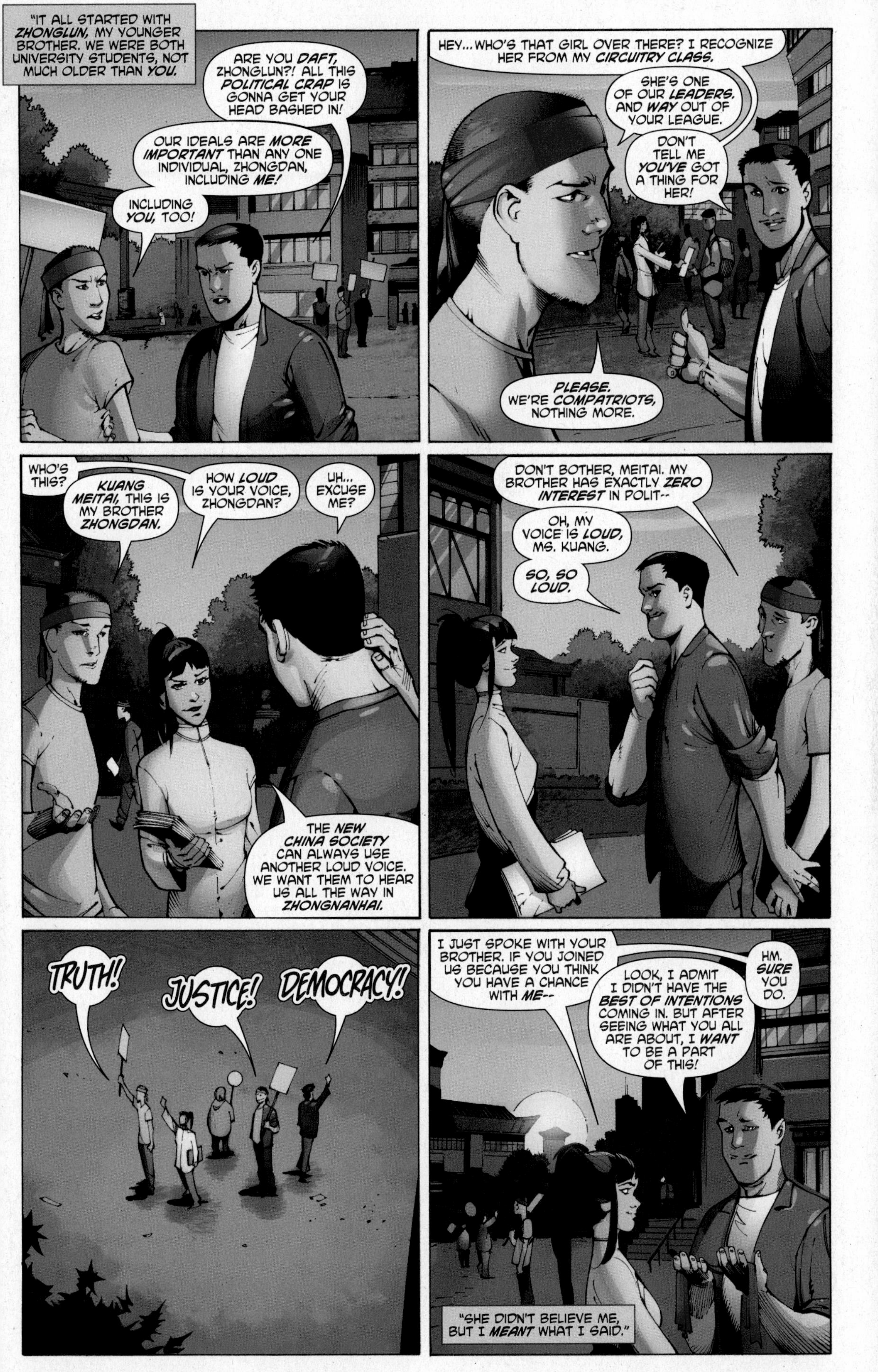
"IT ALL STARTED WITH ZHONGLUN, MY YOUNGER BROTHER. WE WERE BOTH UNIVERSITY STUDENTS, NOT MUCH OLDER THAN YOU.
ARE YOU DAFT, ZHONGLUN?! ALL THIS POLITICAL CRAP IS GONNA GET YOUR HEAD BASHED IN!
OUR IDEALS ARE MORE IMPORTANT THAN ANY ONE INDIVIDUAL, ZHONGDAN, INCLUDING ME!
INCLUDING YOU, TOO!
HEY... WHO'S THAT GIRL OVER THERE? I RECOGNIZE HER FROM MY CIRCUITRY CLASS.
SHE'S ONE OF OUR LEADERS. AND WAY OUT OF YOUR LEAGUE.
DON'T TELL ME YOU'VE GOT A THING FOR HER!
PLEASE. WE'RE COMPATRIOTS, NOTHING MORE.
WHO'S THIS?
KUANG MEITAI, THIS IS MY BROTHER ZHONGDAN.
HOW LOUD IS YOUR VOICE, ZHONGDAN?
UH... EXCUSE ME?
THE NEW CHINA SOCIETY CAN ALWAYS USE ANOTHER LOUD VOICE. WE WANT THEM TO HEAR US ALL THE WAY IN ZHONGNANHAI.
DON'T BOTHER, MEITAI. MY BROTHER HAS EXACTLY ZERO INTEREST IN POLIT--
OH, MY VOICE IS LOUD, MS. KUANG.
SO, SO LOUD.
TRUTH!
JUSTICE!
DEMOCRACY!
I JUST SPOKE WITH YOUR BROTHER. IF YOU JOINED US BECAUSE YOU THINK YOU HAVE A CHANCE WITH ME--
HM. SURE YOU DO.
LOOK, I ADMIT I DIDN'T HAVE THE BEST OF INTENTIONS COMING IN. BUT AFTER SEEING WHAT YOU ALL ARE ABOUT, I WANT TO BE A PART OF THIS!
"SHE DIDN'T BELIEVE ME, BUT I MEANT WHAT I SAID."

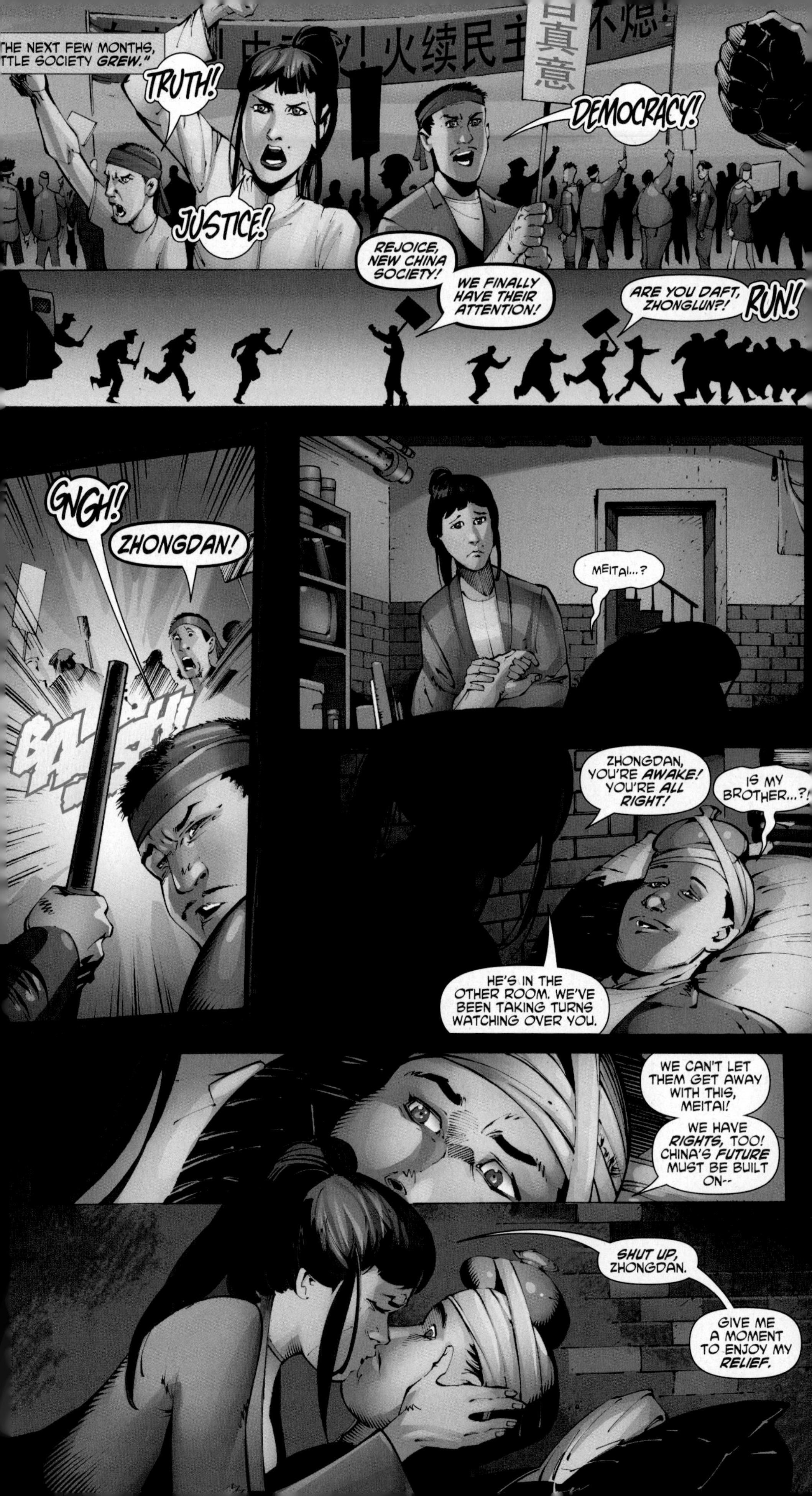

THE NEXT FEW MONTHS,
TTLE SOCIETY *GREW*."
TRUTH!
DEMOCRACY!
JUSTICE!
REJOICE, NEW CHINA SOCIETY!
WE FINALLY HAVE THEIR ATTENTION!
ARE YOU DAFT, ZHONGLUN?!
RUN!
GNGH!
ZHONGDAN!
BASH!
MEITAI...?
ZHONGDAN, YOU'RE *AWAKE!* YOU'RE *ALL RIGHT!*
IS MY BROTHER...?!
HE'S IN THE OTHER ROOM. WE'VE BEEN TAKING TURNS WATCHING OVER YOU.
WE CAN'T LET THEM GET AWAY WITH THIS, MEITAI!
WE HAVE *RIGHTS*, TOO! CHINA'S *FUTURE* MUST BE BUILT ON--
SHUT UP, ZHONGDAN.
GIVE ME A MOMENT TO ENJOY MY *RELIEF*.

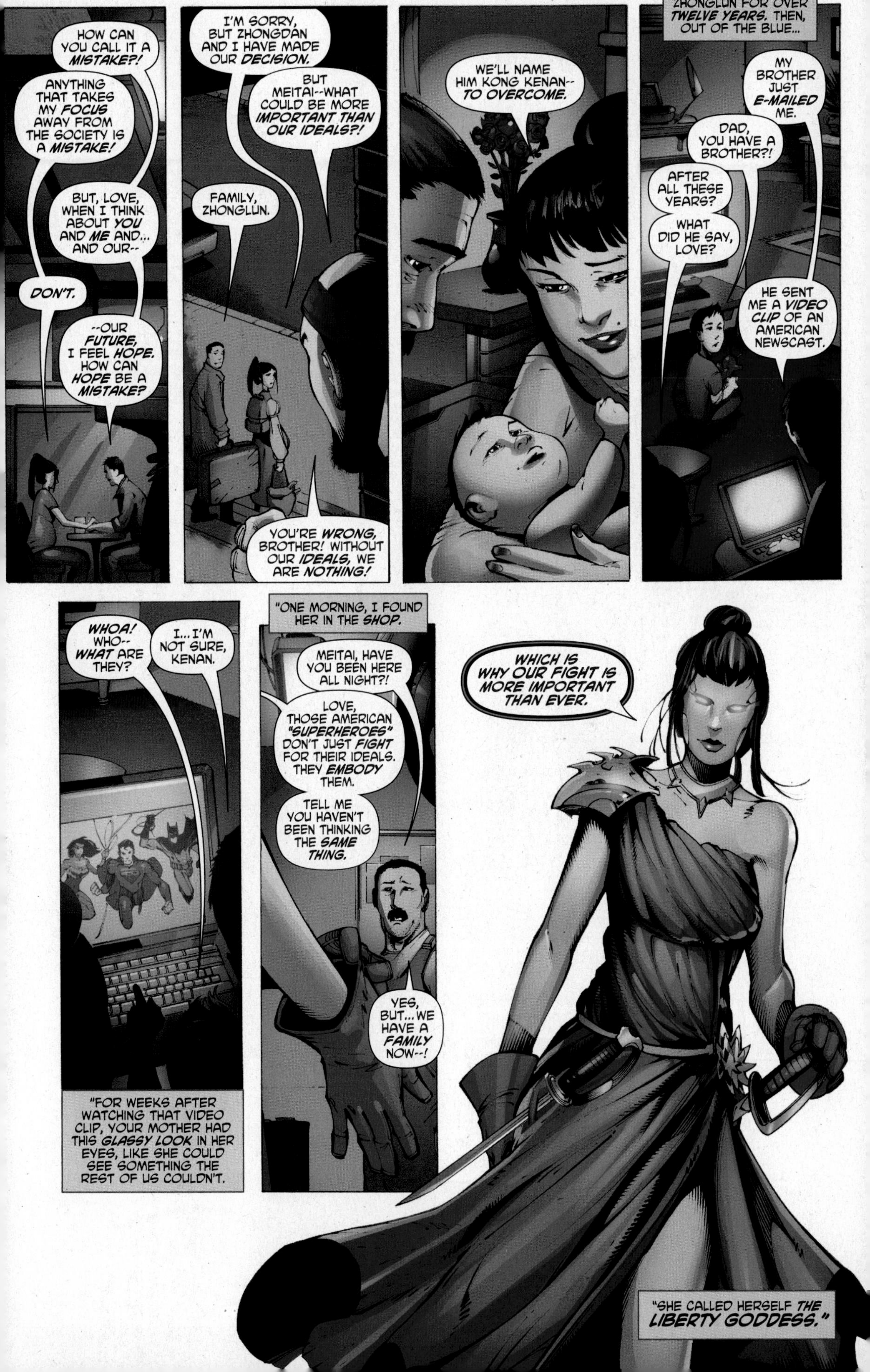
HOW CAN YOU CALL IT A MISTAKE?!
ANYTHING THAT TAKES MY FOCUS AWAY FROM THE SOCIETY IS A MISTAKE!
BUT, LOVE, WHEN I THINK ABOUT YOU AND ME AND... AND OUR--
DON'T.
--OUR FUTURE, I FEEL HOPE. HOW CAN HOPE BE A MISTAKE?
I'M SORRY, BUT ZHONGDAN AND I HAVE MADE OUR DECISION.
BUT MEITAI--WHAT COULD BE MORE IMPORTANT THAN OUR IDEALS?!
FAMILY, ZHONGLUN.
YOU'RE WRONG, BROTHER! WITHOUT OUR IDEALS, WE ARE NOTHING!
WE'LL NAME HIM KONG KENAN--TO OVERCOME.
"I DIDN'T HEAR FROM ZHONGLUN FOR OVER TWELVE YEARS. THEN, OUT OF THE BLUE...
MY BROTHER JUST E-MAILED ME.
DAD, YOU HAVE A BROTHER?!
AFTER ALL THESE YEARS?
WHAT DID HE SAY, LOVE?
HE SENT ME A VIDEO CLIP OF AN AMERICAN NEWSCAST.
WHOA! WHO--WHAT ARE THEY?
I... I'M NOT SURE, KENAN.
"FOR WEEKS AFTER WATCHING THAT VIDEO CLIP, YOUR MOTHER HAD THIS GLASSY LOOK IN HER EYES, LIKE SHE COULD SEE SOMETHING THE REST OF US COULDN'T.
"ONE MORNING, I FOUND HER IN THE SHOP.
MEITAI, HAVE YOU BEEN HERE ALL NIGHT?!
LOVE, THOSE AMERICAN "SUPERHEROES" DON'T JUST FIGHT FOR THEIR IDEALS. THEY EMBODY THEM.
TELL ME YOU HAVEN'T BEEN THINKING THE SAME THING.
YES, BUT... WE HAVE A FAMILY NOW--!
WHICH IS WHY OUR FIGHT IS MORE IMPORTANT THAN EVER.
"SHE CALLED HERSELF THE LIBERTY GODDESS."

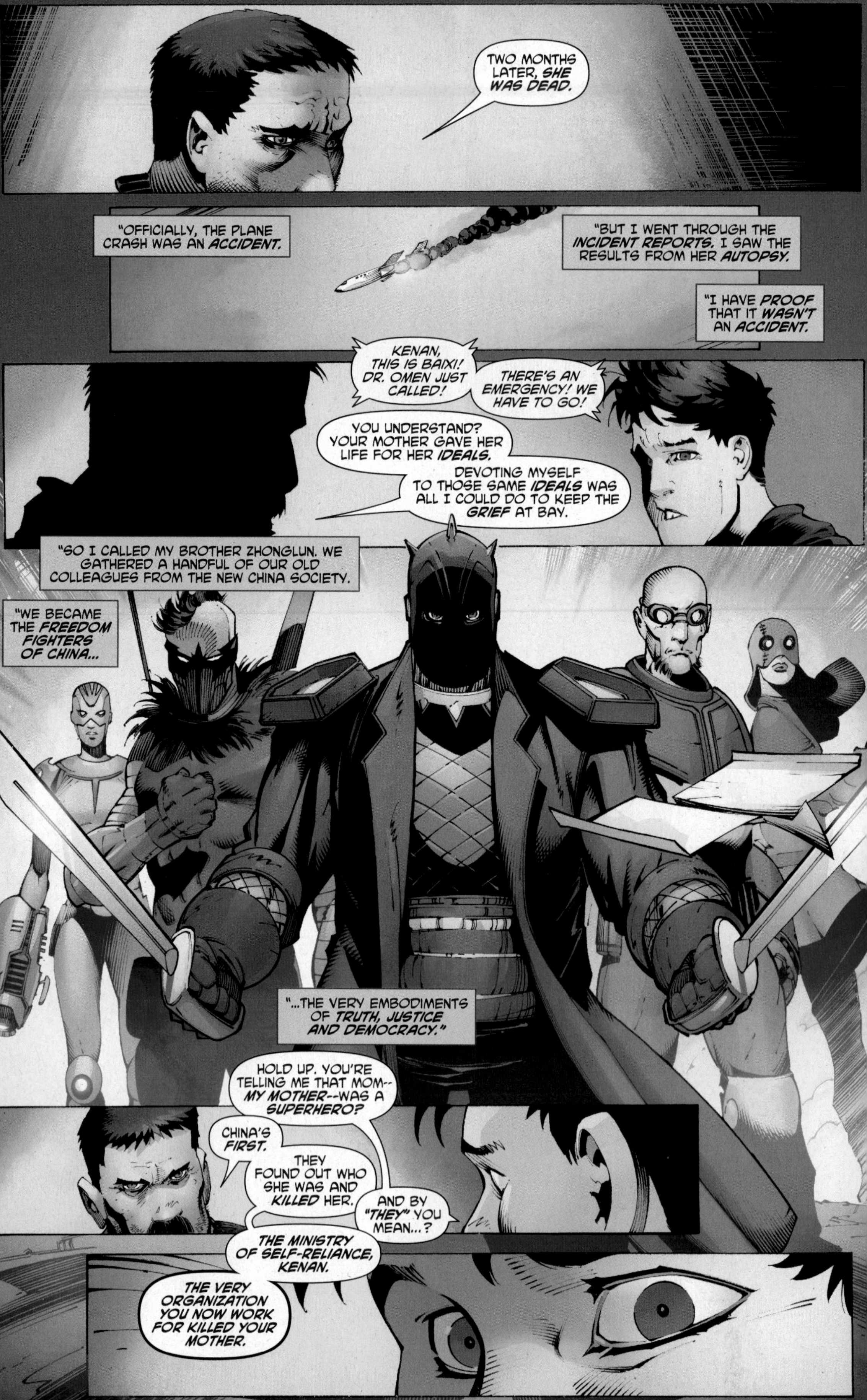
TWO MONTHS LATER, SHE WAS DEAD.
"OFFICIALLY, THE PLANE CRASH WAS AN ACCIDENT.
"BUT I WENT THROUGH THE INCIDENT REPORTS. I SAW THE RESULTS FROM HER AUTOPSY.
"I HAVE PROOF THAT IT WASN'T AN ACCIDENT.
KENAN, THIS IS BAIXI! DR. OMEN JUST CALLED!
THERE'S AN EMERGENCY! WE HAVE TO GO!
YOU UNDERSTAND? YOUR MOTHER GAVE HER LIFE FOR HER IDEALS.
DEVOTING MYSELF TO THOSE SAME IDEALS WAS ALL I COULD DO TO KEEP THE GRIEF AT BAY.
"SO I CALLED MY BROTHER ZHONGLUN. WE GATHERED A HANDFUL OF OUR OLD COLLEAGUES FROM THE NEW CHINA SOCIETY.
"WE BECAME THE FREEDOM FIGHTERS OF CHINA...
"...THE VERY EMBODIMENTS OF TRUTH, JUSTICE AND DEMOCRACY."
HOLD UP. YOU'RE TELLING ME THAT MOM-- MY MOTHER--WAS A SUPERHERO?
CHINA'S FIRST.
THEY FOUND OUT WHO SHE WAS AND KILLED HER.
AND BY "THEY" YOU MEAN...?
THE MINISTRY OF SELF-RELIANCE, KENAN.
THE VERY ORGANIZATION YOU NOW WORK FOR KILLED YOUR MOTHER.

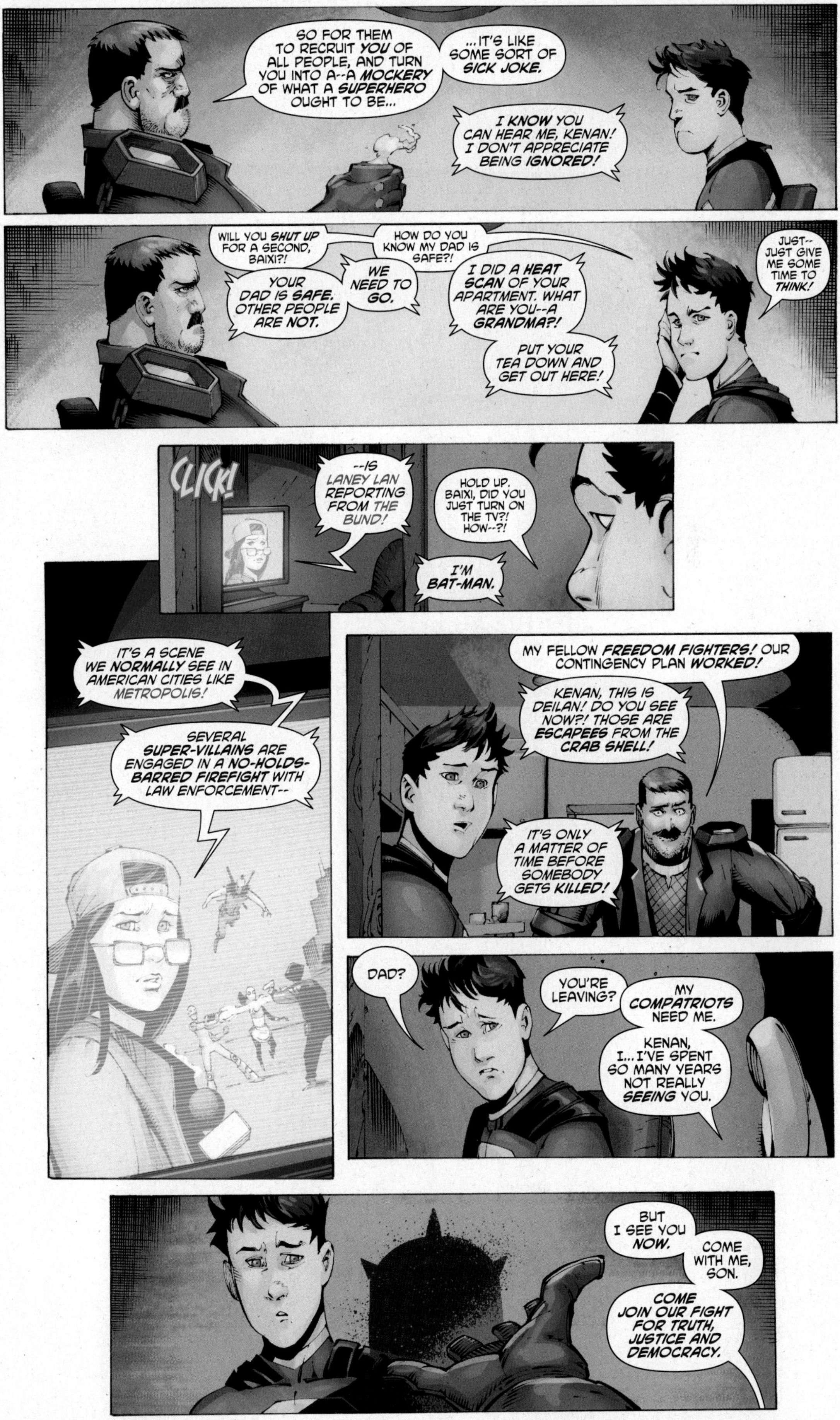

SO FOR THEM TO RECRUIT YOU OF ALL PEOPLE, AND TURN YOU INTO A--A MOCKERY OF WHAT A SUPERHERO OUGHT TO BE...
...IT'S LIKE SOME SORT OF SICK JOKE.
I KNOW YOU CAN HEAR ME, KENAN! I DON'T APPRECIATE BEING IGNORED!
WILL YOU SHUT UP FOR A SECOND, BAIXI?!
HOW DO YOU KNOW MY DAD IS SAFE?!
YOUR DAD IS SAFE. OTHER PEOPLE ARE NOT.
WE NEED TO GO.
I DID A HEAT SCAN OF YOUR APARTMENT. WHAT ARE YOU--A GRANDMA?!
PUT YOUR TEA DOWN AND GET OUT HERE!
JUST-- JUST GIVE ME SOME TIME TO THINK!
CLICK!
--IS LANEY LAN REPORTING FROM THE BUND!
HOLD UP. BAIXI, DID YOU JUST TURN ON THE TV?! HOW--?!
I'M BAT-MAN.
IT'S A SCENE WE NORMALLY SEE IN AMERICAN CITIES LIKE METROPOLIS!
SEVERAL SUPER-VILLAINS ARE ENGAGED IN A NO-HOLDS-BARRED FIREFIGHT WITH LAW ENFORCEMENT--
MY FELLOW FREEDOM FIGHTERS! OUR CONTINGENCY PLAN WORKED!
KENAN, THIS IS DEILAN! DO YOU SEE NOW?! THOSE ARE ESCAPEES FROM THE CRAB SHELL!
IT'S ONLY A MATTER OF TIME BEFORE SOMEBODY GETS KILLED!
DAD?
YOU'RE LEAVING?
MY COMPATRIOTS NEED ME.
KENAN, I...I'VE SPENT SO MANY YEARS NOT REALLY SEEING YOU.
BUT I SEE YOU NOW.
COME WITH ME, SON.
COME JOIN OUR FIGHT FOR TRUTH, JUSTICE AND DEMOCRACY.

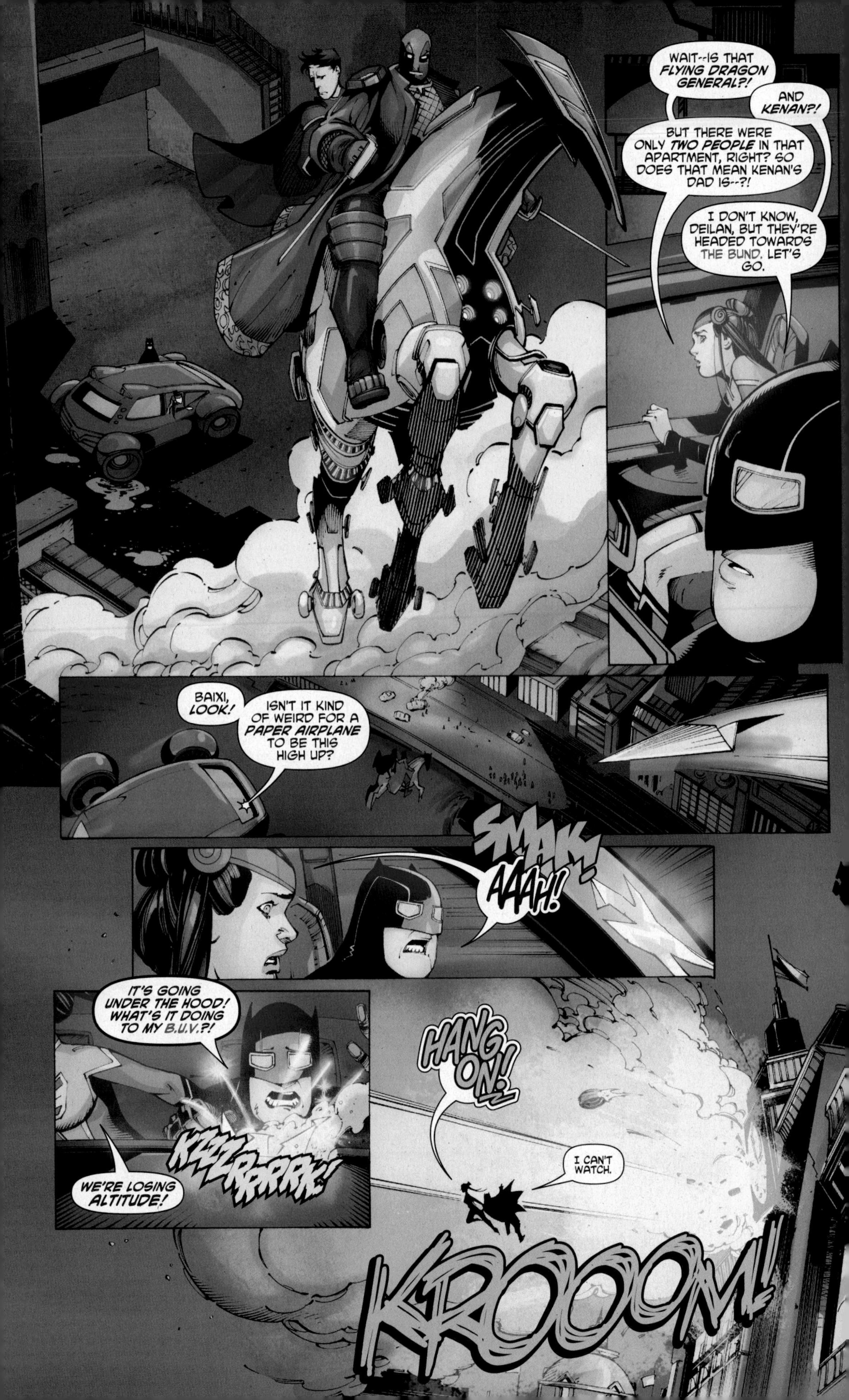
WAIT--IS THAT FLYING DRAGON GENERAL?!
AND KENAN?!
BUT THERE WERE ONLY TWO PEOPLE IN THAT APARTMENT, RIGHT? SO DOES THAT MEAN KENAN'S DAD IS--?!
I DON'T KNOW, DEILAN, BUT THEY'RE HEADED TOWARDS THE BUND. LET'S GO.
BAIXI, LOOK!
ISN'T IT KIND OF WEIRD FOR A PAPER AIRPLANE TO BE THIS HIGH UP?
SMAK!
AAAH!
IT'S GOING UNDER THE HOOD! WHAT'S IT DOING TO MY B.U.V.?!
KZZZRRRRK!
WE'RE LOSING ALTITUDE!
HANG ON!
I CAN'T WATCH.
KROOOM!

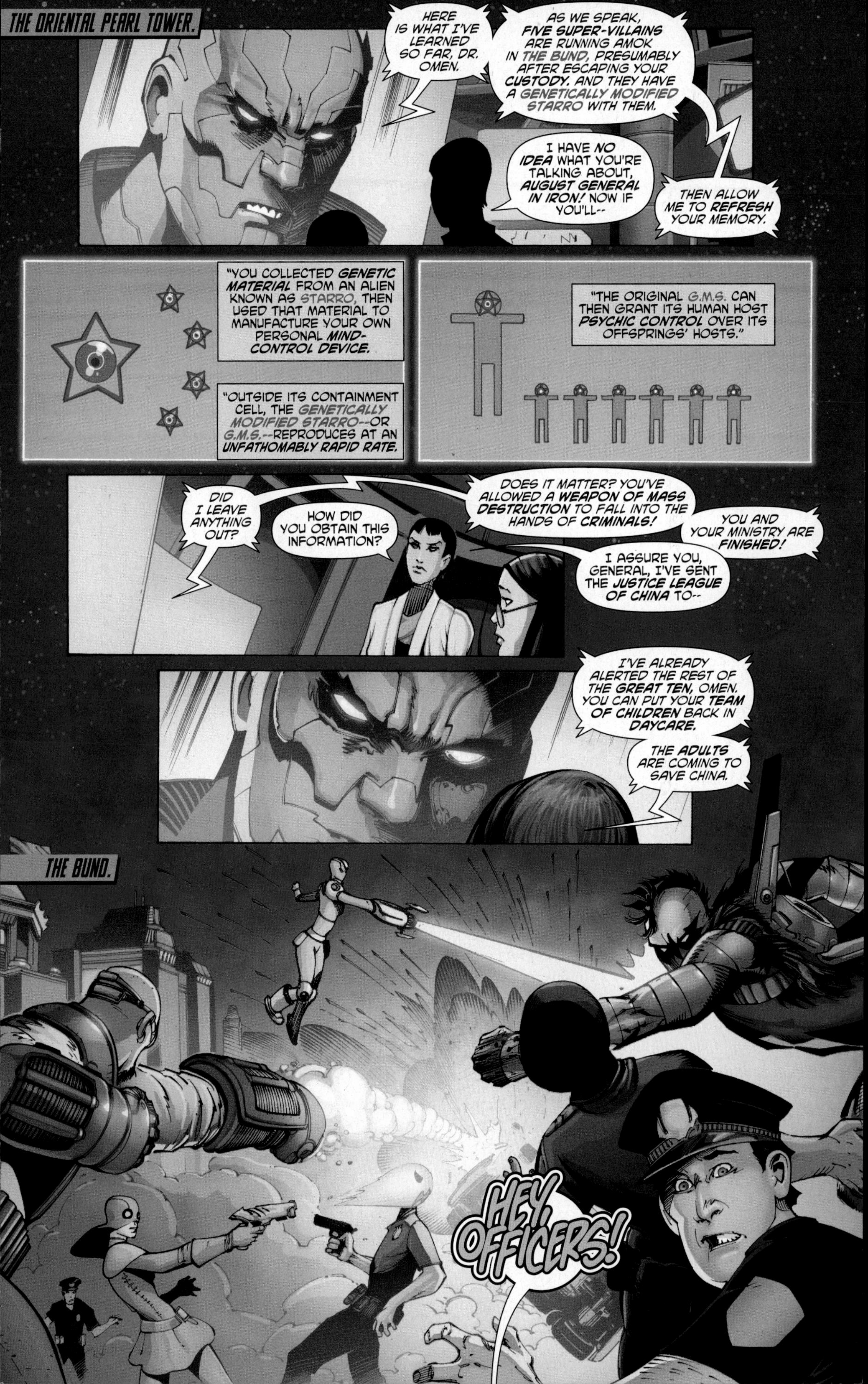
THE ORIENTAL PEARL TOWER.
HERE IS WHAT I'VE LEARNED SO FAR, DR. OMEN.
AS WE SPEAK, FIVE SUPER-VILLAINS ARE RUNNING AMOK IN THE BUND, PRESUMABLY AFTER ESCAPING YOUR CUSTODY. AND THEY HAVE A GENETICALLY MODIFIED STARRO WITH THEM.
I HAVE NO IDEA WHAT YOU'RE TALKING ABOUT, AUGUST GENERAL IN IRON! NOW IF YOU'LL--
THEN ALLOW ME TO REFRESH YOUR MEMORY.
"YOU COLLECTED GENETIC MATERIAL FROM AN ALIEN KNOWN AS STARRO, THEN USED THAT MATERIAL TO MANUFACTURE YOUR OWN PERSONAL MIND-CONTROL DEVICE.
"OUTSIDE ITS CONTAINMENT CELL, THE GENETICALLY MODIFIED STARRO--OR G.M.S.--REPRODUCES AT AN UNFATHOMABLY RAPID RATE.
"THE ORIGINAL G.M.S. CAN THEN GRANT ITS HUMAN HOST PSYCHIC CONTROL OVER ITS OFFSPRINGS' HOSTS."
DID I LEAVE ANYTHING OUT?
HOW DID YOU OBTAIN THIS INFORMATION?
DOES IT MATTER? YOU'VE ALLOWED A WEAPON OF MASS DESTRUCTION TO FALL INTO THE HANDS OF CRIMINALS!
YOU AND YOUR MINISTRY ARE FINISHED!
I ASSURE YOU, GENERAL, I'VE SENT THE JUSTICE LEAGUE OF CHINA TO--
I'VE ALREADY ALERTED THE REST OF THE GREAT TEN, OMEN. YOU CAN PUT YOUR TEAM OF CHILDREN BACK IN DAYCARE.
THE ADULTS ARE COMING TO SAVE CHINA.
THE BUND.
HEY, OFFICERS!

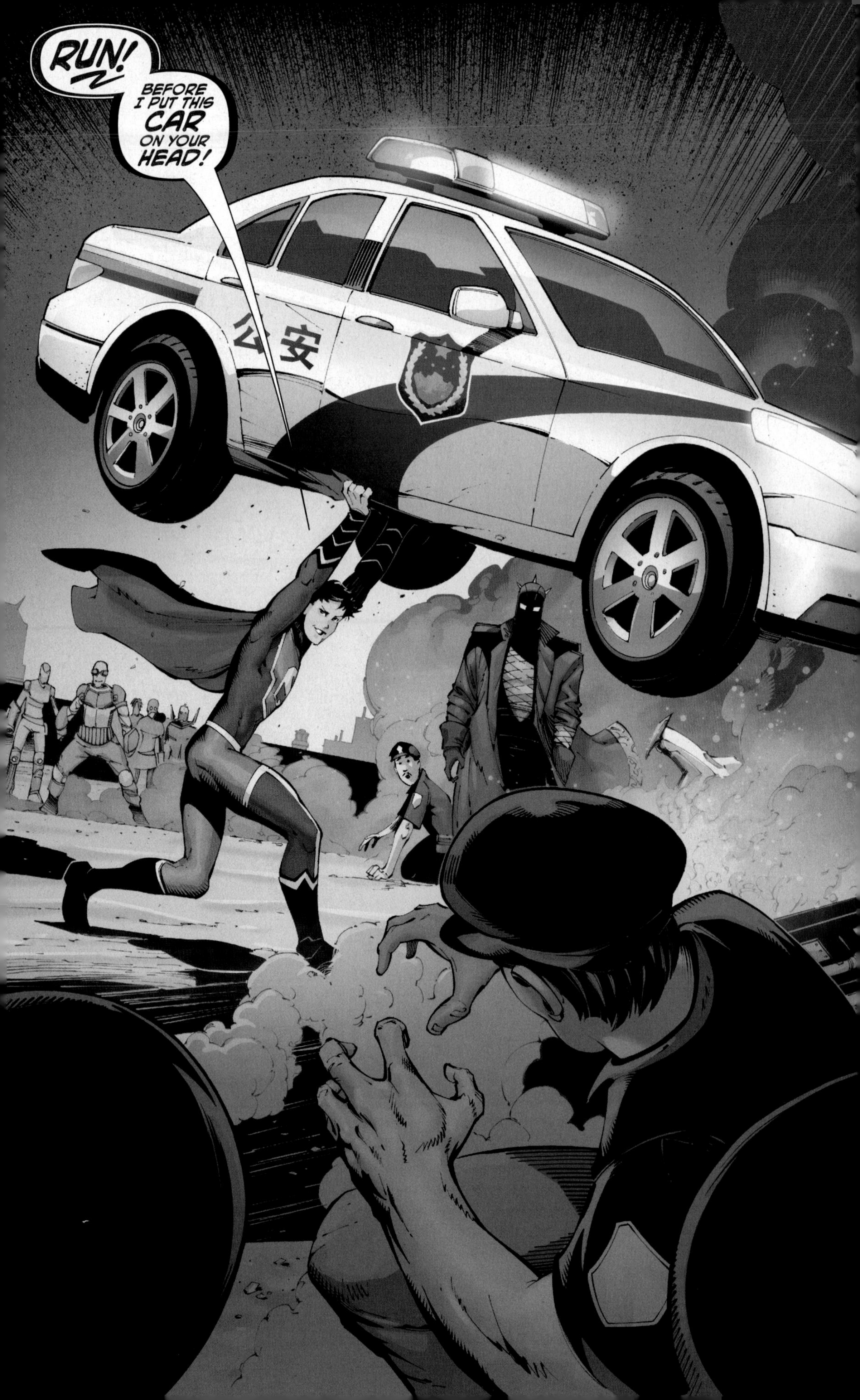
RUN!
BEFORE I PUT THIS CAR ON YOUR HEAD!
公安

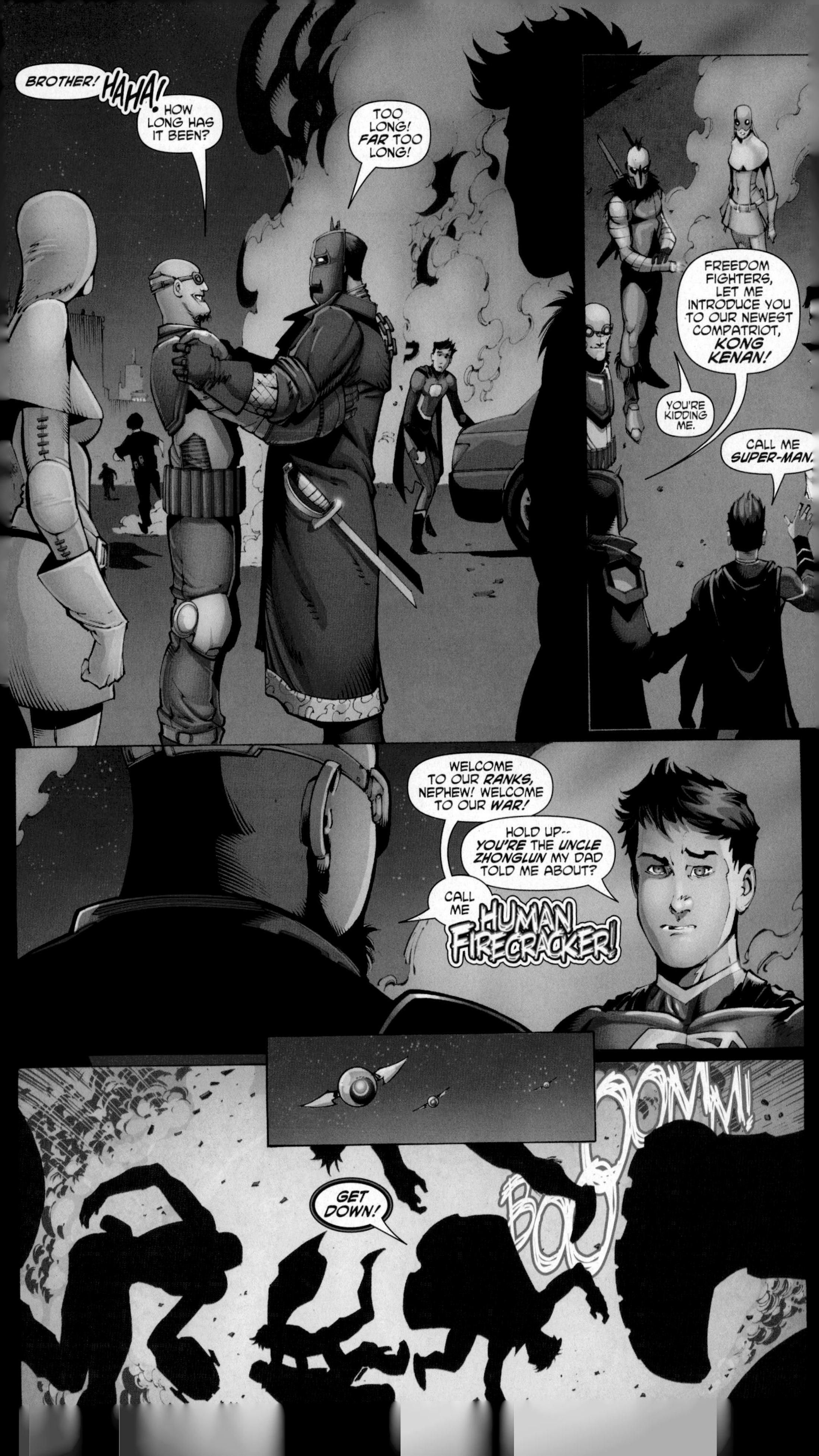

BROTHER! HAHA! HOW LONG HAS IT BEEN?
TOO LONG! FAR TOO LONG!
FREEDOM FIGHTERS, LET ME INTRODUCE YOU TO OUR NEWEST COMPATRIOT, KONG KENAN!
YOU'RE KIDDING ME.
CALL ME SUPER-MAN.
WELCOME TO OUR RANKS, NEPHEW! WELCOME TO OUR WAR!
HOLD UP-- YOU'RE THE UNCLE ZHONGLUN MY DAD TOLD ME ABOUT?
CALL ME HUMAN FIRECRACKER!
DOOMM!
GET DOWN!
BOOM

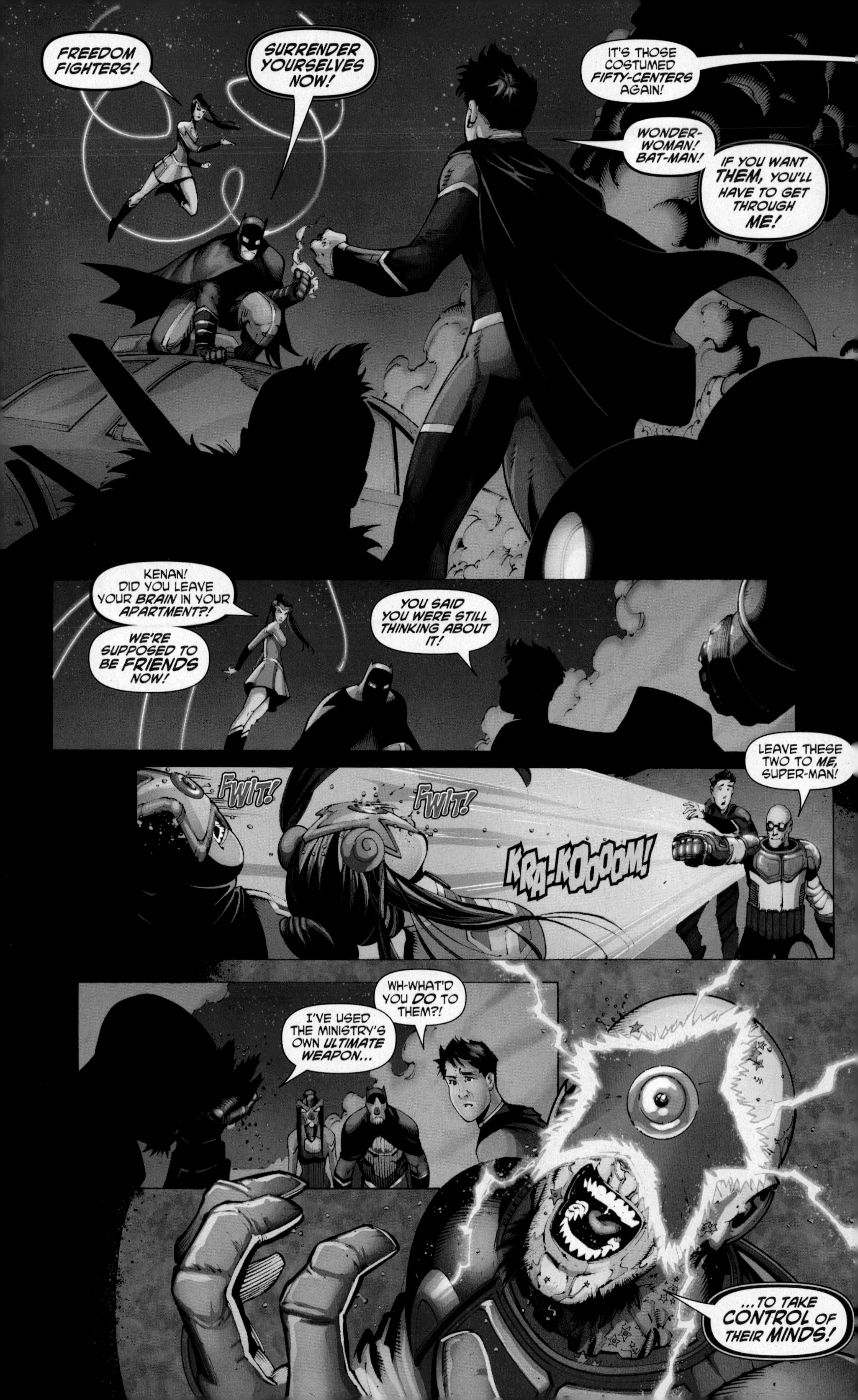
FREEDOM FIGHTERS!
SURRENDER YOURSELVES NOW!
IT'S THOSE COSTUMED FIFTY-CENTERS AGAIN!
WONDER-WOMAN! BAT-MAN!
IF YOU WANT THEM, YOU'LL HAVE TO GET THROUGH ME!
KENAN! DID YOU LEAVE YOUR BRAIN IN YOUR APARTMENT?!
WE'RE SUPPOSED TO BE FRIENDS NOW!
YOU SAID YOU WERE STILL THINKING ABOUT IT!
FWIT!
FWIT!
KRA-KOOOOM!
LEAVE THESE TWO TO ME, SUPER-MAN!
WH-WHAT'D YOU DO TO THEM?!
I'VE USED THE MINISTRY'S OWN ULTIMATE WEAPON...
...TO TAKE CONTROL OF THEIR MINDS!

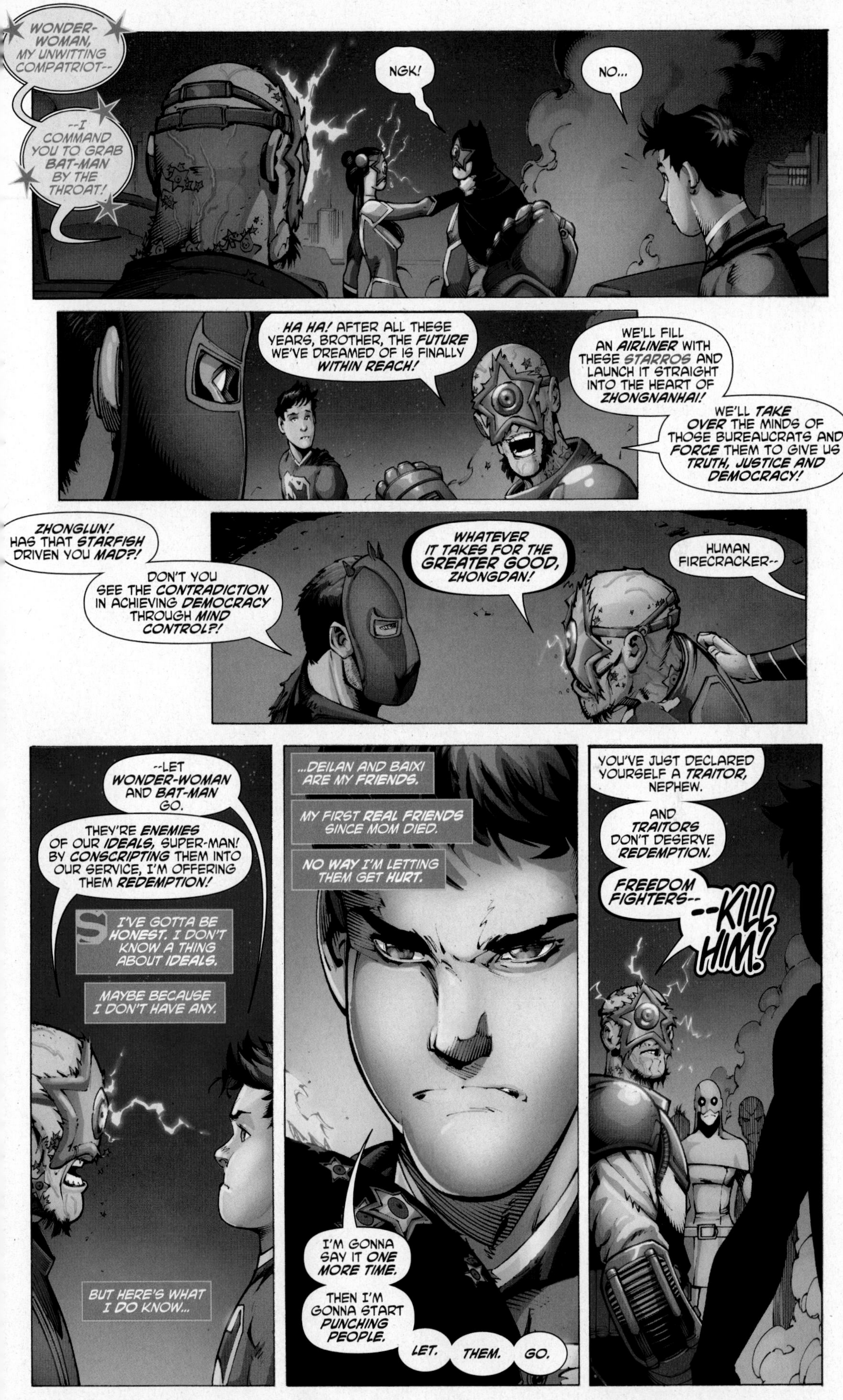
WONDER-WOMAN, MY UNWITTING COMPATRIOT--
--I COMMAND YOU TO GRAB BAT-MAN BY THE THROAT!
NGK!
NO...
HA HA! AFTER ALL THESE YEARS, BROTHER, THE FUTURE WE'VE DREAMED OF IS FINALLY WITHIN REACH!
WE'LL FILL AN AIRLINER WITH THESE STARROS AND LAUNCH IT STRAIGHT INTO THE HEART OF ZHONGNANHAI!
WE'LL TAKE OVER THE MINDS OF THOSE BUREAUCRATS AND FORCE THEM TO GIVE US TRUTH, JUSTICE AND DEMOCRACY!
ZHONGLUN! HAS THAT STARFISH DRIVEN YOU MAD?!
DON'T YOU SEE THE CONTRADICTION IN ACHIEVING DEMOCRACY THROUGH MIND CONTROL?!
WHATEVER IT TAKES FOR THE GREATER GOOD, ZHONGDAN!
HUMAN FIRECRACKER--
--LET WONDER-WOMAN AND BAT-MAN GO.
THEY'RE ENEMIES OF OUR IDEALS, SUPER-MAN! BY CONSCRIPTING THEM INTO OUR SERVICE, I'M OFFERING THEM REDEMPTION!
I'VE GOTTA BE HONEST. I DON'T KNOW A THING ABOUT IDEALS.
MAYBE BECAUSE I DON'T HAVE ANY.
BUT HERE'S WHAT I DO KNOW...
...DEILAN AND BAIXI ARE MY FRIENDS.
MY FIRST REAL FRIENDS SINCE MOM DIED.
NO WAY I'M LETTING THEM GET HURT.
I'M GONNA SAY IT ONE MORE TIME.
THEN I'M GONNA START PUNCHING PEOPLE.
LET.
THEM.
GO.
YOU'VE JUST DECLARED YOURSELF A TRAITOR, NEPHEW.
AND TRAITORS DON'T DESERVE REDEMPTION.
FREEDOM FIGHTERS--
--KILL HIM!

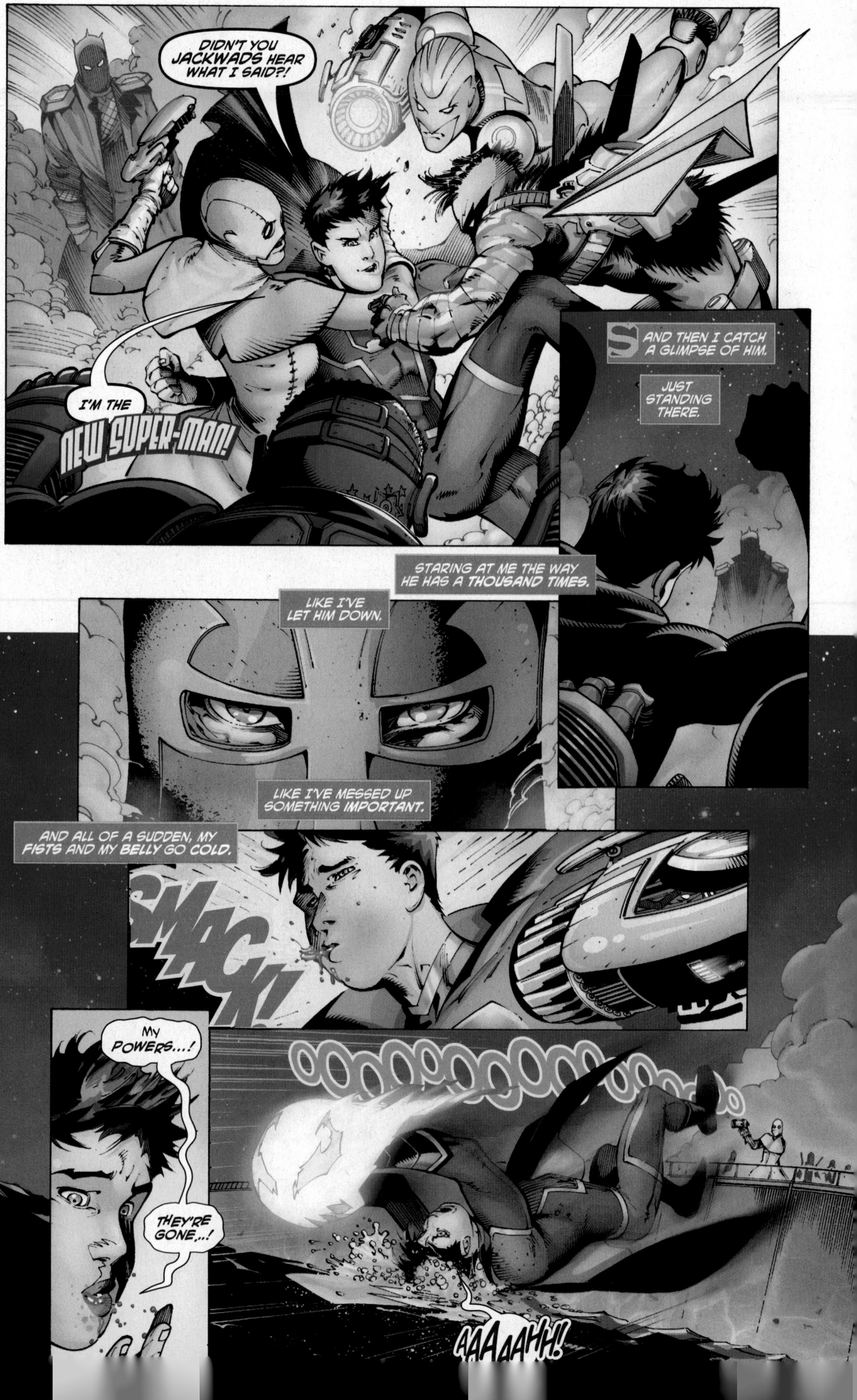

DIDN'T YOU JACKWADS HEAR WHAT I SAID?!
I'M THE NEW SUPER-MAN!
AND THEN I CATCH A GLIMPSE OF HIM.
JUST STANDING THERE.
STARING AT ME THE WAY HE HAS A THOUSAND TIMES.
LIKE I'VE LET HIM DOWN.
LIKE I'VE MESSED UP SOMETHING IMPORTANT.
AND ALL OF A SUDDEN, MY FISTS AND MY BELLY GO COLD.
SMACK!
MY POWERS...!
THEY'RE GONE...!
AAAAAHH!

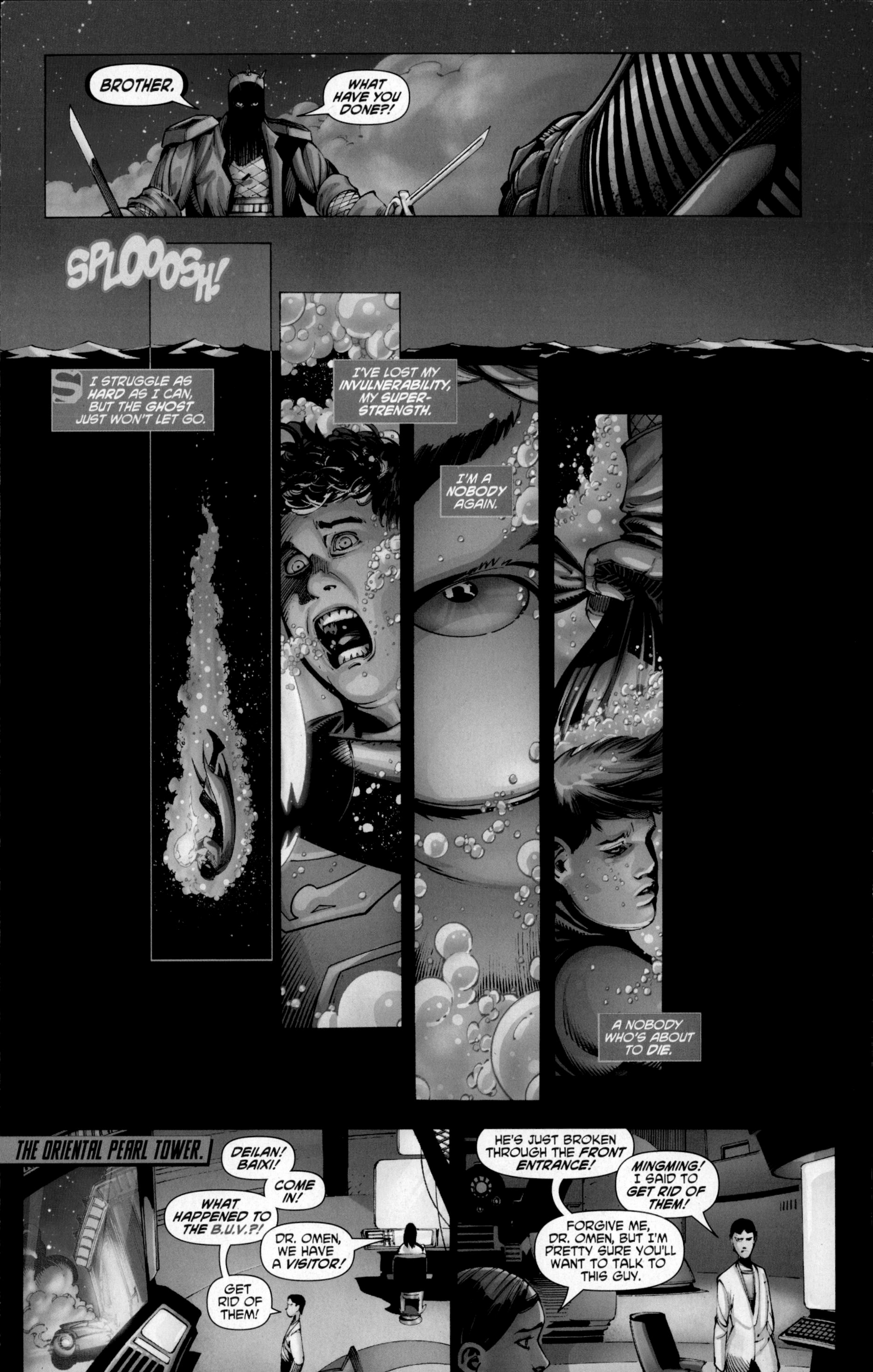
BROTHER.
WHAT HAVE YOU DONE?!
SPLOOOSH!
I STRUGGLE AS HARD AS I CAN, BUT THE GHOST JUST WON'T LET GO.
I'VE LOST MY INVULNERABILITY, MY SUPER-STRENGTH.
I'M A NOBODY AGAIN.
A NOBODY WHO'S ABOUT TO DIE.
THE ORIENTAL PEARL TOWER.
DEILAN! BAIXI!
COME IN!
WHAT HAPPENED TO THE B.U.V.?!
DR. OMEN, WE HAVE A VISITOR!
GET RID OF THEM!
HE'S JUST BROKEN THROUGH THE FRONT ENTRANCE!
MINGMING! I SAID TO GET RID OF THEM!
FORGIVE ME, DR. OMEN, BUT I'M PRETTY SURE YOU'LL WANT TO TALK TO THIS GUY.

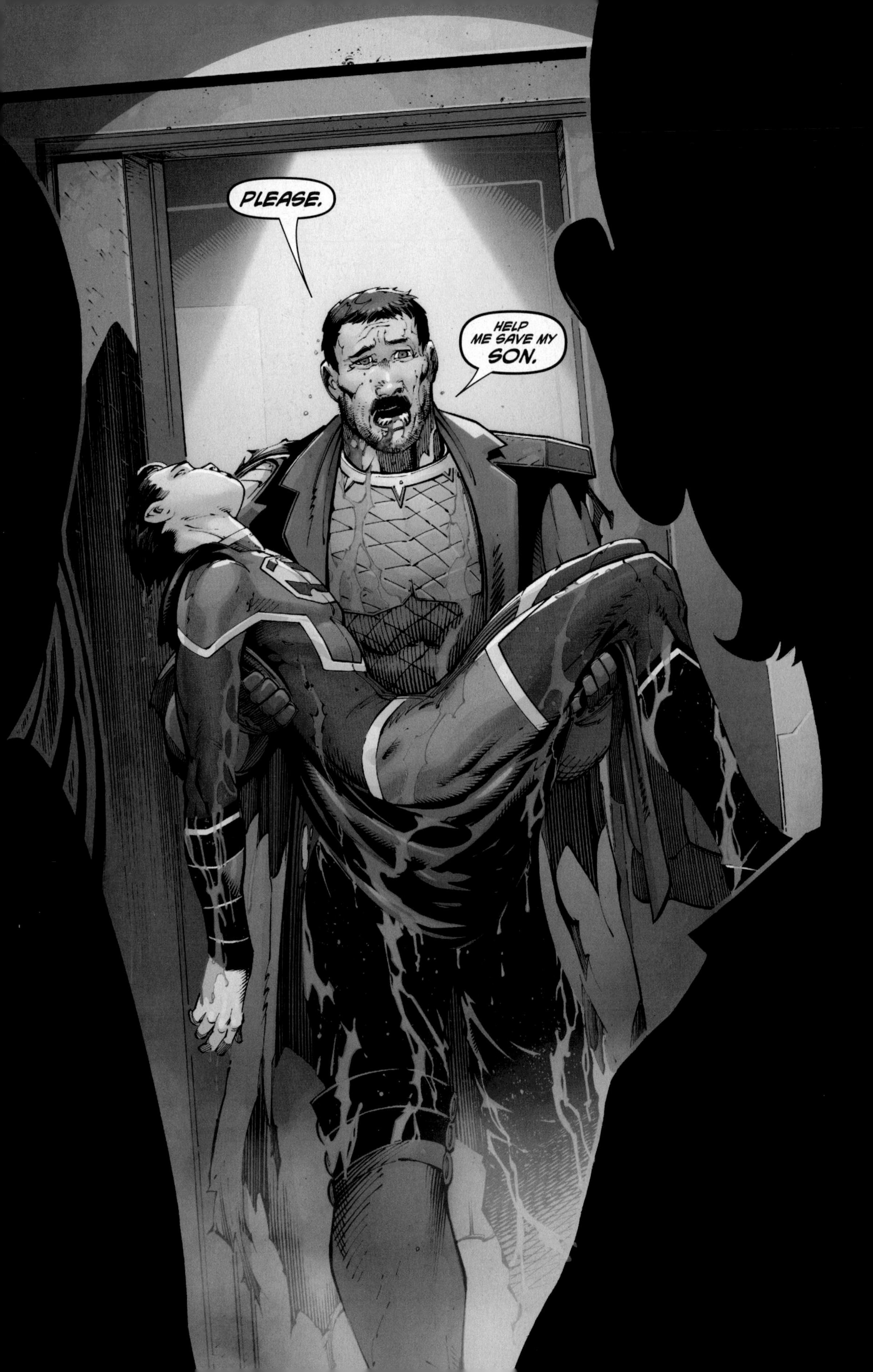
PLEASE.
HELP ME SAVE MY SON.

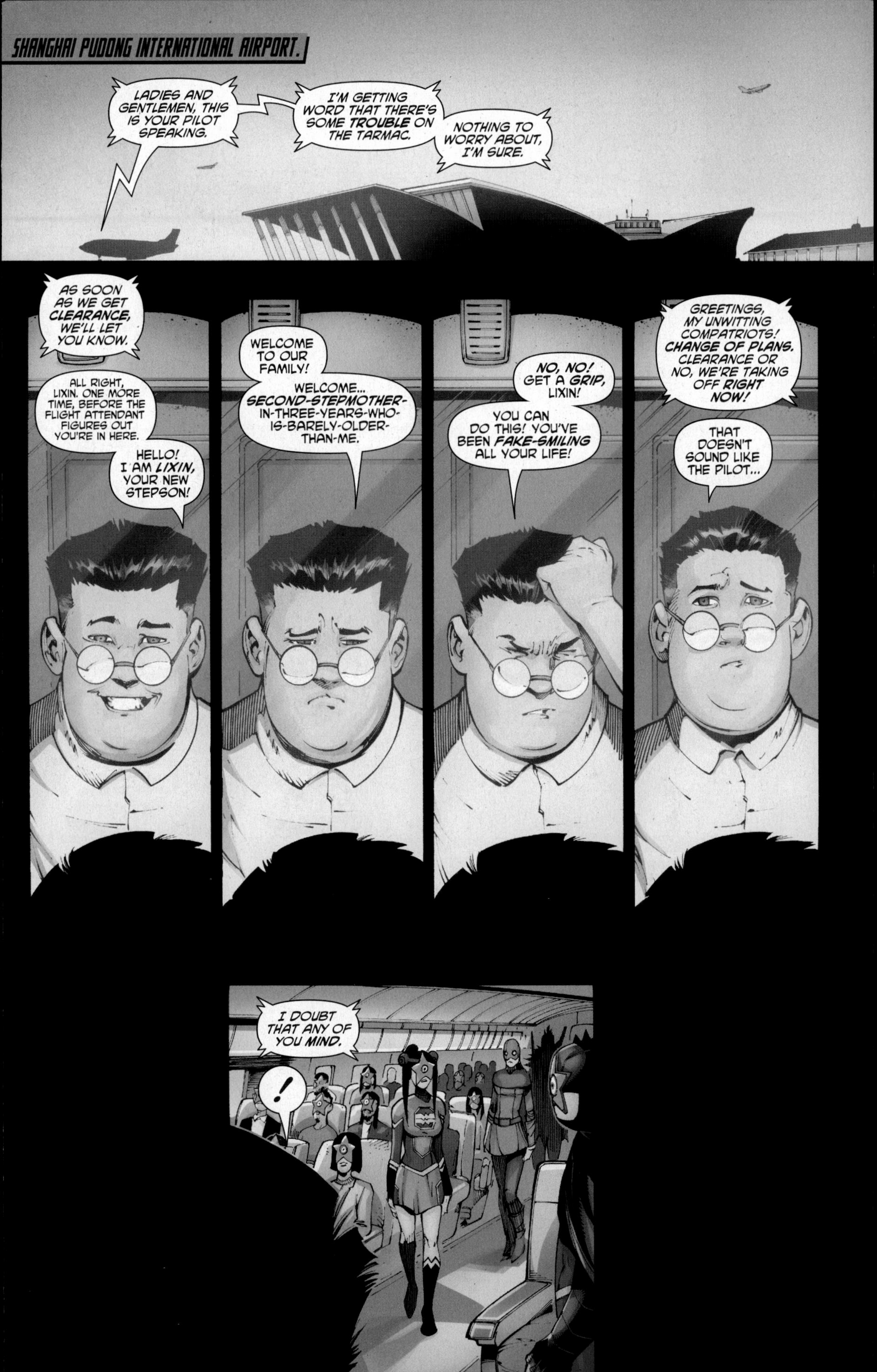
SHANGHAI PUDONG INTERNATIONAL AIRPORT.
LADIES AND GENTLEMEN, THIS IS YOUR PILOT SPEAKING.
I'M GETTING WORD THAT THERE'S SOME TROUBLE ON THE TARMAC.
NOTHING TO WORRY ABOUT, I'M SURE.
AS SOON AS WE GET CLEARANCE, WE'LL LET YOU KNOW.
ALL RIGHT, LIXIN. ONE MORE TIME, BEFORE THE FLIGHT ATTENDANT FIGURES OUT YOU'RE IN HERE.
HELLO! I AM LIXIN, YOUR NEW STEPSON!
WELCOME TO OUR FAMILY!
WELCOME... SECOND-STEPMOTHER-IN-THREE-YEARS-WHO-IS-BARELY-OLDER-THAN-ME.
NO, NO! GET A GRIP, LIXIN!
YOU CAN DO THIS! YOU'VE BEEN FAKE-SMILING ALL YOUR LIFE!
GREETINGS, MY UNWITTING COMPATRIOTS! CHANGE OF PLANS. CLEARANCE OR NO, WE'RE TAKING OFF RIGHT NOW!
THAT DOESN'T SOUND LIKE THE PILOT...
I DOUBT THAT ANY OF YOU MIND.
!

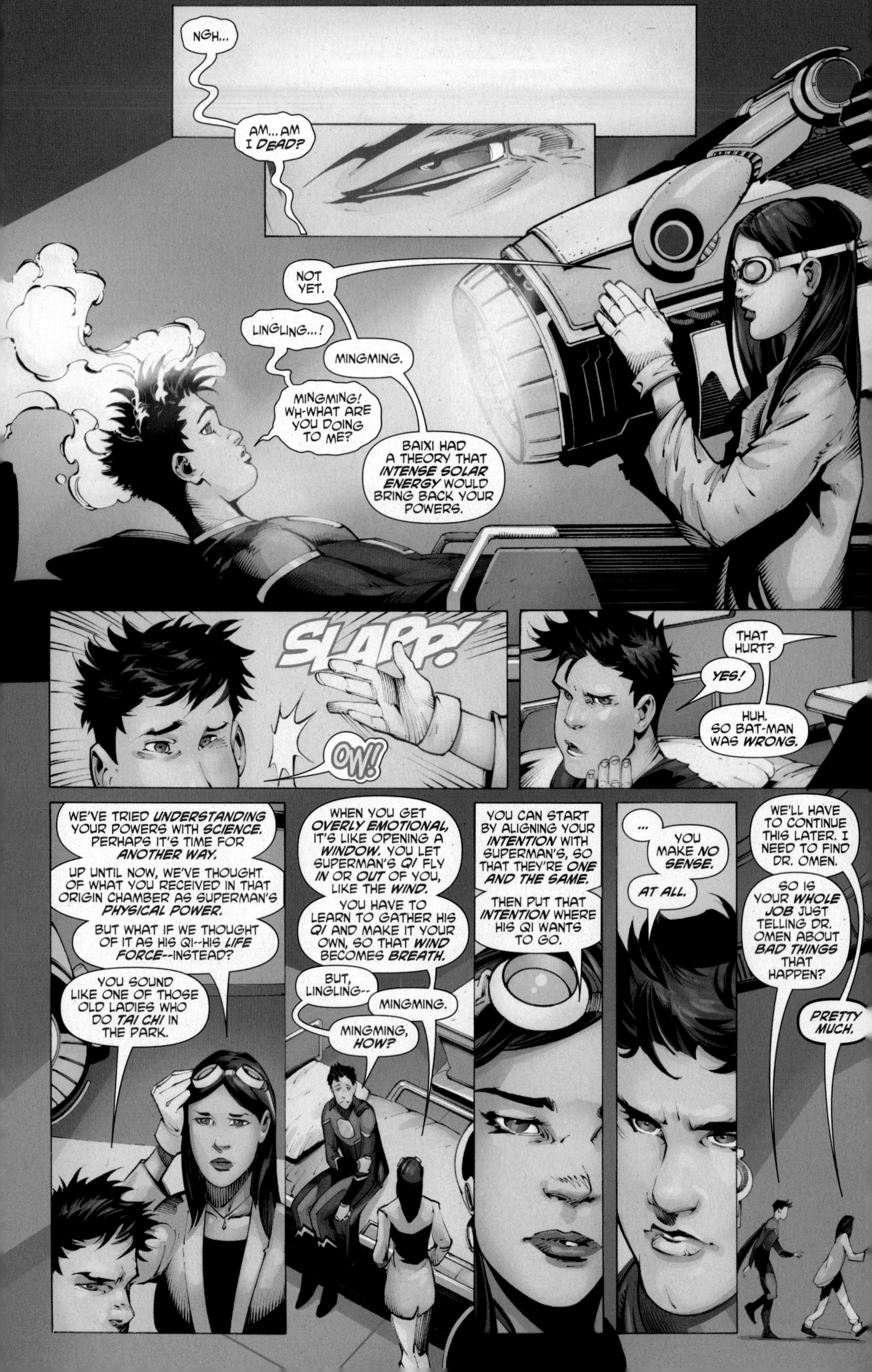
NGH...
AM...AM I DEAD?
NOT YET.
LINGLING...!
MINGMING.
MINGMING! WH-WHAT ARE YOU DOING TO ME?
BAIXI HAD A THEORY THAT INTENSE SOLAR ENERGY WOULD BRING BACK YOUR POWERS.
SLAPP!
OW!!
THAT HURT?
YES!
HUH. SO BAT-MAN WAS WRONG.
WE'VE TRIED UNDERSTANDING YOUR POWERS WITH SCIENCE. PERHAPS IT'S TIME FOR ANOTHER WAY.
UP UNTIL NOW, WE'VE THOUGHT OF WHAT YOU RECEIVED IN THAT ORIGIN CHAMBER AS SUPERMAN'S PHYSICAL POWER.
BUT WHAT IF WE THOUGHT OF IT AS HIS QI--HIS LIFE FORCE--INSTEAD?
YOU SOUND LIKE ONE OF THOSE OLD LADIES WHO DO TAI CHI IN THE PARK.
WHEN YOU GET OVERLY EMOTIONAL, IT'S LIKE OPENING A WINDOW. YOU LET SUPERMAN'S QI FLY IN OR OUT OF YOU, LIKE THE WIND.
YOU HAVE TO LEARN TO GATHER HIS QI AND MAKE IT YOUR OWN, SO THAT WIND BECOMES BREATH.
BUT, LINGLING--
MINGMING.
MINGMING, HOW?
YOU CAN START BY ALIGNING YOUR INTENTION WITH SUPERMAN'S, SO THAT THEY'RE ONE AND THE SAME.
THEN PUT THAT INTENTION WHERE HIS QI WANTS TO GO.
...
YOU MAKE NO SENSE.
AT ALL.
WE'LL HAVE TO CONTINUE THIS LATER. I NEED TO FIND DR. OMEN.
SO IS YOUR WHOLE JOB JUST TELLING DR. OMEN ABOUT BAD THINGS THAT HAPPEN?
PRETTY MUCH.

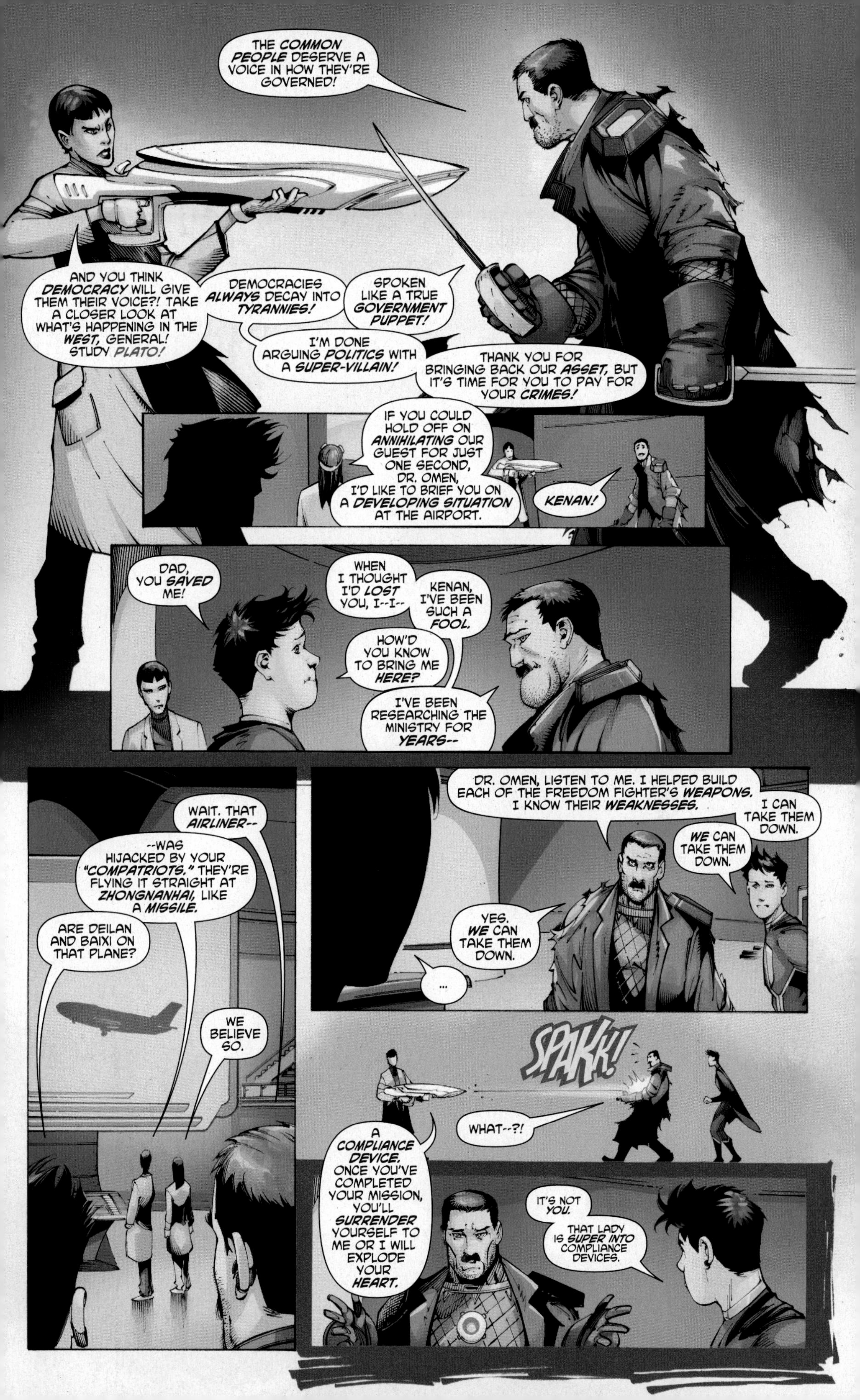
THE COMMON PEOPLE DESERVE A VOICE IN HOW THEY'RE GOVERNED!
AND YOU THINK DEMOCRACY WILL GIVE THEM THEIR VOICE?! TAKE A CLOSER LOOK AT WHAT'S HAPPENING IN THE WEST, GENERAL! STUDY PLATO!
DEMOCRACIES ALWAYS DECAY INTO TYRANNIES!
SPOKEN LIKE A TRUE GOVERNMENT PUPPET!
I'M DONE ARGUING POLITICS WITH A SUPER-VILLAIN!
THANK YOU FOR BRINGING BACK OUR ASSET, BUT IT'S TIME FOR YOU TO PAY FOR YOUR CRIMES!
IF YOU COULD HOLD OFF ON ANNIHILATING OUR GUEST FOR JUST ONE SECOND, DR. OMEN, I'D LIKE TO BRIEF YOU ON A DEVELOPING SITUATION AT THE AIRPORT.
KENAN!
DAD, YOU SAVED ME!
WHEN I THOUGHT I'D LOST YOU, I--I--
KENAN, I'VE BEEN SUCH A FOOL.
HOW'D YOU KNOW TO BRING ME HERE?
I'VE BEEN RESEARCHING THE MINISTRY FOR YEARS--
WAIT. THAT AIRLINER--
--WAS HIJACKED BY YOUR "COMPATRIOTS." THEY'RE FLYING IT STRAIGHT AT ZHONGNANHAI, LIKE A MISSILE.
ARE DEILAN AND BAIXI ON THAT PLANE?
WE BELIEVE SO.
DR. OMEN, LISTEN TO ME. I HELPED BUILD EACH OF THE FREEDOM FIGHTER'S WEAPONS. I KNOW THEIR WEAKNESSES.
I CAN TAKE THEM DOWN.
WE CAN TAKE THEM DOWN.
YES. WE CAN TAKE THEM DOWN.
...
SPAKK!
WHAT--?!
A COMPLIANCE DEVICE. ONCE YOU'VE COMPLETED YOUR MISSION, YOU'LL SURRENDER YOURSELF TO ME OR I WILL EXPLODE YOUR HEART.
IT'S NOT YOU.
THAT LADY IS SUPER INTO COMPLIANCE DEVICES.

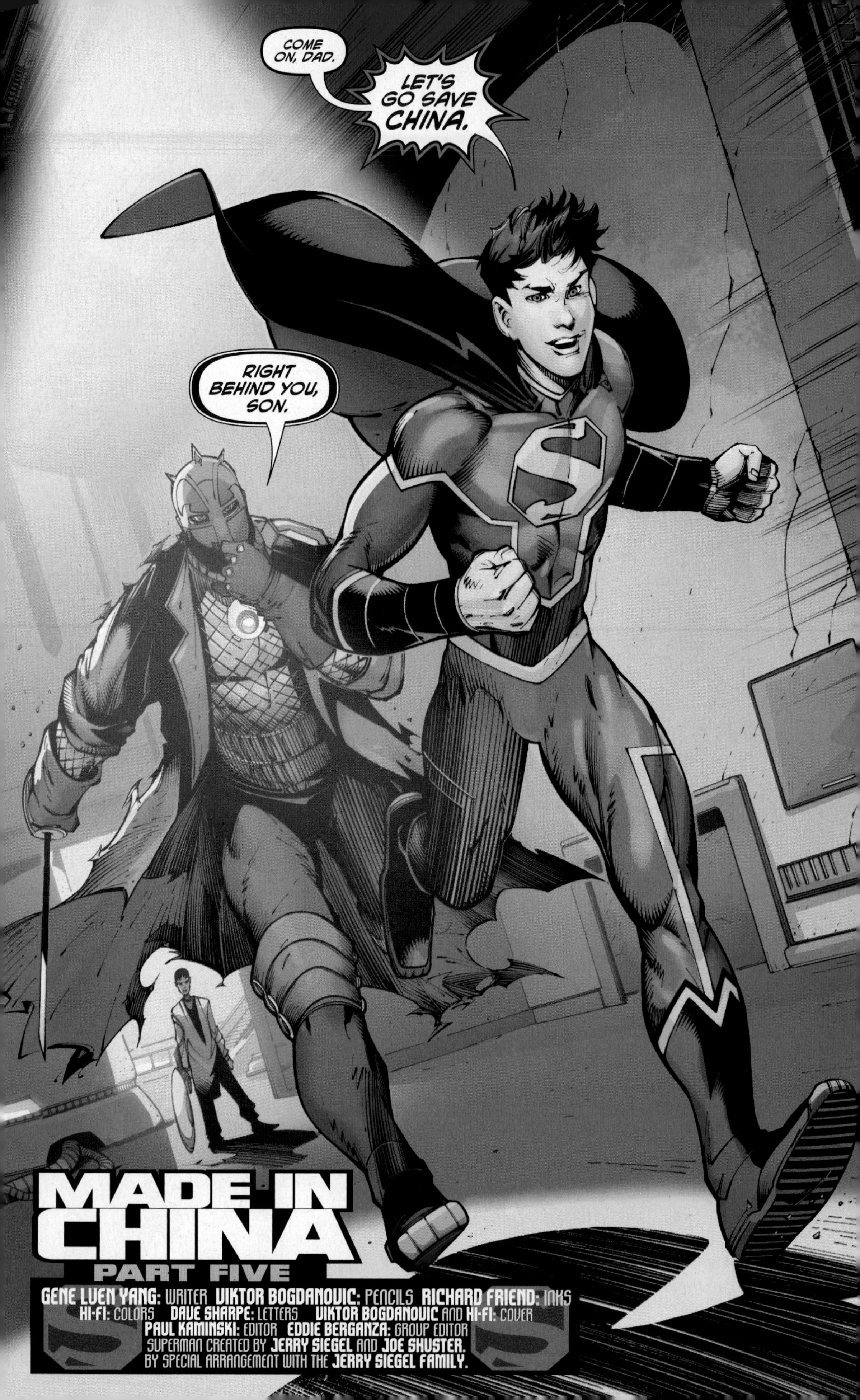

COME ON, DAD.
LET'S GO SAVE CHINA.
RIGHT BEHIND YOU, SON.
MADE IN CHINA
PART FIVE
GENE LUEN YANG: WRITER VIKTOR BOGDANOVIC: PENCILS RICHARD FRIEND: INKS
HI-FI: COLORS DAVE SHARPE: LETTERS VIKTOR BOGDANOVIC AND HI-FI: COVER
PAUL KAMINSKI: EDITOR EDDIE BERGANZA: GROUP EDITOR
SUPERMAN CREATED BY JERRY SIEGEL AND JOE SHUSTER.
BY SPECIAL ARRANGEMENT WITH THE JERRY SIEGEL FAMILY.

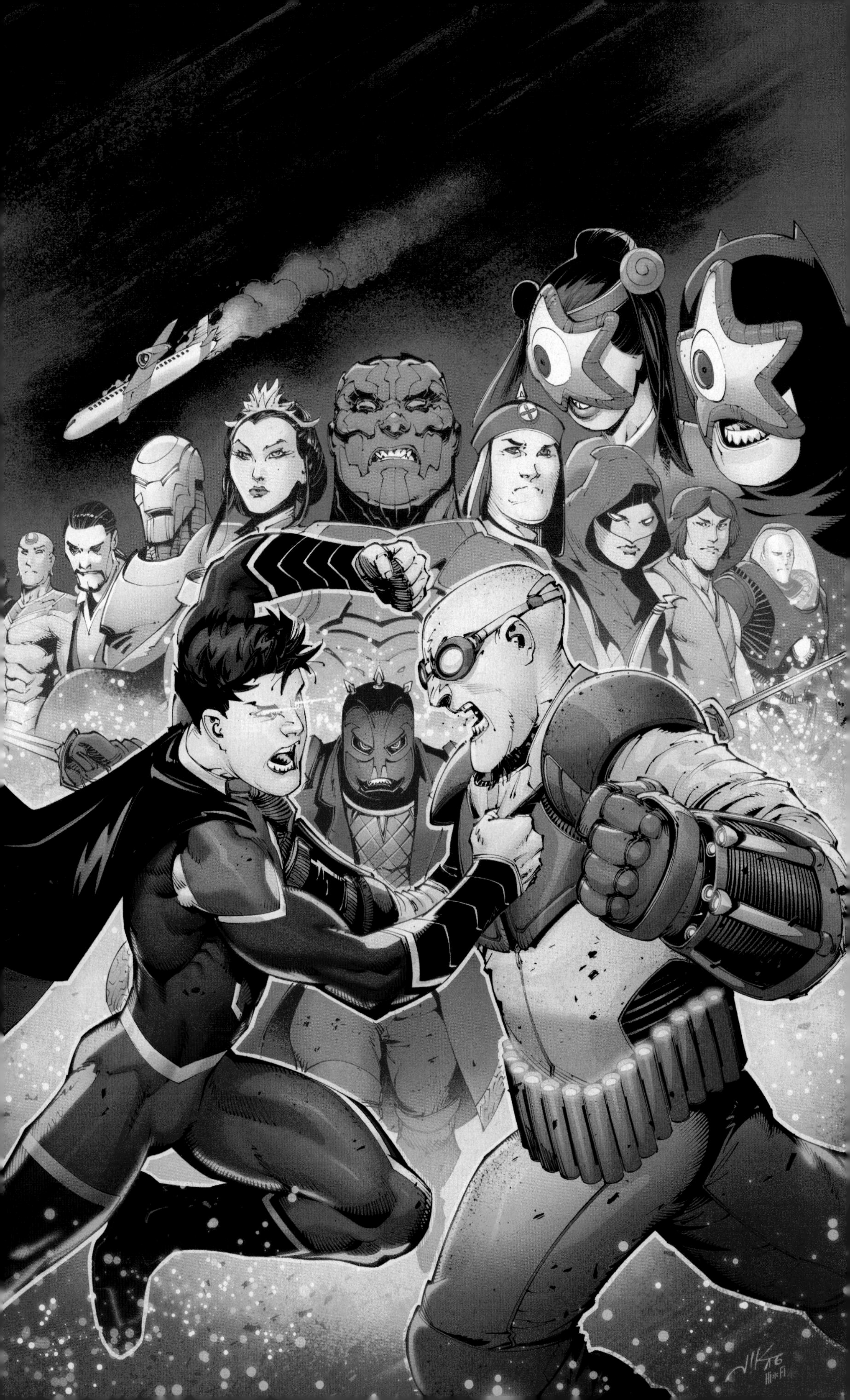

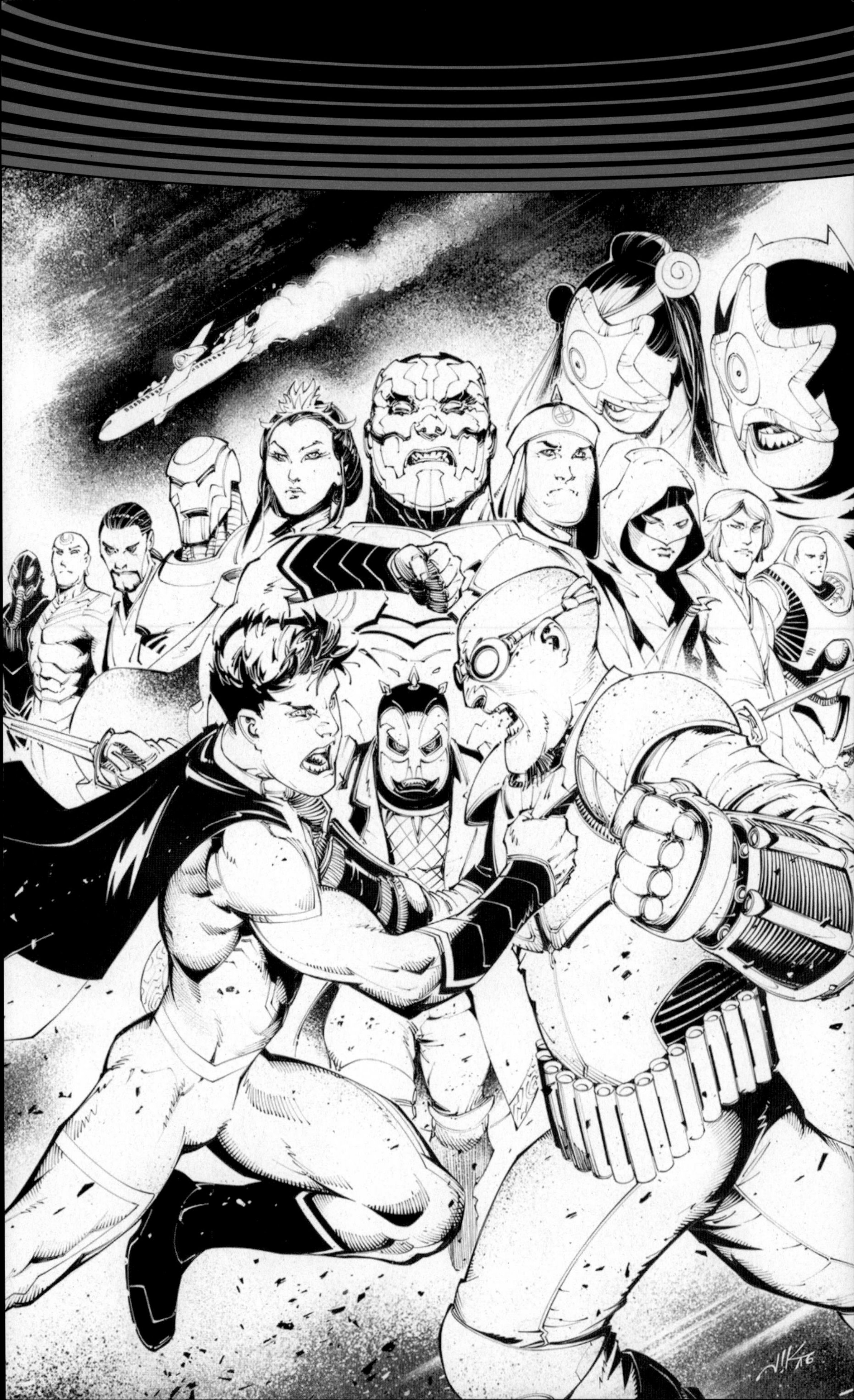

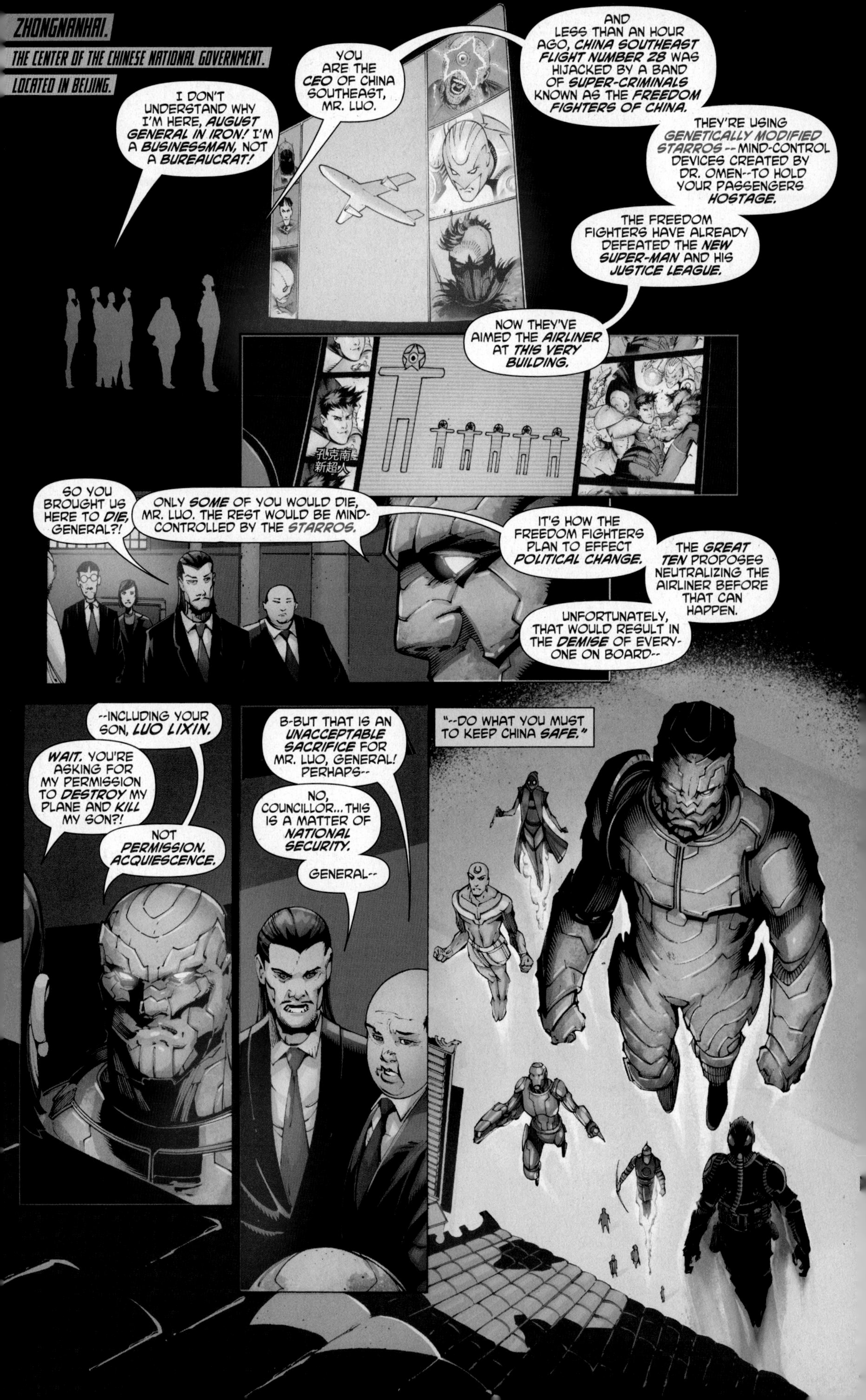
ZHONGNANHAI.
THE CENTER OF THE CHINESE NATIONAL GOVERNMENT.
LOCATED IN BEIJING.
I DON'T UNDERSTAND WHY I'M HERE, AUGUST GENERAL IN IRON! I'M A BUSINESSMAN, NOT A BUREAUCRAT!
YOU ARE THE CEO OF CHINA SOUTHEAST, MR. LUO.
AND LESS THAN AN HOUR AGO, CHINA SOUTHEAST FLIGHT NUMBER 28 WAS HIJACKED BY A BAND OF SUPER-CRIMINALS KNOWN AS THE FREEDOM FIGHTERS OF CHINA.
THEY'RE USING GENETICALLY MODIFIED STARROS--MIND-CONTROL DEVICES CREATED BY DR. OMEN--TO HOLD YOUR PASSENGERS HOSTAGE.
THE FREEDOM FIGHTERS HAVE ALREADY DEFEATED THE NEW SUPER-MAN AND HIS JUSTICE LEAGUE.
NOW THEY'VE AIMED THE AIRLINER AT THIS VERY BUILDING.
孔克南
新超人
SO YOU BROUGHT US HERE TO DIE, GENERAL?!
ONLY SOME OF YOU WOULD DIE, MR. LUO. THE REST WOULD BE MIND-CONTROLLED BY THE STARROS.
IT'S HOW THE FREEDOM FIGHTERS PLAN TO EFFECT POLITICAL CHANGE.
THE GREAT TEN PROPOSES NEUTRALIZING THE AIRLINER BEFORE THAT CAN HAPPEN.
UNFORTUNATELY, THAT WOULD RESULT IN THE DEMISE OF EVERY-ONE ON BOARD--
--INCLUDING YOUR SON, LUO LIXIN.
WAIT. YOU'RE ASKING FOR MY PERMISSION TO DESTROY MY PLANE AND KILL MY SON?!
NOT PERMISSION. ACQUIESCENCE.
B-BUT THAT IS AN UNACCEPTABLE SACRIFICE FOR MR. LUO, GENERAL! PERHAPS--
NO, COUNCILLOR... THIS IS A MATTER OF NATIONAL SECURITY.
GENERAL--
"--DO WHAT YOU MUST TO KEEP CHINA SAFE."

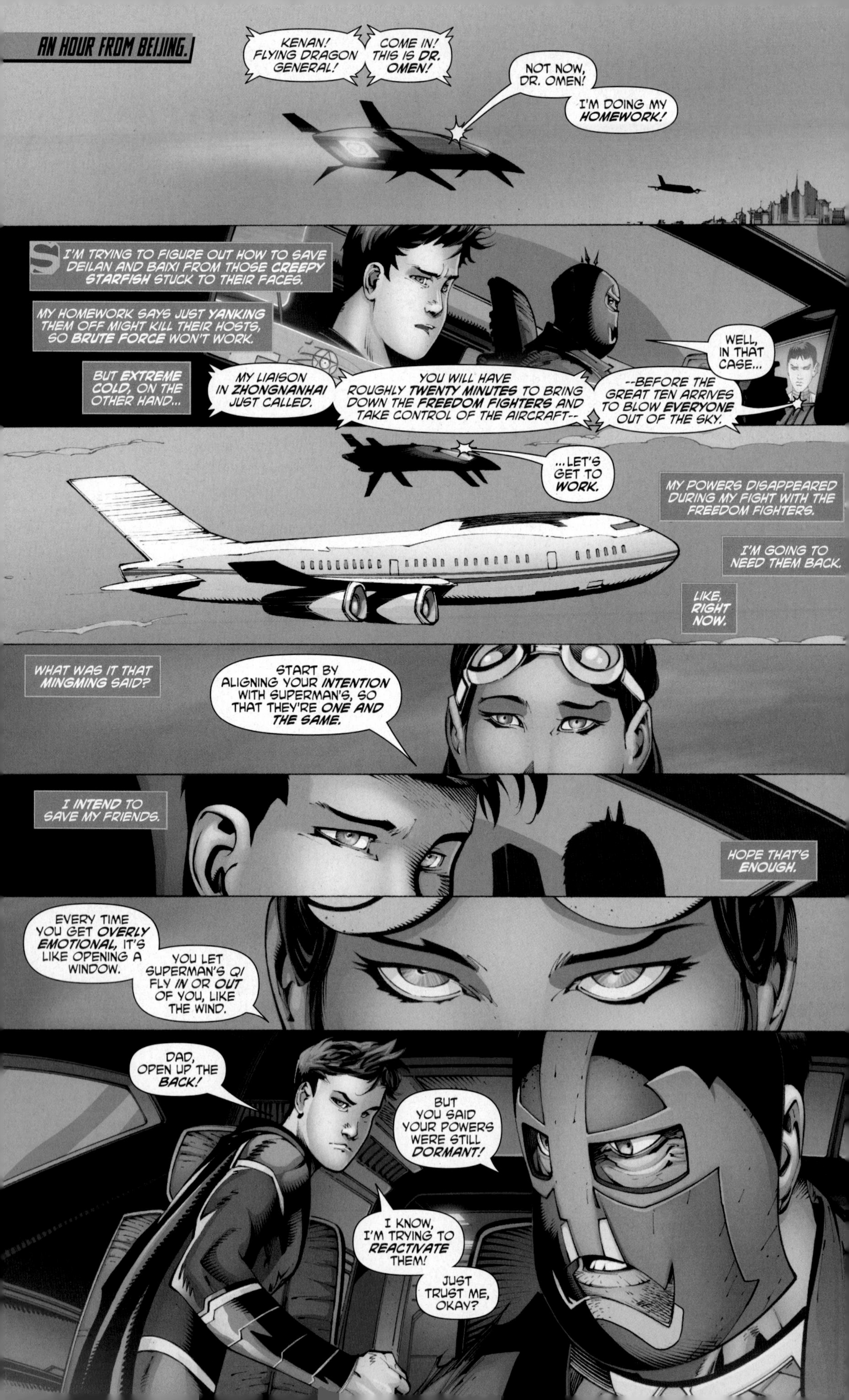
AN HOUR FROM BEIJING.
KENAN! FLYING DRAGON GENERAL!
COME IN! THIS IS DR. OMEN!
NOT NOW, DR. OMEN!
I'M DOING MY HOMEWORK!
I'M TRYING TO FIGURE OUT HOW TO SAVE DEILAN AND BAIXI FROM THOSE CREEPY STARFISH STUCK TO THEIR FACES.
MY HOMEWORK SAYS JUST YANKING THEM OFF MIGHT KILL THEIR HOSTS, SO BRUTE FORCE WON'T WORK.
BUT EXTREME COLD, ON THE OTHER HAND...
MY LIAISON IN ZHONGNANHAI JUST CALLED.
YOU WILL HAVE ROUGHLY TWENTY MINUTES TO BRING DOWN THE FREEDOM FIGHTERS AND TAKE CONTROL OF THE AIRCRAFT--
--BEFORE THE GREAT TEN ARRIVES TO BLOW EVERYONE OUT OF THE SKY.
WELL, IN THAT CASE...
...LET'S GET TO WORK.
MY POWERS DISAPPEARED DURING MY FIGHT WITH THE FREEDOM FIGHTERS.
I'M GOING TO NEED THEM BACK.
LIKE, RIGHT NOW.
WHAT WAS IT THAT MINGMING SAID?
START BY ALIGNING YOUR INTENTION WITH SUPERMAN'S, SO THAT THEY'RE ONE AND THE SAME.
I INTEND TO SAVE MY FRIENDS.
HOPE THAT'S ENOUGH.
EVERY TIME YOU GET OVERLY EMOTIONAL, IT'S LIKE OPENING A WINDOW.
YOU LET SUPERMAN'S QI FLY IN OR OUT OF YOU, LIKE THE WIND.
DAD, OPEN UP THE BACK!
BUT YOU SAID YOUR POWERS WERE STILL DORMANT!
I KNOW, I'M TRYING TO REACTIVATE THEM!
JUST TRUST ME, OKAY?

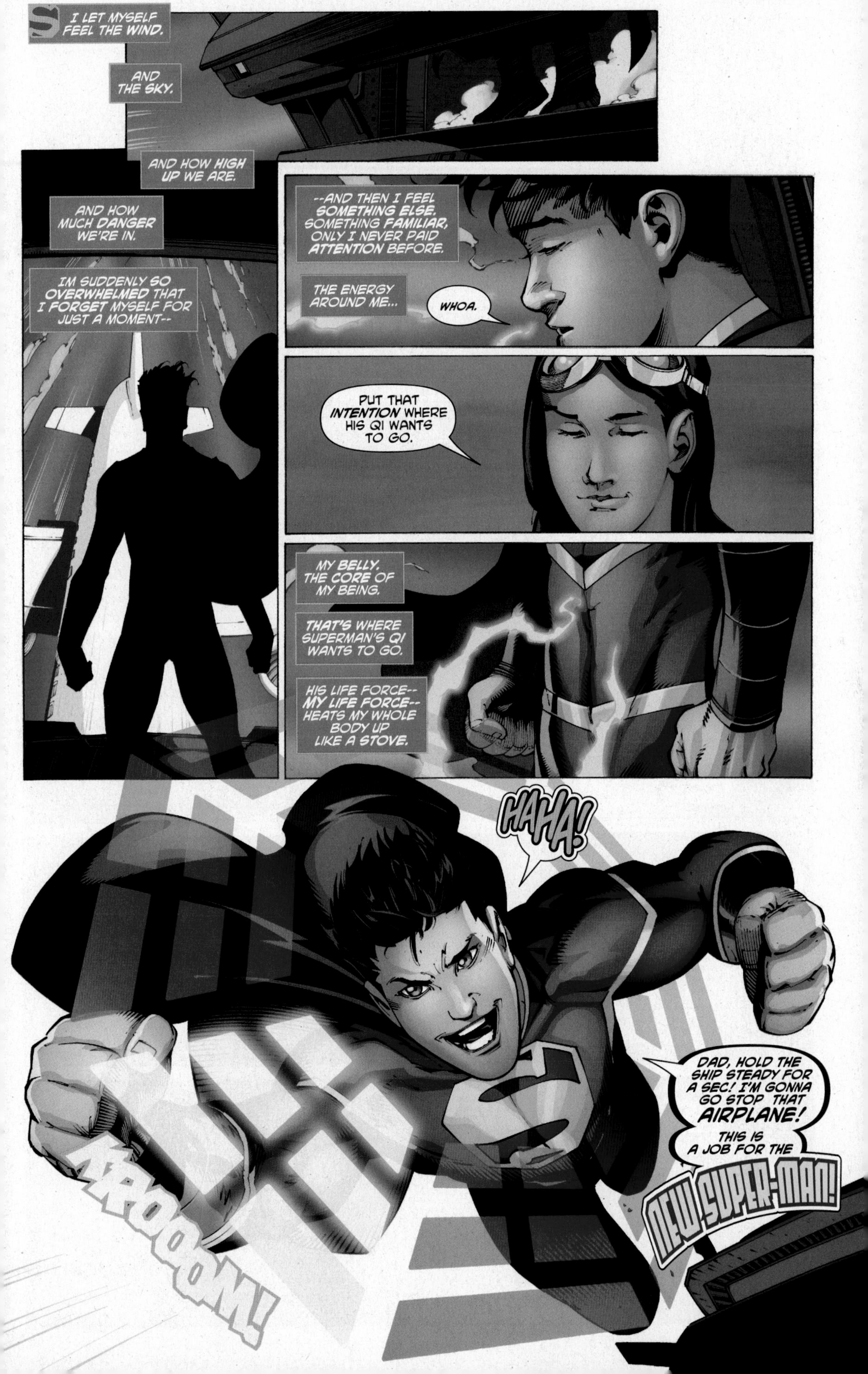
I LET MYSELF FEEL THE WIND.
AND THE SKY.
AND HOW HIGH UP WE ARE.
AND HOW MUCH DANGER WE'RE IN.
IM SUDDENLY SO OVERWHELMED THAT I FORGET MYSELF FOR JUST A MOMENT--
--AND THEN I FEEL SOMETHING ELSE. SOMETHING FAMILIAR, ONLY I NEVER PAID ATTENTION BEFORE.
THE ENERGY AROUND ME...
WHOA.
PUT THAT INTENTION WHERE HIS QI WANTS TO GO.
MY BELLY. THE CORE OF MY BEING.
THAT'S WHERE SUPERMAN'S QI WANTS TO GO.
HIS LIFE FORCE-- MY LIFE FORCE-- HEATS MY WHOLE BODY UP LIKE A STOVE.
HAHA!
DAD, HOLD THE SHIP STEADY FOR A SEC! I'M GONNA GO STOP THAT AIRPLANE!
THIS IS A JOB FOR THE
NEW SUPER-MAN!
KROOOM!

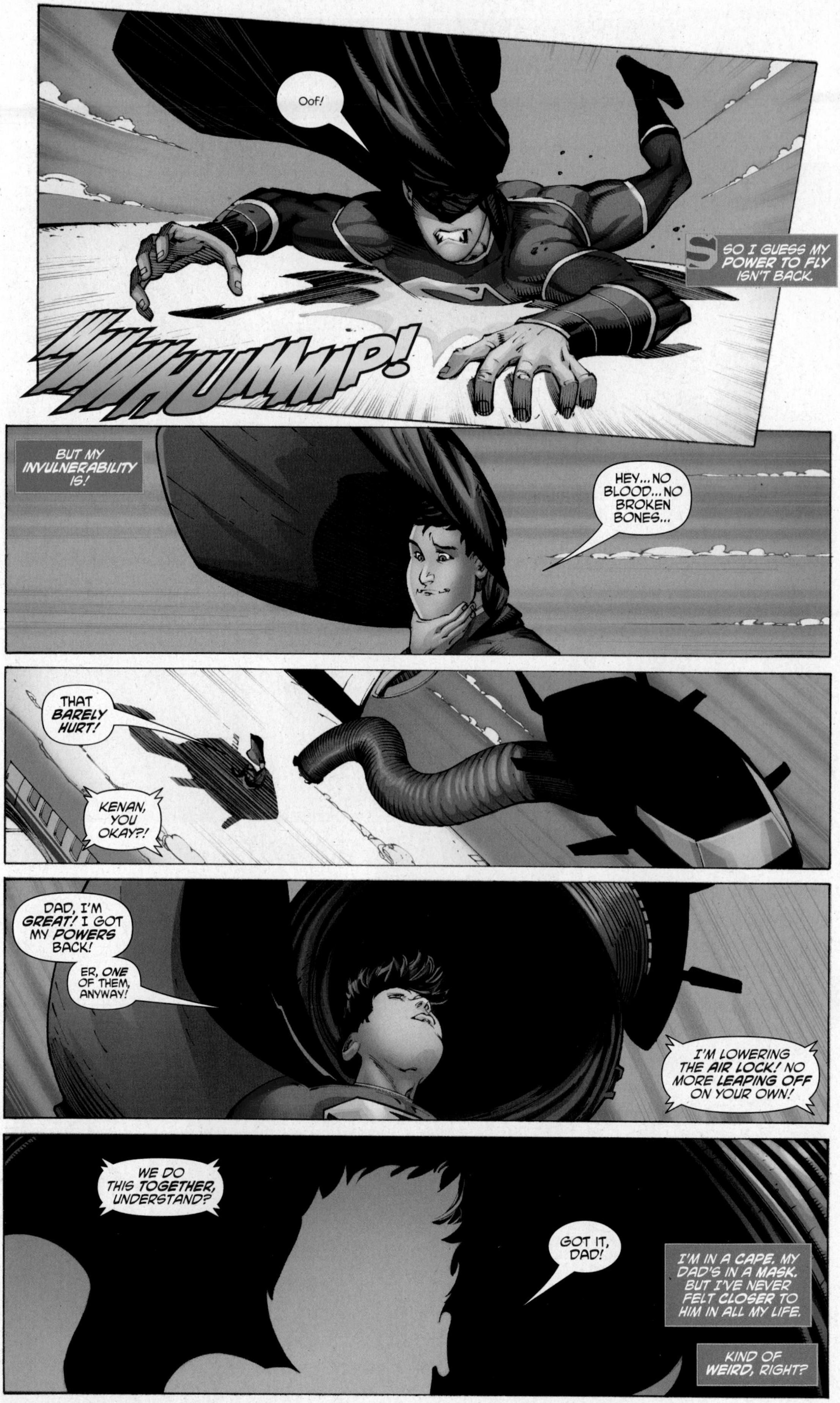
Oof!
SO I GUESS MY POWER TO FLY ISN'T BACK.
WWHUMMP!
BUT MY INVULNERABILITY IS!
HEY...NO BLOOD...NO BROKEN BONES...
THAT BARELY HURT!
KENAN, YOU OKAY?!
DAD, I'M GREAT! I GOT MY POWERS BACK!
ER, ONE OF THEM, ANYWAY!
I'M LOWERING THE AIR LOCK! NO MORE LEAPING OFF ON YOUR OWN!
WE DO THIS TOGETHER, UNDERSTAND?
GOT IT, DAD!
I'M IN A CAPE, MY DAD'S IN A MASK. BUT I'VE NEVER FELT CLOSER TO HIM IN ALL MY LIFE.
KIND OF WEIRD, RIGHT?

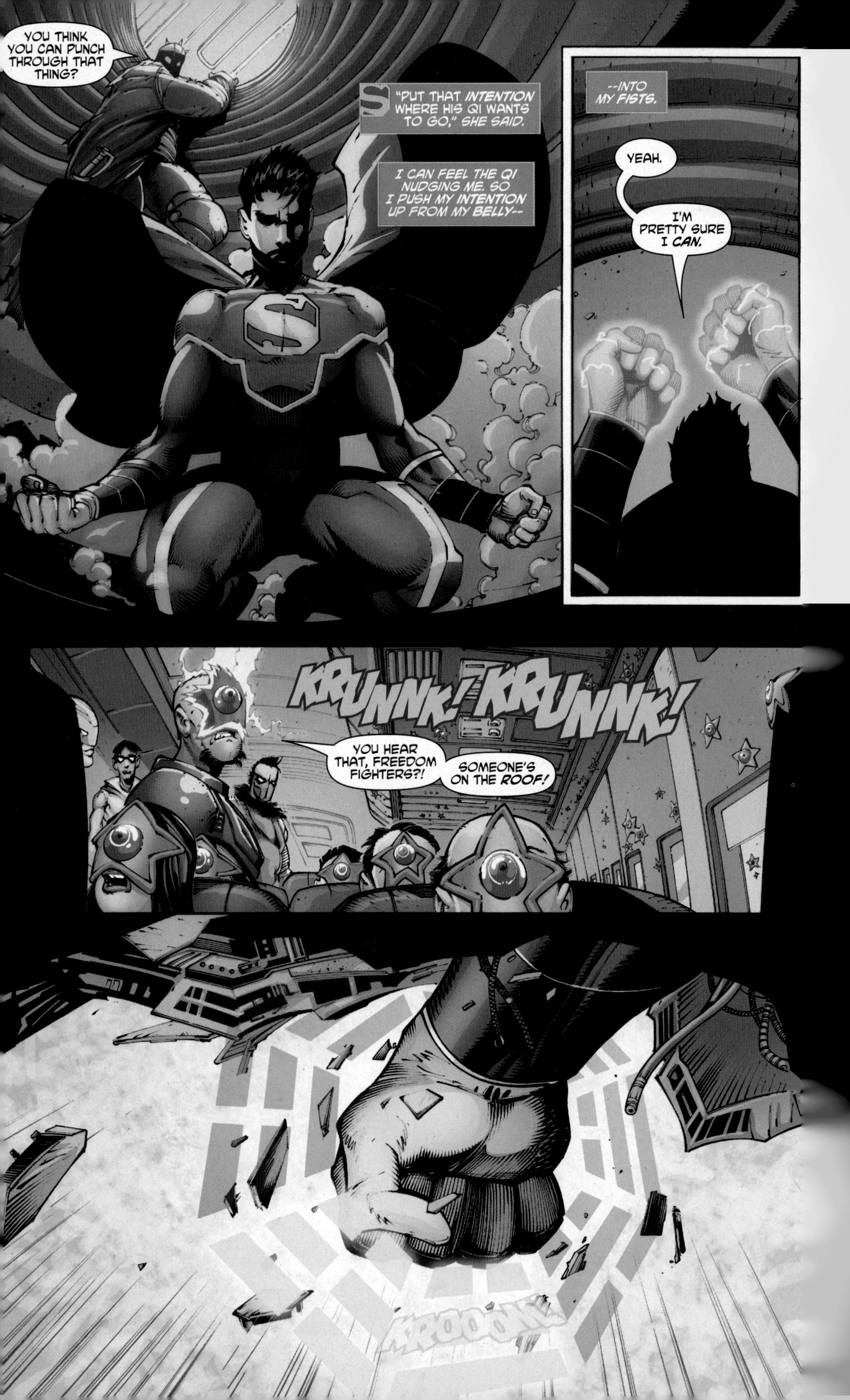

YOU THINK YOU CAN PUNCH THROUGH THAT THING?
"PUT THAT *INTENTION* WHERE HIS QI WANTS TO GO," SHE SAID.
I CAN FEEL THE QI NUDGING ME. SO I PUSH MY *INTENTION* UP FROM MY *BELLY*--
--INTO MY *FISTS.*
YEAH.
I'M PRETTY SURE I *CAN.*
KRUNNK! KRUNNK!
YOU HEAR THAT, FREEDOM FIGHTERS?!
SOMEONE'S ON THE *ROOF!*

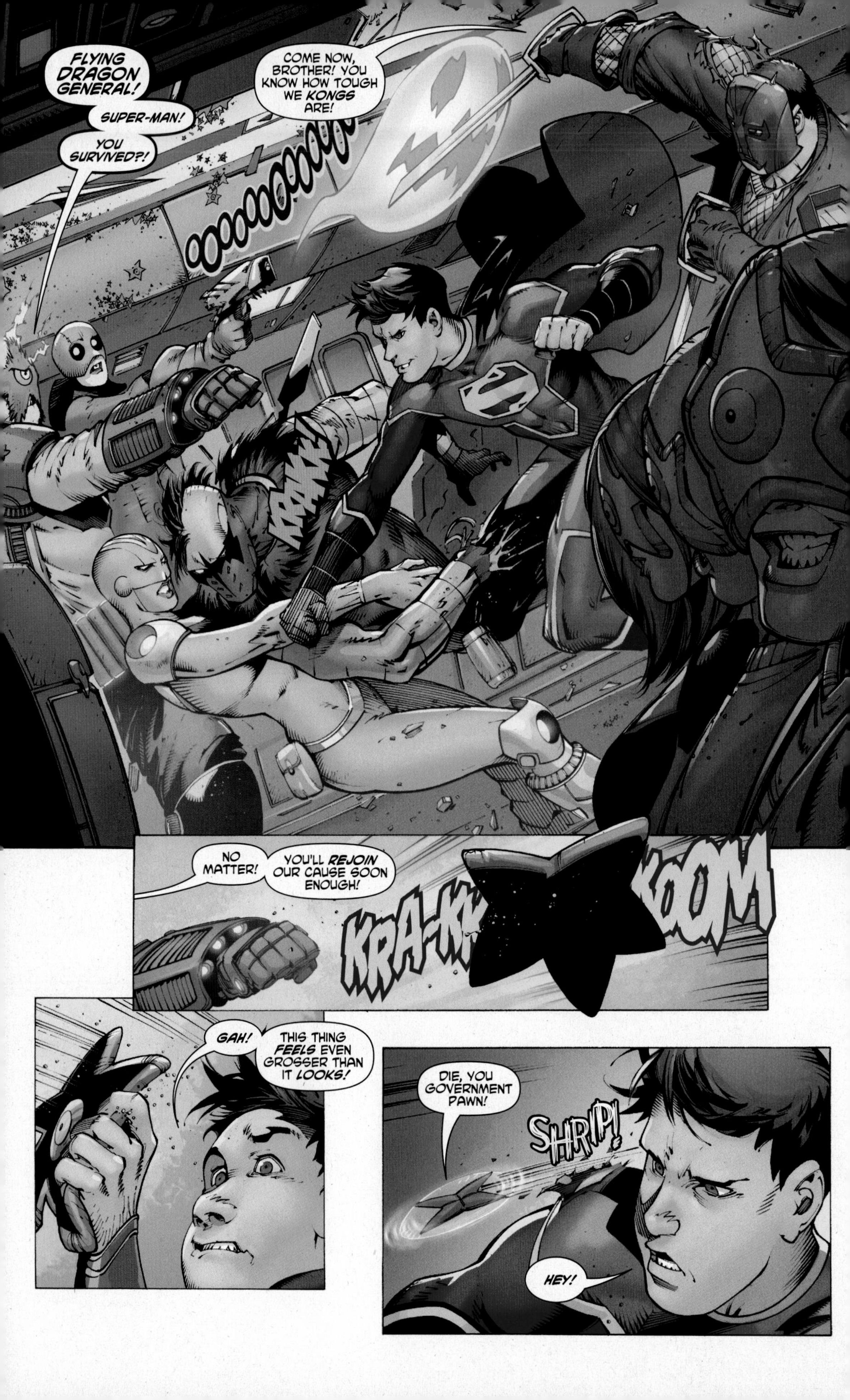
FLYING DRAGON GENERAL!
SUPER-MAN!
YOU SURVIVED?!
COME NOW, BROTHER! YOU KNOW HOW TOUGH WE KONGS ARE!
KRAKK!
NO MATTER!
YOU'LL REJOIN OUR CAUSE SOON ENOUGH!
KRA-KOOM
GAH!
THIS THING FEELS EVEN GROSSER THAN IT LOOKS!
DIE, YOU GOVERNMENT PAWN!
SHRIP!
HEY!

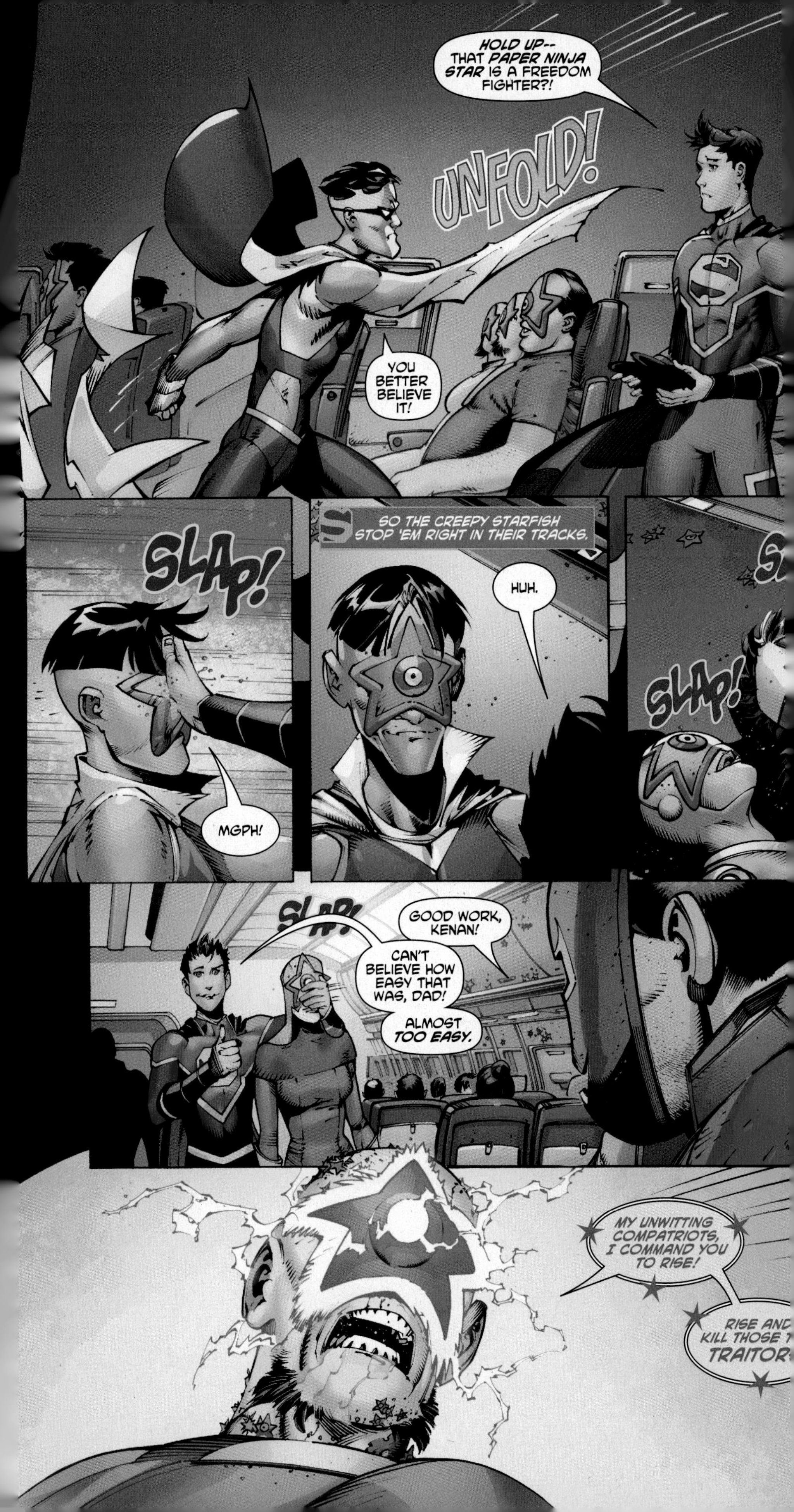

HOLD UP-- THAT PAPER NINJA STAR IS A FREEDOM FIGHTER?!
UNFOLD!
YOU BETTER BELIEVE IT!
SLAP!
MGPH!
SO THE CREEPY STARFISH STOP 'EM RIGHT IN THEIR TRACKS.
HUH.
SLAP!
SLAP!
GOOD WORK, KENAN!
CAN'T BELIEVE HOW EASY THAT WAS, DAD!
ALMOST TOO EASY.
MY UNWITTING COMPATRIOTS, I COMMAND YOU TO RISE!

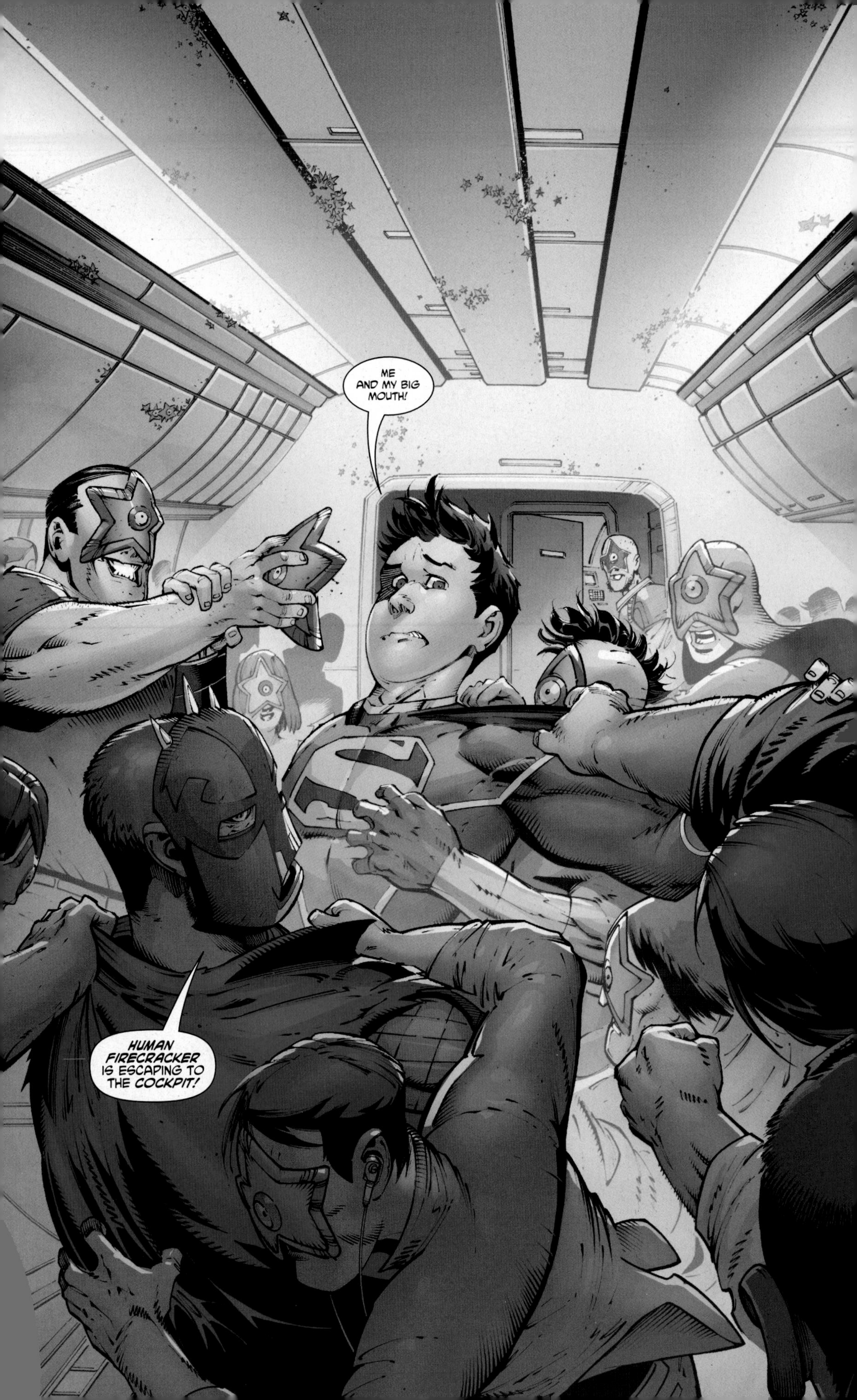
ME AND MY BIG MOUTH!
HUMAN FIRECRACKER IS ESCAPING TO THE COCKPIT!

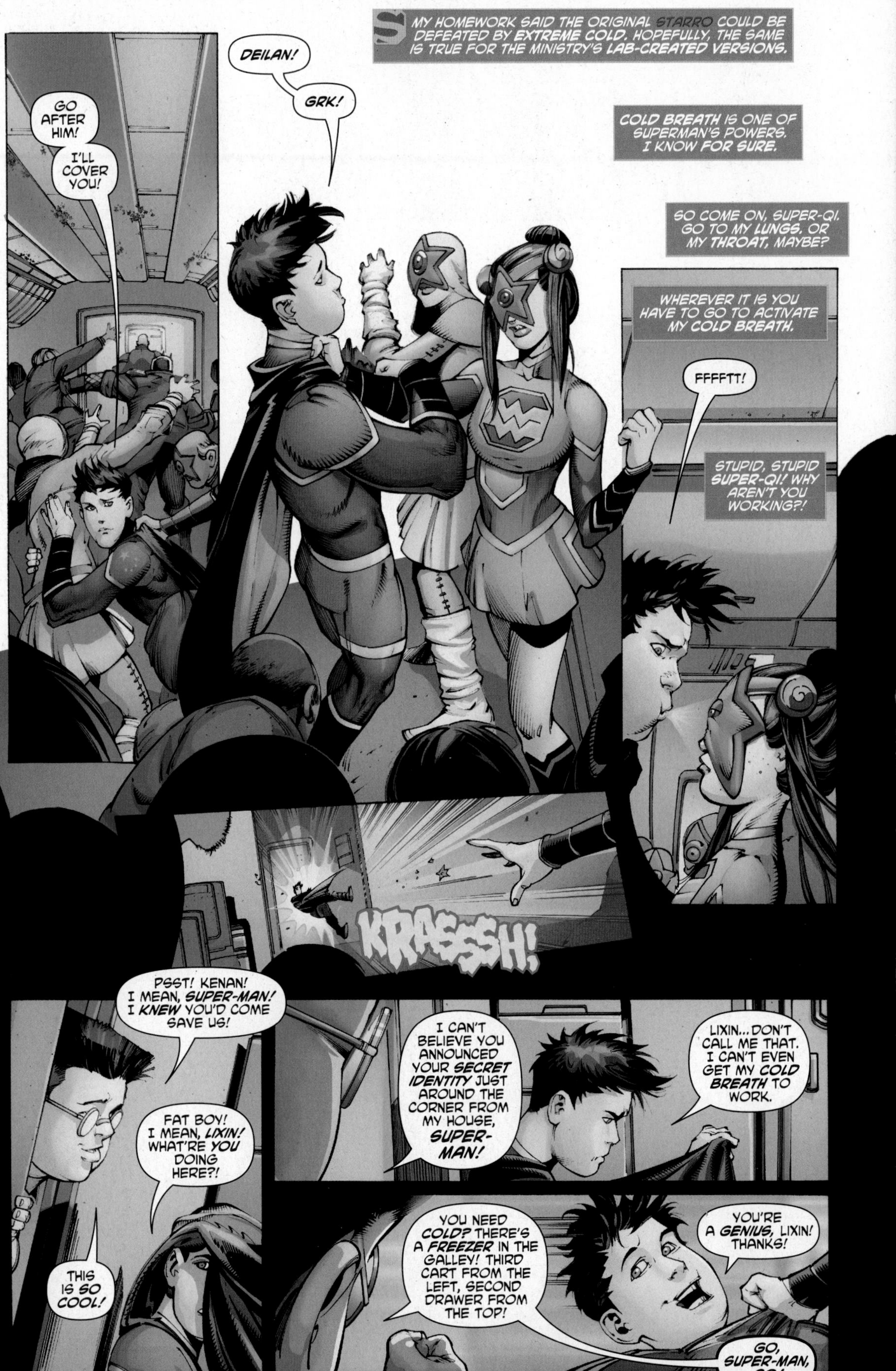
MY HOMEWORK SAID THE ORIGINAL STARRO COULD BE DEFEATED BY EXTREME COLD. HOPEFULLY, THE SAME IS TRUE FOR THE MINISTRY'S LAB-CREATED VERSIONS.
GO AFTER HIM! I'LL COVER YOU!
DEILAN!
GRK!
COLD BREATH IS ONE OF SUPERMAN'S POWERS. I KNOW FOR SURE.
SO COME ON, SUPER-QI. GO TO MY LUNGS. OR MY THROAT, MAYBE?
WHEREVER IT IS YOU HAVE TO GO TO ACTIVATE MY COLD BREATH.
FFFFTT!
STUPID, STUPID SUPER-QI! WHY AREN'T YOU WORKING?!
KRASSSH!
PSST! KENAN! I MEAN, SUPER-MAN! I KNEW YOU'D COME SAVE US!
FAT BOY! I MEAN, LIXIN! WHAT'RE YOU DOING HERE?!
THIS IS SO COOL!
I CAN'T BELIEVE YOU ANNOUNCED YOUR SECRET IDENTITY JUST AROUND THE CORNER FROM MY HOUSE, SUPER-MAN!
LIXIN... DON'T CALL ME THAT. I CAN'T EVEN GET MY COLD BREATH TO WORK.
YOU NEED COLD? THERE'S A FREEZER IN THE GALLEY! THIRD CART FROM THE LEFT, SECOND DRAWER FROM THE TOP!
YOU'RE A GENIUS, LIXIN! THANKS!
GO, SUPER-MAN, GO!

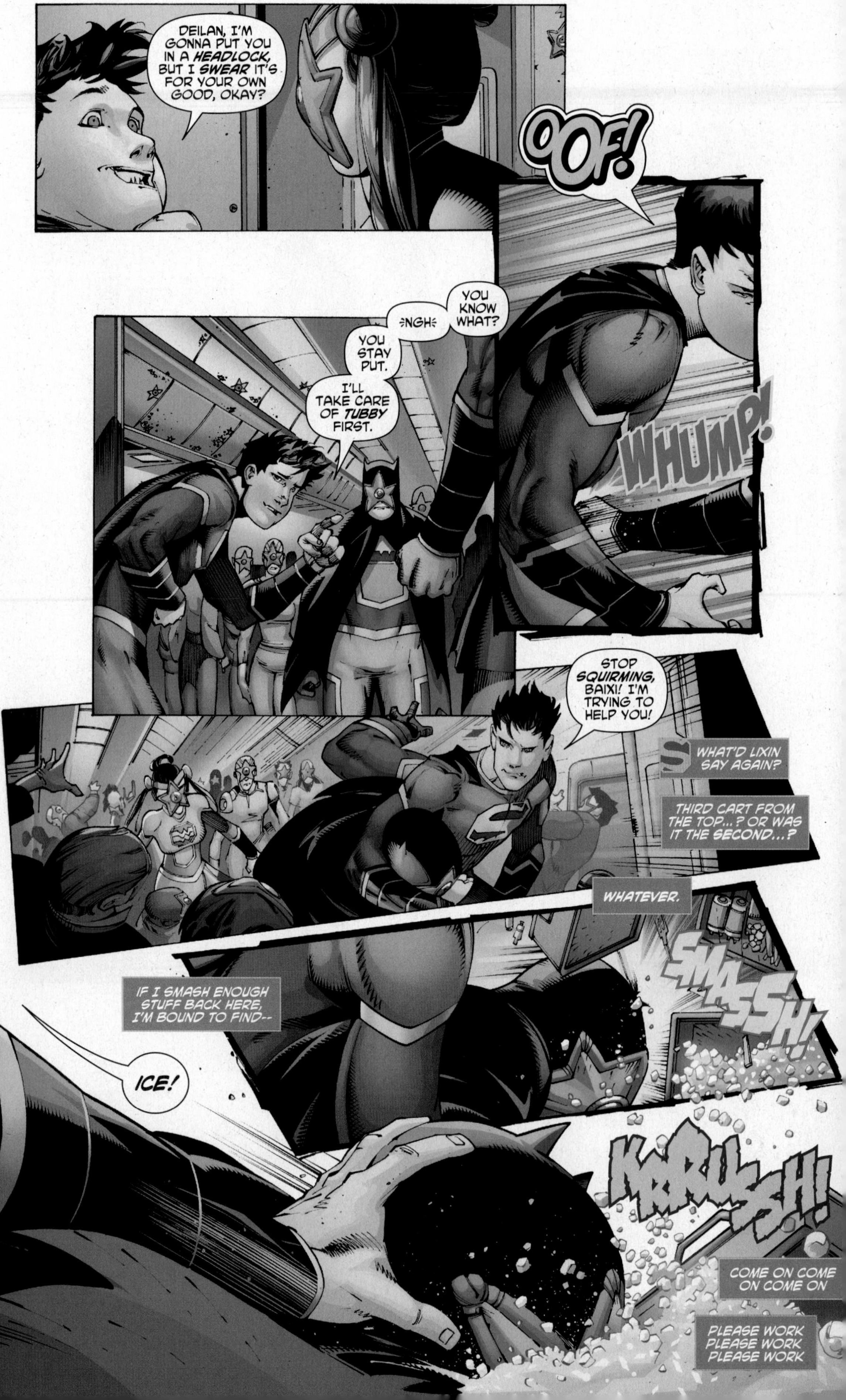
DEILAN, I'M GONNA PUT YOU IN A HEADLOCK, BUT I SWEAR IT'S FOR YOUR OWN GOOD, OKAY?
OOF!
WHUMP!
NGH
YOU KNOW WHAT?
YOU STAY PUT.
I'LL TAKE CARE OF TUBBY FIRST.
STOP SQUIRMING, BAIXI! I'M TRYING TO HELP YOU!
WHAT'D LIXIN SAY AGAIN?
THIRD CART FROM THE TOP...? OR WAS IT THE SECOND...?
WHATEVER.
SMASSH!
IF I SMASH ENOUGH STUFF BACK HERE, I'M BOUND TO FIND--
ICE!
KRUSSH!
COME ON COME ON COME ON
PLEASE WORK PLEASE WORK PLEASE WORK

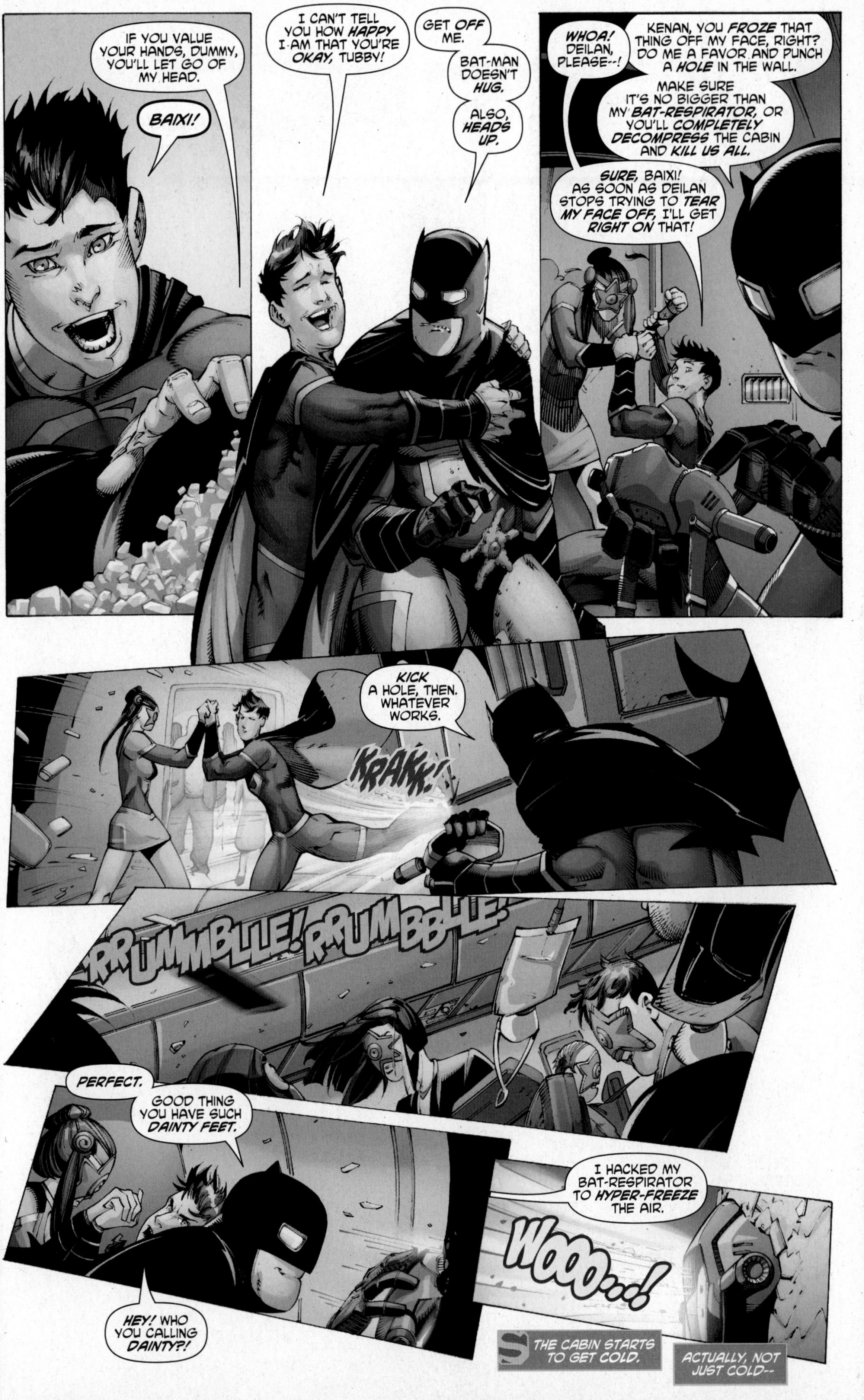
IF YOU VALUE YOUR HANDS, DUMMY, YOU'LL LET GO OF MY HEAD.
BAIXI!
I CAN'T TELL YOU HOW HAPPY I AM THAT YOU'RE OKAY, TUBBY!
GET OFF ME.
BAT-MAN DOESN'T HUG.
ALSO, HEADS UP.
WHOA! DEILAN, PLEASE--!
KENAN, YOU FROZE THAT THING OFF MY FACE, RIGHT? DO ME A FAVOR AND PUNCH A HOLE IN THE WALL.
MAKE SURE IT'S NO BIGGER THAN MY BAT-RESPIRATOR, OR YOU'LL COMPLETELY DECOMPRESS THE CABIN AND KILL US ALL.
SURE, BAIXI! AS SOON AS DEILAN STOPS TRYING TO TEAR MY FACE OFF, I'LL GET RIGHT ON THAT!
KICK A HOLE, THEN. WHATEVER WORKS.
KRAKK!
RRUMMBLLE! RRUMBBLLE!
PERFECT.
GOOD THING YOU HAVE SUCH DAINTY FEET.
HEY! WHO YOU CALLING DAINTY?!
I HACKED MY BAT-RESPIRATOR TO HYPER-FREEZE THE AIR.
WOOO...!
THE CABIN STARTS TO GET COLD.
ACTUALLY, NOT JUST COLD--

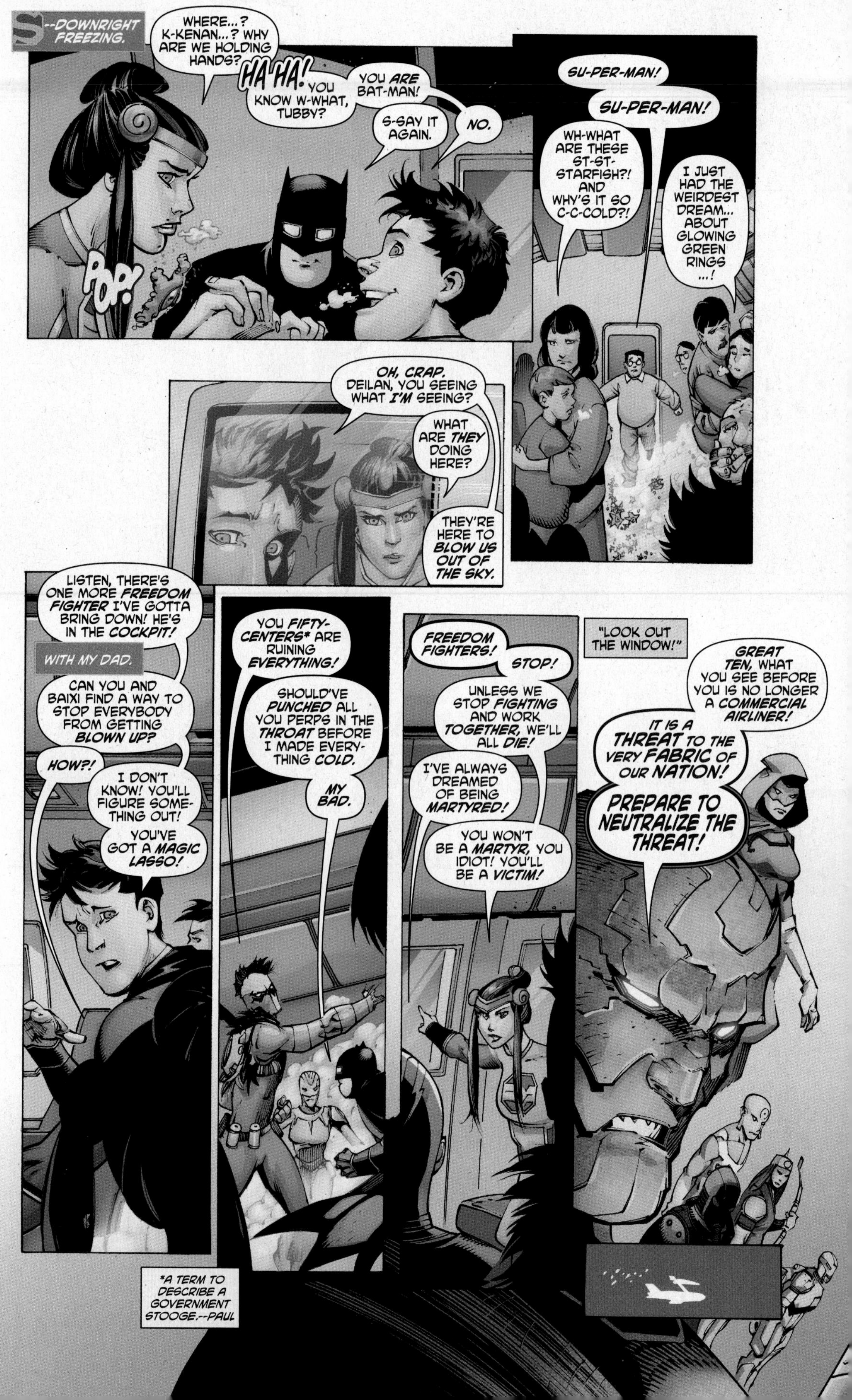
S--DOWNRIGHT FREEZING.
WHERE...? K-KENAN...? WHY ARE WE HOLDING HANDS?
HA HA!
YOU KNOW W-WHAT, TUBBY?
YOU ARE BAT-MAN!
S-SAY IT AGAIN.
NO.
POP!
SU-PER-MAN!
SU-PER-MAN!
WH-WHAT ARE THESE ST-ST-STARFISH?! AND WHY'S IT SO C-C-COLD?!
I JUST HAD THE WEIRDEST DREAM... ABOUT GLOWING GREEN RINGS ...!
OH, CRAP. DEILAN, YOU SEEING WHAT I'M SEEING?
WHAT ARE THEY DOING HERE?
THEY'RE HERE TO BLOW US OUT OF THE SKY.
LISTEN, THERE'S ONE MORE FREEDOM FIGHTER I'VE GOTTA BRING DOWN! HE'S IN THE COCKPIT!
WITH MY DAD.
CAN YOU AND BAIXI FIND A WAY TO STOP EVERYBODY FROM GETTING BLOWN UP?
HOW?!
I DON'T KNOW! YOU'LL FIGURE SOMETHING OUT!
YOU'VE GOT A MAGIC LASSO!
YOU FIFTY-CENTERS* ARE RUINING EVERYTHING!
SHOULD'VE PUNCHED ALL YOU PERPS IN THE THROAT BEFORE I MADE EVERYTHING COLD.
MY BAD.
*A TERM TO DESCRIBE A GOVERNMENT STOOGE.--PAUL
FREEDOM FIGHTERS!
STOP!
UNLESS WE STOP FIGHTING AND WORK TOGETHER, WE'LL ALL DIE!
I'VE ALWAYS DREAMED OF BEING MARTYRED!
YOU WON'T BE A MARTYR, YOU IDIOT! YOU'LL BE A VICTIM!
"LOOK OUT THE WINDOW!"
GREAT TEN, WHAT YOU SEE BEFORE YOU IS NO LONGER A COMMERCIAL AIRLINER!
IT IS A THREAT TO THE VERY FABRIC OF OUR NATION!
PREPARE TO NEUTRALIZE THE THREAT!

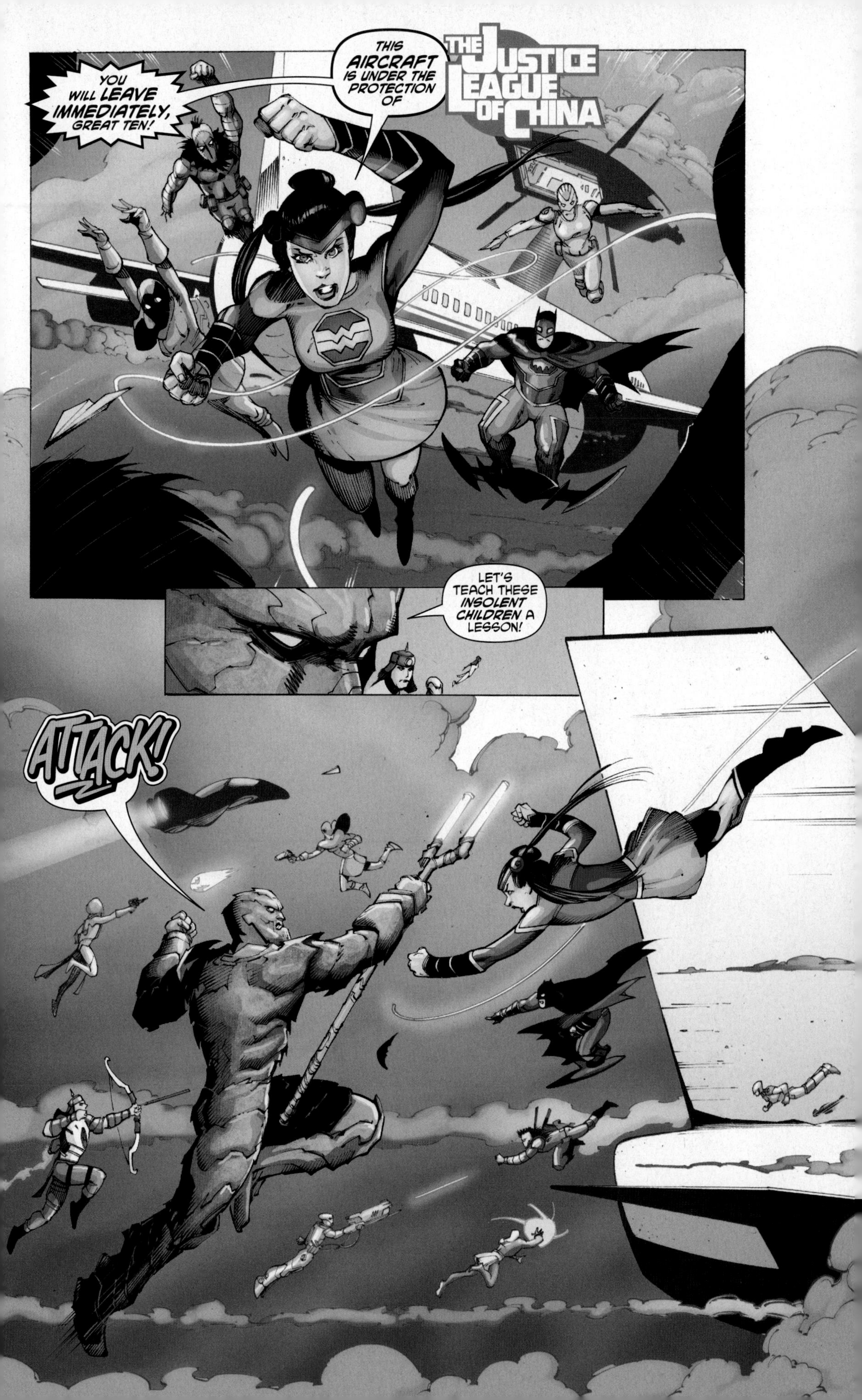
YOU WILL LEAVE IMMEDIATELY, GREAT TEN!
THIS AIRCRAFT IS UNDER THE PROTECTION OF
THE JUSTICE LEAGUE OF CHINA
LET'S TEACH THESE INSOLENT CHILDREN A LESSON!
ATTACK!

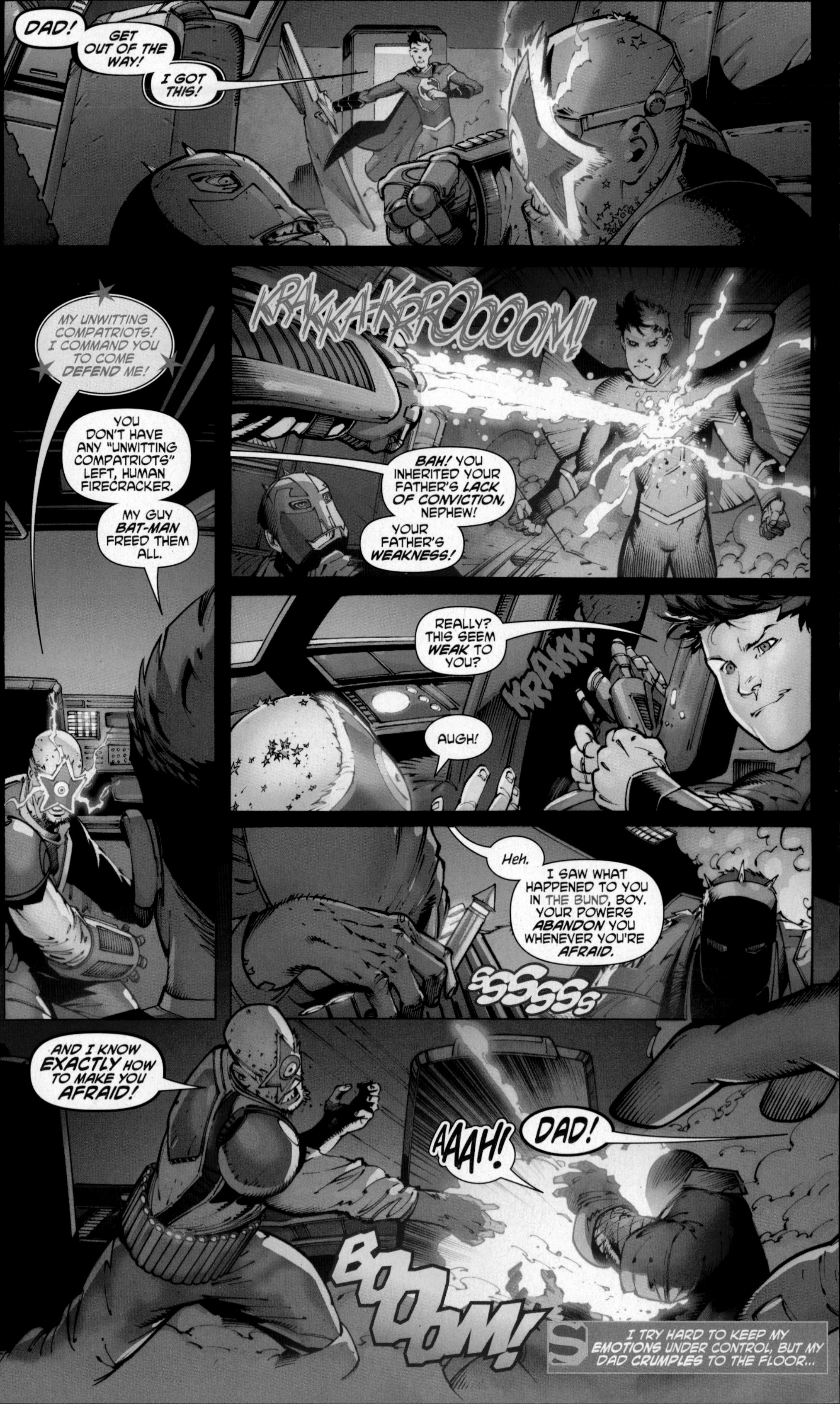

DAD!
GET OUT OF THE WAY!
I GOT THIS!
KRAKKA-KROOOOOM!
MY UNWITTING COMPATRIOTS! I COMMAND YOU TO COME DEFEND ME!
YOU DON'T HAVE ANY "UNWITTING COMPATRIOTS" LEFT, HUMAN FIRECRACKER.
MY GUY BAT-MAN FREED THEM ALL.
BAH! YOU INHERITED YOUR FATHER'S LACK OF CONVICTION, NEPHEW!
YOUR FATHER'S WEAKNESS!
REALLY? THIS SEEM WEAK TO YOU?
KRAKK
AUGH!
Heh.
I SAW WHAT HAPPENED TO YOU IN THE BUND, BOY. YOUR POWERS ABANDON YOU WHENEVER YOU'RE AFRAID.
SSSSSS
AND I KNOW EXACTLY HOW TO MAKE YOU AFRAID!
AAAH!
DAD!
BOOOOM!
I TRY HARD TO KEEP MY EMOTIONS UNDER CONTROL, BUT MY DAD CRUMPLES TO THE FLOOR...

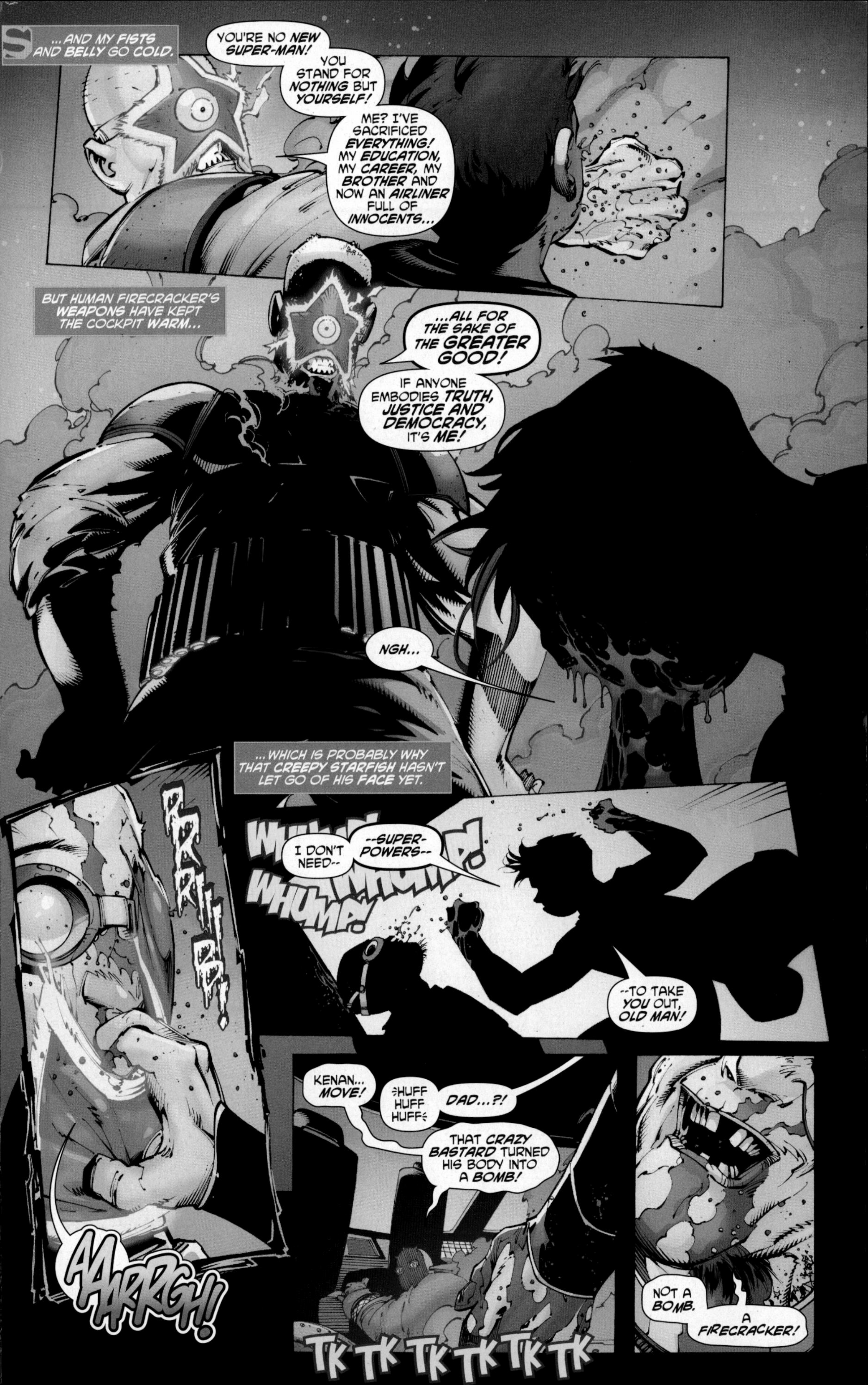
...AND MY FISTS AND BELLY GO COLD.
YOU'RE NO NEW SUPER-MAN!
YOU STAND FOR NOTHING BUT YOURSELF!
ME? I'VE SACRIFICED EVERYTHING! MY EDUCATION, MY CAREER, MY BROTHER AND NOW AN AIRLINER FULL OF INNOCENTS...
BUT HUMAN FIRECRACKER'S WEAPONS HAVE KEPT THE COCKPIT WARM...
...ALL FOR THE SAKE OF THE GREATER GOOD!
IF ANYONE EMBODIES TRUTH, JUSTICE AND DEMOCRACY, IT'S ME!
NGH...
...WHICH IS PROBABLY WHY THAT CREEPY STARFISH HASN'T LET GO OF HIS FACE YET.
RRRIIIBB!
WHUMP!
I DON'T NEED--
--SUPER-POWERS--
WHUMP!
WHUMP!
--TO TAKE YOU OUT, OLD MAN!
AAARRGH!
KENAN... MOVE!
HUFF HUFF HUFF
DAD...?!
THAT CRAZY BASTARD TURNED HIS BODY INTO A BOMB!
TK TK TK TK TK TK
NOT A BOMB.
A FIRECRACKER!

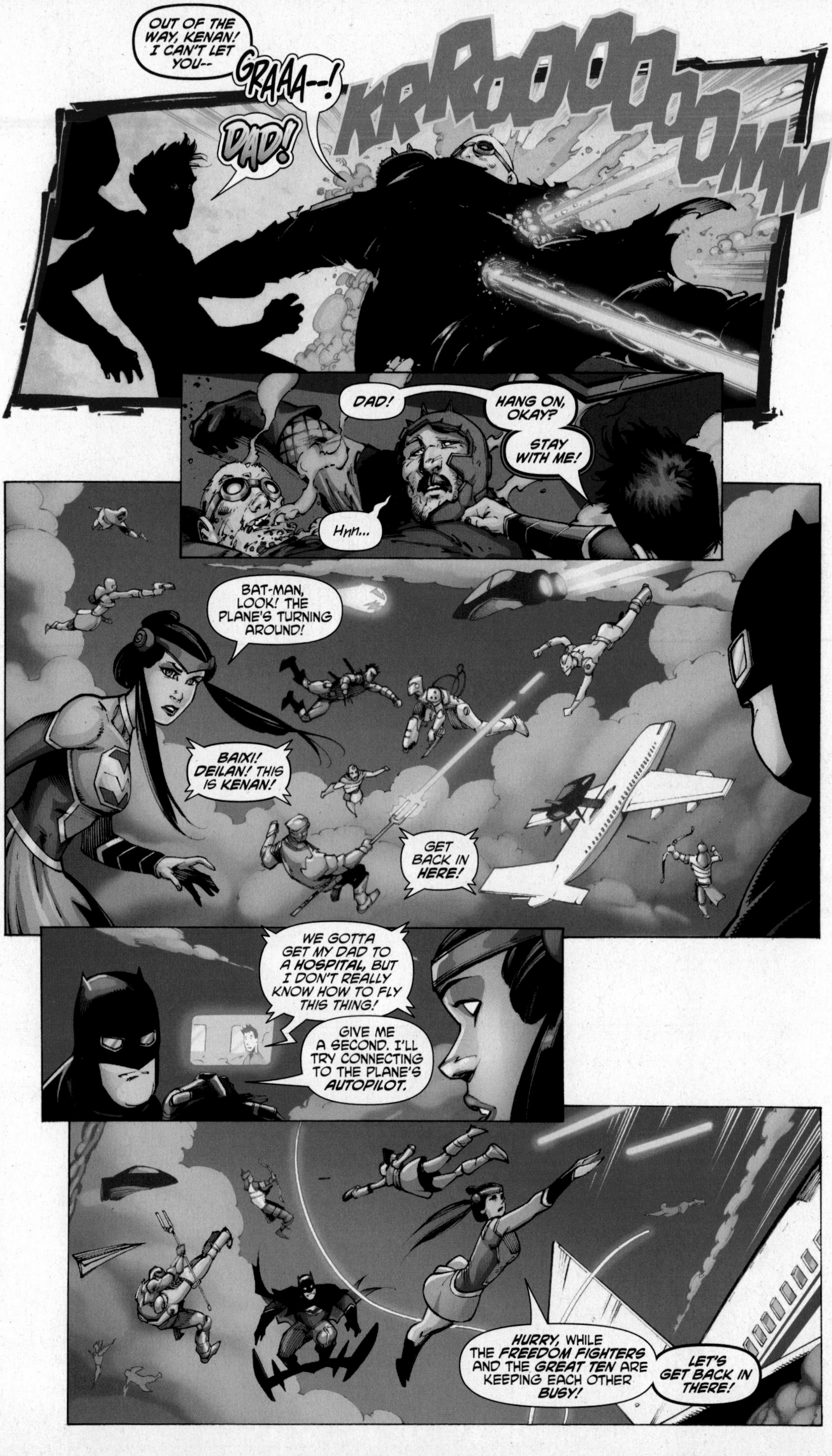
OUT OF THE WAY, KENAN! I CAN'T LET YOU--
GRAAA--!
KRROOOOOOOMM
DAD!
DAD!
HANG ON, OKAY?
STAY WITH ME!
Hnn...
BAT-MAN, LOOK! THE PLANE'S TURNING AROUND!
BAIXI! DEILAN! THIS IS KENAN!
GET BACK IN HERE!
WE GOTTA GET MY DAD TO A HOSPITAL, BUT I DON'T REALLY KNOW HOW TO FLY THIS THING!
GIVE ME A SECOND. I'LL TRY CONNECTING TO THE PLANE'S AUTOPILOT.
HURRY, WHILE THE FREEDOM FIGHTERS AND THE GREAT TEN ARE KEEPING EACH OTHER BUSY!
LET'S GET BACK IN THERE!

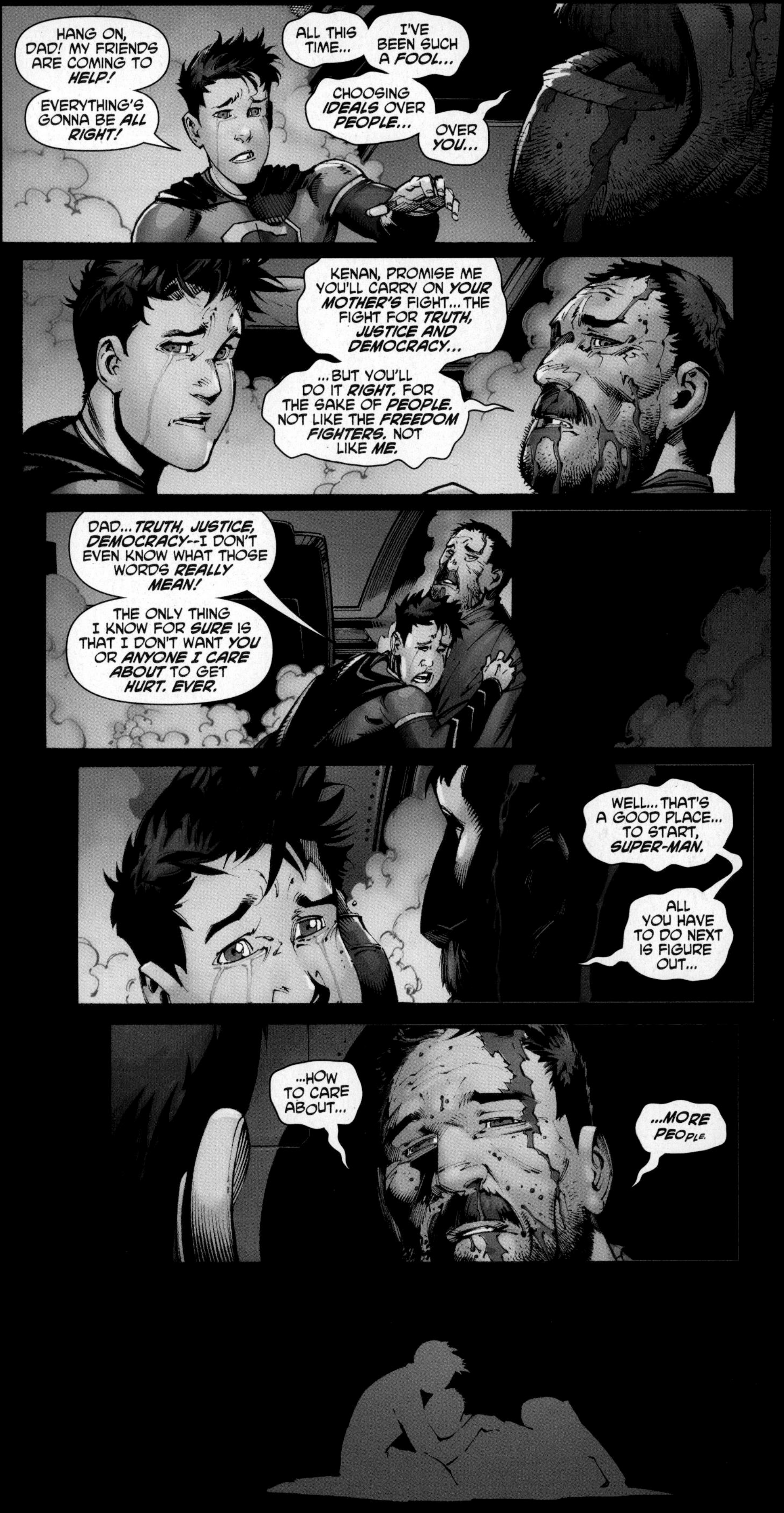
HANG ON, DAD! MY FRIENDS ARE COMING TO *HELP!*
EVERYTHING'S GONNA BE *ALL RIGHT!*
ALL THIS TIME...
I'VE BEEN SUCH A *FOOL*...
CHOOSING *IDEALS* OVER *PEOPLE*...
OVER *YOU*...
KENAN, PROMISE ME YOU'LL CARRY ON *YOUR MOTHER'S* FIGHT... THE FIGHT FOR *TRUTH, JUSTICE AND DEMOCRACY*...
...BUT YOU'LL DO IT *RIGHT*. FOR THE SAKE OF *PEOPLE*. NOT LIKE THE *FREEDOM FIGHTERS*. NOT LIKE *ME*.
DAD... *TRUTH, JUSTICE, DEMOCRACY*--I DON'T EVEN KNOW WHAT THOSE WORDS *REALLY MEAN!*
THE ONLY THING I KNOW FOR *SURE* IS THAT I DON'T WANT *YOU* OR *ANYONE I CARE ABOUT* TO GET *HURT. EVER.*
WELL... THAT'S A GOOD PLACE... TO START, *SUPER-MAN.*
ALL YOU HAVE TO DO NEXT IS FIGURE OUT...
...HOW TO CARE ABOUT...
...MORE PEOPLE.

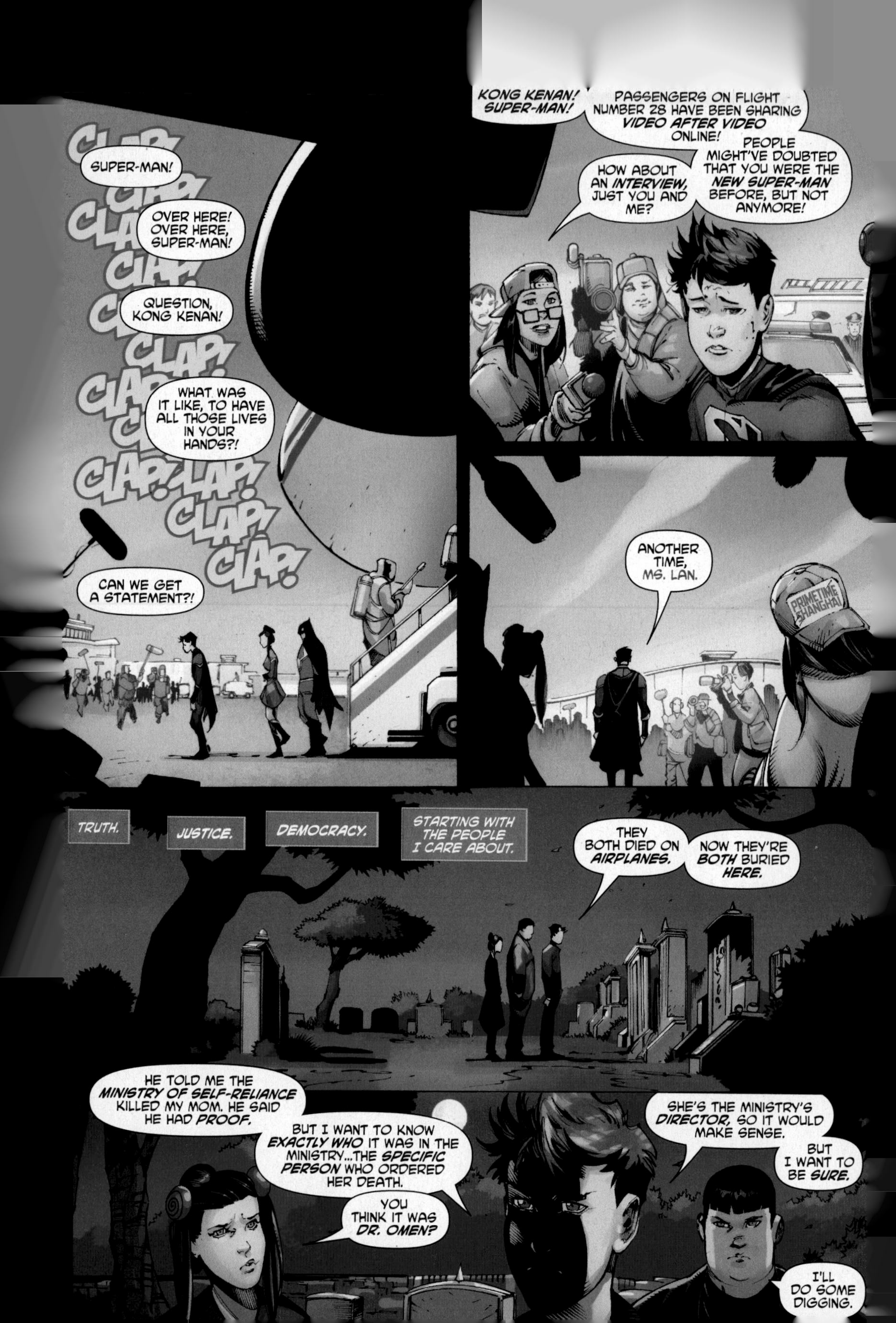

CLAP! CLAP! CLAP! CLAP! CLAP! CLAP! CLAP! CLAP! CLAP! CLAP! CLAP! CLAP!
SUPER-MAN!
OVER HERE! OVER HERE, SUPER-MAN!
QUESTION, KONG KENAN!
WHAT WAS IT LIKE, TO HAVE ALL THOSE LIVES IN YOUR HANDS?!
CAN WE GET A STATEMENT?!
KONG KENAN! SUPER-MAN!
PASSENGERS ON FLIGHT NUMBER 28 HAVE BEEN SHARING VIDEO AFTER VIDEO ONLINE!
PEOPLE MIGHT'VE DOUBTED THAT YOU WERE THE NEW SUPER-MAN BEFORE, BUT NOT ANYMORE!
HOW ABOUT AN INTERVIEW, JUST YOU AND ME?
ANOTHER TIME, MS. LAN.
PRIMETIME SHANGHAI
TRUTH.
JUSTICE.
DEMOCRACY.
STARTING WITH THE PEOPLE I CARE ABOUT.
THEY BOTH DIED ON AIRPLANES.
NOW THEY'RE BOTH BURIED HERE.
HE TOLD ME THE MINISTRY OF SELF-RELIANCE KILLED MY MOM. HE SAID HE HAD PROOF.
BUT I WANT TO KNOW EXACTLY WHO IT WAS IN THE MINISTRY...THE SPECIFIC PERSON WHO ORDERED HER DEATH.
YOU THINK IT WAS DR. OMEN?
SHE'S THE MINISTRY'S DIRECTOR, SO IT WOULD MAKE SENSE.
BUT I WANT TO BE SURE.
I'LL DO SOME DIGGING.

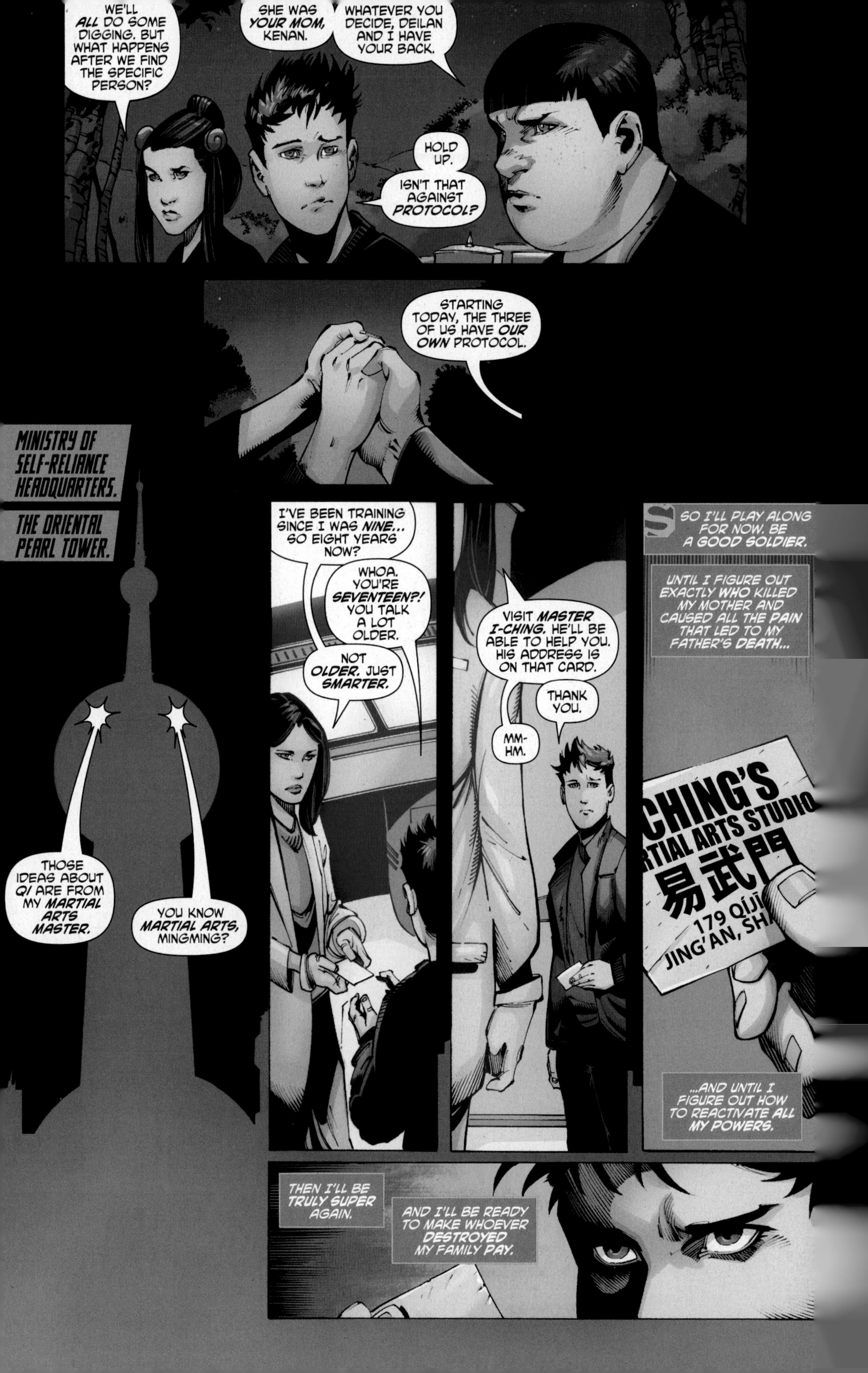
WE'LL ALL DO SOME DIGGING. BUT WHAT HAPPENS AFTER WE FIND THE SPECIFIC PERSON?
SHE WAS YOUR MOM, KENAN.
WHATEVER YOU DECIDE, DEILAN AND I HAVE YOUR BACK.
HOLD UP.
ISN'T THAT AGAINST PROTOCOL?
STARTING TODAY, THE THREE OF US HAVE OUR OWN PROTOCOL.
MINISTRY OF SELF-RELIANCE HEADQUARTERS.
THE ORIENTAL PEARL TOWER.
THOSE IDEAS ABOUT QI ARE FROM MY MARTIAL ARTS MASTER.
YOU KNOW MARTIAL ARTS, MINGMING?
I'VE BEEN TRAINING SINCE I WAS NINE... SO EIGHT YEARS NOW?
WHOA. YOU'RE SEVENTEEN?! YOU TALK A LOT OLDER.
NOT OLDER. JUST SMARTER.
VISIT MASTER I-CHING. HE'LL BE ABLE TO HELP YOU. HIS ADDRESS IS ON THAT CARD.
THANK YOU.
MM-HM.
SO I'LL PLAY ALONG FOR NOW. BE A GOOD SOLDIER.
UNTIL I FIGURE OUT EXACTLY WHO KILLED MY MOTHER AND CAUSED ALL THE PAIN THAT LED TO MY FATHER'S DEATH...
CHING'S
RTIAL ARTS STUDIO
易武門
179 QÍJ
JING'AN, SH
...AND UNTIL I FIGURE OUT HOW TO REACTIVATE ALL MY POWERS.
THEN I'LL BE TRULY SUPER AGAIN.
AND I'LL BE READY TO MAKE WHOEVER DESTROYED MY FAMILY PAY.

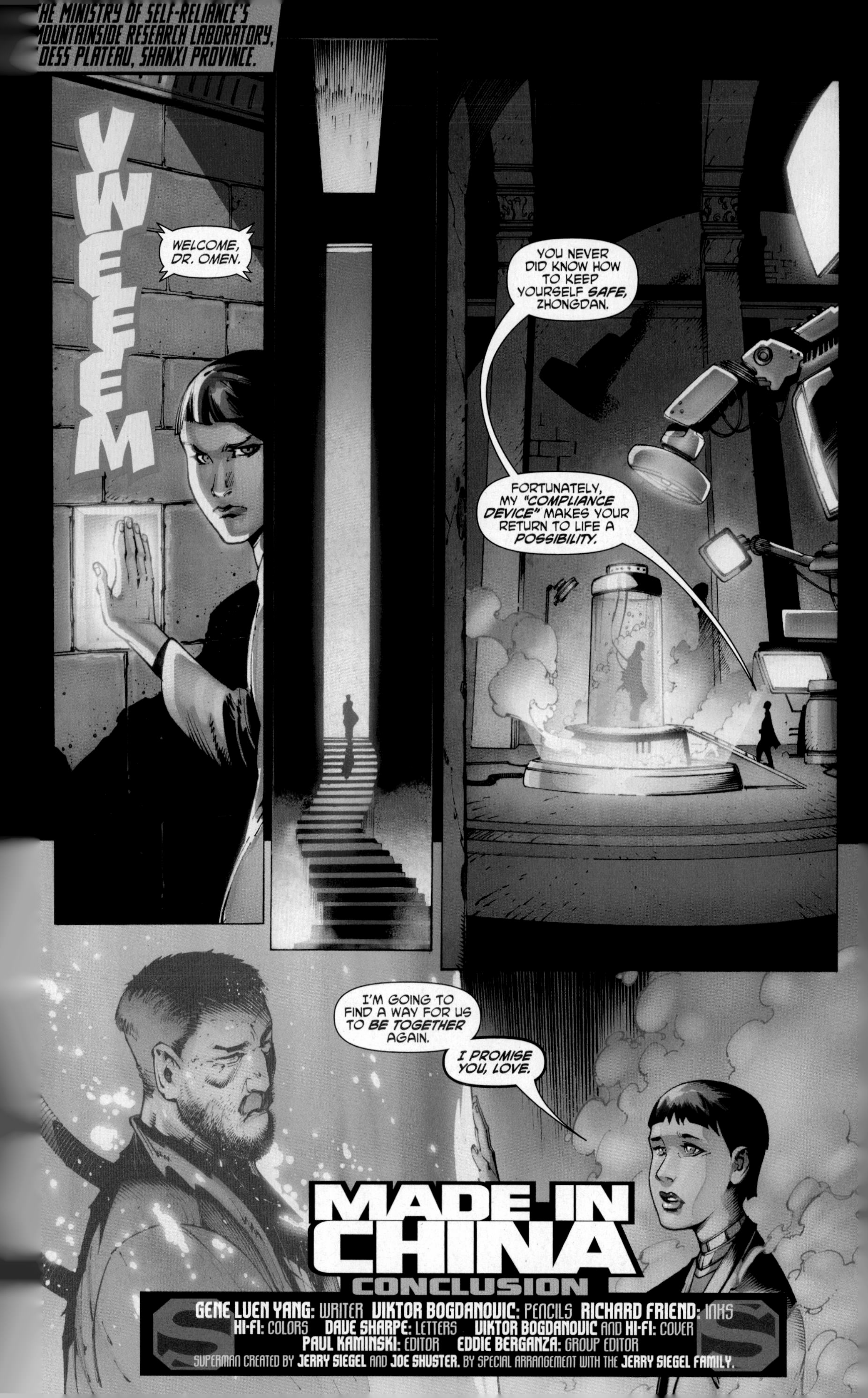

THE MINISTRY OF SELF-RELIANCE'S MOUNTAINSIDE RESEARCH LABORATORY, LOESS PLATEAU, SHANXI PROVINCE.
VWEEM
WELCOME, DR. OMEN.
YOU NEVER DID KNOW HOW TO KEEP YOURSELF SAFE, ZHONGDAN.
FORTUNATELY, MY "COMPLIANCE DEVICE" MAKES YOUR RETURN TO LIFE A POSSIBILITY.
I'M GOING TO FIND A WAY FOR US TO BE TOGETHER AGAIN.
I PROMISE YOU, LOVE.
MADE IN CHINA
CONCLUSION
GENE LUEN YANG: WRITER VIKTOR BOGDANOVIC: PENCILS RICHARD FRIEND: INKS
HI-FI: COLORS DAVE SHARPE: LETTERS VIKTOR BOGDANOVIC AND HI-FI: COVER
PAUL KAMINSKI: EDITOR EDDIE BERGANZA: GROUP EDITOR
SUPERMAN CREATED BY JERRY SIEGEL AND JOE SHUSTER. BY SPECIAL ARRANGEMENT WITH THE JERRY SIEGEL FAMILY.

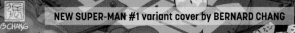
NEW SUPER-MAN #1 variant cover by BERNARD CHANG

NEW SUPER-MAN #2 variant cover by BERNARD CHANG

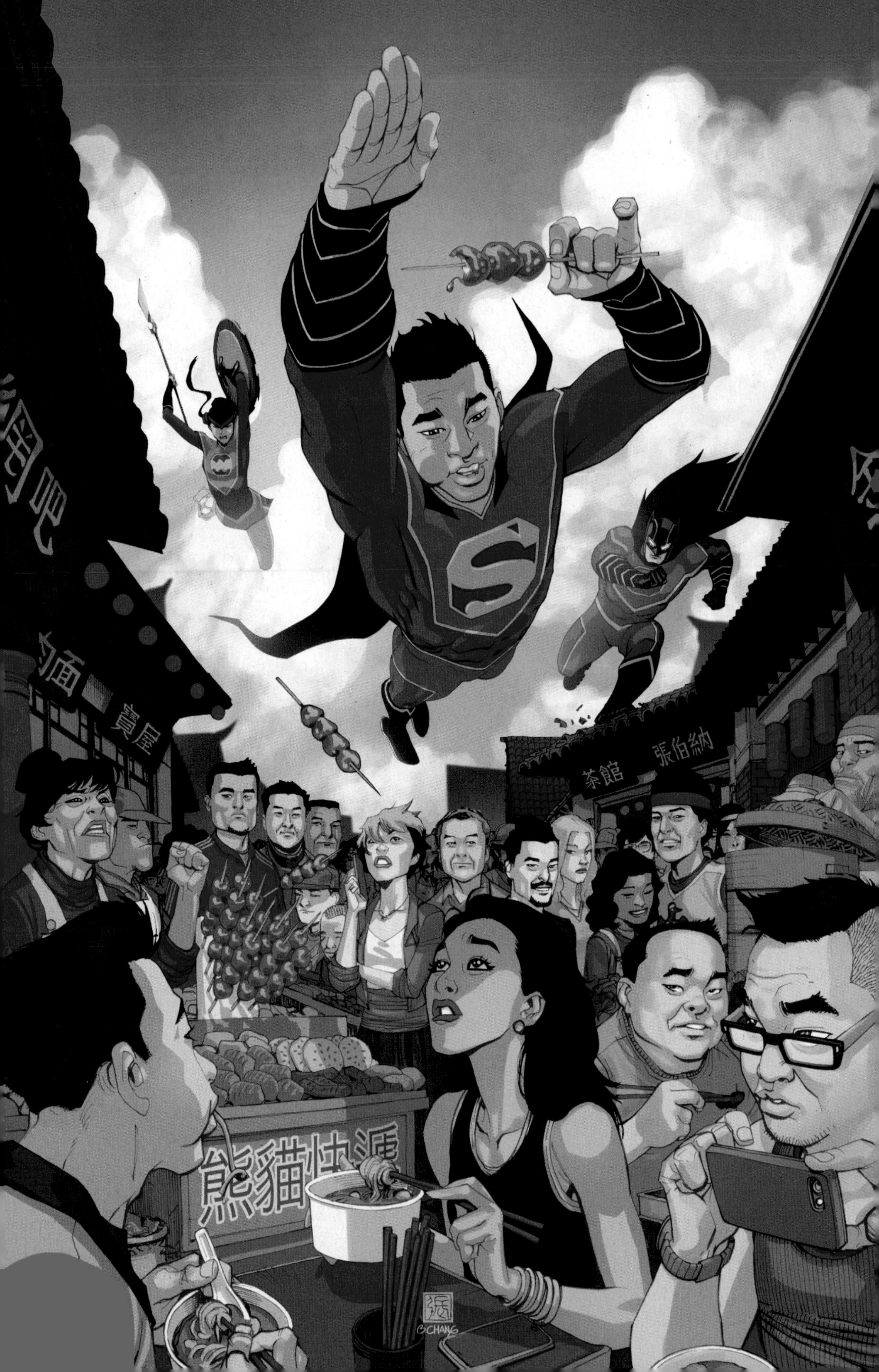
茶館
張伯納
熊貓快遞
B CHANG

NEW SUPER-MAN #3 variant cover by PHILIP TAN and ELMER SANTOS

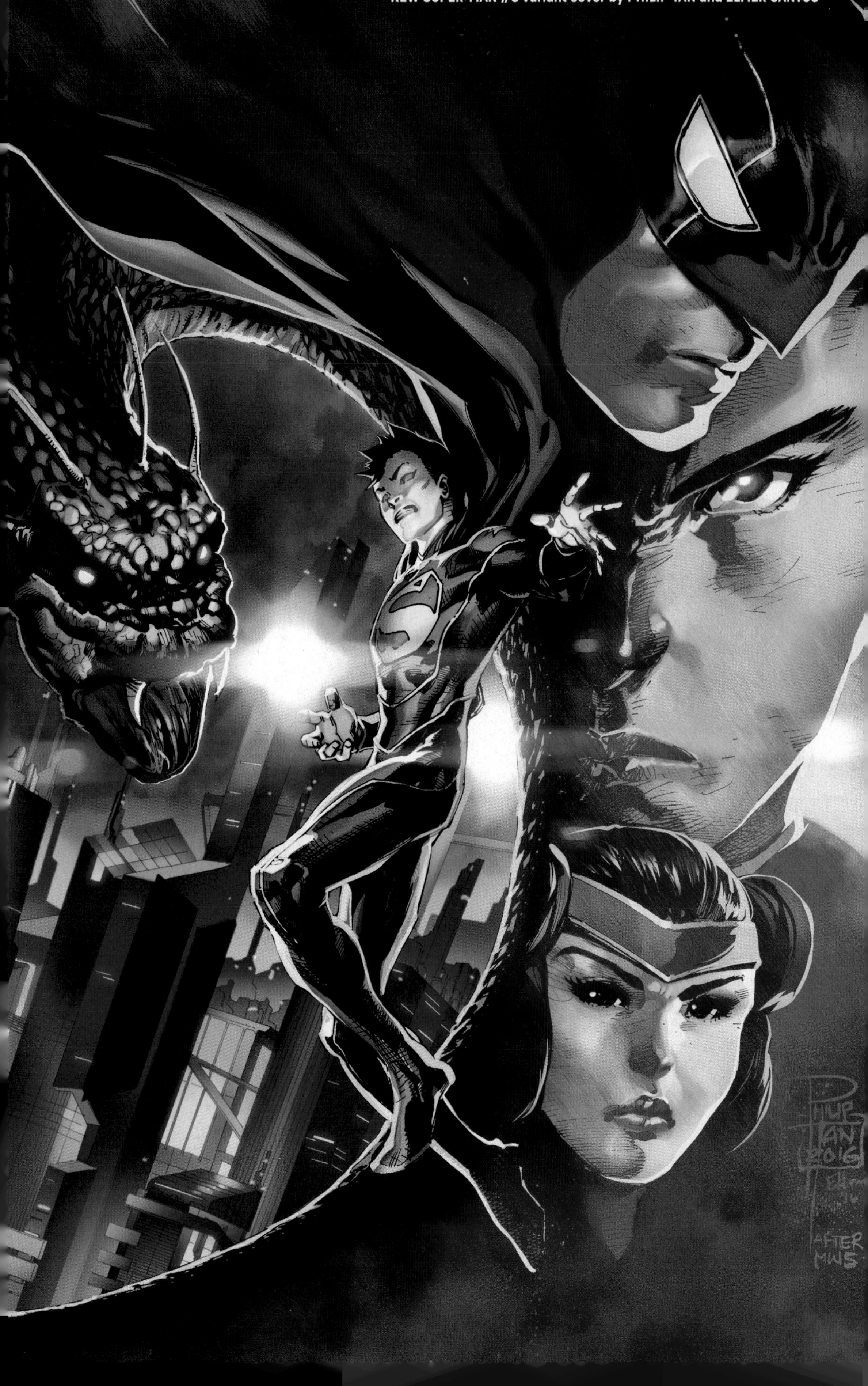

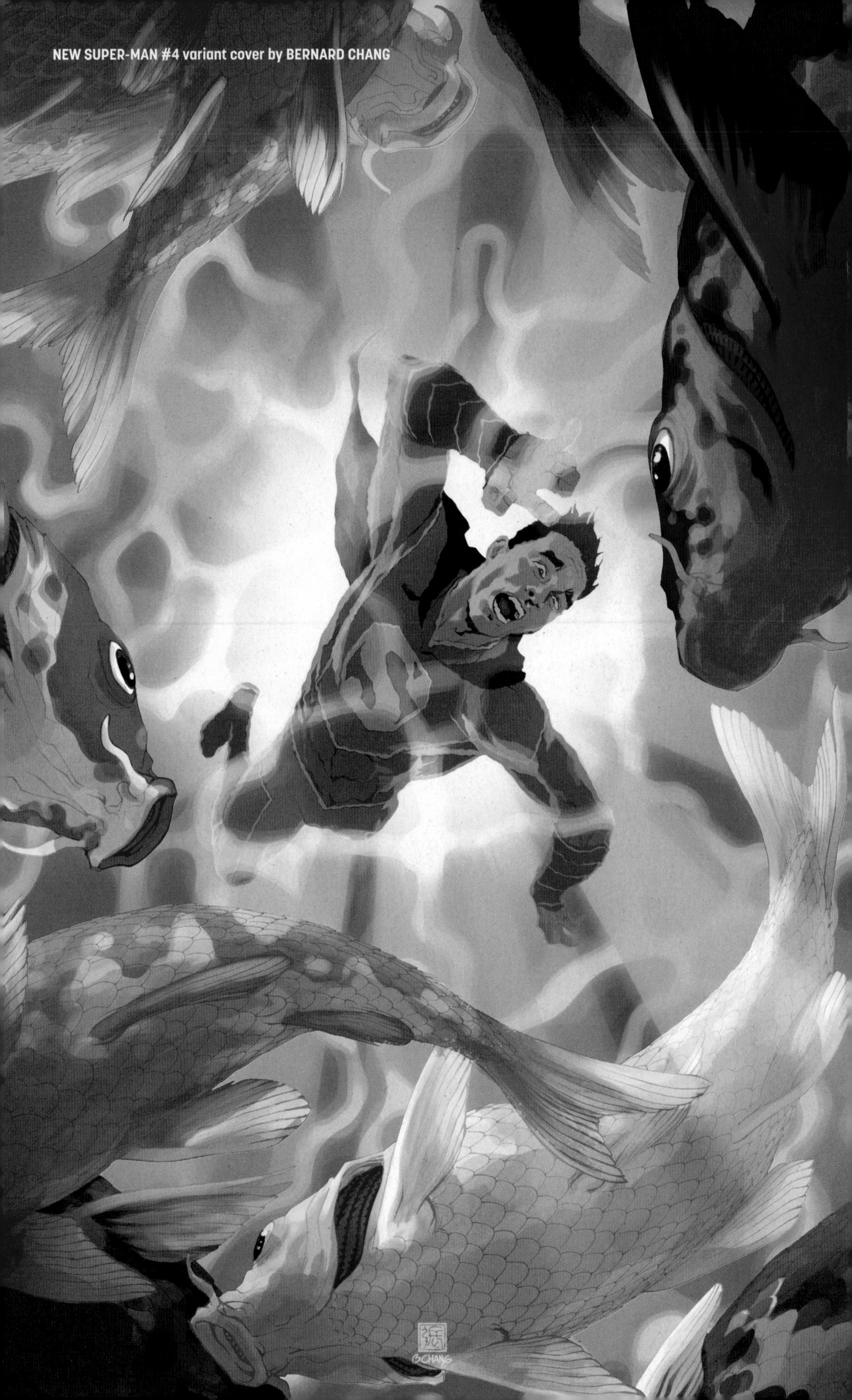
NEW SUPER-MAN #4 variant cover by BERNARD CHANG

NEW SUPER-MAN #5 variant cover by BERNARD CHANG

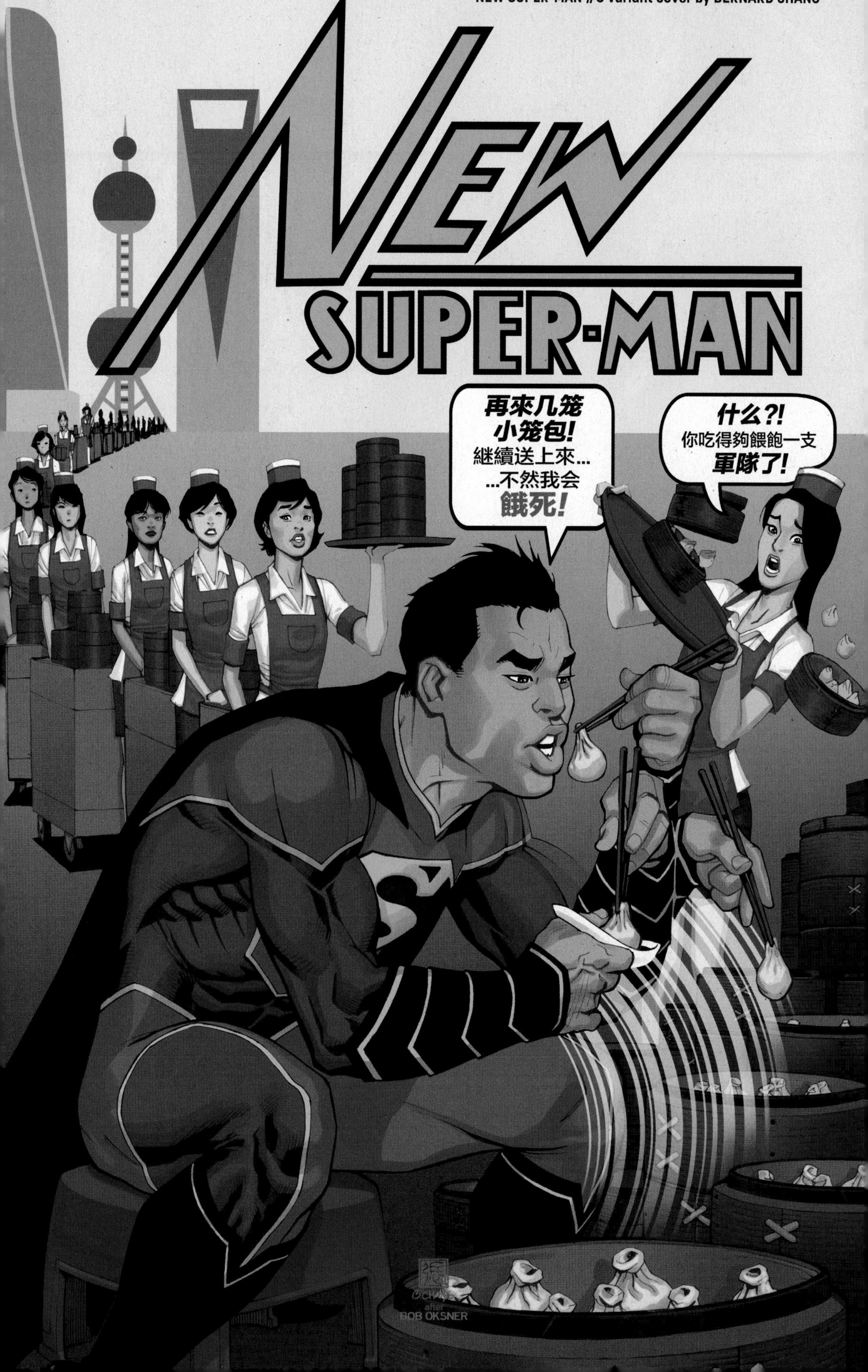
NEW
SUPER-MAN
再來几笼
小笼包!
継續送上來...
...不然我会
餓死!
什么?!
你吃得夠餵飽一支
軍隊了!
B.CHANG
after
BOB OKSNER

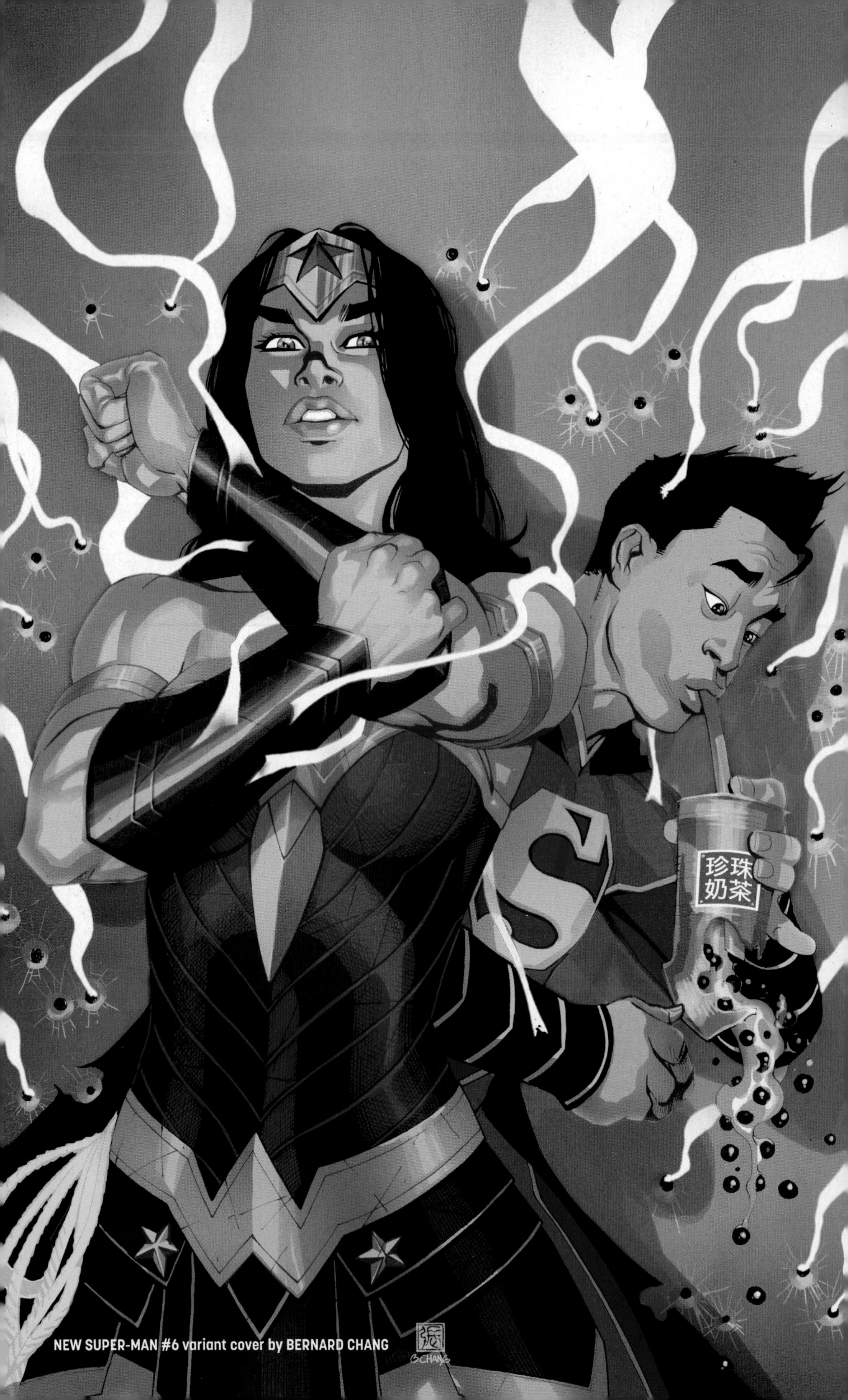
珍珠奶茶
BCHANG

NEW SUPER-MAN #6 variant cover by BERNARD CHANG

NEW SUPER-MAN promotional piece by VIKTOR BOGDANOVIC and BLOND

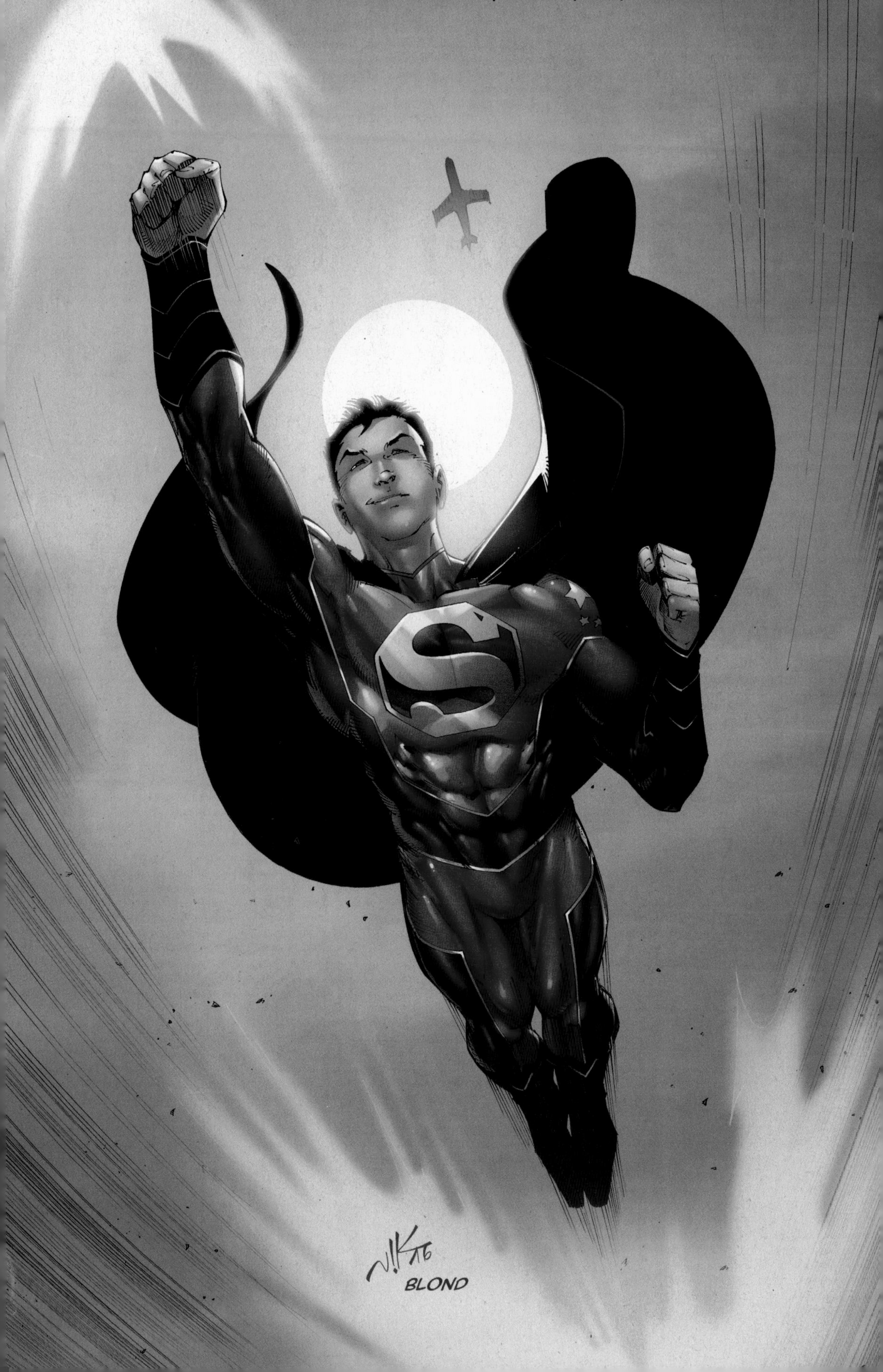
BLOND

CHARACTER SKETCHES
by VIKTOR BOGDANOVIC

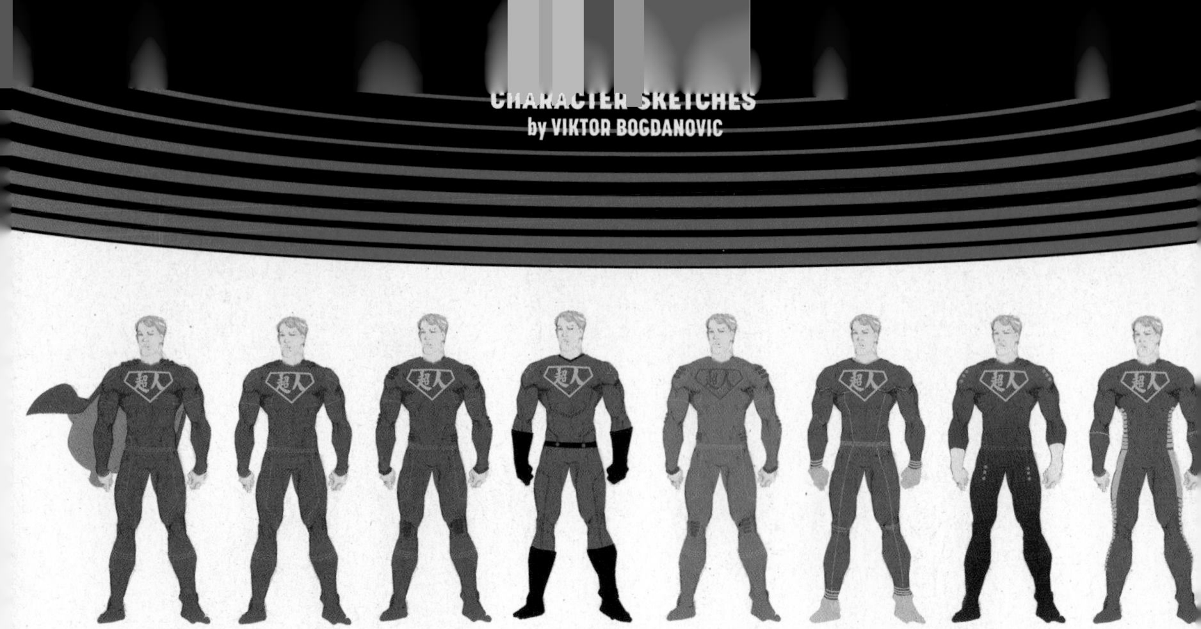

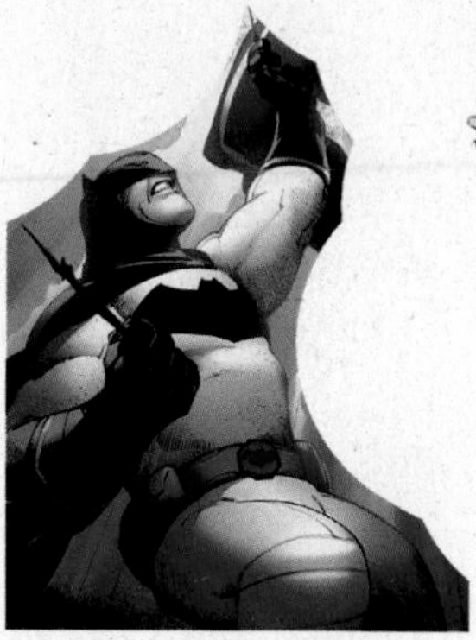

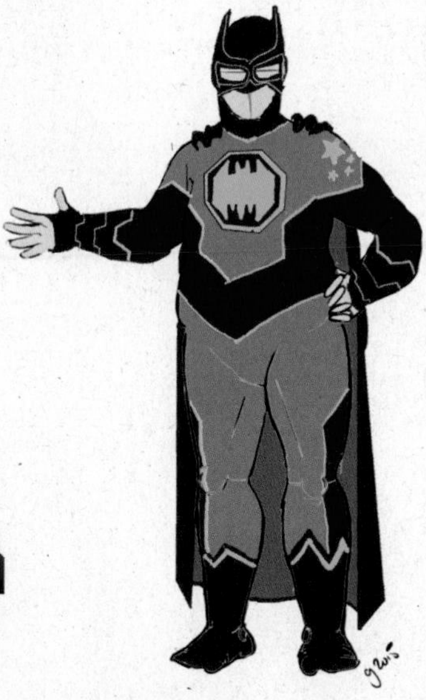

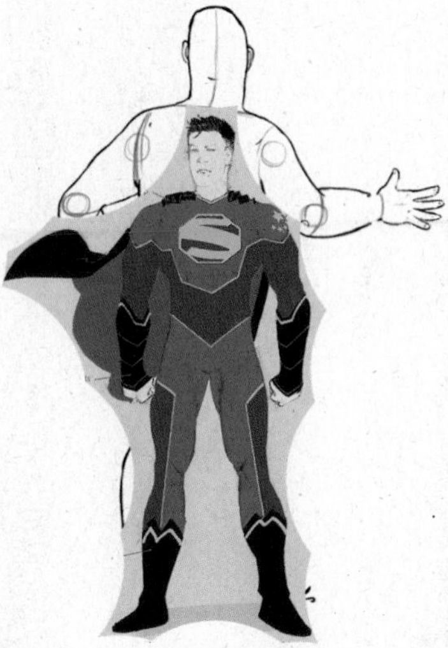

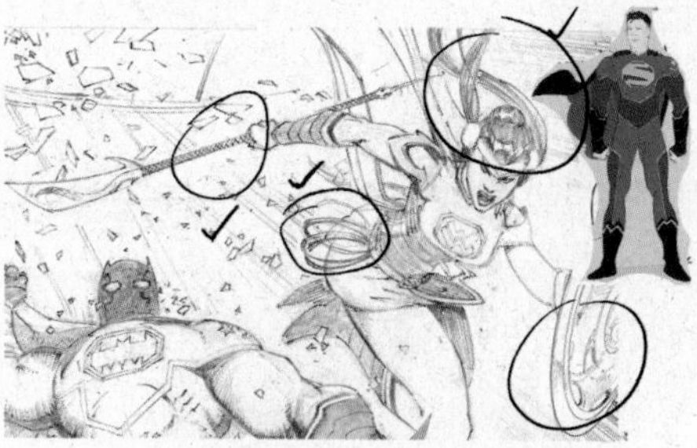

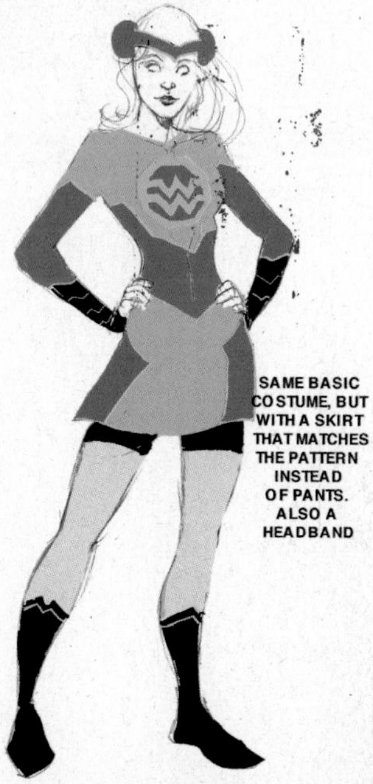
SAME BASIC COSTUME, BUT WITH A SKIRT THAT MATCHES THE PATTERN INSTEAD OF PANTS. ALSO A HEADBAND

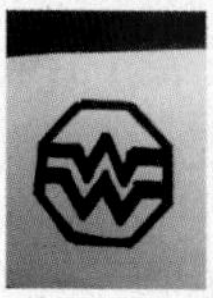

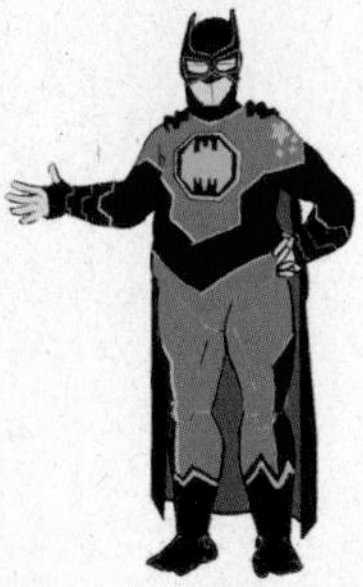